React in Action

React in Action

MARK TIELENS THOMAS

MANNING

SHELTER ISLAND

For online information and ordering of this and other Manning books, please visit
www.manning.com. The publisher offers discounts on this book when ordered in quantity.
For more information, please contact

> Special Sales Department
> Manning Publications Co.
> 20 Baldwin Road
> PO Box 761
> Shelter Island, NY 11964
> Email: orders@manning.com

 Manning Publications Co.
20 Baldwin Road
PO Box 761
Shelter Island, NY 11964

Development editor:	Marina Michaels
Technical development editor:	Nickie Bruckner
Project manager:	Janet Vail
Copy editor:	Corbin Collins
Technical proofreader:	German Frigerio
Proofreader:	Melody Dolab
Typesetter:	Dennis Dalinnik
Cover designer:	Marija Tudor

ISBN: 9781617293856
Printed in the United States of America
1 2 3 4 5 6 7 8 9 10 – DP – 23 22 21 20 19 18

This book is dedicated to my wife, Haley. Stay forever.

brief contents

contents

preface

When I first started learning about and using React, the JavaScript community was just beginning to settle down from a period of rapid innovation and disruption (read: turbulence). React was gaining in popularity, but the JavaScript community still seemed like the Wild West in many ways. I was excited about React as a technology because it showed real promise. The mental model seemed solid, components made building UIs easier, the API was flexible and expressive, and the whole project seemed like it was "just right." Postulations about its API surface, usability, and theoretical underpinnings aside, there was also the fact that it seemed really cool to me and I enjoyed working with it.

Since then, quite a bit has changed—and at the same time not much has changed at all. React has remained largely the same in terms of its fundamental concepts and API, although a body of knowledge and best practices have emerged and evolved, and more people use it. An open source ecosystem of libraries and related technologies has flourished. There are conferences, meetups, and communities that involve React to one degree or another. In version 16, the React core team rewrote the internal architecture of React in a way that both maintained backward compatibility and paved the way for a slew of future innovations. All these "changes without too much change" point to what I believe is one of React's greatest strengths: a maintained tension between stability and innovation that drives adoption without leaving people in the dust.

For all these reasons and more, React has continued to take hold as a technology and has only become more popular. It's in use in one way or another at many large companies, at countless startups, and at every sort of company in between. And many companies that don't currently use React are trying to switch over to it to modernize their frontend applications.

React hasn't only grown in popularity with respect to the web—it's also made inroads into other platforms. React Native, the port of React to mobile platforms, has also been a major innovation. It demonstrates React's "learn once, write anywhere" approach. This idea of React as a platform means you're not limited to using it for browser-based applications.

Let's forget the hype around React and focus on what this book should do for you. My primary hopes for *React in Action* are that it equips you to understand and work with React effectively and, even more, that it makes you better at building user interfaces overall, even if in a small way. My aim is not to engage in buzzword-driven development or push you toward "magical" technologies. Rather, my wager is that a robust mental model and deep understanding coupled with practical examples will put you in a place to do incredible things with React, whether on your own or with others.

acknowledgments

Don't wait for things to be perfect before you share them with others. Show early and show often. It'll be pretty when we get there, but it won't be pretty along the way.

—Ed Catmull, *Creativity, Inc.: Overcoming the Unseen Forces That Stand in the Way of True Inspiration*

Few worthwhile endeavors are undertaken alone. In many cases, a single person or handful of people is entirely credited with success, but this singular attribution belies the larger network of contributors who work toward an end. Those who would claim to have "done it alone" often fail to realize the ways in which others have helped them, whether by example or by instruction. What's more, failure to realize the strength of working in a community pushes success and excellence even further out of reach. Working alone means being limited to what you, and only you, can do. Collaboration provides a path to excellence by opening us to humility, new ideas, different perspectives, and invaluable feedback.

I won't be so foolish as to think, even for a second, that I've written this book by myself. My fingers pushed keys, and my name will be on the cover, but that doesn't mean this was a one-person show. No, this book—like all the things in my life that I'm grateful for—is the result of a rich community of smart, humble, loving people willing to be patient, kind, and sometimes firm with me.

First, I would like to thank my wife, Haley. She's my joy, my best friend, my creative partner. She's put up with this book for a long time. Late nights, more late nights, and endless talking about the book. She—the brilliant and better writer—helped me when

I had writer's block. She encouraged me when I felt as if finishing the book was impossible. She's always constant in love and in prayer. She's always comforted me in low times, challenged me when I doubted myself, and celebrated with me in times of joy. She's been incredible through the entire process and I can't wait to return the favor and help her with the many books she'll write in the future. I'm always and immeasurably grateful for her.

I would also like to thank the other people in my life who have supported me in this process. I'm humbled and thankful to have an incredible family. My mom and dad, Annmarie and Mitchell, have been encouraging throughout the writing of this book (and my whole life). They've also promised to read it in its entirety, though I won't hold them to that. My brothers, David and Peter, have also been supportive and encouraging. They haven't promised to read the book, though, so I'll be reading it aloud to them for the next year (or however long it takes). My friends from church, childhood, and work have also been incredibly helpful. They did me the great service of always asking, "Is it done yet?" to spur me on, and they put up with my explanations of React. I would also like to thank my professors, especially Dr. Diana Pavlac Glyer, for teaching me to think and to write.

The folks at Manning have been very helpful in this process. I want to extend a special thank you to Marina Michaels (development editor), Nickie Bruckner (technical development editor), and German Frigerio (technical proofer). They spent countless hours reading and helping with my writing. This book wouldn't exist without them. I would also like to thank Brian Sawyer for reaching out to me about writing the book and Marjan Bace for giving me the opportunity to write the book in the first place. Everyone at Manning is committed to helping people everywhere learn important, impactful skills and concepts in effective ways. I firmly believe in and am excited to help further Manning's educational mission.

about this book

React in Action is about React, the library for building user interfaces on the web. It covers the core concepts and APIs involved in building React applications. You'll build a sample social networking application with React over the course of the book. This app will cover a variety of topics, ranging from adding dynamic data to rendering on the server.

Audience

This book is written for people who want to learn React. It doesn't matter if you're a software engineer, a VP of engineering, a CTO, a designer, an engineering manager, a university or coding boot camp student, or someone who's just curious about React. Depending on what your needs are, you can focus on different parts of the book, too. I cover React from a high level during the first part of the book and get more specific and advanced as we go.

You'll have a better experience reading the book if you have some basic familiarity with JavaScript. This book uses a lot of JavaScript, but it isn't about JavaScript. I don't cover fundamental concepts in JavaScript, although I do lightly touch on them if they're relevant to a discussion about React. You should be able to work through the examples if you have a basic proficiency with JavaScript and understand how asynchronous programming in JavaScript works.

React in Action also assumes that you know some of the basics of building a front-end web application from a technology perspective—knowing about the basic browser APIs will be helpful. You'll work with things like the Fetch API to make network requests, set and get cookies, and work with user events (typing, clicks, and so on). You'll also interact heavily with libraries (although not too many!). Familiarity with the basics of a modern frontend application will help you get the most out of this book.

Fortunately, I've abstracted away all the complexity around tooling and the build process that's also a requisite part of building modern web applications. The source code for the project includes all the necessary dependencies and build tools, so you don't have to understand, for example, how Webpack and Babel work in order to enjoy this book. All in all, you should have at least a basic proficiency with JavaScript and some frontend web application concepts to fully enjoy *React in Action.*

Roadmap

React in Action's 13 chapters are divided into 3 parts.

Part 1, "Meet React," introduces you to React. Chapter 1 covers core ideas of React at a high level. It talks about some of the key points of React, shows how it might fit into your development process, and looks at what React does and doesn't do. Chapter 2 is the "show me the code" chapter. You'll dive into React's APIs and build a simple comment box with React components.

Part 2, "Components and data in React," is where you'll start to go deeper with React. You'll see how data flows in React in chapter 3 and look at the component life-cycle API and start building the Letters Social sample project in chapter 4. This project will take us through the remainder of the book. Chapter 4 goes over setting up the project from the application source code and explains how to work with it for the rest of the book.

Chapters 5 through 9 are an even deeper dive into React. Chapter 5 covers working with forms and gives you another opportunity to work with data and data flow in React. Chapter 6 follows in the same vein and builds on the work done in chapter 5 to create a more complex React component for displaying maps.

Chapters 7 and 8 tackle routing, a crucial part of almost any modern frontend application. You'll build a router from scratch and get your app set up to handle multiple pages. You'll keep going with routing in chapter 8 and integrate the Firebase platform so you can authenticate users. Chapter 9 closes out part 3 by introducing testing React apps and components.

Part 3, "React application architecture," covers more advanced topics in React and focuses especially on transitioning your application to use Redux. Chapters 10 and 11 introduce Redux, a state-management solution. Once your app is transitioned to use Redux, we'll explore server-side rendering in chapter 12. This chapter also covers switching out your custom-built router for React Router. Chapter 13 briefly discusses React Native, another React project that allows you to write JavaScript React apps for mobile devices (iOS and Android).

About the code

React in Action uses two main groups of source code. For the first two chapters, you'll work with code outside the project repository. You'll be able to run these code samples on Codesandbox.io, an online code playground. It takes care of bundling your code and running it in real time, so you don't have to worry about setting up a build process.

In chapter 4, you'll get set up with the project source code. It's available for download at the book's website, www.manning.com/books/react-in-action, and on GitHub online at https://github.com/react-in-action/letters-social, and the final result of the project is live at https://social.react.sh. Each chapter or range of chapters has its own branch in Git, so you can easily switch into a later chapter or follow the progression of the project throughout the book. The source code all lives on GitHub, so feel free to ask questions on GitHub or on the book's forum at https://forums.manning.com/forums/react-in-action.

The JavaScript for the app should all be formatted using Prettier (https://github.com/prettier/prettier), written using the most current ECMAScript specification (which is ES2017 at time of writing). Prettier uses concepts, syntax, and methods available in that specification. The project includes an ESLint configuration, but if you prefer to modify it to suit your own needs, feel free.

Software and hardware requirements

React in Action doesn't have any strict hardware requirements. You're free to use any type of computer (physical or a virtual provider like Cloud9 https://c9.io), although I won't address inconsistencies caused by differences in development environments. If these issues come up for individual packages, the repositories for those packages or Stack Overflow (https://stackoverflow.com) are the best place to seek help.

As for software, here are a few requirements and recommendations:

- The build process for the sample project uses node.js (https://nodejs.org), so you'll need to install the latest stable version. See chapter 4 for more on getting set up with node.js.
- You'll also need a text editor and a web browser. I recommend something like Visual Studio Code (https://code.visualstudio.com), Atom (https://atom.io), or Sublime Text (www.sublimetext.com).
- You'll use Chrome as the main browser for the course of the book, especially its developer tools. Download it at www.google.com/chrome.

about the author

Mark Tielens Thomas is a full-stack software engineer and author. He and his wife live and work in southern California. Mark enjoys tackling large-scale engineering problems and leading teams to deliver high-impact, high-value solutions. He loves Jesus, good coffee, too many books, fast APIs, and beautiful systems. He writes for Manning and on his personal blog at https:// ifelse.io.

about the cover illustration

The caption for the illustration on the cover of *React in Action* is "The Capitan Pasha, Derya Bey, admiral of the Turkish navy." The capitan pasha was a high-admiral with supreme command of the navy of the Ottoman Empire. The illustration is taken from a collection of costumes of the Ottoman Empire published on January 1, 1802, by William Miller of Old Bond Street, London. The title page is missing from the collection, and we have been unable to track it down to date. The book's table of contents identifies the figures in both English and French, and each illustration bears the names of two artists who worked on it, both of whom would no doubt be surprised to find their art gracing the front cover of a computer programming book ... two hundred years later.

The collection was purchased by a Manning editor at an antiquarian flea market in the "Garage" on West 26th Street in Manhattan. The seller was an American based in Ankara, Turkey, and the transaction took place just as he was packing up his stand for the day. The Manning editor didn't have on his person the substantial amount of cash that was required for the purchase, and a credit card and check were both politely turned down. With the seller flying back to Ankara that evening, the situation was getting hopeless. What was the solution? It turned out to be nothing more than an old-fashioned verbal agreement sealed with a handshake. The seller simply proposed that the money be transferred to him by wire, and the editor walked out with the bank information on a piece of paper and the portfolio of images under his arm. Needless to say, we transferred the funds the next day, and we remain grateful and impressed by this unknown person's trust in one of us. It recalls something that might have happened a long time ago.

We at Manning celebrate the inventiveness, the initiative, and, yes, the fun of the computer business with book covers based on the rich diversity of regional life of two centuries ago, brought back to life by the pictures from this collection.

Part 1

Meet React

If you've worked on frontend JavaScript applications in the past two years, you've probably heard of React. You might have heard of it even if you're just starting out building user interfaces. Even if you're hearing about React for the first time in this book, I've still got you covered: there are many hugely popular applications that use React. If you use Facebook, watch Netflix, or learn about computer science through Khan Academy, you've used an application built with React.

React is a library for building user interfaces. It was created by engineers at Facebook and since its release has made waves in the JavaScript communities. It's gained in popularity over the past few years and is the tool of choice for many teams and engineers building dynamic user interfaces. In fact, the combination of React's API, mental model, and robust community have led to the development of React for other platforms, including mobile and even virtual reality.

In this book, you'll explore React and see why it's been such a successful and useful open source project. In part 1, you'll start with the basics of React and learn them from the ground up. Because the tooling involved in building robust JavaScript UI applications can be incredibly complex, we'll avoid getting bogged down in tools and focus on learning the ins and outs of the React API. We'll also avoid "magic" and work toward a concrete understanding of React and how it works.

In chapter 1, you'll learn about React at a high level. We'll cover some important ideas like components, the virtual DOM, and some of the tradeoffs of React. In chapter 2, you'll take a whirlwind tour through React's APIs and build a simple comment-box component to get your hands dirty with React.

Meet React

If you work as a web engineer in the tech industry, chances are you've heard of React. Maybe it was somewhere online like Twitter or Reddit. Maybe a friend or colleague mentioned it to you or you heard a talk about it at a meetup. Wherever it was, I bet that what you heard was probably either glowing or a bit skeptical. Most people tend to have a strong opinion about technologies like React. Influential and impactful technologies tend to generate that kind of response. For these technologies, often a smaller number of people initially "get it" before the technology catches on and moves to a broader audience. React started this way, but now enjoys immense popularity and use in the web engineering world. And it's popular for

3

good reason: it has a lot to offer and can reinvigorate, renew, or even transform how you think about and build user interfaces.

1.1   *Meet React*

React is a JavaScript library for building user interfaces across a variety of platforms. React gives you a powerful mental model to work with and helps you build user interfaces in a declarative and component-driven way. We'll unpack these ideas and much more over the course of the book, but that's what React is in the broadest, briefest sense.

Where does React fit into the broader world of web engineering? You'll often hear React talked about in the same space as projects like Vue, Preact, Angular, Ember, Webpack, Redux and other well-known JavaScript libraries and frameworks. React is often a major part of front-end applications and shares similar features with the other libraries and frameworks just mentioned. In fact, many popular front-end technologies are more like React in subtle ways now than in the past. There was a time when React's approach was novel, but other technologies have since been influenced by React's component-driven, declarative approach. React continues to maintain a spirit of rethinking established best practices, with the main goal being providing developers with an expressive mental model and a performant technology to build UI applications.

What makes React's mental model powerful? It draws on deep areas of computer science and software engineering techniques. React's mental model draws broadly on functional and object-oriented programming concepts and focuses on components as primary units for building with. In React applications, you create interfaces from components. React's rendering system manages these components and keeps the application view in sync for you. Components often correspond to aspects of the user interface, like datepickers, headers, navbars, and others, but they can also take responsibility for things like client-side routing, data formatting, styling, and other responsibilities of a client-side application.

Components in React should be easy to think about and integrate with other React components; they follow a predictable lifecycle, can maintain their own internal state, and work with "regular old JavaScript." We'll dive into these ideas over the course of the rest of the book, but we can look at them at a high level right now. Figure 1.1 gives you an overview of the major ingredients that go into a React application. Let's look at each part briefly:

- *Components*—Encapsulated units of functionality that are the primary unit in React. They utilize data (*properties* and *state*) to render your UI as output; we'll explore how React components work with data later in chapter 2 onward. Certain types of React components also provide a set of lifecycle methods that you can hook into. The *rendering process* (outputting and updating a UI based on your data) is predictable in React, and your components can hook into it using React's APIs.
- *React libraries*—React uses a set of core libraries. The core React library works with the `react-dom` and `react-native` libraries and is focused on component

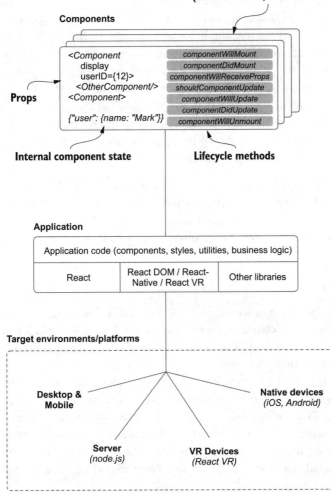

Figure 1.1 React allows you to create user interfaces from components. Components maintain their own state, are written in and work with "vanilla" JavaScript, and inherit a number of helpful APIs from React. Most React apps are written for browser-based environments, but can also be used in native environments like iOS and Android. For more about React Native, see Nader Dabit's *React Native in Action*, also available from Manning.

specification and definition. It allows you to build a tree of components that a renderer for the browser or another platform can use. `react-dom` is one such renderer and is aimed at browser environments and server-side rendering. The React Native libraries focus on native platforms and let you create React applications for iOS, Android, and other platforms.

- *Third-party libraries*—React doesn't come with tools for data modeling, HTTP calls, styling libraries, or other common aspects of a front-end application. This leaves you free to use additional code, modules, or other tools you prefer in your application. And even though these common technologies don't come bundled with React, the broader ecosystem around React is full of incredibly useful libraries. In this book, we'll use a few of these libraries and devote chapters 10 and 11 to looking at Redux, a library for state management.
- *Running a React application*—Your React application runs on the platform you're building for. This book focuses on the web platform and builds a browser and server-based application, but other projects like React Native and React VR open the possibility of your app running on other platforms.

We'll spend lots of time exploring the ins and outs of React in this book, but you may have a few questions before getting started. Is React something for you? Who else is using React? What are some of the tradeoffs of using React or not? These are important questions about a new technology that you'll want answered before adopting it.

1.1.1   Who this book is for

This book is for anyone who's working on or interested in building user interfaces. Really, it's is for anyone who's curious about React, even if you don't work in UI engineering. You'll get the most out of this book if you have some experience with using JavaScript to build front-end applications.

You can learn how to build applications with React as long as you know the basics of JavaScript and have some experience building web applications. I don't cover the fundamentals of JavaScript in this book. Topics like prototypal inheritance, ES2015+ code, type coercion, syntax, keywords, asynchronous coding patterns like async/await, and other fundamental topics are beyond the scope of this book. I do lightly cover anything that's especially pertinent to React but don't dive deep into JavaScript as a language.

This doesn't mean you can't learn React or won't get anything from this book if you don't know JavaScript. But you'll get much more if you take the time to learn JavaScript first. Charging ahead without a working knowledge of JavaScript will make things more difficult. You might run into situations where things might seem like "magic" to you—things will work, but you won't understand why. This usually hurts rather than helps you as a developer, so ... last warning: get comfortable with the basics of JavaScript before learning React. It's a wonderfully expressive and flexible language. You'll love it!

You may already know JavaScript well and may have even dabbled in React before. This wouldn't be too surprising given how popular React has become. If this is you, you'll be able to gain a deeper understanding of some of the core concepts of React. But I don't cover highly specific topics you may be looking for if you've been working with React for a while. For those, see other React-related Manning titles like *React Native in Action.*

You may not fit into either group and may want a high-level overview of React. This book is for you, too. You'll learn the fundamental concepts of React and you'll have access to a sample application written in React—check out the running app at https://social.react.sh. You'll be able to see the basics of building a React application in practice and how it might be suited to your team or next project.

1.1.2 A note on tooling

If you've worked extensively on front-end applications in the past few years, you won't be surprised by the fact that the tooling around applications has become as much a part of the development process as frameworks and libraries themselves. You're likely using something like Webpack, Babel, or other tools in your applications today. Where do these and other tools fit into this book, and what you need to know?

You don't need to be a master of Webpack, Babel, or other tools to enjoy and read this book. The sample application I've created utilizes a handful of important tools, and you can feel free to read through the configuration code for these in the sample application, but I don't cover these tools in depth in this book. Tooling changes quickly, and more importantly, it would be well outside the scope of this book to cover these topics in depth. I'll be sure to note anywhere tooling is relevant to our discussion, but besides that I'll avoid covering it.

I also feel that tooling can be a distraction when learning a new technology like React. You're already trying to get your head around a new set of concepts and paradigms—why clutter that with learning complex tooling too? That's why chapter 2 focuses on learning "vanilla" React first before moving on to features like JSX and JavaScript language features that require build tools. The one area of tooling that you'll need to be familiar with is npm. npm is the package management tool for JavaScript, and you'll use it to install dependencies for your project and run project commands from the command line. It's likely you're already familiar with npm, but if not, don't let that dissuade you from reading the book. You only need the most basic terminal and npm skills to go forward. You can learn about npm at https://docs.npmjs .com/getting-started/what-is-npm.

1.1.3 Who uses React?

When it comes to open source software, who is (and who isn't) using it is more than just a matter of popularity. It affects the experience you'll have working with the technology (including availability of support, documentation, and security fixes), the level of innovation in the community, and the potential lifetime of a certain tool. It's generally more fun, easier, and overall a smoother experience to work with tools that have a vibrant community, a robust ecosystem, and a diversity of contributor experience and background.

React started as a small project but now has broad popularity and a vibrant community. No community is perfect, and React's isn't either, but as far as open source communities go, it has many important ingredients for success. What's more, the React community also includes smaller subsets of other open source communities. This can be daunting because the ecosystem can seem vast, but it also makes the community robust and diverse. Figure 1.2 shows a map of the React ecosystem. I mention various libraries and projects throughout the course of the book, but if you're curious to learn more about the React ecosystem, I've put together a guide at https://ifelse.io/react-ecosystem. I'll keep this updated over time and ensure it evolves as the ecosystem does.

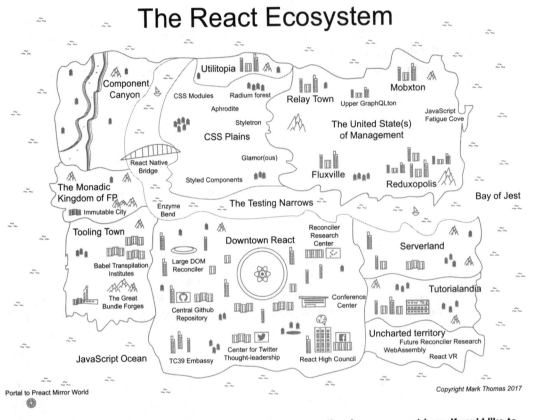

Figure 1.2   A map of the React ecosystem is diverse—even more so than I can represent here. If you'd like to learn more, check out my guide at https://ifelse.io/react-ecosystem, which will help you find your way in the React ecosystem when starting out.

The primary way you might interact with React is probably in open source, but you likely use apps built with it every day. Many companies use React in different and exciting ways. Here are a few of the companies using React to power their products:

- Facebook
- Netflix
- New Relic
- Uber
- Wealthfront
- Heroku
- PayPal
- BBC
- Microsoft
- NFL
- And more!

- Asana
- ESPN
- Walmart
- Venmo
- Codecademy
- Atlassian
- Asana
- Airbnb
- Khan Academy
- FloQast

These companies aren't blindly following the trends of the JavaScript community. They have exceptional engineering demands that impact a huge number of users and must deliver products on hard deadlines. Someone saying, "I heard React was good; we should React-ify everything!" won't fly with managers or other engineers. Companies and developers want good tools that help them think better and move quickly so they can build high-impact, scalable, and reliable applications.

1.2   *What does React not do?*

So far, I've been talking about React at a high-level: who uses it, who this book is for, and so on. My primary goals in writing this book are to teach you how to build applications with React and empower you as an engineer. React isn't perfect, but it's genuinely been a pleasure to work with, and I've seen teams do great things with it. I love writing about it, building with it, hearing talks about it at conferences, and engaging in the occasional spirited debate about this or that pattern.

But I would be doing you a disservice if I didn't talk about some of the downsides of React and describe what it *doesn't* do. Understanding what something can't do is as important as understanding what it can do. Why? The best engineering decisions and thinking usually happen in terms of tradeoffs instead of opinions or absolutes ("React is fundamentally better than tool *X* because I like it more"). On the former point: you're probably not dealing with two totally different technologies (COBOL versus JavaScript); hopefully you're not even considering technologies that are fundamentally unsuited to the task at hand. And to the latter point: building great projects and solving engineering challenges should never be about opinions. It's not that people's opinions don't matter—that's certainly not true—it's that opinions don't make things work well or at all.

1.2.1 Tradeoffs of React

If tradeoffs are the bread and butter of good software evaluation and discussion, what tradeoffs are there with React? First, React is sometimes called *just the view*. This can be misconstrued or misunderstood because it can lead you to think React is just a templating system like Handlebars or Pug (née Jade) or that it has to be part of an MVC (model-view-controller) architecture. Neither is true. React can be both of those things, but it can be much more. To make things easier, I'll describe React more in terms of what it *is* than what it's not ("just the view," for example). React is a *declarative, component-based* library for building user interfaces that works on a variety of platforms: web, native, mobile, server, desktop, and even on virtual reality platforms going forward (React VR).

This leads to our first tradeoff: React is primarily concerned with the *view* aspects of UI. This means it's not built to do many of the jobs of a more comprehensive framework or library. A quick comparison to something like Angular might help drive this point home. In its most recent major release, Angular has much more in common with React than it previously did in terms of concepts and design, but in other ways it covers much more territory than React. Angular includes opinionated solutions for the following:

- HTTP calls
- Form building and validation
- Routing
- String and number formatting
- Internationalization
- Dependency injection
- Basic data modeling primitives
- Custom testing framework (although this isn't as important a distinction as the other areas)
- Service workers included by default (a worker-style approach to executing JavaScript)

That's a lot, and in my experience there are generally two ways people tend to react[1] to all these features coming with a framework. Either it's along the lines of "Wow, I don't have to deal with all those myself" or it's "Wow, I don't get to choose how I do anything." The upside of frameworks like Angular, Ember, and the like is that there's usually a well-defined way to do things. For example, routing in Angular is done with the built-in Angular Router, HTTP tasks are all done with the built-in HTTP routines, and so on.

There's nothing fundamentally wrong with this approach. I've worked on teams where we used technologies like this and I've worked on teams where we went the

---

[1] Pun not intended but, hey, it's a book about React, so there it is.

more flexible direction and chose technologies that "did one thing well." We did great work with both kinds of technologies, and they served their purposes well. My personal preference is toward the choose-your-own, does-one-thing-well approach, but that's really neither here nor there; it's all about tradeoffs. React doesn't come with opinionated solutions for HTTP, routing, data modeling (although it certainly has opinions about data flow in your views, which we'll get to), or other things you might see in something like Angular. If your team sees this as something you absolutely can't do without in a singular framework, React might not be your best choice. But in my experience, most teams want the flexibility of React coupled with the mental model and intuitive APIs that it brings.

One upside to the flexible approach of React is that you're free to pick the best tools for the job. Don't like the way X HTTP library works? No problem—swap it out for something else. Prefer to do forms in a different way? Implement it, no problem. React provides you with a set of powerful primitives to work with. To be fair, other frameworks like Angular will usually allow you to swap things out too, but the de facto and community-backed way of doing things will usually be whatever is built-in and included.

The obvious downside to having more freedom is that if you're used to a more comprehensive framework like Angular or Ember, you'll need to either come up with or find your own solution for different areas of your application. This can be a good thing or a bad thing, depending on factors like developer experience on your team, engineering management preferences, and other factors specific to your situation. There are plenty of good arguments for the one-size-fits-all as well as the does-one-thing-well approaches. I tend to be more convinced by the approach that lets you adapt and make flexible, case-by-case decisions about tooling over time in a way that entrusts engineering teams with the responsibility to determine or create the right tools. There's also the incredibly broader JavaScript ecosystem to consider—you'll be hard-pressed to find *nothing* aimed at a problem you're solving. But at the end of the day, the fact remains that excellent, high-impact teams use both sorts of approaches (sometimes at the same time!) to build out their products.

I'd be remiss if I didn't mention lock-in before moving on. It's an unavoidable fact that JavaScript frameworks are rarely truly interoperable; you can't usually have an app that's part Angular, part Ember, part Backbone, and part React, at least not without segmenting off each part or tightly controlling how they interact. It doesn't usually make sense to put yourself in that sort of situation when you can avoid it. You usually go with one and maybe temporarily, at most, two primary frameworks for a particular application.

But what happens when you need to change? If you use a tool with wide-ranging responsibilities like Angular, migrating your app is likely going to be a complete rewrite due to the deep idiomatic integration of your framework. You can rewrite smaller parts of the application, but you can't just swap out a few functions and expect everything to work. This is an area where React can shine. It employs relatively few "magic" idioms. That doesn't mean it makes migration painless, but it does help you to potentially forgo incurring the cost of a tightly integrated framework like Angular if you migrate to or from it.

Another tradeoff you make when choosing React is that it's primarily developed and built by Facebook and is meant to serve the UI needs of Facebook. You might have a hard time working with React if your application is fundamentally different than the UI needs of Facebook's apps. Fortunately, most modern web apps are in React's technological wheelhouse, but there are certainly apps that aren't. These might also include apps that don't work within the conventional UI paradigms of modern web apps or apps that have very specific performance needs (such as a high-speed stock ticker). Yet even these can often be addressed with React, though some situations require more-specific technologies.

One last tradeoff we should discuss is React's implementation and design. Baked into the core of React are systems that handle updating the UI for you when the data in your components change. They execute changes that you can hook into using certain methods called *lifecycle methods*. I cover these extensively in later chapters. React's systems that handle updating your UI make it much easier to focus on building modular, robust components that your application can use. The way React abstracts away most of the work of keeping a UI up-to-date with data is a big part of why developers enjoy working with it so much and why it's a powerful primitive in your hands. But it shouldn't be assumed that there are no downsides or tradeoffs made with respect to the "engines" that power the technology.

React is an abstraction, so the costs of it being an abstraction still remain. You don't get as much visibility into the system you're using because it's built in a particular way and exposed through an API. This also means you'll need to build your UI in an idiomatically React way. Fortunately, React's APIs provide "escape hatches" that let you drop down into lower levels of abstraction. You can still use other tools like jQuery, but you'll need to use them in a React-compatible way. This again is a tradeoff: a simpler mental model at the cost of not being able to do absolutely everything how you'd like.

Not only do you lose some visibility to the underlying system, you also buy into the way that React does things. This tends to impact a narrower slice of your application stack (only views instead of data, special form-building systems, data modeling, and so on), but it affects it nonetheless. My hope is that you'll see that the benefits of React far outweigh the cost of learning it and that the tradeoffs you make when using it generally leave you in a much better place as a developer. But it would be disingenuous for me to pretend that React will magically solve all your engineering challenges.

1.3   *The virtual DOM*

We've talked a little bit about some of the high-level features of React. I've posited that it can help you and your team become better at creating user interfaces and that part of this is due to the mental model and APIs that React provides. What's behind all that? A major theme in React is a drive to simplify otherwise complex tasks and abstract unnecessary complexity away from the developer. React tries to do just enough to be performant while freeing you up to think about other aspects of your application. One of the main ways it does that is by encouraging you to be *declarative* instead of *imperative*. You get to declare how your components should behave and look under different states, and React's internal machinery handles the complexity of managing updates, updating the UI to reflect changes, and so on.

One of the major pieces of technology driving this is the virtual DOM. A *virtual DOM* is a data structure or collection of data structures that mimics or mirrors the Document Object Model that exists in browsers. I say *a* virtual DOM because other frameworks such as Ember employ their own implementation of a similar technology. In general, a virtual DOM will serve as an intermediate layer between the application code and the browser DOM. The virtual DOM allows the complexity of change detection and management to be hidden from the developer and moved to a specialized layer of abstraction. In the next sections, we'll look from a high level at how this works in React. Figure 1.3 shows a simplified overview of the DOM and virtual DOM relationship that we'll explore shortly.

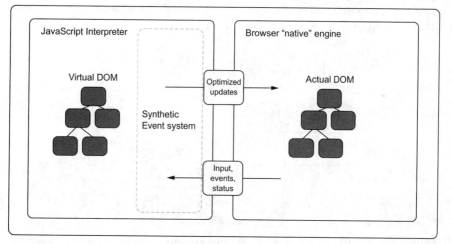

Figure 1.3 The DOM and virtual DOM. React's virtual DOM handles change detection in data as well as translating browser events into events that React components can understand and react to. React's virtual DOM also aims to optimize changes made to the DOM for the sake of performance.

1.3.1 The DOM

The best way to ensure that we understand React's virtual DOM is to start by checking our understanding of the DOM. If you already feel you have a deep understanding of the DOM, feel free to move ahead. But if not, let's start with an important question: what is the DOM? The DOM, or *Document Object Model*, is a programming interface that allows your JavaScript programs to interact with different types of documents (HTML, XML, and SVG). There are standards-driven specifications for it, which means that a public working group has created a standard set of features it should have and ways it should behave. Although other implementations exist, the DOM is mostly synonymous with web browsers like Chrome, Firefox, and Edge.

The DOM provides a structured way of accessing, storing, and manipulating different parts of a document. At a high level, the DOM is a tree structure that reflects the hierarchy of an XML document. This tree structure is comprised of sub-trees that are in turn made of nodes. You'll probably know these as the `div`s and other elements that make up your web pages and applications.

You've probably used the DOM API before—but you may not have known you were using it. Whenever you use a method in JavaScript that accesses, modifies, or stores information related to something in an HTML document, you're almost certainly using the DOM or its related APIs (see https://developer.mozilla.org/en-US/docs/Web/API for more on web APIs). This means that not all the methods you've used in JavaScript are necessarily part of the JavaScript language itself (`document.findElemenyById`, `querySelectorAll`, `alert`, and so on). They're part of the bigger collection of *web APIs*—the DOM and other APIs that go into a browser—that allow you to interact with documents. Figure 1.4 shows a simplified version of the DOM tree structure you've probably seen in your web pages.

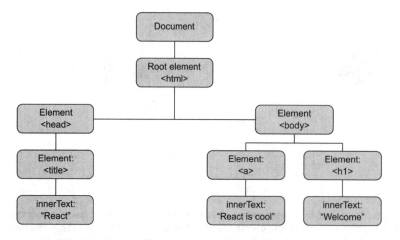

Figure 1.4   Here's a simple version of the DOM tree structure, using elements you're probably familiar with. The DOM API that's exposed to JavaScript lets you performs operations on these elements in the tree.

Common methods or properties you may have used to update or query a web page might include `getElementById`, `parent.appendChild`, `querySelectorAll`, `innerHTML`, and others. These are all provided by the host environment (in this case, the browser) and allow JavaScript to interact with the DOM. Without this ability, we'd have far less interesting web apps to use and perhaps no books about React to write!

Interacting with the DOM is usually straightforward but can get complicated in the context of a large web application. Fortunately, we don't often need to directly interact with the DOM when building applications with React—we mostly leave that to React. There are cases when we want to reach out past the virtual DOM and interact with the DOM directly, and we'll cover those in future chapters.

1.3.2 The virtual DOM

The web APIs in browsers let us interact with web documents with JavaScript via the DOM. But if we can already do this, why do we need something else in between? I want to first state that React's implementation of a virtual DOM doesn't mean that the regular web APIs are bad or inferior to React. Without them, React can't work. There are, however, certain pain points of working directly with the DOM in larger web applications. Generally, these pain points arise in the area of change detection. When data changes, we want to update the UI to reflect that. Doing that in a way that's efficient and easy to think about can be difficult, so React aims to solve that problem.

Part of the reason for that problem is the way browsers handle interactions with the DOM. When a DOM element is accessed, modified, or created, the browser is often performing a query across a structured tree to find a given element. That's just to access an element, which is usually only the first part of an update. More often than not, it may have to reperform layout, sizing, and other actions as part of a *mutation*— all of which can tend to be computationally expensive. A virtual DOM won't get you around this, but it can help updates to the DOM be optimized to account for these constraints.

When creating and managing a sizeable application that deals with data that changes over time, many changes to the DOM may be required, and often these changes can conflict or are done in a less-than-optimal way. That can result in an overly complicated system that's difficult for engineers to work on and likely a subpar experience for users—lose-lose. Thus performance is another key consideration in React's design and implementation. Implementing a virtual DOM helps address this, but it should be noted that it's designed to be just "fast enough." A robust API, simple mental model, and other things like cross-browser compatibility end up being more important outcomes of React's virtual DOM than an extreme focus on performance. The reason I make this point is that you may hear the virtual DOM talked about as a sort of silver bullet for performance. It is performant, but it's no magic performance bullet, and at the end of the day, many of its other benefits are more important for working with React.

1.3.3   *Updates and diffing*

How does the virtual DOM work? React's virtual DOM has a few similarities to another software world: 3D gaming. 3D games sometimes employ a rendering process that works very roughly as follows: get information from the game server, send it to the game world (the visual representation that the user sees), determine what changes need to be made to the visual world, and then let the graphics card determine the minimum changes necessary. One advantage of this approach is that you only need the resources for dealing with incremental changes and can generally do things much quicker than if you had to update everything.

That's a gross oversimplification of the way 3D games are rendered and updated, but the general ideas give us a good example to think of when looking at how React performs updates. DOM mutation done poorly can be expensive, so React tries to be efficient in its updates to your UI and employs methods similar to 3D games.

As figure 1.5 shows, React creates and maintains a virtual DOM in memory, and a renderer like React-DOM handles updating the browser DOM based on changes. React can perform intelligent updates and only do work on parts that have changed because it can use *heuristic diffing* to calculate which parts of the in-memory DOM require changes to the DOM. Theoretically, this is much more streamlined and elegant than "dirty checking" or other more brute-force approaches, but a major practical implication is that developers have less complicated state tracking to reason about.

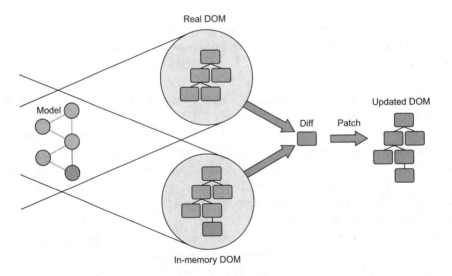

Figure 1.5   React's diffing and update procedure. When a change happens, React determines differences between the actual and in-memory DOMs. Then it performs an efficient update to the browser's DOM. This process is often referred to as a *diff* ("what changed?") and patch ("update only what changed") process.

1.3.4 *Virtual DOM: Need for speed?*

As I've noted, there's more to the virtual DOM than speed. It's performant by design and generally results in snappy, speedy applications that are fast enough for modern web application needs. Performance and a better mental model have been so appreciated by engineers that many popular JavaScript libraries are creating their own versions or variations of a virtual DOM. Even in these cases, people tend to think that the virtual DOM is primarily focused on performance. Performance is a key feature of React, but it's secondary to simplicity. The virtual DOM is part of what enables you to defer thinking about complicated state logic and focus on other, more important parts of your application. Together, speed and simplicity mean happier users and happier developers—a win-win!

I've spent some time talking about the virtual DOM, but I don't want to give you the idea that it will be an important part of working with React. In practice, you won't need to be thinking extensively about how the virtual DOM is accomplishing your data updates or making your changes to your application. That's part of the simplicity of React: you're freed up to focus on the parts of your application that need the most focus.

1.4 *Components: The fundamental unit of React*

React doesn't just use a novel approach to dealing with changing data over time; it also focuses on components as a paradigm for organizing your application. Components are the most fundamental unit of React. There are several different ways you can create components with React, which future chapters will cover. Thinking in terms of components is essential for grasping not only how React was meant to work but also how you can best use it in your projects.

1.4.1 *Components in general*

What is a component? It's a part of a larger whole. The idea of components is likely familiar to you, and you probably see them often even though you might not realize it. Using components as mental and visual tools when designing and building user interfaces can lead to better, more intuitive application design and use. A component can be whatever you determine it to be, although not everything makes sense as a component. For example, if you decide that the entirety of an interface is a component, with no child components or further subdivisions, you're probably not helping yourself. Instead, it's helpful to break different parts of an interface into parts that can be composed, reused, and easily reorganized.

To start thinking in terms of components, we'll look at an example interface and break it down into its constituent parts. Figure 1.6 shows an example of an interface you'll be working on later in the book. User interfaces often contain elements that are reused or repurposed in other parts of the interface. And even if they're not reused, they're at least distinct. These different elements, the distinct elements of an interface, can be thought of as components. The interface on the left in figure 1.6 is broken down into components on the right.

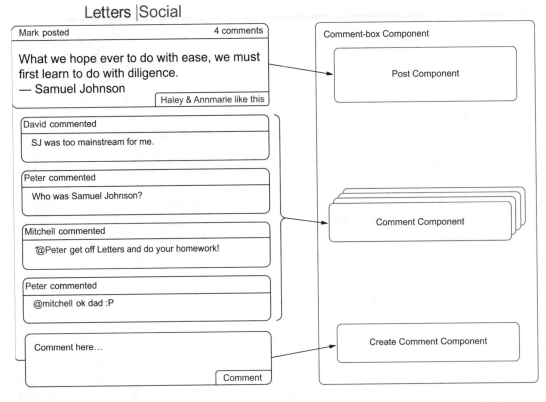

Figure 1.6   An example of an interface broken into components. Each distinct section can be thought of as a component. Items that repeat in a uniform nature can be thought of as one component that gets reused over different data.

Exercise 1.1   Component thinking

Visit a popular site that you enjoy and use often (like GitHub, for example) and break down the interface into components. As you go, you'll probably find yourself dividing things into separate parts. When does it make sense to stop breaking things down? Should an individual letter be a component? When might it make sense for a component to be something small? When would it make sense to consider a grouping of things as one component?

1.4.2   *Components in React: Encapsulated and reusable*

React components are well encapsulated, reusable, and composable. These character-istics help enable a simpler and more elegant way of thinking about and building user interfaces. Your application can be comprised of clear, concise groups instead of being a spaghetti-code mess. Using React to build your application is almost like building your project with LEGOs, except that you can't run out of pieces. You'll encounter bugs, but thankfully there are no pieces to step on.

In exercise 1.1, you practiced thinking with components and broke an interface into some constituent components. You could have done it any number of ways, and it's possible you might not have been especially organized or consistent. That's fine. But when you work with components in React, it will be important to consider organization and consistency in component design. You'll want to design components that are self-contained and focus on a particular concern or a handful of related concerns.

This lends itself towards components that are portable, logically grouped, and easy to move around and reuse throughout your application. Even if it takes advantage of other libraries, a well-designed React component should be fairly self-contained. Breaking your UI into components allows you to work more easily on different parts of the application. Boundaries between components mean that functionality and organization can be well-defined, whereas self-contained components mean they can be reused and moved around more easily.

Components in React are meant to work together. This means you can *compose* together components to form new *composite* components. Component composition is one of the most powerful aspects of React. You can create a component once and make it available to the rest of your application for reuse. This is often especially helpful in larger applications. If you're on a medium-to-large team, you could publish components to a private registry (npm or otherwise) that other teams could easily pull down and use in new or existing projects. This might not be a realistic scenario for all sizes of teams, but even smaller teams will benefit from the code reuse that React components promote.

A final aspect of React components is *lifecycle methods*. These are predictable, well-defined methods you can use as your component moves through different parts of its lifecycle (mounting, updating, unmounting, and so on). We'll spend a lot of time on these methods in future chapters.

1.5 *React for teams*

You now know a little bit more about components in React. React can make your life easier as an individual developer. But what about on a team? Overall, what makes React so appealing to individual developers is also what can make it a great fit for teams. Like any technology, React isn't a perfect solution for every use case or project, no matter the hype or what fanatical developers may try to convince you of. As you've already seen, there are many things that React doesn't do. But the things it does do, it does extremely well.

What makes React a great tool for larger teams and larger applications? First, there's the simplicity of using it. *Simplicity* is not the same thing as *ease*. Easy solutions are often dirty and quick, and worst of all, they can incur technical debt. Truly simple technology is flexible and robust. React provides powerful abstractions that can still

be worked with along with ways to drop down into the lower-level details when necessary. Simple technology is easier to understand and work with because the difficult
work of streamlining and removing what's not necessary has been done. In many ways
React has made simple easy, providing an effective solution without introducing harm-
ful "black magic" or an opaque API.

All this is great for the individual developer, but the effect is amplified across larger
teams and organizations. Although there's certainly room for React to improve and
keep growing, the hard work of making it a simple and flexible technology pays off for
engineering teams. Simpler technologies with good mental models tend to create less
of a mental burden for engineers and let them move faster and have a higher impact.
As a bonus, a simpler set of tools is easier to learn for new employees. Trying to ramp
up a new team member to an overly complex stack will not only cost time for the train-
ing engineers, it will also probably mean that the new developer will be unable to
make meaningful contributions for some time. Because React seeks to carefully rethink
established best practices, there's the initial cost in paradigm switch, but after that it's
often a big, long-term win.

Although it's certainly a different tool than others in the same space, React is a
fairly lightweight library in terms of responsibility and functionality. Where something
like Angular may require you to "buy in" to a more comprehensive API, React is only
concerned with the view of your application. This means it's much more trivial to integrate it with your current technologies, and it will leave you room to make choices
about other aspects. Some opinionated frameworks and libraries require an all-or-
nothing adoption stance, but React's "just the view" scope and general interoperability with JavaScript mean this isn't always the case.

Instead of going all-in, you can incrementally transition different projects or tools
over to React without having to make a drastic change to your structure, build stack,
or other related areas. That's a desirable trait for almost any technology, and it's how
React was first tried out at Facebook—in one small project area. From there it grew
and took hold as more and more teams saw and experienced its benefits. What does
all this mean for your team? It means you can evaluate React without having to take
the risk of completely rewriting the product using React.

The simplicity, un-opinionated nature, and performance of React make it a great
fit for projects small and large alike. As you keep exploring React, you'll see how it can
be a good fit for your team and projects.

1.6   *Summary*

React is a library for creating user interfaces that was initially built and open
sourced by Facebook. It's a JavaScript library built with simplicity, performance, and
components in mind. Rather than provide a comprehensive set of tools for creating
applications, it allows you to choose how to implement your data models, server
calls, and other application concerns, and what to implement them with. These key
reasons and others are why React can be a great tool for small and large applications

and teams alike. Here are some of the benefits of React briefly summarized for a few typical roles:

- *Individual developer*—Once you learn React, your applications can be easier to rapidly build out. They will tend to be easier to work on for larger teams, and sophisticated features can be easier to implement and maintain.
- *Engineering manager*—There's an initial cost for developers as they learn React, but eventually they'll be able to more easily and quickly develop complex applications.
- *CTO or upper management*—React, like any technology, is an investment with risks. But the eventual gains in productivity and reduced mental burdens often outweigh time sunk into ramping up. That's not the case for every team, but it's true for many.

All in all, React can be relatively easy for onboarding engineers to learn, can reduce the total amount of unnecessary complexity in an application, and can reduce technical debt by promoting code reuse. Take a second to review some of what you've learned about React so far:

- React is a library for building user interfaces, originally created by engineers at Facebook.
- React provides a simple, flexible API that's based around components.
- Components are the fundamental unit of React, and they're used extensively in React applications.
- React implements a virtual DOM that sits between your program and the browser DOM.
- The virtual DOM allows for efficient updates to the DOM using a fast diffing algorithm.
- The virtual DOM allows for excellent performance, but the biggest win is the mental model that it affords.

Now that you know a little more about the background and design of React, we can really dive in. In the next chapter, you'll create your first component and take a closer look at how React works. You'll be learning more about the virtual DOM, components in React, and how you can create components of your own.

\<Hello World /\>: our first component

Chapter 1 talked about React in mostly theoretical terms. If you're a "show me the code!" kind of person, this chapter is for you. We'll start looking at React up close in this chapter. As we get into some of React's API, you'll build a simple comment box that will help you see the mechanics of React in action and start to solidify a mental model of how React works. We'll start by building React components without any "syntactic sugar" or conveniences that might obscure the underlying technology. We'll explore JSX (a lightweight markup language that helps us build React components more easily) at the end of the chapter. In later chapters, we'll get more complex and see how to create a full app out of React components (Letters Social—check it out at https://social.react.sh), but in this chapter, we'll keep our scope limited to just a few related components.

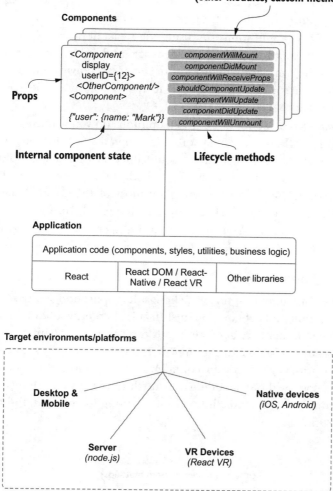

Figure 2.1 This is React at a very high level, which you may recognize from chapter 1. With React you can use components to build user interfaces that can run on browsers and native platforms like iOS and Android. It isn't a comprehensive framework—it leaves you the freedom to choose what libraries you use for data modeling, styling, HTTP calls, and more. You can run React apps in browsers and, with the help of React Native, on mobile devices.

Before diving in, let's take a brief, high-level look at React again to orient ourselves. Figure 2.1 gives you an overview of the core aspects of most React applications. Let's look at each part:

- *Components*—Encapsulated units of functionality that are the fundamental unit of React. These are what your views are made from. They're JavaScript functions or classes that receive properties as inputs and maintain their own internal state. React provides a set of lifecycle methods for certain types of components so you can hook into the different component-management steps.

- *React libraries*—React applications run using the React libraries. The core React library (`react`) is supported by the `react-dom` and `react-native` libraries. React DOM handles rendering in browser or server-side environments, whereas React Native provides native bindings that mean you can create React applications for iOS or Android.

- *Third-party libraries*—React doesn't enforce opinions on you with regard to data modeling, HTTP calls, specific areas of styling such as look and feel, or other aspects of your application. For these, you'll integrate other technologies to build out your application as you see fit. Not all libraries are compatible with React, but there are ways you can integrate most of them with React. We'll explore using non-React code in React apps in chapters 4, 10, and 11.

- *Running a React application*—Your React application, created from components, runs on a platform of your choice: web, mobile, or native.

2.1   Introducing React components

Components are the fundamental unit of a client-side application written in React. You'll definitely be creating lots of components! In this chapter, you'll build a simple comment box from components to get your hands dirty and take a whirlwind tour of React. But first let's take a little time to explore "thinking in components" and see how that might shake out with regard to your comment box. For most of the book, we'll usually dive into the code without spending too much time planning things out, but for this first foray into React we'll do a little bit of planning to get our mindset right. Have a look at figure 2.2.

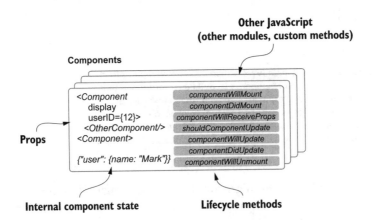

Figure 2.2   Overview of a React component. We'll be exploring each of these key parts for the rest of the book.

In this book, we'll pretend that we're employees of a fictional startup called Letters. You'll build a next-generation social network (where you can post, comment, and like—truly ground-breaking). In this chapter, we're exploring React as a potential technology choice for your company. You've been tasked with creating a simple set of components to get a feel for the technology. You have some really rough mockups that the design team gave you, but that's about it. Figure 2.3 shows a pretty version of what you'll be building.

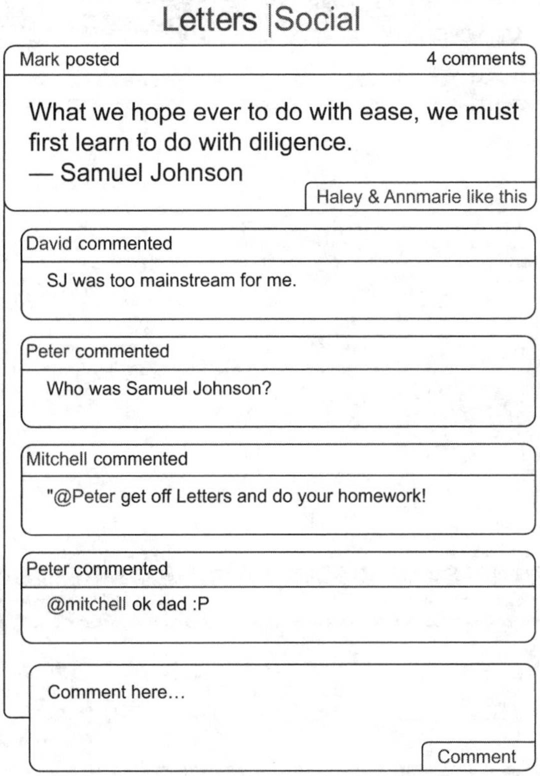

Figure 2.3 **Rough comment box mockup. You'll create a UI where users can add comments to a post and view previous comments.**

How should you get started building this? Let's begin with understanding the data your application needs and then seeing how you can turn that into components. How should you translate the mockup into components? You could just dive in and start trying to create components without knowing anything about React, but without understanding how they work or what purpose they'd serve, you could end up creating something messy or not idiomatic to React. We'll do some planning in the next few sections so you have a better idea about how to structure and design your comment box.

Exercise 2.1   Revisit your interface breakdown

Before moving on, take some time to revisit an exercise from the last chapter. You looked at a web interface and took some time to break it down on your own. Take a minute to revisit the same interface and see if you'd do anything differently now that you know more about components in React. Would you group things together differently? Here's the same marked-up GitHub profile interface from chapter 1 to jog your memory:

2.1.1   Understanding the application data

Besides the mockup, we need something else before we can plan how your components will be organized. We need to know what information the API will provide to your application. Based on the mockup, you can probably already guess some of the data that you might be getting back. Getting a sense of the shape of your application data will be an important part of the planning we're doing before starting to create your UI.

Web APIs

You may have heard the term *API* used frequently in your job or in your learning. If you're already familiar with this concept, feel free to move on. If not, this section might help you. What is an API? An API, or, *application programming interface*, is a set of routines and protocols for building software. That might sound vague, and it is a pretty general definition. API is a broad term, applying to everything from company platforms to open source libraries.

In web development and engineering, API has become almost synonymous with a remote, web-based *public* API. This means that an API is usually a way of exposing defined ways to interact with a program or platform, usually over the internet, and for people to use and consume. There are many examples, but two of the more familiar ones are the Facebook and Stripe APIs. They provide a set of methods to interact with their programs and data over the web.

The back-end infrastructure team at Letters, our fictional company, has created such an API for you to use. There are many different forms and types of web-based APIs, but the one that you'll work with in this book is that of a *RESTful JSON API*. This means that a server will give you data in the JSON format and the available data organized around resources like users, posts, comments, and so on. RESTful JSON APIs are a common style of remote API, so this likely won't be the only time you work with one if you haven't already.

The following listing shows an example of data you'll receive from the API for your comment box and how it might match up to your mockup.

Listing 2.1 Sample JSON API

```
{
  "id": 123,
  "content": "What we hope ever to do with ease, we must first learn to do
      with diligence. — Samuel Johnson",
  "user": {
    "name": "Mark Thomas",
    "id": 1
  },
  "comments": [{
    "id": 0,
    "user": "David",
    "content": "too. mainstream."
  }, {
    "id": 1,
    "user": "Peter",
    "content": "Who was Samuel Johnson?"
  }, {
    "id": 2,
    "user": "Mitchell",
    "content": "@Peter get off Letters and do your homework!"
  }, {
```

This didn't appear in the visual mockup, but that doesn't mean you don't need this piece of data.

You've received a collection of comment objects.

Comments have IDs too.

```
      "id": 3,
      "user": "Peter",
      "content": "@mitchell ok dad :P"
   }]
}
```

The API returns a JSON response containing a single post. It has some important properties, including id, content, author, and comments. id is a number, content and author are strings, and comments is an array of objects. Each comment has its own ID, a user who made the comment, and the content of the comment.

2.1.2   *Multiple components: Composition and parent-child relationships*

You have the data we need and a mockup, but how do you go about forming components to use that data? For one, you need to know how components can be organized with other components. React components are organized into tree structures. Like DOM elements, React components can be nested and can contain other components. They can also appear "next to" other components, which means that they occur at the same level as other components (see figure 2.4).

That brings up an important question: what sort of relationships can components have? You might think there would be quite a few different types of relationships that can be created using components, and in one sense, you're right. Components can be used in flexible ways. Because they're self-contained and tend not to carry around any "baggage," they're said to be *composable.*

Composable components are often easily moved around and can be reused to create other components. You can think of them almost like LEGO bricks. Each LEGO brick is self-contained, so it can be easily moved around—you don't have to bring a whole set with the one brick—and it easily fits in with other components. Portability isn't the be-all, end-all, but it's often a feature of well-designed React components.

Because components are composable, they can be used in many places throughout your application. Wherever a component is used, it probably helps form a certain type of relationship: *parent* and *child.* If a component contains another component, it's said to be the parent. A component within another component is said to be a child. Components that exist at the same level don't share any sort of direct relationship, even though they might be right next to each other. They only "care" about their parents and children.

Figure 2.4 shows how components can relate to each other in a parent-child way and be composed together to create new components. Note the lack of direct relationship between the two sibling components despite a direct parent-child relationship. I'll cover more on this when we explore data flow in React.

2.1.3   *Establishing component relationships*

We have a sense of the data and visual appearance of your interface as well as the parent-child relationship components can form. Now you can get started on defining

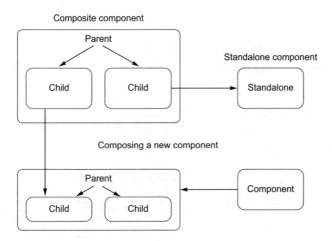

Composite component

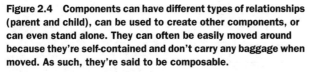

Composing a new component

Figure 2.4 Components can have different types of relationships (parent and child), can be used to create other components, or can even stand alone. They can often be easily moved around because they're self-contained and don't carry any baggage when moved. As such, they're said to be composable.

your component hierarchy, which is the process of applying what you've learned so far. You'll establish what will be a component and where it will go. This process of establishing component relationships won't look the same for every team or every project. Component relationships are also likely to change over time, so don't expect perfection your first time around. Easier iteration in a UI is part of what makes React pleasant to work with.

Take a minute or two to try breaking down the mockup into components before we move on. You've done this a couple times now, but practicing thinking with components will only make working with React easier. As you practice, remember the following:

- Ensure that components are grouped together in a way that makes sense; components should be organized around related functionality. If it's untenable to move components around in your application, you might be creating too rigid a hierarchy. This isn't always the case, but it's good to watch out for.
- If you see an interface element repeated multiple times, that's usually a good candidate for becoming a component.
- You won't get everything perfect the first time, and that's okay. It's normal to iteratively improve your code. The initial planning isn't meant to eliminate future change, but to set the proper starting direction.

With these guidelines in mind, you can look at the available data and mockup and start by breaking things up into a few components. Figure 2.5 shows one way of breaking up the interface into components.

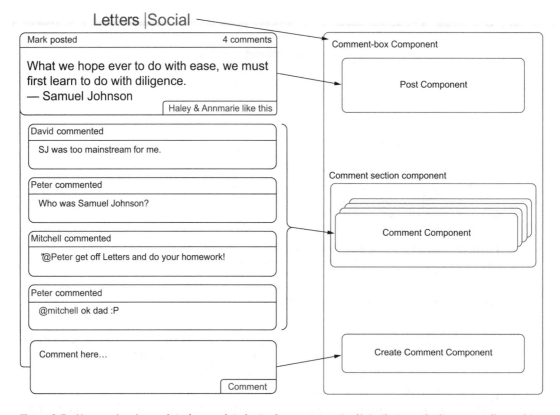

Figure 2.5   You can break your interface up into just a few components. Note that you don't necessarily need to create components for every single element of the interface, although it might make sense to decompose more parts into components as an application grows. Also, you'll notice that the same comment component will be used for each of the comments attached to a post. And note that I've diagrammed things here on the side for readability; you might have instead drawn lines right on top of everything.

With React you can be flexible in designing your application. We've come up with four components, but there are many ways that you might have gone about dividing things up. React enforces a parent-child relationship between components, but beyond that you're free to define your hierarchy in whatever way makes the most sense to you and your team. There might be, for example, cases where you break a small section of the UI into many different parts. The size of the UI isn't directly related to how many or how few components it should be comprised from.

Now that we've gone through some initial planning, you're ready to dive in and start creating your comment box UI. In the next section, you'll start creating React components. You won't use any syntactic helpers like JSX. Instead, we'll focus on "raw" React and you'll get a feel for the core mechanics of the technology before moving on to use such helpers.

You might get frustrated by having to forgo some of the helpers that you'd use during normal React development. I'm glad about that, because it will probably mean that you'll more genuinely appreciate and understand the abstractions you'll be working with. It's not always the case, but in my experience starting with the lower-level elements of a new technology will generally better equip you to work with it for the long term. We don't need to write our JavaScript programs in assembly code, certainly, but we also don't want to use a technology with an incomplete understanding of the core mechanics.

2.2 Creating components in React

In this section, you'll create some React components and run them in a browser. For now, you won't need to use node.js or any anything else to get everything set up and running. You'll run code in the browser via CodeSandbox (https://codesandbox.io). If you'd prefer to edit the files locally, you can click Download in the CodeSandbox code editor and get the code for that example.

You'll use three libraries for your first components: React, React DOM, and prop-types. React DOM is a renderer for React that was split off from the main React library to better separate concerns; it handles rendering components to the DOM or to a string for server-side rendering. The prop-types library is a development library that will help you do some typechecking on data passed to your components.

You'll start creating the comment box component by creating some of the constituent parts first. This will help you get a better sense of what's going to happen overall when React creates and renders your components. You need to add a new DOM element with an ID of root as well as some basic code that uses React DOM. The following listing shows the bare-bones starting place for your component. For each listing, I'll include a link to an online running version of the code you can easily edit and play around with.

Listing 2.2   Starting out

```
//... index.js
const node = document.getElementById("root");    ⟵  Store a reference to the root
                                                      element—you'll render your React
                                                      app into this DOM element.

//... index.html
<div id="root"></div>    ⟵  In the index.html file you've
                             created a div with the id 'root'.
```

Code for listing 2.2 is available online at https://codesandbox.io/s/vj9xkqzkvy.

2.2.1 Creating React elements

So far, your code won't do much of anything except download the React libraries and find the root DOM element. To make something substantial happen, you need to use React DOM. You'll need to call its render method for React to create and manage your component. You'll call this method with a component to render and container

(which will be the DOM element you stored in a variable earlier). The signature of
`ReactDOM.render` looks like this:

```
ReactDOM.render(
  ReactElement element,
  DOMElement container,
  [function callback]
) -> ReactComponent
```

React DOM needs an element of type `ReactElement` and a DOM element. You've created a valid DOM element that you can use, but now you need to create a React element. But what's a React element?

> **DEFINITION**   A *React element* is a light, stateless, immutable primitive in React.
> There are two types: `ReactComponentElement` and `ReactDOMElement`. React-
> DOMElements are virtual representations of DOM elements. `ReactComponent-`
> `Elements` reference either a function or a class corresponding to a React
> component.

Elements are the descriptors we use to tell React what we want to see on the screen and
are a central concept in React. Most of your components will be collections of React
elements; they'll create a "boundary" of sorts around a portion of your UI so you can
group functionality, markup, and styles together. But what does it mean for a React
element to be a virtual representation of a DOM element? This means that React elements are to React what DOM elements are to the DOM—the basic primitives that
compose a UI. When you're creating plain old HTML markup, you use a variety of element types (`div`, `span`, `section`, `p`, `img`, and so on) to contain and structure information. In React, you can use React elements—which tell React about either React
components or regular DOM elements you want rendered—to compose and build
your UI.

Maybe the parallel between DOM elements and React elements didn't click for
you immediately. That's okay. Remember how React is supposed to help you by creating a better mental model to work with? The parallel between DOM elements and
React elements is one way in which it does that. It means that you get a familiar mental
structure to work with: a tree structure of elements that are like regular DOM elements. Figure 2.6 will help you visualize some of the similarities between React elements and DOM elements.

Another way to think of React elements is as a set of basic instructions for React to
use, like a blueprint for a DOM element. React elements are what React DOM will take
and use to update the DOM. In figure 2.7 React elements are being used in the overall
process of a React application.

You now know a little more about React elements in general, but how do they get
created and what goes into creating them? You create React elements with `React`

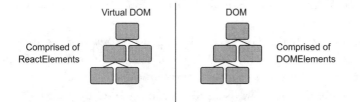

Figure 2.6 The virtual and "real" DOM share a similar tree-like structure, which makes it easy for you to think about the structure of your components and overall application in React in similar ways. The DOM is comprised of DOMElements (HTMLElements and SVGElements), whereas React's virtual DOM is comprised of React elements.

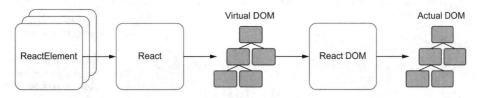

Figure 2.7 React elements are what React uses to create a virtual DOM that React DOM will manage and use to reconcile and update the actual DOM. They are simple blueprints for React to use in creating and managing elements.

.createElement—go figure! Let's look at its function signature to find out how you should use it:

```
React.createElement(
  String/ReactClass type,
  [object props],
  [children...]
) -> React Element
```

React.createElement takes a string or component (either a class extending React.Component or a function), a props object, and children and returns a React element. Remember, a React element is a lightweight representation of something you want React to render. It can indicate either a DOM element or another React component.

Let's look more closely at each of these basic instructions:

- type—You can pass in either a string that is the tag name of the HTML element to be created ("div", "span", "a", and so on) or a React class, which we'll look at shortly. Think of this argument as React asking, "What type of thing am I going to be creating?"

- props—Short for *properties.* The props object provides a way of specifying which attributes will be defined on the HTML element (if in the context of a React-DOMElement) or will be available to a component class instance.

- children...—Remember how I said React components are *composable?* This is where you can do some composing. Using children..., the arguments passed after type and props let you nest, order, and even further nest other React elements. As you can see in listing 2.3, you can nest React elements by nesting calls to React.createElement in children....

React.createElement asks, "What am I creating?", "How should I configure it?", and "What does it contain?" The following listing shows how you might use React .createElement.

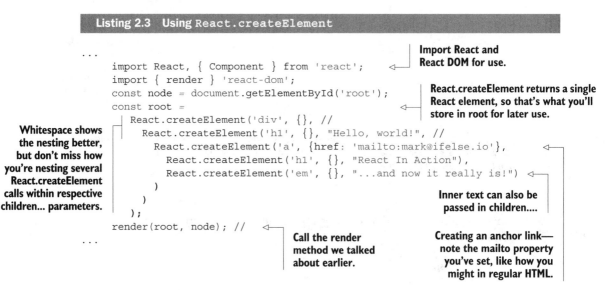

Listing 2.3   Using `React.createElement`

```
...
    import React, { Component } from 'react';      ←┐ Import React and
                                                      React DOM for use.
    import { render } 'react-dom';
    const node = document.getElementById('root');
    const root =                                   ←┐ React.createElement returns a single
                                                      React element, so that's what you'll
      React.createElement('div', {}, //               store in root for later use.
        React.createElement('h1', {}, "Hello, world!", //
          React.createElement('a', {href: 'mailto:mark@ifelse.io'},  ←
            React.createElement('h1', {}, "React In Action"),
            React.createElement('em', {}, "...and now it really is!")  ←
          )
        )
      );
    render(root, node); //   ←
    ...
```

Whitespace shows the nesting better, but don't miss how you're nesting several React.createElement calls within respective children... parameters.

Call the render method we talked about earlier.

Inner text can also be passed in children....

Creating an anchor link—note the mailto property you've set, like how you might in regular HTML.

Code for listing 2.3 is available online at https://codesandbox.io/s/qxx7z86q4w.

2.2.2   Rendering your first component

You should now be able see something besides a blank page, as shown in figure 2.8. You just created your first React component! Using the developer tools for your browser, try opening up the page and inspecting the HTML. You should see HTML elements that correspond to what you created using React. Note that the properties you passed have made it through, too, so you can click the link and send me an email telling me how much you're loving learning about React.

This is great, but you may be wondering how React turns your many React .createElements into what you see on the screen. React uses the React elements you provide to create a virtual DOM that React DOM can use as it manages the browser

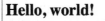

Hello, world!

React In Action

...and now it really is!

Figure 2.8   Your first component. It's not much, but you've successfully created a component using React.

DOM. Remember from figure 2.4 that the virtual and real DOMs share similar structures? Well, React needs to form its own virtual DOM tree structure from your React elements before it can do its work.

To do that, React will recursively evaluate all of the children... properties of every React.createElement call, passing the result up to the parent element. You can think of React doing this as being like a small child asking, "What is *X*?" repeatedly until they understand every little thing about *X*. Figure 2.9 shows how you might think about React evaluating nested React elements. Follow the arrows down and across to the right to see how React examines the children... of every React element until it can form a complete tree.

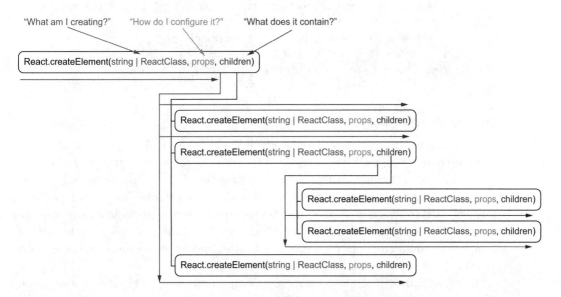

Figure 2.9   React will recursively evaluate a series of React elements to determine how it should form a virtual DOM tree structure for your components. It will also check for more React elements in children... to evaluate. React will go through every possible path, like a child asking, "What is X?" until they know everything. You can follow the arrows down and across to the right to get a sense of how React might evaluate nested React elements as well as what each parameter is asking.

Now that you've created your first component, you may have a few questions and even some concerns. Even with some formatting help, it's clear that it will be difficult to read through components that are nested even a few levels deep. We'll explore better ways to write components, so don't worry—you won't be nesting `React.create-Element` hundreds of times. Using it now will give you a better sense of what `React.createElement` does and will hopefully help you appreciate JSX when you start using it that much more.

You also may be concerned that what you've created seems too simple. So far, React seems like it might be a verbose JavaScript templating system. But there's much more that React can do: enter components.

Exercise 2.2   React elements

Before moving on to components, check your understanding of React elements. Either on paper or in your mind, list out a few of the characteristics of a React element. Here are a few characteristics of React elements to refresh your memory before moving on:

- React elements take a string to create a type of DOM element (div, a, p, and so on).
- You can provide configuration to the React element via a props object; these are analogous to attributes DOM elements can have (`<img src="aUrl"/>`, for example).
- React elements are nestable and you can provide other React elements as the children of an element.
- React uses React elements to create a virtual DOM that `React DOM` can use as it updates the browser DOM.
- React elements are what components are made from in React.

2.2.3   *Creating React components*

As you can probably already tell, using only React elements and `React.createElement` to create parts of your UI doesn't do much for you beyond managing the DOM. You could still pass in event handlers as props to handle clicks or input changes, pass in other data to display, and even nest elements. But you'd still be missing the *persistent state* provided by React, lifecycle methods that would give you predictable ways to work with a component, and, for that matter, any sort of logical grouping together that a component could give you. You definitely want to find a way to group React elements together.

You can do that through components. Components serve to bundle up and group functionality, markup, styles, and other related bits of your UI together. They act as a sort of boundary around parts of your UI that can also contain other components. Components can then be independent, reusable pieces that allow you think about each piece in isolation.

You can create two primary types of components using functions and JavaScript classes. I'll cover the first type, *stateless functional components,* in future chapters. For now we'll talk about the second type: *stateful* React components created with JavaScript classes. From here on, when I refer to a React component, I'm referring to a component that's a created from either a class or a function.

2.2.4 *Creating React classes*

To start really building something, you need more than just React elements; you need components. As mentioned, React components (components created from functions) are like React elements but with more features. Components in React are classes that help group together React elements and functionality. They can be created as classes that extend the `React.Component` base class or functions. This section explores React classes and how to use this type of component in React. Let's look at how you create a React class:

```
class MyReactClassComponent extends Component {
    render() {}
}
```

Rather than invoke a specific method from the React library as you did with `React.createElement`, creating a component from `React.Component` is done by declaring a JavaScript class that inherits from the `React.Component` abstract base class. That inheriting class will typically need to define at least a render method that will return a single React element or an array of React elements. The old way to create React classes was with the `createClass` method. This has since changed with the advent of classes in JavaScript and is now discouraged, although you can still use the `create-react-class` module, available on npm. For more on using React without ES2015+ JavaScript, check out https://reactjs.org/docs/react-without-es6.html.

2.2.5 *The render method*

We'll start our exploration of creating components as React classes with the `render` method mentioned earlier. This is one of the most common methods you'll see in React applications, and almost any component that renders something to a screen will have a `render` method. We'll eventually explore components that don't directly render anything but instead modify or enhance other components (known sometimes as *higher-order* components).

The render method needs to return exactly one React element. In this way, the render method is similar to how React elements are created—they can be nested but at the topmost level there's a single node. However, unlike React elements, the `render` methods of React classes have access to embedded data (persisted internal component state) as well as component methods and additional methods inherited from the `React.Component` abstract base class (all of which I'll cover). The persistent state I mentioned is available to the entire component because React creates a "backing instance" for this type of component. That's also why you'll hear these sorts of components referred to as *stateful* components.

All this means that React will create and keep track of a special data object for an instance of a React class (not the blueprint itself) that stays around over time and can be updated through special React functions. I'll cover this more in future chapters, but figure 2.10 illustrates how React classes get backing instances and React elements don't.

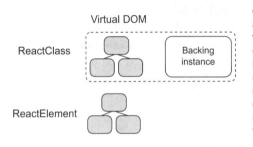

Virtual DOM

ReactClass

Backing instance

ReactElement

Figure 2.10   React will create a backing instance in memory for components created as React component classes. As you can see, React component classes get one, and React elements and non-React class components don't. Remember that React elements are mirrors of the DOM and components are ways to group them together. The backing instance is a way of providing data storage and access for a specific component. The data stored in the instance will be made available to the component's render method through specific API methods. This means that you get access to data that you can change and that will persist over time.

When using a React class to create a component, you also have access to props—data that you can pass to your component and that it can in turn pass to child components. You may remember this props data as a parameter you passed to React.create-Element. As before, you can use it to specify properties of components at the time of creation. Props shouldn't be modified within a component, but you'll soon discover ways for updating data in React components.

In listing 2.5 in the next section you'll see a React class component in action and how you've created more nested React elements and passed in your custom data using this.props. When you see props being used with React classes, it's as if you were creating a custom HTML element like Jedi and giving it a custom attribute like "name": <Jedi name="Obi Wan"/>. I'll cover the this JavaScript keyword more in future chapters, but note that in this case the reserved JavaScript keyword this points to the component instance.

2.2.6   *Property validation via PropTypes*

You know that React class components are free to use custom properties, and this sounds great; it's as if you can create your own custom HTML elements but with even more functionality. Remember that with great power comes great responsibility. You need to provide some sort of way to validate which properties you'll be using so you can prevent bugs and plan the sorts of data your components will use. To do that, you can use validators available from a namespace within React: PropTypes. The PropTypes set of validators used to be included with the React core library, but was later broken out and deprecated within React in version 15.5. To use `PropTypes`, you'll need to install the `prop-types` package, which is still part of the React toolchain but is no longer included in the core library. This package will be included in the application source code and the CodeSandbox examples that you've been using in this chapter.

The `prop-types` library provides a set of validators that will let you specify what props your component needs or expects. For example, if you were going to build a ProfilePicture component, it wouldn't be of much use without a picture (or the logic to handle not having one available). You could use `PropTypes` to specify which props your ProfilePicture component would need to work and what those props would look like.

You can think of `PropTypes` as providing a sort of contract that can be fulfilled or broken by other developers and your future self. Using `PropTypes` isn't strictly necessary for React to work, but should be used for bug prevention and ease of debugging. Another benefit of using `PropTypes` is that if you specify what props you expect first, you get a chance to think through what your component will need to work.

When using `PropTypes`, you need to add a `propTypes` property to the `React` `.Component` class via a static class property or by simple property assignment after the class definition. Note the lowercasing of the property on the class but not the one from the `React` object, as it can be easy to mix them up. Listing 2.4 shows how you can use `PropTypes`, as well as return React elements from React class components. In this listing, you'll bring together a few things: creating a `React` class that you can pass to `createElement`, adding a `render` method, and specifying `propTypes`.

Listing 2.4 Using `PropTypes` and the `render` method

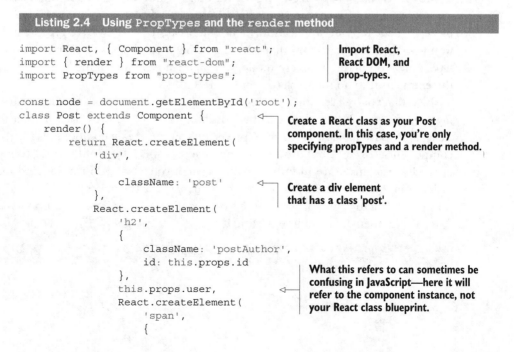

```
import React, { Component } from "react";        Import React,
import { render } from "react-dom";              React DOM, and
import PropTypes from "prop-types";              prop-types.

const node = document.getElementById('root');
class Post extends Component {                   Create a React class as your Post
    render() {                                   component. In this case, you're only
        return React.createElement(              specifying propTypes and a render method.
            'div',
            {
                className: 'post'                Create a div element
            },                                   that has a class 'post'.
            React.createElement(
                'h2',
                {
                    className: 'postAuthor',
                    id: this.props.id
                },                               What this refers to can sometimes be
                this.props.user,                 confusing in JavaScript—here it will
                React.createElement(             refer to the component instance, not
                    'span',                      your React class blueprint.
                    {
```

```
                        className: 'postBody'
                    },
                    this.props.content
                )
            )
        );
    }
}

Post.propTypes = {
    user: PropTypes.string.isRequired,
    content: PropTypes.string.isRequired,
    id: PropTypes.number.isRequired
};

const App = React.createElement(Post, {
    id: 1,
    content: ' said: This is a post!',
    user: 'mark'
});

render(App, node);

...
```

Using className instead of class for the Dom element's CSS class name

Again, the content prop is the inner content of a span element you're creating.

Properties can be optional or required, have a type, and can even be required to have a certain "shape" (an object with certain properties, for example).

Pass the Post React Class to React.createElement along with some props to create something. React DOM can render—try changing the data to see how the render for your component output changes.

Code for listing 2.4 is available online at https://codesandbox.io/s/3yj462omrq.

You should see some text appear: "mark said: This is a post!" If you hadn't provided any of the required props, you'd see a warning in the developer console. Failure to provide certain props might break your app because of what components need to work, but the validation step won't. In other words, if you forget to provide a crucial piece of data to your application, it might break, but using PropTypes validation won't—it'll just let you know that you forgot the prop. Because PropTypes only does type evaluation in development mode, your app running in production won't expend the extra effort to do the work of PropTypes.

Now that you're creating a component and passing in some data, you can try nesting components. I've mentioned this possibility before, and it's part of what makes React a pleasure to work with and so powerful: you can create components from other components. Listing 2.5 illustrates this and shows a special use of the children property. I'll cover this more in future chapters when you work with routing and higher-order components. When you use the this.props.children prop, it's like an outlet for nested data to come through. In this case, you'll create a Comment component, pass it as the argument, and achieve nesting it.

Listing 2.5   Adding a nested component

```
//...
      this.props.user,
      React.createElement(
        "span",
        {
```

```
            className: "postBody"
        },
        this.props.content          Add this.props.children to
    ),                              the Post component so it
    this.props.children    ◁───     can render children.
//...
class Comment extends Component {   ◁───   Create a Comment component,
    render() {                              similarly to how you created a
        return React.createElement(         Post component.
            'div',
            {
                className: 'comment'
            },
            React.createElement(
                'h2',
                {
                    className: 'commentAuthor'
                },
                this.props.user,
                React.createElement(
                    'span',
                    {
                        className: 'commentContent'
                    },
                    this.props.content
                )
            )
        );
    }
}

                                    Declare
                                    propTypes.
Comment.propTypes = {          ◁───┘
    id: PropTypes.number.isRequired,
    content: PropTypes.string.isRequired,
    user: PropTypes.string.isRequired
};

const App = React.createElement(
    Post,
    {
        id: 1,
        content: ' said: This is a post!',
        user: 'mark'
    },
    React.createElement(Comment, {    ◁───   Nest the Comment
        id: 2,                              component within the
        user: 'bob',                       Post component.
        content: ' commented: wow! how cool!'
    })
);

ReactDOM.render(App, node);
```

Code for listing 2.5 is available online at https://codesandbox.io/s/k2vn448pn3.

Now that you've created a nested component, you should be able to see more in your browser. Next, we'll see how you can use the embedded state mentioned earlier that comes with React classes to create dynamic components.

Exercise 2.3   Reverse engineering a component tree

Before moving on, check your understanding by reverse-engineering a component tree from a site like GitHub. Open your developer tools, pick a DOM element that's not too deeply nested, and reconstruct a React class from it. Consider the following DOM element:

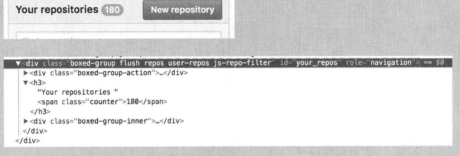

How would you structure a similar component structure but in React? (Feel free to not add every CSS class name.)

2.3   *The life and times of a component*

In this section, you're going to add to your Post and Comment components to make them interactive. Earlier, we discovered that components created as React classes get some special ways to store and access data through "backing instances." To understand how, let's revisit the big picture of how React works. Figure 2.11 sums up what you've learned so far. You can create components from React classes that are made from React elements (elements that map to the DOM). What I'm calling *React classes* are sub-classes of `React.Component` that `React.createElement` can use.

Components created from React classes have backing instances that let you store data and need to have a `render` method that returns exactly one React element. React will take React elements and create an in-memory virtual DOM from them, and it will handle managing and updating the DOM.

You've added a `render` method and some `PropTypes` validation to your React classes. But you're going to need more than that to create dynamic components. React classes can have some special methods that will be called in a certain order as React manages the virtual DOM. `render`, which you've used to return React elements, is just one of those methods.

In addition to the reserved lifecycle methods, you can add your own methods. React gives you the freedom and flexibility to add whatever functionality you need to

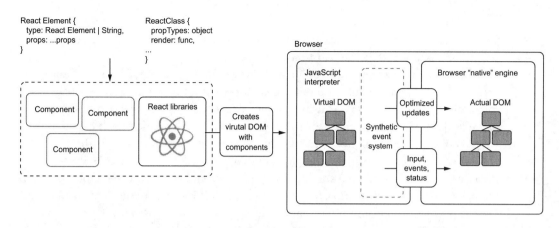

Figure 2.11   Zooming in on rendering in React. React classes and React elements are used by React to create an in-memory virtual DOM that manages the real DOM. It also creates a "synthetic" event system so that you can still react to events from the browser (such as clicks, scrolls, and other user-caused events).

your components. Pretty much anything that's valid JavaScript is useable in React. If you look back at figure 1.1 in chapter 1, you'll notice that lifecycle methods, special properties, and custom code make up most of a React component. What's left?

2.3.1   A React state of mind

Along with custom methods and lifecycle methods, React classes also gives you state (data) that can persist with the component. This comes from the backing instance I've mentioned. *State* is a big topic—I won't cover it all in this chapter, but you can learn enough about it for now to be able to make your components interactive and lively. What's state? Another way to think about it is as *information about something at a given time.* You could, for example, get the "state" of your friend by asking "How are you today?"

There are two general types of state: *mutable* and *immutable.* A simple way to think about the difference between them is to think in terms of time. Can something change after being created? If so, it can be called mutable. If not, it can be called immutable. There are in-depth academic areas of study on these topics, so I won't go into depth on them here.

In React, components created as JavaScript classes (https://developer.mozilla.org/en-US/docs/Web/JavaScript/Reference/Classes) that extend `React.Component` may have both mutable and immutable state, whereas components created from functions (stateless functional components) only have access to immutable state (props). I'll cover these in future chapters; for now I'll stick to components that inherit from `React.Component` and get state and additional methods. In these sorts of components, state is accessible from the `this.state` property of the instance of the class. The immutable state made available to you is accessed with `this.props`, which you've been using already to create static components.

`this.props` shouldn't be modified from within the component. You'll see ways to provide data that changes over time to components in future chapters. For now, all you need to know is that you can't directly mutate `this.props`.

You may be wondering how you might use `state` and `props` in React. The answer is pretty much how you would use data passed to or used in a function. That includes calculations, display, parsing, business logic, and any other data-related tasks. In fact, props and state are the primary ways that you can utilize dynamic or static data in your UI (showing user information, passing data to event handlers, and so forth).

State and props are vehicles for the data that make up your app and make it useful. If you're creating a social network application (and you will in future chapters), you'll often use a combination of props and state to build components that display and update user information, updates, and more. If you're using React for data visualization, you might use props and state as inputs for visualization libraries like `D3.js`. Whatever you're building, you'll probably use state and props to manage and funnel information within your React application.

Exercise 2.4   Mutable vs. immutable

Before moving on, check your understanding by thinking about the differences between the two main types of data in React: mutable and immutable. Mark each statement as true or false:

- Mutable means that data can change over time: T | F
- State is accessed with the `this.state` property in React: T | F
- `props` is a mutable object provided by React: T | F
- Immutable data doesn't change over time: T | F
- Props are accessed via `this.props`: T | F

2.3.2   Setting initial state

When should you use state and how do you get started using it? For now, the simple answer is *when you want to make changes to data stored within a component*. I said props were immutable (not modifiable), so if you need to change data, you need mutable state. In React, data that tends to need to be mutable often comes from or is the result of user input (often text, files, toggled options, and so on), but could be many other things. To keep track of user interactions with form elements, you need to provide an initial state and then change that state over time. You can use the constructor of the component to set the initial state for your component, a comment box component that builds on the ideas and concepts from earlier code listings. It will allow you to add comments to a post via a simple form. The following listing shows how to set up the component and set initial state.

Listing 2.6 Setting initial state

```
//...
class CreateComment extends Component {
    constructor(props) {
        super(props);
        this.state = {
            content: '',
            user: ''
        };
    }
    render() {
        return React.createElement(
            'form',
            {

                className: 'createComment'
            },
            React.createElement('input', {
                type: 'text',
                placeholder: 'Your name',
                value: this.state.user
            }),
            React.createElement('input', {
                type: 'text',
                placeholder: 'Thoughts?'
            }),
            React.createElement('input', {
                type: 'submit',
                value: 'Post'
            })
        );
    }
}
CreateComment.propTypes = {
    content: React.PropTypes.string
};
//...
const App = React.createElement(
    Post,
    {
        id: 1,
        content: ' said: This is a post!',
        user: 'mark'
    },
    React.createElement(Comment, {
        id: 2,
        user: 'bob',
        content: ' commented: wow! how cool!'
    }),
    React.createElement(CreateComment)
);
```

Call super in the class constructor and assign the initial state object to the instance of the class's state property—note that you won't normally assign state like this except in the constructor of the component class.

Create a component as a React class that will have some input fields for the user—I'll cover forms in more detail in future chapters.

Add CreateComment to the App component.

The code for listing 2.6 is available online at https://codesandbox.io/s/p5r3kwqx5q.

To update the state that you initialized in the component class's constructor, you need to use a special method; you can't just overwrite this.state like you might in a non-React situation. That's because React needs to keep track of state and ensure that the virtual DOM and real DOM are kept in sync. To update state within a React class component, you'll use this.setState; look at the basic usage. It takes an updater function to use for updating state and doesn't return anything:

```
setState(
    function(prevState, props) -> nextState,
    callback
)-> void
```

this.setState takes an updater function that returns object that will get shallowly merged into state. For example, if you had initially set a property of username to be an empty string, you'd use this.setState to set a new username value for your component's state. React will take that value and update the backing instance and DOM with your new value.

One key difference between updating or reassigning a value in JavaScript and using setState is that React can choose to batch updates based on state changes to maximize efficiency. This means that when you call setState to perform a state update, it won't necessarily happen right away. Think of it more as an acknowledgement that React will update the DOM based on new state in the most efficient way possible, as soon as possible.

What would cause React to update? JavaScript is event-driven, so it'll probably be in response to some sort of user input (at least in the browser). That might be a click, key press, or many of the other events supported by browsers. How do events work with React? React implements a synthetic event system as a part of the virtual DOM that will translate events in the browser into events for your React application. You can set up event handlers that can respond to events from the browser, as you normally would in JavaScript. One difference is that React event handlers are set up on React elements or components themselves (as opposed to using addEventListener). You can update the state of your component using the data from these events (text from an input, a radio button value, or even the target of the event).

Listing 2.7 shows how to put into practice what you've learned about setting initial state and setting up event handlers. There are many different events you can listen for in the browser, encompassing virtually every possible user interaction (clicking, typing, forms, scrolling, and so on). Here we're most concerned with two main ones: when the form input values change, and when the form is submitted. By listening for those events, you can receive and use data to create new comments.

Listing 2.7   Setting up event handlers

```
...
class CreateComment extends Component {
    constructor(props) {
```

```
        super(props);
        this.state = {
            content: '',
            user: ''
        };
        this.handleUserChange = this.handleUserChange.bind(this);
        this.handleTextChange = this.handleTextChange.bind(this);
        this.handleSubmit = this.handleSubmit.bind(this);
    }
    handleUserChange(event) {
        const val = event.target.value;
        this.setState(() => ({
            user: val
        }));
    }
    handleTextChange(event) {
        const val = event.target.value;
        this.setState(() => ({
            content: val
        }));
    }
    handleSubmit(event) {
        event.preventDefault();
        this.setState(() => ({
            user: '',
            content: ''
        }));
    }
    render() {
        return React.createElement(
            'form',
            {
                className: 'createComment',
                onSubmit: this.handleSubmit
            },
            React.createElement('input', {
                type: 'text',
                placeholder: 'Your name',
                value: this.state.user,
                onChange: this.handleUserChange
            }),
            React.createElement('input', {
                type: 'text',
                placeholder: 'Thoughts?',
                value: this.state.content,
                onChange: this.handleTextChange
            }),
            React.createElement('input', {
                type: 'submit',
                value: 'Post'
            })
        );
    }
}
CreateComment.propTypes = {
```

Because components created with classes don't auto bind component methods, you need to bind them to this in the constructor.

Assign an event handler to handle changes to the author field—you get the value of the input element with event.target.value and use this.setState to update the component's state.

Create an event handler with similar functionality for the comment content.

Event handler for form submission event

Reset the input field after submission so the user can submit further comments.

```
    onCommentSubmit: PropTypes.func.isRequired,
    content: PropTypes.string
};
...
```

The code for listing 2.7 is available online at https://codesandbox.io/s/x9mxo31pxp.

Did you notice how you used `.bind` in the constructor of the component class? In previous versions of React, React would *auto bind* methods to the instance of your component for you. With the switch to JavaScript classes, though, you need to bind methods yourself. If you define a component method and it's not working, confirm that you've correctly bound your methods—it can be easy to forget when first starting out with React.

Next, try leaving out the `onChange` event handlers and see if you can type anything into the form inputs. You won't be able to because React is ensuring that the DOM stays in sync with the virtual DOM, which isn't being updated and thus won't let the DOM change. If this doesn't make perfect sense right now, don't worry—chapters 5 and 6 cover forms more extensively.

Now that you have a way of listening for events and modifying the component's state, you can implement a way to create new comments using unidirectional data flow. In React, data flows top-down, as an input from parents to children. When you create composite components, you can pass information to child components via props and make use of it in child components. That means you could store the data from the `CreateComment` component in a parent component and from there pass the data to child components. But how can you get the data from a new comment (in the form that the user types text into) in a child component back into the parent and into the child? Figure 2.12 shows an example of the sort of data flow you need.

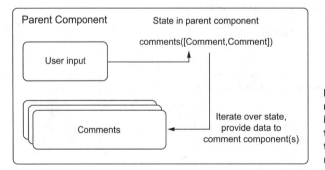

Figure 2.12 To add a post, you need to capture the data from input fields and somehow send it to the parent component, and then that updated data will be used to render out the posts.

How can you make this happen? One kind of data we haven't looked at passing via props is functions. Because functions can be passed as arguments to other functions in JavaScript, you can use this to your advantage. You can define a method on a parent component and give it to the child component as a property. That way, the child component can send data back up to its parent without having to know how the parent will handle the data. If you needed to change what happened with the data, you wouldn't need to do anything to the CreateComment component. To execute a function passed as a prop, the child only needs to call the method and pass any data to it. The following listing shows how to use functions as props.

Listing 2.8 Using functions as props

```
//...
class CreateComment extends Component {
    constructor(props) {
        super(props);
        this.state = {
            content: '',
            user: ''
        };
        this.handleUserChange = this.handleUserChange.bind(this);
        this.handleTextChange = this.handleTextChange.bind(this);
        this.handleSubmit = this.handleSubmit.bind(this);
    }
    handleUserChange(event) {
        this.setState(() => ({
            user: event.target.value
        }));
    }
    handleTextChange(event) {
        this.setState(() => ({
            content: event.target.value
        }));
    }
    handleSubmit(event) {
        event.preventDefault();
        this.props.onCommentSubmit({                       Call the onCommentSubmit
            user: this.state.user.trim(),                  function that's been passed as a
            content: this.state.content.trim()             prop by the parent—you're
        });                                                passing in data from the form
        this.setState(() => ({                             and resetting the form so the
            user: '',                                      user knows their action was
            text: ''                                       successful.
        }));
    }
    render() {
        return React.createElement(
            'form',
            {
                className: 'createComment',
                onSubmit: this.handleSubmit        <─┐  Don't forget to bind the
            },                                        │  method you've set up to the
            React.createElement('input', {            │  onSubmit event—without it,
                type: 'text',                         │  there won't be any connection
                placeholder: 'Your name',             │  between the right event and
                value: this.state.user,               │  your method.
                onChange: this.handleUserChange
            }),
            React.createElement('input', {
                type: 'text',
```

```
                placeholder: 'Thoughts?',
                value: this.state.content,
                onChange: this.handleTextChange
            }),
            React.createElement('input', {
                type: 'submit',
                value: 'Post'

            })
        );
    }
}
}

//...
```

The code for listing 2.8 is available online at https://codesandbox.io/s/p3mk26v3lx.

Now that your component can pass new comment data to a parent, you'll need to include some mock data so you can get started commenting. In future chapters, you'll work with the Fetch API and a RESTful JSON API, but using some fake data you create will be fine for now. The following listing shows how you might go about mocking out some basic post data with associated comments.

Listing 2.9   Mocking out API data

```
...
const data = {                              Set up the mock data
    post: {                                 for your CommentBox
        id: 123,                            component.
        content:
            'What we hope ever to do with ease, we must first learn to do
            with diligence. — Samuel Johnson',
        user: 'Mark Thomas',
    },
    comments: [
        {
            id: 0,                                    ◁──┐
            user: 'David',
            content: 'such. win.',
        },
        {
            id: 1,                                    ◁──┤  You'll use
            user: 'Haley',                               these
            content: 'Love it.',                         comment
        },                                               objects as
        {                                                the existing
            id: 2,                                    ◁──┤  comments.
            user: 'Peter',
            content: 'Who was Samuel Johnson?',
        },
        {
            id: 3,                                    ◁──┘
            user: 'Mitchell',
```

```
          content: '@Peter get off Letters and do your homework',
      },
      {
          id: 4,
          user: 'Peter',
          content: '@mitchell ok :P',
      },
    ],
};
...
```

You'll use these comment objects as the existing comments.

Next, you need a way to show all the comments. In React, that's easy to do. You already have a component that will display a comment. Because all you need to work with React components is regular JavaScript, you can use the `.map()` function to return a new array of React elements. You can't use `.forEach()` in-line because it doesn't return an array and would leave `React.createElement()` with nothing to use. You could, however, build an array using `forEach` and then pass that in.

Aside from iterating over the existing comments, you need to define a method you can pass to the CreateComment component. It needs to modify the list of comments in its state by receiving data from the child component. Both the submission method and the state need to go in a new parent component: CommentBox. The following listing shows how to create the component and set up these methods.

Listing 2.10 Handling comment submissions and iterating over elements

```
...
class CommentBox extends Component {
    constructor(props) {
        super(props);
        this.state = {
            comments: this.props.comments
        };
        this.handleCommentSubmit = this.handleCommentSubmit.bind(this);
    }
    handleCommentSubmit(comment) {
        const comments = this.state.comments;
        // note that we didn't directly modify state
        comment.id = Date.now();
        const newComments = comments.concat([comment]);
        this.setState({
            comments: newComments
        });
    }
    render() {
        return React.createElement(
            'div',
            {
                className: 'commentBox'
            },
            React.createElement(Post, {
```

Pass in the comments data at the topmost level to CommentBox.

Never directly modify state— instead, make a copy.

```
            id: this.props.post.id,
            content: this.props.post.content,
            user: this.props.post.user
        }),
        this.state.comments.map(function(comment) {
            return React.createElement(Comment, {
                key: comment.id,
                id: comment.id,
                content: comment.content,
                user: comment.user
            });
        }),
        React.createElement(CreateComment, {
            onCommentSubmit: this.handleCommentSubmit
        })
        );
    }
}

CommentBox.propTypes = {
    post: PropTypes.object,
    comments: PropTypes.arrayOf(PropTypes.object)
};

const App = React.createElement(CreateComment);

ReactDOM.render(
    React.createElement(CommentBox, {

        comments: data.comments,
        post: data.post
    }),
    node
);

...
```

As before, pass in the data variable at the topmost level to access the post data.

Map over the comments in this.state.comments and return a React element for each one.

Give the parent's handleComment-Submit method to the CreateComment component to use.

Pass in the mock data to the CommentBox component as a prop.

The code for listing 2.10 is available online at https://codesandbox.io/s/z6o64oljn4.

At this point you have an unsightly, untested, but functional component that will perform validation on props, update state, and enable you to add new comments. It doesn't look like much, so I leave it as a challenge to you to make the comment box worthy of our fictional company, Letters.

2.4   *Meet JSX*

You've created your first dynamic React component. If you found it easy, great! If you found parts of the code hard to read through with all the nested `React.create-Elements`, that's fine, too. We're about to discuss some easier ways to create components, but needed to focus on the fundamentals first. Learning almost anything else in the reverse way ("magic" and ease first, fundamentals and details later) is usually much easier, but it can inhibit you in the long run because you haven't done the hard work of understanding how an underlying mechanism works. If you look back at your mock data, you may remember this quote, which is timely:

What we hope ever to do with ease, we must first learn to do with diligence.

—Samuel Johnson

2.4.1 *Creating components using JSX*

It's important to master the fundamentals, but that doesn't mean we have to make things difficult for ourselves. There are, it turns out, easier and better ways to create React components than only using `React.createElement`. Meet JSX: the better way.

What is JSX? It's an XML-like syntax extension to ECMAScript without any defined semantics, intended specifically for use by preprocessors. In other words, JSX is an extension of JavaScript that's similar to XML and is only intended for use by code-transformation tools. It's not something you'll see incorporated into the ECMAScript specification at any point.

JSX helps by allowing you to write XML-style (think HTML) code in place of using `React.createClass`. In other words, it lets you write code that *looks* like HTML but isn't. A JSX preprocessor program like Babel—a transpiler that turns your JavaScript code into code that's compatible with older browsers—will go through and convert all your JSX code to regular JavaScript like we've written so far. One implication is that running untransformed JSX code natively in the browser won't work—you'll get all sorts of syntax errors when your JavaScript is parsed.

Writing XML-style, HTML-like code in your JavaScript might set your warning instincts off, but there are plenty of good reasons to use JSX, and I'll cover them. For now, look at listing 2.11 to see what your comment box component might look like with JSX. I've omitted some code to make it easier to focus on the JSX syntax. Note that Babel is included as part of the environment on CodeSandbox. Normally, you'll use a build tool like Webpack to transpile your JavaScript, but you can also import Babel and have it work without a build step. That's much slower, though, and should never be done in production. You can learn more at https://babeljs.io.

Listing 2.11 Rewriting components using JSX

```
...
    class CreateComment extends Component {
    constructor(props) {
        super(props);
        this.state = {
            content: '',
            user: ''
        };
        this.handleUserChange = this.handleUserChange.bind(this);
        this.handleTextChange = this.handleTextChange.bind(this);
        this.handleSubmit = this.handleSubmit.bind(this);
    }
    //...
```

```
        render() {
            return (
                <form onSubmit={this.handleSubmit} className="createComment">
                    <input
                        value={this.state.user}
                        onChange={this.handleUserChange}
                        placeholder="Your name"
                        type="text"
                    />
                    <input
                        value={this.state.content}
                        onChange={this.handleTextChange}
                        placeholder="Thoughts?"
                        type="text"
                    />
                    <button type="submit">Post</button>
                </form>
            );
        }
    }

    class CommentBox extends Component {
    //...
        render() {
            return (
                <div className="commentBox">
                    <Post
                        id={this.props.post.id}
                        content={this.props.post.content}
                        user={this.props.post.user}
                    />
                    {this.state.comments.map(function(comment) {
                        return (
                            <Comment
                                key={comment.id}
                                content={comment.content}
                                user={comment.user}
                            />
                        );
                    })}
                    <CreateComment
                      onCommentSubmit={this.handleCommentSubmit}
                    />
                </div>
            );
        }
    }

    CommentBox.propTypes = {
        post: PropTypes.object,
        comments: PropTypes.arrayOf(PropTypes.object)
    };

    ReactDOM.render(
        <CommentBox
```

Instead of creating props on an object, in JSX you create them like you would in HTML—to pass in expressions, you use the {} syntax.

This is the Post React class you created before—note now it's much clearer that it's a custom component you created and looks like it would belong right at home in HTML.

Use regular JavaScript inside of {} to iterate over comments and create a comment component for each.

Pass in the handleComment-Submit handler as a property.

```
            comments={data.comments}
            post={data.post}
        />,
        node
    );
```

> At the top level, CommentBox is also a custom component you give props to and pass to React DOM to render.

```
    . . . . . .
```

The code for listing 2.11 is available online at https://codesandbox.io/s/vnwz6y28x5.

2.4.2   *Benefits of JSX and differences from HTML*

Now that you've seen JSX in action, you may feel a little less skeptical about it. If you're still wary, it's important to consider the many benefits it brings to working with components in React. Here are two of those benefits:

- *Similarity to HTML and simpler syntax*—If writing `React.createElement` repeatedly felt tedious or if you found the nesting hard to follow, you're not alone. JSX's similarity to HTML makes declaring your component's structure in a familiar way much easier and dramatically improves readability.
- *Declarative and encapsulated*—By including the code that will make up your view alongside any related methods, you create a group of functionality. Essentially everything you need to know about the component is in one place. Nothing is unnecessarily hidden from you, which means you can reason about your components more easily and be more fully aware of how it works as a system.

It may feel like a trip back to the late 90s to be writing your markup right alongside your JavaScript, but that doesn't mean it's a bad idea.

It's important to note that JSX is not HTML (or XML)—it will only transpile into regular React code just like you've used so far, and it doesn't share the exact same syntax and conventions. There are subtle differences that you'll need to look out for. Future chapters will go into these differences more fully, but I'll note a few of them briefly:

- *HTML tags versus React components*—Custom React components you created using `React.createClass` are by convention capitalized so you can determine the difference between custom and native HTML components.
- *Attribute expressions*—When you want to use a JavaScript expression as an attribute value, wrap the expression in a pair of curly braces (`<Comment a={this.props.b}/>`) instead of quotes (`<User a="this.props.b"/>`) as shown in listing 2.8.
- *Boolean attributes*—Omitting the value of an attribute (`<Plan active/>`, `<Input checked/>`) causes JSX to treat it as `true`. To pass a false value, you have to use an attribute expression (`attribute={false}`).
- *Nested expressions*—To insert the value of an expression *inside* an element, you also use a pair of curly braces (`<p>{this.props.content}</p>`).

There are subtle differences in JSX and even the occasional "gotcha," but later chapters will cover all that and more. You'll be using JSX extensively in your components, and now that you've started using JSX, you'll be able to create, read through, and think about your components that much more easily.

2.5   *Summary*

We spent a lot of time talking about components in this chapter, so let's review some of the key points:

- There are two main types of elements that we work with to create components in React: React elements and React classes. React elements are "what you want to see on the screen" and are comparable to DOM elements. React classes, on the other hand, are JavaScript classes that inherit from the `React.Component` class. These are what we normally call *components* in general. They're created from either classes (usually extending `React.Component`) or functions (stateless functional components, covered in later chapters).
- React classes get access to state that can change over time (mutable state), but all React elements get access to props that shouldn't be modified (immutable state).
- React classes also have special methods called *lifecycle methods* that will be called by React in a particular order during the rendering and update process. This makes your components more predictable to work with and allows you to easily hook into the component update process.
- React classes can have custom methods defined on them to perform tasks such as mutating state.
- React components communicate via props and have child-parent relationships. Parent components can pass data to children, but children can't modify parents. They can pass data back to parents via callbacks, but don't have direct access to parents.
- JSX is an XML-like extension of JavaScript that lets you write components in a much easier and more familiar way. It may feel strange at first to write what looks like HTML in your JavaScript, but JSX can make writing markup in React more familiar and is generally easier to read than `React.createElement` calls.

You created your first component, but you've only brushed the surface of what's possible with React. In the next chapter, you'll start to explore how to work with more complicated data, learn about different types of components, and delve further into state as we expand your React horizons.

Components and data in React

In part 1, you looked at React at a high level, took a whirlwind tour through some of its APIs, and built a handful of components. Hopefully this gave you a better overall sense of what React is and how it works as a technology. But a quick tour won't allow you to take full advantage of React so you can build robust, dynamic user interfaces with it.

That's where part 2 comes in. In part 2, you'll start to explore React more thoroughly and take a careful look at its APIs. We'll look at how you can create components and some of the different types of components that you can create. In chapter 3, we'll look at how data flows through a React application. This will help you understand how React works with data in components.

In chapter 4, you'll look at lifecycle methods in React and start to build a project that you'll focus on for the rest of the book: a social networking app called Letters Social. If you want to peek ahead at the final project you can visit https://social.react.sh. Chapter 4 will help you understand the React Component API and show you how to get set up to build the Letters Social project.

In chapters 5 and 6, we'll look at forms in React. Forms are an important part of most web applications, and we'll explore how they can work in React. You'll add forms to Letters Social and create a user interface that allows users to create posts and integrate Mapbox to add mapped locations to posts.

In chapters 7 and 8, we'll dive into routing. Routing is another critical part of modern front-end web applications. You'll build a router from scratch with

React and add multiple pages to Letters Social. Towards the end of the chapter, you'll integrate Firebase so users can log into your application.

As we wrap up part 2 in chapter 9, we'll focus on testing. Testing is an important part of all software and React is no different. You'll explore using Jest and Enzyme, among other tools, to test your React components.

Data and
data flow in React

Chapter 2 was a whirlwind tour of React. We spent some time learning about React at a high level, looked at some of the concepts behind its design and API, and we even went through building a simple comment box with React components. In chapter 4 you'll start to work more extensively with components and start building the Letters Social sample project. But before you do that, you need to know a little bit more about how to work with data in React and understand how it flows in React applications. That's what this chapter is about.

3.1   *Introducing state*

Chapter 2 gave you a few glimpses of working with data in React components, but we'll need to spend more time focusing on it if you want to build more substantial React applications. In this section, you'll learn about the following:

- State
- How React handles state
- How data flows through components

Modern web applications are usually built as data-first applications. Granted, there are many static sites (my blog is one—https://ifelse.io), but even these are updated over time and generally considered to be in a different category from modern web applications. Most web apps that people use on a regular basis are highly dynamic and filled with data that changes over time.

Think of an application like Facebook. As a social network, data is the lifeblood of everything it's useful for. It provides a variety of ways to interact with other people over the internet, and all these ways are done via modifying and receiving data in your browser (or other platforms). Many other applications contain incredibly complex data which needs to be represented in a UI people can understand and easily use. Developers also need to be able to maintain and reason about these interfaces and how data flows through them, so how an application deals with data is as important as its ability to handle changing data over time. The sample application you'll start building in the next chapter, Letters Social (check it out at https://social.react.sh), will use lots of changing data, though it won't be nearly as complex as most consumer or business apps. I'll be more explicit about it in this chapter, but we'll continue to learn about working with data in React for the rest of the book.

3.1.1   *What is state?*

Let's take a brief and simplified look at state so you can have a better understanding of it when we look at state in React. If you've never explicitly thought or heard about state in a program before, you've probably at least seen it before. Most of the programs you've written probably had some kind of state to them. If you've ever worked with a front-end framework like Vue, Angular, or Ember, you've almost certainly written UIs that had some aspect of state to them. React components can have state, too. But what exactly are we talking about when we say *state*? Try this definition:

> **STATE**   All the information a program has access to at a given instant in time.

That's a simplified definition that probably ignores some academic nuances, but it's good enough for our purposes. Many papers have been written by scholars dedicated to precisely defining state in computer systems, but for us state is the information at an instant in time that a program has access to. This includes, among other things, all the values you can reference without doing any further assignment or calculation at a given moment in time—in other words, it's a snapshot of what you know about a program at an instant.

For example, this might include any variables you previously created or other available values. When you change a variable (and aren't just using it to get at a value), you change the state of a program, and it's no longer the same as it was before. You can retrieve state at a given moment by only fetching or getting values, but when you change something over time, the state of a program has changed. Technically, the underlying state of your machine is changing every moment you're using it, but we're only concerned with the state of your program here.

Let's look at some code and step through simplified program state in the nest listing. We won't go into all the underlying allocations or processes that happen behind the scenes—we're just trying to think more explicitly about the data in our programs so that thinking about React components will be easier.

Listing 3.1 Simple program state

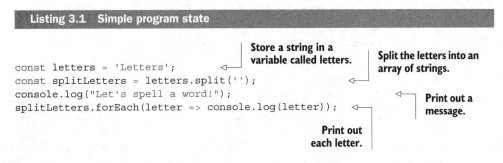

Listing 3.1 shows a simple script that does some basic assignment and manipulation of data and logs it out. It's boring, but we can use it to learn more about state. JavaScript employs what are called *run to completion* semantics, meaning that programs will be executed from top to bottom, in the order that you think they would be. JavaScript engines will often optimize your code in a way that you might not expect, but it should still run in a way consistent with your original code.

Try reading the code in listing 3.1 from top to bottom, one line at a time. If you want to use the browser debugger to do this, head to https://codesandbox.io/s/n9mvol5x9p. The dev tools for your browser should open up, and you can step through each line of the code and see all the variable assignments and more.

For our purposes, let's consider each line of code to be a moment in time. Working with our simplified definition of state as "all the information available to a program at a given moment in time," how would you describe the state of the application at each given moment? Note that we're keeping things simple and omitting things like closures, garbage collection, and so on:

1 `letters` is a variable with a string "Letters" assigned to it.
2 `splitLetters` is created by splitting every character from `letters`, which is still available.
3 All information from steps 1 and 2 is still available; a message is sent to the console.

4 Our program iterates over each item in the array and logs out a character. This process will probably occur over several moments in time, so the program also has the information available from the `Array.forEach` method available to it.

As the program moved forward in execution, the state changed over time, and more information became available because you haven't deleted anything or changed references. Table 3.1 shows how the available information increases as the program moves forward in time.

Table 3.1 State step-by-step

Step	State available to program
1	letters = "Letters"
2	letters = "Letters" splitLetters = ["L", "e", "t", "t", "e", "r", "s"]
3	letters = "Letters" splitLetters = ["L", "e", "t", "t", "e", "r", "s"]
4	letters = "Letters" splitLetters = ["L", "e", "t", "t", "e", "r", "s"] for sub-steps 0 through the length of splitLetters: letter = "L" (then "e", "t", etc.)

Try walking through some of your own code and thinking about what information is available to the program at each line. We tend to simplify our code—and rightly so, because we don't have to think about every possible dimension of it at once—but there can be a nontrivial amount of information available even for simpler programs.

One takeaway we can reflect on is that when a running program becomes reasonably complex (as even most simple UIs can tend to be), reasoning about it can become difficult. By that I mean that the complexity of a system can be hard to keep in your head all at once, and the logic in a system can make it hard to think through. This is true for most programs, but when it comes to building UIs, it can be especially difficult.

The UI for modern browser apps often represents the intersection of a multitude of technologies, including servers providing data, styling and layout APIs, JavaScript frameworks, browser APIs, and so on. Advances in UI frameworks have aimed to simplify this problem, but it remains a challenge. The challenge often only increases with the greater expectations people have for web apps as these apps become more and more widespread and embedded in society and daily life. If React is to be useful, it will need to help us by reducing or shielding us from the immensely complex state of some modern UIs. I hope you'll come to see that React does do this. But how? One way is by providing two specific APIs to work with data: props and state.

3.1.2 *Mutable and immutable state*

In React applications, there are two primary ways that you can work with state in components: through state that you can change, and through state that you shouldn't. We're oversimplifying here: there are many types of data and state that will exist in your application. You could represent data in many different ways, like binary trees, Maps or Sets, or regular JavaScript objects. But the way that you can communicate and interact with state in your React components fall into these two categories. In React, these are known as *state* (data you can change within a component) and *props* (data a component receives that shouldn't be changed by the component).

You may have heard of state and props referred to as being mutable and immutable. That's partly true, because JavaScript doesn't natively support truly immutable objects (outside of, maybe, Symbols). In React components, state is generally mutable, and props shouldn't be changed. Let's explore the ideas of mutability and immutability a little more before we dive all the way into React-specific APIs.

You saw in chapter 2 that when we call state mutable we mean we can overwrite or update that data (for example, a variable that you can overwrite). Immutable state, on the other hand, can't be changed. There are also immutable data structures, which can be changed but only in controlled ways (this is sort of how the state API works in React). When you work with Redux in chapters 10 and 11, you'll emulate immutable data structures.

We can slightly expand our notions of mutable and immutable to include their corresponding data structure types:

- *Immutable*—An immutable, persistent data structure supports multiple versions over time but can't be directly overwritten; immutable data structures are generally persistent.
- *Mutable*—A mutable, ephemeral data structure supports only a single version over time; mutable data structures are overwritten when they change and don't support additional versions.

Figure 3.1 visualizes these ideas.

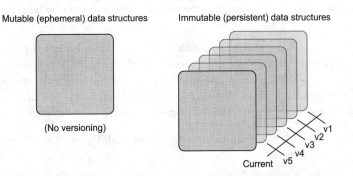

Mutable (ephemeral) data structures   Immutable (persistent) data structures

(No versioning)

v1
v2
v3
v4
Current   v5

Figure 3.1   Persistence and ephemerality in immutable and mutable data structures. Immutable or persistent data structures usually record a history and don't change but rather make versions of what changed over time. Ephemeral data structures, on the other hand, usually don't record history and get wiped out with each update.

Another way to think of the difference between immutable and mutable data structures is to think of each as having different capacities or memories. Ephemeral data structures only have the capacity to store a moment's worth of data, whereas persistent data structures can keep track of changes over time. This is where the immutability of immutable data structures becomes clearer: only copies of state are made—they're not replaced. The old state is replaced by the new one, but the data isn't replaced. Figure 3.2 shows how changes are made.

Mutable (ephemeral) data structures

 Immutable (persistent) data structures

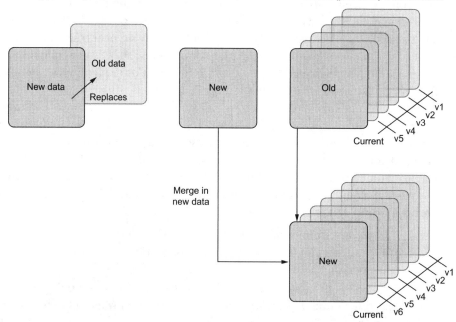

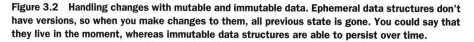

Figure 3.2 Handling changes with mutable and immutable data. Ephemeral data structures don't have versions, so when you make changes to them, all previous state is gone. You could say that they live in the moment, whereas immutable data structures are able to persist over time.

TIP   Another way you can think of immutability versus mutability is by thinking of the difference between Save and Save As. With many computer programs, you can save a file as it is at the moment or save a copy of the current file under a different name. Immutability is similar in that when you save to it, you're saving a copy, whereas mutable data can be overwritten in-place.

Even though JavaScript doesn't support truly immutable data structures natively, React exposes component state in a mutable way (changeable via `setState`) and props as read-only. There's a lot more to immutability and immutable data structures in general, but we don't need to concern ourselves with them much more than we already have. If you're still curious to learn more, an entire body of academic research is focused on this sort of question. There are also ways you can use immutable data structures extensively throughout your JavaScript apps (React or not) with libraries like Immutable JS (see https://facebook.github.io/immutable-js/ for more information), but in React we'll only deal with the props and state APIs.

3.2 State in React

You've learned a little bit more about state and (im)mutability. How does all this fit into React? Well, we've already seen a little of the props and state APIs in the last chapter, so you can probably guess that they must be important parts of how you build components. In fact, they're the two main ways that React components deal with data and communicate with each other.

3.2.1 Mutable state in React: Component state

Let's start with the state API. Although we can say that all components have some kind of "state" (the general concept) to them, not all components in React have local component state. From here on out, when I refer to state I'm talking about the React API, not the general concept. Components that inherit from the `React.Component` class will get access to this API. React will create and keep track of a backing instance for components created in this way. These components will also get access to a series of lifecycle methods discussed in the next chapter.

You can access state in your components that inherit from `React.Component` via `this.state`. In this case, `this` refers to the instance of the class, and `state` is the special property that React will keep track of for you. You might think you can update `state` just by assigning to it or by mutating a property in it, but that's not the case. Let's look at an example of component state in a simple React component in the following listing. You can create this code on your local machine or, even more easily, at https://codesandbox.io/s/ovxpmn340y.

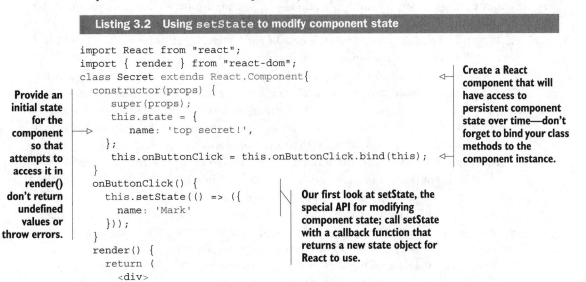

Listing 3.2 Using `setState` to modify component state

```
import React from "react";
import { render } from "react-dom";
class Secret extends React.Component{
  constructor(props) {
    super(props);
    this.state = {
      name: 'top secret!',
    };
    this.onButtonClick = this.onButtonClick.bind(this);
  }
  onButtonClick() {
    this.setState(() => ({
      name: 'Mark'
    }));
  }
  render() {
    return (
      <div>
```

Provide an initial state for the component so that attempts to access it in render() don't return undefined values or throw errors.

Create a React component that will have access to persistent component state over time—don't forget to bind your class methods to the component instance.

Our first look at setState, the special API for modifying component state; call setState with a callback function that returns a new state object for React to use.

```
        <h1>My name is {this.state.name}</h1>
            <button onClick={this.onButtonClick}>reveal the secret!</button>    ◁─┐
    </div>
    )                                                          Bind the name-revealing
  }                                                            function to the click event
}                                                              emitted by the button.

render(
    <Secret/>,                                        Render top-level components to an
    document.getElementById('root')   ◁──             HTML element at the topmost level of an
);                                                    application—identify your container however
                                                      you like, as long as ReactDOM can find it.
```

Listing 3.2 creates a simple component that will reveal a secret name when you click a button using setState to update the component state. Notice that setState is available on this because the component inherits from the React.Component class.

When you click the button, a click event will be fired, and the function you've told React to respond with will be executed. When it's executed, it will call the setState method with an object as a parameter. That object has a property, name, that points to a string. React will schedule an update to state. When this work has occurred, React DOM will update the DOM if necessary. Your render function will be called again, but this time with a different value available to the JSX expression syntax ({}) that contains this.state.name. It will read "Mark" instead of "top secret!" and my secret identity will be blown!

Usually, you want to use setState sparingly when possible due to the performance and complexity hit you incur (React has to keep track of something else for you, and you have to mentally keep track of another piece of data). There are patterns that enjoy significant popularity in the React community that allow you to rarely use component state at all (including Redux, Mobx, Flux, and others), and these are great to explore as options for your application—in fact, we'll look at Redux in chapters 10 and 11. Although it's better to usually use a stateless functional component, or rely on a pattern like Redux, using the setState API isn't a bad practice by itself—it's still the main API in React for changing data in a component.

Before moving on, it's important to note that you should never directly modify this.state in React components. If you try to modify this.state directly, calling setState() afterwards could replace the mutation you made, and—even worse—React won't have any idea about the change you made to state. Even though you can think about component state as something you can change, you should treat the this.state objects as if they're immutable within your components (like props).

This is also important because setState() doesn't immediately mutate this.state. Instead, it creates a pending state *transition* (more on rendering and change detection in the next chapter). Accessing this.state after calling this method can potentially return the existing value. All these things make for potentially tricky debugging situations, so just use setState() to mutate component state.

Even in a small interaction like the one in listing 3.2, there's quite a bit going on. We'll keep breaking down all the various steps that occur when React performs updates on your components in future chapters, but for the moment it's important to look more closely at your component's render method. Note that even though you performed a state mutation and changed data around, it happened in a relatively understandable and predictable way.

Even better, you could declare what you wanted your component's appearance and structure to look like once. You didn't have to do tons of extra work for the two different states it could exist in (with or without the top-secret name revealed). React handled all underlying state binding and update procedures, and you only had to say, "The name should go here." React helped by not forcing you to think about every piece of state at every point in time, like you had to in section 3.1.1.

Let's look at the setState API a little more closely. It's the primary way for changing dynamic state in React components, and you'll use it often in your application. Let's look at the method signature to see what you need to pass to it:

```
setState(
  updater,
  [callback]
) -> void
```

setState takes a function to use to set the new state for the component and an optional callback function. The updater function has this signature:

```
(prevState, props) => stateChange
```

With past versions of React you could pass an object instead of a function as the first argument to setState. A key difference from current versions of React (16 and up) is that it could imply that setState was synchronous in nature, whereas what happens is that React will schedule a change to state. The callback format better communicates this idea and is generally more consistent with React's overall declarative asynchronous paradigms: you allow the system (React) to schedule updates where order but not time are guaranteed. This is in line with a more declarative approach to UI and is generally much easier to think about than having to imperatively specify updates to data at different times (often a source of race conditions).

If you need to make an update to state that depends on the current state or props, you can access those through the prevState and props arguments. That's often useful when you want to do something like toggle a Boolean and need to know the exact last value before performing an update.

Let's focus on the mechanics of setState a little more. Using the object returned from your updater function, it performs a shallow merge into current state. This means you can yield an object and React will merge top-level properties on the object into state. For example, say you have an object with properties A and B. B has some deeply nested properties to it, and A is just a string ('hi!'). Because a shallow merge is being performed, only the top-level properties and what they reference will get preserved, not every part of B. React won't find some deeply nested property of B for you to update. One way around this is to make a copy of the object, deeply update it, and then use that. You can also use a library like `immutable.js` (https://facebook.github .io/immutable-js/) to make working with data structures in React easier.

setState is a straightforward API to use; you give your ReactClass component some data to merge into the current state, and React will handle it for you. And if you need to listen for the completion of the process for some reason, you can hook into it with the optional `callback` function. Listing 3.3 shows an example of a `setState` shallow merge in action. As before, you can easily create and run your React component on CodeSandbox at https://codesandbox.io/s/0myo6ny4ww. This should save you the trouble of having to set everything up on your machine.

Listing 3.3 Shallow merging with `setState`

```
import React from "react";
import { render } from "react-dom";
class ShallowMerge extends React.Component {
  constructor(props) {
    super(props);
    this.state = {
      user: {
        name: 'Mark',  //          ◁──┐  name exists in the
        colors: {                      initial state under
          favorite: '',                the user property...
        }
      }
    };
    this.onButtonClick = this.onButtonClick.bind(this);
  }
  onButtonClick() {
    this.setState({
      user: {  //                 ◁──┐  ...but not in the state you're
        colors: {                      setting—if it had been a level
          favorite: 'blue'             up, a shallow merge wouldn't
        }                              have worked.
      }
    });
  }
  render() {
    return (
      <div>
        <h1>My favorite color is {this.state.user.colors.favorite} and my
      name is {this.state.user.name}</h1>
        <button onClick={this.onButtonClick}>show the color!</button>
      </div>
    )
  }
}

render(
  <ShallowMerge />,
  document.getElementById('root')
);
```

Forgetting about shallow merges can be a common source of bugs when first learning React. In this example, when you click the button the name property nested within the user key of the initial state will be overwritten because it doesn't exist in the new state. You wanted to keep both pieces of state, but one ended up overwriting the other.

> ### Exercise 3.1 Thinking about the setState API
> This chapter has talked about React's component API for managing state in components. One of the things mentioned has been that you need to modify state through the setState API, not directly. Why do you think that would be a problem and why won't that work? Try it out at https://codesandbox.io/s/j7p824jxnw.

3.2.2 Immutable state in React: Props

We've talked about how React lets you work with data in a mutable way via state and setState, but what about immutable data in React? In React, props are the primary way to pass immutable data. Any component can receive props (not just those that inherit from React.Component) and use them in their constructor, render, and lifecycle methods.

Props in React are more or less immutable. You can use libraries and other tools to emulate immutable data structures in your components, but the React props API is semi-immutable by itself. React uses the native JavaScript Object.freeze (https://developer.mozilla.org/en-US/docs/Web/JavaScript/Reference/Global_Objects/Object/freeze) method if available to prevent new properties from being added to it or existing properties from being removed. Object.freeze also prevents existing properties (or their enumerability, configurability, or writability) from being changed and prevents the prototype from being changed, too. This goes a long way toward preventing you from mutating the props object, but it's not technically a truly immutable object (although you can essentially think of it that way).

Props are data that gets passed to React components, either from a parent or from the defaultProps static method on the component itself. Whereas component state is localized to a single component, props are usually passed from a parent component. If you're thinking, "Can I use state in a parent component to pass props to a child component?" you're onto something. State in one component can be props for another.

Props are usually passed in JSX as attributes, but if you're using React.createElement you can pass them directly into a child component via that interface. You can pass any valid JavaScript data as a prop to another component—even other components (which are only classes after all). Once props are passed into a component for use, you shouldn't change them from within the component. You can try, but you'll probably get a nice error like Uncaught TypeError: Cannot assign to read-only property '<myProperty>' of object '#<Object>'—or worse, your React app won't work as expected because you're violating the expected use.

Listing 3.4 in the next section shows some ways you can access props and how not to assign to them. As noted before, properties can change over time, but not from within the component. This is part of one-way data flow—a topic covered in later chapters. In short, *one-way* means changing data flows down through components from parent components to children. A parent component using state (inheriting from `React.Component`) can change its state, and that changed state can be what is passed down as properties to child components, thus changing properties.

Exercise 3.2   Calling setState in a render method

We've established that `setState` is how you can update a component's state. Where can you call `setState`? We'll look at which points of the component lifecycle allow you to call `setState` in the next chapter, but for now let's focus on just the `render` method. What do you think happens when `setState` is called in a component's `render` method? Try it at https://codesandbox.io/s/48zv2nwqww.

3.2.3   *Working with props: PropTypes and default props*

When working with props, you have a few APIs available to you that can help you during development: PropTypes and default props. PropTypes provides a typechecking functionality in which you can specify what sort of props your component will expect to receive when used. You can specify data types and even tell the component consumer what sort of shape of data they need to provide (an object with a user property that has certain keys, for example). In past versions of React, PropTypes was part of the core `React` library, but now lives alone as the `prop-types` package (https://github.com/facebook/prop-types).

The `prop-types` library isn't magic—it's a set of functions and properties that can help do typechecking on inputs. It's also not specific to React—you could just as easily use it in another library where you wanted to do typechecking on inputs. You could, for example, bring `prop-types` into another component-driven framework similar to React, like Preact (https://preactjs.com), and use it similarly.

To set PropTypes for a component, you provide a static property on the class called `propTypes`. Notice in listing 3.4 that the name of the static property you set on a component class is lowercase, whereas the name of the object you access from the `prop-types` library is uppercase (`PropTypes`). To specify which props your component needs, you add the name of the prop you want to validate and assign it a property from the `prop-types` library's default export (`import PropTypes from 'prop-types'`). Using PropTypes, you can declare just about any type, shape, and requirement type (optional or mandatory) for your props.

Another tool you can use to make your development experience easier is default props. Remember how you can provide an initial state to your component using the class `constructor`? You can do something similar for props, too. You can provide a static property called `defaultProps` to provide default props to your component.

Using default props can be helpful to ensure that your component will have what it needs to run, even if someone using the component forgets to provide a prop to it. The following listing shows an example of using PropTypes and default props in a component. Run the code at https://codesandbox.io/s/31ml5pmk4m.

Listing 3.4 Immutable props in React components

```
import React from "react";
import { render } from "react-dom";
import PropTypes from "prop-types";

class Counter extends React.Component {               Specify an object
  static propTypes = {                                with a "shape."
    incrementBy: PropTypes.number,
    onIncrement: PropTypes.func.isRequired            You can chain any propTypes
  };                                                  with isRequired to make sure a
  static defaultProps = {                             warning is shown if the prop
    incrementBy: 1                                    isn't shown.
  };

  constructor(props) {
    super(props);
    this.state = {
      count: 0
    };
    this.onButtonClick = this.onButtonClick.bind(this);
  }
  onButtonClick() {
    this.setState(function(prevState, props) {
      return { count: prevState.count + props.incrementBy };
    });
  }
  render() {
    return (
      <div>
        <h1>{this.state.count}</h1>
        <button onClick={this.onButtonClick}>++</button>
      </div>
    );
  }
}

render(<Counter incrementBy={1} />, document.getElementById("root"));
```

3.2.4 Stateless functional components

What do you do if you want to create a simple component that only uses props and no state? It turns out this is a common use case, especially with some of the common React-friendly application architectural patterns that we'll explore later in the book, like Flux and Redux. In these cases, you often want to keep state in a centralized location and not distributed across your components. But only using props is also useful in other situations. It would be nice to incur less of a resource usage penalty for your app if React didn't have to manage a backing instance for you.

As it turns out, there is a type of component you can create that only uses props: a stateless functional component. These components are sometimes called *stateless* components, *functional* components, and other similar names by developers, which can make it hard to keep track of what's being talked about. They usually mean the same thing: a React component that doesn't inherit from `React.Component` and therefore doesn't get access to component state or other lifecycle methods.

A stateless functional component is, not surprisingly, just that: a component that doesn't have access to or use the React state API (or the other methods inherited from `React.Component`). It is stateless not because it doesn't have any kind of (general) state whatsoever, but because it doesn't get a backing instance that React will manage for you. This means no lifecycle methods (covered in Chapter 4), no component state, and potentially less memory.

Stateless functional components are functional because they can be written as named functions or anonymous function expressions assigned to a variable. They only take props and, because they return the same output based on a given input, are essentially considered pure. This makes them fast, as React will potentially be able to make optimizations by avoiding unnecessary lifecycle checks or memory allocations. The following listing shows a simple example of a stateless functional component. Run the code at https://codesandbox.io/s/l756002969.

Listing 3.5 Stateless functional components

```
import React from "react";
import { render } from "react-dom";
import PropTypes from "prop-types";

function Greeting(props) {
  return <div>Hello {props.for}!</div>;
}
Greeting.propTypes = {
    for: PropTypes.string.isRequired
};

Greeting.defaultProps = {
    for: 'friend'
};

render(<Greeting for="Mark" />, mountNode);

// Or using an arrow function
// const Greeting = (props) => <div>Hello {props.for}</div>;
//... specify props and default props same as before
// render(<Greeting name="Mark" />, document.getElementById("root"));
```

For either form of stateless functional component, you can specify propTypes and default props as properties on the function or variable.

Stateless functional components can be created with functions or anonymous functions.

Stateless functional components can be powerful, especially when used in combination with a parent component that has a backing instance. Rather than having to set state across multiple components, you can create a single stateful parent component and use lightweight child components for the rest. In chapters 10 and 11, we'll look at using Redux to take this pattern to a whole new level. In React applications that use Redux, you usually end up creating fewer stateful components (although there are still cases where this makes sense) and instead centralize state in a single location (the store).

> **Exercise 3.3   Using state in one component to modify props in another**
> This chapter has talked about props and state as the primary ways you can work with and pass around data in React components. You should never directly modify either state or props, but with `setState` you can tell React to update a component's state. How would you use state in one component to modify the props in another? Head to https://codesandbox.io/s/38zq71q75 to try it out.

3.3   *Component communication*

When you built your simple comment box component, you saw that you can create components from other components. That's one reason why React is great. You can easily build other components from subcomponents while keeping things nicely bundled up. You're also easily able to express *is-a* and *has-a* relationships between components. That means you can think about components as *having a* part to them as well as *being a* certain thing.

It's great that you can mix and match components and flexibly build things, but how do you get them to talk to each other? Many frameworks and libraries offer a framework-specific method to get different parts of the application to talk to each other. In Angular.js or Ember.js, you may have heard of or used a service to communicate between different parts of your application. Usually these are broadly available, long-lived objects that you can store state in and access from different parts of your application.

Does React use services or something similar? No. In React, if you want components to communicate with each other, you pass props, and when you pass props, you're doing two simple things:

- Accessing data in the parent (either state or props)
- Passing that data to a child component

The following listing shows an example of both the parent-child relationship you're familiar with and the owner-ownee relationship. Run it at https://codesandbox.io/s/pm18mlz8jm.

Listing 3.6   Passing props from parent to child

```
import React from "react";
import { render } from "react-dom";
import PropTypes from "prop-types";
```

Create a
stateless
functional
component
that returns
an example
image.

```
const UserProfile = props => {
  return <img src={`https://source.unsplash.com/user/${props.username}`} />;
};
UserProfile.propTypes = {
  pagename: PropTypes.string
};

UserProfile.defaultProps = {
  pagename: "erondu"
};

const UserProfileLink = props => {
  return <a href={`https://ifelse.io/${props.user-
    name}`}>{props.username}</a>;
};

const UserCard = props => {
  return (
    <div>
      <UserProfile username={props.username} />
      <UserProfileLink username={props.username} />
    </div>
  );
};

render(<UserCard username="erondu" />, document.getElementById("root"));
```

Remember, you can still specify default props and propTypes even on stateless functional components.

UserCard is a parent to UserProfile and UserProfileLink.

3.4   *One-way data flow*

If you've developed web applications using frameworks before, you may be familiar with the term *two-way data binding*. Data binding is the process that establishes a connection between the application UI and other data. In practice, this is often manifested as something like a library or framework connecting app data like models (a user) to the user interface and keeps them in sync. They're synchronized and are therefore bound together. Another way to think of this that'll be more helpful in React is as a *projection*: UI is the data projected into a view, and when the data changes, the view changes, as illustrated in figure 3.3.

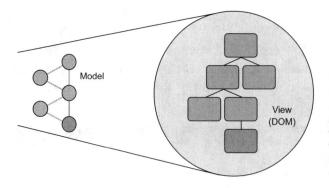

Model

View
(DOM)

Figure 3.3   Data binding usually refers to the process of setting up a connection between data in your app and the view (the display of that data). Another way to think of this is as a projection of the data into something the user can see (for example, a view).

Another way to think about data binding is as data *flow:* how does data move through different parts of your application? Essentially, you're asking, "What can update what, from where, and how?" It's important to understand how the tools you're using shape, manipulate, and move data around if you want to use them well. Different libraries and frameworks take different approaches to data flow (React is no different in having its own opinion about how to do this).

In React, data flows in one direction. That means that rather than flow between entities in a horizontal way where each can update the other, a hierarchy is established. You can pass data through components but can't reach out and modify the state or props of other components without passing props. You also can't modify the data in a parent.

But you can pass data back up the hierarchy via callbacks. When a parent receives a callback from a child component, it can change its data and send the changed data back down to the child components. Even in this scenario with callbacks, data still flows downwards in aggregate and remains determined by the parent passing that data down. That's why we say that in React data flows unidirectionally, as shown in figure 3.4.

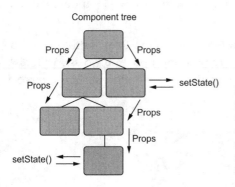

Figure 3.4 **Data flows one way in React. Props are passed from parent to child (from owner to ownee), and children can't edit the state or props of a parent component. Each component that has a backing instance can modify its own state but can't modify anything outside itself apart from setting the props of one of its children.**

Unidirectional flow is especially helpful in building UIs because it tends to make it easier to think about the way data moves through an application. Thanks to the hierarchy of components and the way props and state are localized to components, it's generally easier to predict how data moves through an application.

It might sound nice in some ways to eschew this hierarchy and have the freedom to modify whatever you want from any part of your application, but in practice that tends to lead to applications that are hard to think about and can result in difficult debugging situations. Later chapters will explore architectural patterns like Flux and Redux that allow you to maintain a unidirectional data flow paradigm while coordinating actions that can occur across components or across your application.

3.5   *Summary*

This chapter discussed the following topics:

- State is the information available to a program at a given moment in time.
- Immutable state doesn't change, whereas mutable state does change.
- Persistent, immutable data structures don't change—they only record their changes and make copies of themselves.
- Ephemeral, mutable data structures are wiped out when they're updated.
- React uses both mutable (local component state) and pseudo-immutable data (props).
- Props are pseudo-immutable and should not be modified once set.
- Component state is tracked by a backing instance and can be modified with setState.
- setState performs a shallow merge of data and updates your component's state, preserving any top-level properties that aren't overwritten.
- Data flows one way in React, from parents to children. Children can yield back data to a parent via a callback, but they can't directly modify the parent's state, and a parent can't directly modify a child's state. Component interaction is done via props instead.

In chapter 4, we'll build on your knowledge of state in React and look at how to use lifecycle methods to hook into React's render and update process. We'll also start to explore change detection in React and you'll start to build out the Letters Social app using your newly learned React skills!

4

Rendering and
lifecycle methods in React

This chapter covers

- Getting set up with the application repository
- The rendering process
- Lifecycle methods
- Updating React components
- Creating a newsfeed using React

In this chapter, you're going to start to pull together some of the concepts and skills we've covered so far to create your first React app. In past chapters, we've talked about dealing with data in React and the different ways that you can work with mutable (changeable) and immutable (unchangeable) data. But to build even more robust components, you need to take advantage of the full component API, dive into lifecycle methods, and learn about the rendering process in React.

We'll take a look at *rendering*, the process that React uses to turn your data into a user interface, and some ways to interact with a component over its lifecycle, called *lifecycle methods*. You'll combine this with some of what you already know about reading and modifying data in React (props and state), updating your component state, and passing data to different components.

4.1   *Getting set up with the Letters Social repo*

In this chapter, you're going to start building the application Letters Social. We'll pretend that we're a startup focusing on creating the next great social networking application. Our company, Letters—ingeniously named to differentiate us from web giants like Alphabet—is working on Social. You'll use React to build this application over the course of the book. By the end of the book, Letters Social will be using server-side rendering, Redux, and React. The application, shown in figure 4.1, supports a few features worth noting here so you know what you'll be building over the course of the book:

- Creating posts that have text
- Adding locations to posts with Mapbox
- Liking and commenting on posts
- Providing OAuth authentication via GitHub and Firebase
- Displaying posts in a newsfeed
- Using basic pagination

We'll go through each of these features in this and the following chapters. To make things easier for you, I've created a Git branch for chapters 4 through 12. Each chapter (or paired chapters in some cases) represents the code as it stands at the end of that chapter. For example, if you check out the Git branch for chapters 5 and 6, you'll have the code for the end of those chapters. This will let you look ahead if you like, and you can start from any chapter. If you wanted to work through chapter 9 (covering testing React applications), for instance, you could check out the code for chapters 7 and 8 and start from there. I've tried to make it as easy as possible for you to check out code, but you can use the Git repository and branches however you'd like. Feel free to open pull requests with questions or fork it to use as a starting place for new features you want to add to the app.

You can also read some basic documentation about the files in the source code at https://docs.react.sh. It's not comprehensive, but if you'd like to get a sense of the code and you like JSDoc-style documentation, the docs will be a good place to go. The README for the repo also lists a number of helpful resources. As always, feel free to reach out to me if you have questions (or if you just like the book!). You can do that through the README.

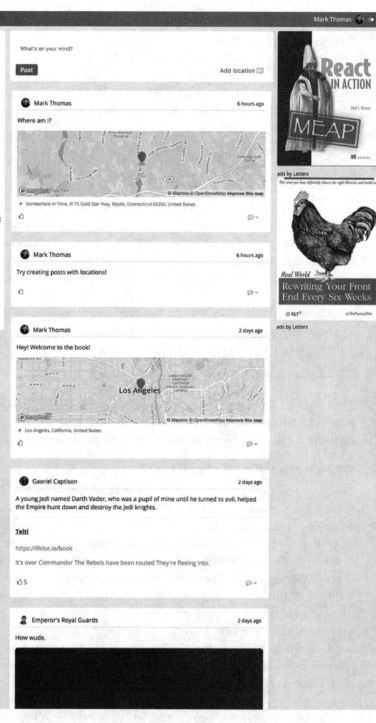

Figure 4.1   Letters Social, the React app that you'll be building in this book. You can check out its source code at https://github.com/react-in-action/letters-social and the app at https://social.react.sh.

4.1.1   Getting the source code

To get the source code, go to https://github.com/react-in-action/letters-social. This is the repository where all the source code related to the book is stored. There are several other repos in the React in Action GitHub Organization, so feel free to check those out, too. The main source code is in the https://github.com/react-in-action/letters-social. Head there and either download the source or use the following command to clone the repository:

```
git clone git@github.com:react-in-action/letters-social.git

git checkout chapter-4
```

That will clone the repository in the current directory and switch to the start branch (the starting branch for the project). The next step is to install dependencies. We'll use npm (www.npmjs.com) in this book for the sake of consistency, but if you prefer to use yarn (another dependency management library that wraps npm, at https://yarn-pkg.com), you can do that, too. You'll just need to ensure that you install with yarn, not npm.

All the modules you'll need for the entire book should be included in package.json in the application source. To install, run the following command in the source code directory:

```
npm install
```

That will install all the dependencies you'll need. If you change versions of node (via nvm or another means), you'll need to reinstall your node modules because different versions of node will compile different modules differently (like node-sass).

4.1.2   Which version of node should I use?

This is a good time to talk about which version of node to use. I recommend using the latest stable version. At the time of writing, that was the 8.X release line. I won't support versions of node earlier than 6.X, and it makes more sense to support 8.X or greater since this isn't a business or production environment where you can't easily switch between versions without extensive testing. Node 8.X also uses a newer version of npm and contains significant speed improvements made to the underlying V8 engine.

If you don't have one of these versions of node on your computer, head to https://nodejs.org to download a copy of the latest stable version of node. Another option is to use the nvm command-line tool to install copies of node locally and be able to switch between them. You can check out the nvm tool at https://github .com/creationix/nvm.

Different versions of node support different features of JavaScript, so it's important to know what the version you're using supports. If you'd like to know more about which features yours supports and which versions others do (or will), check out http://node.green to see feature implementation across versions.

4.1.3   Note on tooling and CSS

As I mention in other places in this book, tooling around JavaScript applications can be a complex and fast-moving target. It's also a domain that deserves its own treatment. For these reasons, I won't be covering how to set up things like Webpack, Babel, or other tools. The application source code has a development and build process in place, and you're free to explore the configuration I've set up, but that's outside the scope of this book, so I won't be covering it.

Another point worth making is about CSS. I've already covered the ways you work with inline styles in React, but CSS is also generally out of the scope of this book. For that reason, I've created all the styles you'll need. Any UI markup you see has styles created for it. Some styles depend on certain types or hierarchies, so if you move different elements around or change CSS class names, you can expect the app to look broken. My aim is to give you one less thing to think about while learning React, but if you're interested in playing around with the app's styling, go right ahead.

4.1.4   Deploying

The app running at https://social.react.sh is deployed to https://zeit.co, but if, for some reason in the future, circumstances arise that require a change, I'll keep the app running at whatever cloud solution makes the most sense at the time. You don't need to be concerned with what the app is hosted on. If at the end of the book you find yourself wanting to fork and add to the app for your own learning and enjoyment, you'll need to determine the best way to deploy the app for yourself. Fortunately, the build and runtime processes are straightforward, so you should find it relatively easy to deploy somewhere else.

4.1.5   The API server and database

To prevent you from having to run a database like MongoDB or PostgreSQL, we'll use a simulated REST API via the `JSON-server` library (https://github.com/typicode/json-server). I've made some modifications to the default server (which you can see in the db folder of the repo) that help make the project a little bit easier. Rather than work with a database, you'll get a lightweight database that works by reading and modifying a JSON file. To create sample data or reset your application data, you can run this command:

```
npm run db:seed
```

That will overwrite the existing JSON database and replace it with new sample data (the users, posts, and comments are all *Star Wars*-themed—may the Force be with you). In later chapters, you'll be able to create a user in the database after you log in. If you rerun the database `seed` command, your user will get overwritten, and you'll have to log out and log back in to get things fixed. That shouldn't happen, and you probably won't need to run the database command more than once, but you should be aware of what it means to reset your data just in case.

I've included a number of helpers to make it easier to make requests to the API. You can see these functions in src/shared/http.js. I'm making use of the `isomorphic-fetch` library (https://github.com/matthew-andrews/isomorphic-fetch) because it mirrors the standard Fetch API available in browsers, but also runs on the server. I'll assume you have some experience with an HTTP library in the browser, but if not you can use the included helper files as a way to start learning about the Fetch API (https://developer.mozilla.org/en-US/docs/Web/API/Fetch_API).

4.1.6   Running the app

The easiest way to get started running the app in development mode will be to run the following:

```
npm run dev
```

There are other commands you can use, too, but the main one you'll want is `dev`. To see the other available commands, you can run this:

```
npm run
```

That should list every available command for the repository. Feel free to try each of them to see how they fit in. The main two you'll be concerned with, though, are `npm run dev` and `npm run db:seed`.

4.2   The render process and lifecycle methods

If you've cloned the repository and installed the dependencies, you should have everything you need. Before you start building Letters Social, though, you'll need to take a look at rendering and lifecycle methods. These are key features of React, and once you know them you'll be better equipped to start building the Letters Social application.

4.2.1   Introducing lifecycle methods

In chapter 2, you saw that you can create and assign functions as handlers for events (clicks, form submissions, and so on) inside your components. That's useful because you can create dynamic components that respond to user events (a key aspect of any modern web application). But what if you want something more? With just this as a feature, it seems like you're still working with regular old HTML and JavaScript. Say you want to get user data from an API or read a cookie for later use, all without waiting for a user-initiated event. These are routine things you'll need to do in web applications—you'll want to do them automatically in some cases, so where would those sorts of things happen? The answer is lifecycle methods.

> **DEFINITION**   *Lifecycle methods* are special methods attached to class-based React components that will be executed at specific points in a component's lifecycle. A *lifecycle* is a way of thinking about a component. A component with a lifecycle has a metaphorical "life"—it has at least a beginning, middle, and end. This mental model makes thinking about a component easier and gives you context

about where a component is in terms of its life. Lifecycle methods aren't unique to React; many UI technologies employ them due to their intuitive and useful nature. The main parts of a React component's life are mounting, updating, and unmounting. Figure 4.2 shows an overview of a component lifecycle and the rendering process (how React manages your components over time).

I've mentioned lifecycle methods in past chapters, but now it's time to really dive in to them to get a sense of what they are and how you can use them. To get started, think about React at a high level again. Take a look at the top of figure 4.2 to refresh your

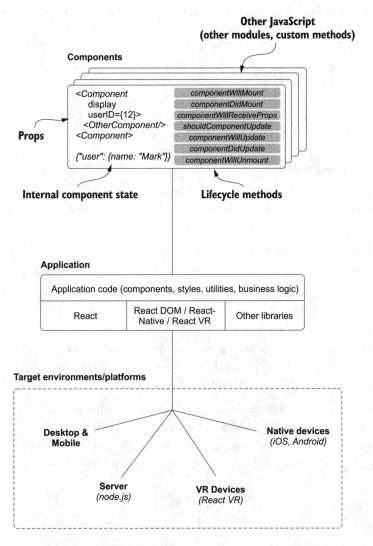

Figure 4.2   Overview of React. React will render (create, manage) components and create user interfaces from them.

memory. I've talked about state in React, creating components with `React.create-Element` and JSX, but we still need to look at the lifecycle methods in depth.

Let's jog your memory from past chapters and review some concepts. What is rendering? One definition of *render* is "to cause to be or become; to make." For our purposes, you can think of rendering as what React does in creating and managing a user interface for you. It's the work of getting your application onto the screen. It's React taking your components and turning them into a UI.

You can hook into this process using the lifecycle methods you're learning about in this chapter. These methods give you the flexibility to do what you need to at the right moment of a component's lifetime. They're only available to components that are created from classes that extend the `React.Component` abstract base class.

Stateless functional components, discussed at the end of chapter 3, don't have lifecycle methods available to them. You also can't use `this.setState` inside them because they don't have backing instances; React doesn't keep track of any internal state for them. They can still have their data updated by a parent via props, but you don't get access to lifecycle methods. That may seem like a hindrance or like they're less powerful, but in many cases they're all you need.

4.2.2 *Types of lifecycle methods*

This section looks at the different lifecycle methods provided by React in different groups and discusses what each one does. Lifecycle methods can be broken into two main groups:

- *Will methods*—Called right before something happens
- *Did methods*—Called right after something happens

There are also a few other methods that don't fit into either of these groups. They're related to initialization and error handling, and one is for updating. Most of the methods are did and will types, however.

We can further break them down into several more types based on what part of the lifecycle they're related to (see figure 4.3). Components have four main parts of their lifecycle and corresponding lifecycle methods for each:

- *Initialization*—When a component class is being instantiated.
- *Mounting*—A component is being inserted into the DOM.
- *Updating*—A component is being updated with new data via state or props.
- *Unmounting*—A component is being removed from the DOM.

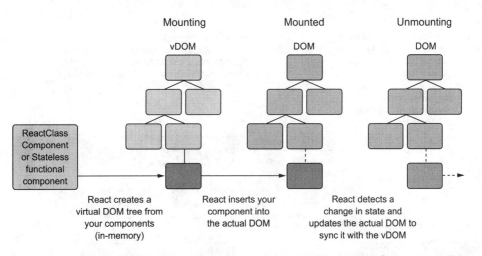

Figure 4.3 Overview of the rendering process and a component's lifecycle. This is the process that React uses as it manages your components for you. The three main parts of a component's life are when it's mounting, mounted, and unmounting. A component is mounting when it's being inserted into the DOM, mounted once it is, and unmounting when it's being removed.

There are lifecycle methods that will be called during initialization as well as before and after component mounting, updating, and unmounting. There aren't that many of these methods, especially when compared to other libraries and frameworks, but it can be easy to mix them up when you're learning React. Forming meaningful mental groups for them will help you navigate the different parts of the render process. Figure 4.4 shows an overview of the whole rendering process in React, which we'll look at more closely over the course of this chapter.

Remember, thinking of user interfaces and components in terms of a lifecycle isn't unique to React or JavaScript. Other technologies have adopted this idea with great success and sometimes even after being inspired by React (http://componentkit.org, for example). But these specific lifecycle methods *are* unique to React. To explore these methods, you'll create two simple components—a parent and child—that will implement all the lifecycle methods we'll look at. Head to https://codesandbox.io/s/ 2vxn9251xy to see how to add these components. You can still download the code from the CodeSandbox and use your browser's developer tools to inspect the console. Listing 4.1 shows the basic setup for these components.

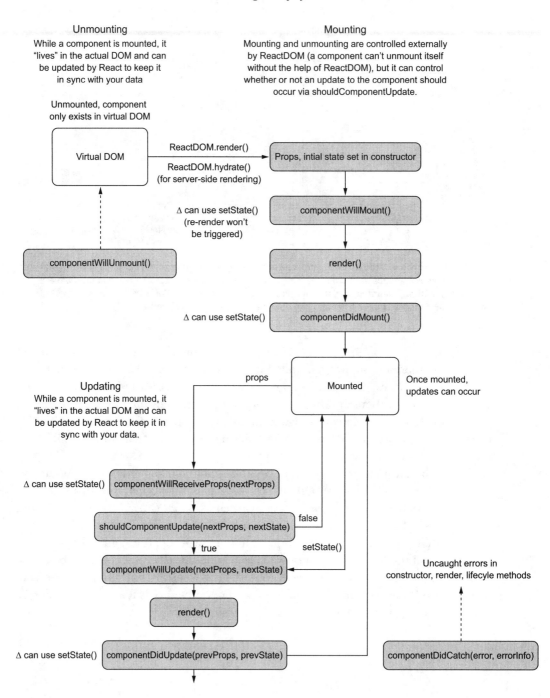

Figure 4.4   Overview of a component lifecycle in React. `ReactDOM` **renders a component and certain lifecycle methods are called as React manages your component.**

Listing 4.1 Exploring lifecycle methods

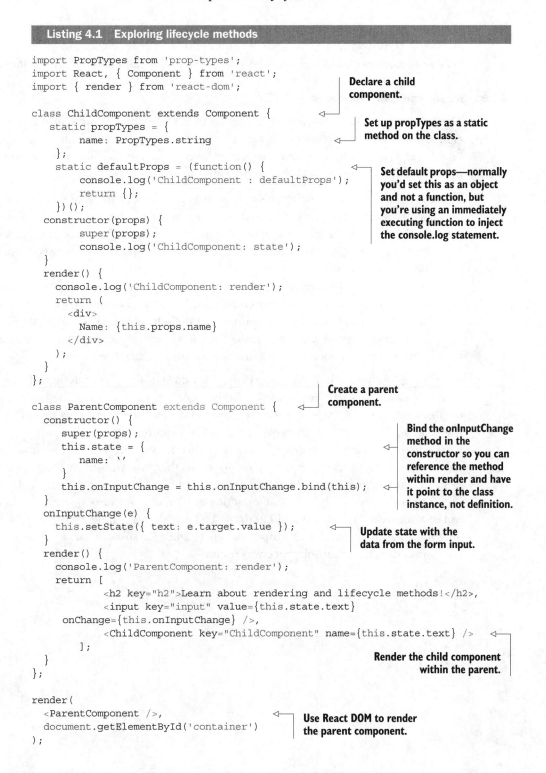

```
import PropTypes from 'prop-types';
import React, { Component } from 'react';
import { render } from 'react-dom';
```
Declare a child component.

```
class ChildComponent extends Component {
    static propTypes = {
        name: PropTypes.string
    };
```
Set up propTypes as a static method on the class.

```
    static defaultProps = (function() {
        console.log('ChildComponent : defaultProps');
        return {};
    })();
```
Set default props—normally you'd set this as an object and not a function, but you're using an immediately executing function to inject the console.log statement.

```
    constructor(props) {
        super(props);
        console.log('ChildComponent: state');
    }
    render() {
        console.log('ChildComponent: render');
        return (
          <div>
            Name: {this.props.name}
          </div>
        );
    }
};
```

```
class ParentComponent extends Component {
```
Create a parent component.

```
    constructor() {
        super(props);
        this.state = {
            name: ''
        }
        this.onInputChange = this.onInputChange.bind(this);
    }
```
Bind the onInputChange method in the constructor so you can reference the method within render and have it point to the class instance, not definition.

```
    onInputChange(e) {
        this.setState({ text: e.target.value });
    }
```
Update state with the data from the form input.

```
    render() {
        console.log('ParentComponent: render');
        return [
            <h2 key="h2">Learn about rendering and lifecycle methods!</h2>,
            <input key="input" value={this.state.text}
        onChange={this.onInputChange} />,
            <ChildComponent key="ChildComponent" name={this.state.text} />
        ];
    }
};
```
Render the child component within the parent.

```
render(
  <ParentComponent />,
  document.getElementById('container')
);
```
Use React DOM to render the parent component.

You don't need your components to do much for you to explore how lifecycle methods work. Here you've set up a parent and child. The parent component listens for changes to an input field and provides new props to the child component via state.

4.2.3   *Initial and "will" methods*

The first group of lifecycle-related properties to explore are the initial properties of a component. These include two properties you've already learned about: `default-Props` and `state` (initial). These properties help provide initial data to your component. Let's revisit these quickly before moving on:

- `defaultProps`–A static property that provides the default props for a component. Sets on `this.props` if that prop is not set by the parent component, is accessed before any components are mounted, and can't rely on `this.props.` or `this.state`. Because `defaultProps` is a static property, it's accessed from the class, not instances.
- `state` *(initial)*—The value of this property in the constructor will be the initial value set for the state of your component. That's especially helpful when you need to provide placeholder content, set default values, or the like. It's similar to default props with the exception that the data is expected to be mutated and only available on components that inherit from `React.Component`.

Even though setting initial state and props isn't done with special methods from the React `Component` class (they use the JavaScript `constructor` method), they're still part of the component lifecycle. It's easy to accidentally exclude them in your mind, but they play an important role in providing data for your components.

To help illustrate the order of rendering and the various lifecycle methods we'll look at, you'll next create two simple components that you can specify lifecycle methods on. You'll create a parent component and a child component so you can see not only the order in which different methods are called, but also how that order is worked out between parents and children. To keep things simple, you'll only be logging information out to the developer console. Figure 4.5 shows what you'll be able to see in your developer console once you're done.

```
⊗ ⊖ ⊗                   Developer Tools - https://jsfiddle.net/nnpe5dp8/
⎘ ⬚  |  Elements   Console   Sources   Network   Timeline   Profiles   Resources   Security   Audits   Augury   Redux                     ⋮
⊘ ▽  top                                    ▼  ☐ Preserve log
‹⋅ undefined
    ChildComponent : getDefaultProps                                                                    embedded:16
    ParentComponent – getDefaultProps                                                                   embedded:61
    ParentComponent – getInitialState                                                                   embedded:64
    ParentComponent – componentWillMount                                                                embedded:68
    ParentComponent – render                                                                            embedded:81
    ChildComponent : componentWillMount                                                                 embedded:19
    ChildComponent – render                                                                             embedded:51
    ChildComponent : componentDidMount                                                                  embedded:22
    ParentComponent – componentDidMount                                                                 embedded:71
    ParentComponent – render                                                                            embedded:81
    ChildComponent : componentWillReceiveProps()                                                        embedded:25
   ▶ Object {text: "1"}                                                                                 embedded:26
    <ChildComponent/> – shouldComponentUpdate()                                                         embedded:29
    nextProps:  ▶ Object {text: "1"}                                                                    embedded:30
    nextnextState:  Object {name: "Mark"}                                                               embedded:31
    <ChildComponent/> – componentWillUpdate                                                             embedded:35
    nextProps:  ▶ Object {text: "1"}                                                                    embedded:36
    nextState:  Object {name: "Mark"}                                                                   embedded:37
    ChildComponent – render                                                                             embedded:51
    ChildComponent – componentDidUpdate                                                                 embedded:40
    previousProps:                                                                                      embedded:41
   ▶ Object {text: ""}                                                                                  embedded:42
    previousState:                                                                                      embedded:43
    Object {name: "Mark"}                                                                               embedded:44
 > |
```

Figure 4.5   Output from the sample components once they've been fleshed out. A lifecycle method will trigger a message being logged to the console at each step, along with any arguments available to those methods. You can see the lifecycle methods in action at https://codesandbox.io/s/2vxn9251xy.

4.2.4   *Mounting components*

Now that you've created your parent and child components, let's look at mounting. *Mounting* is the process of React inserting a component into the DOM. Remember, components only exist in the virtual DOM until React creates them in the real DOM. See figure 4.6 for an overview of mounting and the rendering process for the parent and child components. Mounting methods will let you "hook" into the beginning and end of a component's life and are only fired once because, by definition, there can only be one beginning and end to a component.

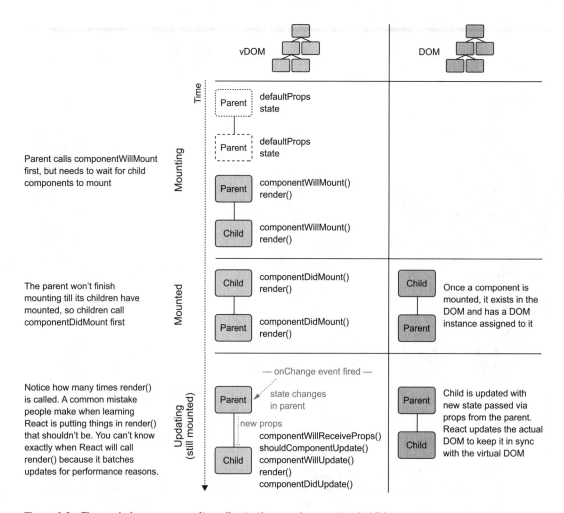

Figure 4.6   The rendering process as it applies to the sample parent and child components

DEFINITION   Mounting is the process of React inserting your components into the real DOM. Once done, your component is "ready," and it's often a good time to do things like perform HTTP calls or read cookies. At this point you'll also be able to access the DOM element via something called a *ref*, discussed in future chapters.

If you look back at figure 4.3, you'll notice that you only have one opportunity to change state before a component is mounted. You can do that by using component-WillMount, which will provide the opportunity to set state or perform other actions before your component mounts. Any changes to state within this method won't trigger a rerender, unlike other updates to state that will trigger the update process seen earlier. It's important to know which methods trigger a rerender and which don't so you can understand how your app will behave as well as debug it if something goes wrong. Figure 4.7 shows the mounting methods in the context of the lifecycle overview we've been working with.

Mounting

Mounting and unmounting are controlled externally
by ReactDOM (a component can't unmount itself
without the help of ReactDOM), but it can control
whether or not an update to the component should
occur via shouldComponentUpdate.

```
                                ReactDOM.render()
    ┌─────────────┐             ────────────────────►  ┌──────────────────────────────────────┐
    │ Virtual DOM │                                     │ Props, intial state set in constructor │
    └─────────────┘             ReactDOM.hydrate()      └──────────────────────────────────────┘
                                (for server-side rendering)              │
                                                                         ▼
                            Δ can use setState()        ┌──────────────────────────────────────┐
                            (re-render won't            │          componentWillMount()          │
                            be triggered)               └──────────────────────────────────────┘
                                                                         │
                                                                         ▼
                                                        ┌──────────────────────────────────────┐
                                                        │                render()                │
                                                        └──────────────────────────────────────┘
                                                                         │
                                                                         ▼
    Uncaught errors in constructor,   Δ can use setState()  ┌──────────────────────────────────────┐
    render, lifecycle methods                               │          componentDidMount()           │
              ▲                                              └──────────────────────────────────────┘
              ┊                                                              │
              ┊                                                              ▼
              ┊                                             ┌──────────────────┐   Once mounted,
    ┌──────────────────────────────────────┐               │     Mounted       │   updates can occur
    │ componentDidCatch(error, errorInfo)    │              └──────────────────┘
    └──────────────────────────────────────┘
```

Figure 4.7 Mounting methods in the context of the larger lifecycle process. Components are added to the DOM, and as they are, several specific methods are fired along the way.

The next method I'll cover is componentDidMount. When React calls this method, you have the opportunity to use componentDidMount as well as access refs on components. In this method, you have access to component state and props as well as the knowledge that your component is ready for updates. That means it's a good place to do things like update your component state with data coming back from a network request. It's also a great place to work with third-party libraries that depend on the DOM, like jQuery and others.

If you execute handlers or other functions in other methods (like render()), you'll end up with unpredictable and unexpected results due to how React works. Render methods need to be *pure* (consistent based on a given input) and are usually called many times over the lifetime of a component. React may even batch updates together, so you can't guarantee that a render will happen at a given time.

Now that we've looked at some of the methods related to mounting, you'll add them to your components so we can see the component lifecycle. The next listing shows how you can add these mounting methods to your components.

Listing 4.2 Mounting methods

```
import PropTypes from 'prop-types';
import React, { Component } from 'react';
import { render } from 'react-dom';

class ChildComponent extends Component {
    static propTypes = {
        name: PropTypes.string
    };
    static defaultProps = (function() {
        console.log('ChildComponent : defaultProps');
        return {};
    })();
    constructor(props) {
        super(props);
        console.log('ChildComponent: state');
        this.state = {
            name: 'Mark'
        };
    }
    componentWillMount() {                                              ◁┐ Add component-
        console.log('ChildComponent : componentWillMount');              │ DidMount and
    }                                                                     │ componentWillMount
    componentDidMount() {                                              ◁┘ to the child component.
        console.log('ChildComponent : componentDidMount');
    }
    render() {
        if (this.state.oops) {
            throw new Error('Something went wrong');
        }
        console.log('ChildComponent: render');
        return [
            <div key="name">Name: {this.props.name}</div>
        ];
    }
}

class ParentComponent extends Component {
    static defaultProps = (function() {
        console.log('ParentComponent: defaultProps');
        return {
            true: false
        };
    })();
    constructor(props) {
        super(props);
```

```
            console.log('ParentComponent: state');
            this.state = { text: '' };
            this.onInputChange = this.onInputChange.bind(this);
    }
    componentWillMount() {
            console.log('ParentComponent: componentWillMount');
    }
    componentDidMount() {
            console.log('ParentComponent: componentDidMount');
    }
    onInputChange(e) {
            const text = e.target.value;
            this.setState(() => ({ text: text }));
    }
    render() {
            console.log('ParentComponent: render');
            return [
                <h2 key="h2">Learn about rendering and lifecycle methods!</h2>,
                <input key="input" value={this.state.text}
        onChange={this.onInputChange} />,
                <ChildComponent key="ChildComponent" name={this.state.text} />
            ];
    }
}

render(<ParentComponent />, document.getElementById('root'));
```

Add component-
DidMount and
componentWillMount
to the parent
component.

Exercise 4.1 Pondering mounting
What does it mean that a component has *mounted*?

4.2.5 *Updating methods*

Once your component is mounted and in the DOM, you'll want to update it. In chapter 3, you saw that you can use this.setState() to perform a shallow merge of new data into the component state, but more than that goes on when you trigger an update. React provides several methods you can use to hook into the update process: shouldComponentUpdate, componentWillUpdate, and componentDidUpdate. Figure 4.8 shows the updating portion of the overall lifecycle chart we looked at earlier.

Unlike with other methods we've seen so far, you're given the option to control whether an update should occur. Another difference between the "update" methods and those related to mounting is that they provide arguments for props and state. You can use these to determine whether an update should occur or to react to changes.

If shouldComponentUpdate returns false for some reason, render() is skipped until the next state change. This means you can prevent your component from unnecessarily updating. Because the component won't update, the next methods, component-WillUpdate and componentDidUpdate, won't be called.

Unless you specify otherwise, shouldComponentUpdate will always return true, but if you're careful to always treat state as immutable and to read only from props and

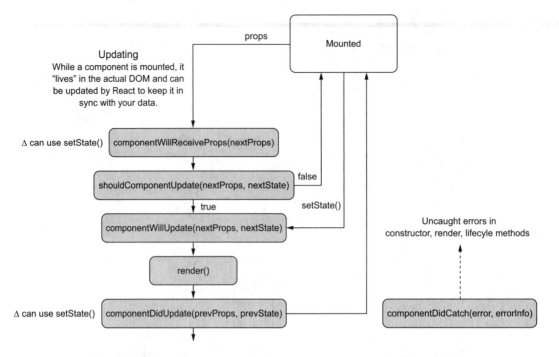

Figure 4.8   Updating lifecycle methods. When a component is being updated, several hooks fire that let you determine whether the component should be updated at all, how to update, and when the update is done.

state in `render()`, then you can override `shouldComponentUpdate` with an implementation that compares the old props and state to their replacements. That can be useful for performance tuning but should be treated as an escape hatch. React already employs sophisticated and advanced methods to determine what should be updated and when.

If you do end up using `shouldComponentUpdate`, it should be in a case where those methods aren't sufficient for some reason. That doesn't mean you should never use it, but you probably won't need to when first starting out with React. Like all the lifecycle methods, it's provided to you but should only be used when necessary. The next listing shows an example of React's update-related lifecycle methods.

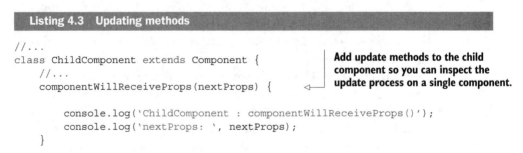

Listing 4.3   Updating methods

```
//...
class ChildComponent extends Component {
    //...
    componentWillReceiveProps(nextProps) {          Add update methods to the child
                                                     component so you can inspect the
                                                     update process on a single component.
        console.log('ChildComponent : componentWillReceiveProps()');
        console.log('nextProps: ', nextProps);
    }
```

```
        shouldComponentUpdate(nextProps, nextState) {          ◁─┐
            console.log('<ChildComponent/> - shouldComponentUpdate()');       **Add update**
            console.log('nextProps: ', nextProps);                           **methods to**
            console.log('nextState: ', nextState);                           **the child**
            return true;                                                     **component**
        }                                                                    **so you can**
        componentWillUpdate(nextProps, nextState) {             ◁─  **inspect the**
            console.log('<ChildComponent/> - componentWillUpdate');          **update**
            console.log('nextProps: ', nextProps);                           **process**
            console.log('nextState: ', nextState);                           **on a single**
        }                                                                    **component.**
        componentDidUpdate(previousProps, previousState) {      ◁─┘
            console.log('ChildComponent: componentDidUpdate');
            console.log('previousProps:', previousProps);
            console.log('previousState:', previousState);
        }
        //...
        render() {
            console.log('ChildComponent: render');
            return [
                <div key="name">Name: {this.props.name}</div>
            ];
        }
    }
}

class ParentComponent extends Component {
    //...
    onInputChange(e) {
        const text = e.target.value;
        this.setState(() => ({ text: text }));
    }
    //...
    render() {
        console.log('ParentComponent: render');
        return [
            <h2 key="h2">Learn about rendering and lifecycle methods!</h2>,
            <input key="input" value={this.state.text}
      onChange={this.onInputChange} />,
            <ChildComponent key="ChildComponent" name={this.state.text} />
        ];
    }
}
//...
```

Now that you've specified update methods for your components, try running them
again and type something into the text box. You'll see a cascading output in the developer console (listing 4.4 shows what the components should output). Take a minute
to look at the order of rendering. Notice anything? The order should cohere with
what you've learned so far in this chapter, but now you get to see how child and parent
component ordering matters. You may remember from chapter 2 that React is recur-
sive in how it forms a tree and renders things—it will exhaustively examine every part
of your components by asking about each component and all of its children.

Because it knows everything it needs to know about your component tree, React can intelligently create components for you in the proper order. You'll notice in listing 4.4 that a child component's mounting occurs before its parent's. This makes sense if you think about what mounting means for the parent: children have to be created before the parent component's mounting can be considered complete. If the child didn't yet exist, the parent couldn't be said to be mounted.

You'll also note that when an update occurs, you'll see the child component receive props because the prop of that child has been changed by the parent via `this.setState()`. From there, the updating methods run in order: `shouldComponent-Update`, `componentWillUpdate`, `componentDidUpdate`. If you for some reason told the component not to update by returning `false` from `shouldComponentUpdate`, those steps would have been skipped.

Listing 4.4   Component update output with text entered

```
ChildComponent  : defaultProps
ParentComponent : defaultProps
ParentComponent : get initial State
ParentComponent : componentWillMount
ParentComponent : render
ChildComponent  : componentWillMount
ChildComponent  : render
ChildComponent  : componentDidMount
ParentComponent : componentDidMount
ParentComponent : render
ChildComponent  : componentWillReceiveProps
Object {text: "Mark"}
<ChildComponent/> : shouldComponentUpdate
nextProps:  Object {text: "Mark"}
nextnextState:  Object {name: "Mark"}
<ChildComponent/> : componentWillUpdate
 nextProps:  Object {text: "Mark"}
 nextState:  Object {name: "Mark"}
 ChildComponent : render
 ChildComponent : componentDidUpdate
 previousProps:  Object {text: ""}
 previousState:  Object {name: "Mark"}
 >
```

"Mark" was pasted in so you don't trigger a whole series of updates for every letter.

4.2.6   *Unmounting methods*

Just as we could listen for the mounting of a component, we can listen for its unmounting. *Unmounting* is the process of removing a component from the DOM. If your application is written all with React, a *router* (explored in chapters 8 and 9) will remove components as you move between different pages. But you can also use React to integrate with other frameworks and libraries, so you might need to perform some other actions when your component unmounts (maybe clearing an interval, toggling a setting, and so on). Regardless of what it is, you can take advantage of `componentWillUnmount` to do any cleanup you need to when a component is being removed. Figure 4.9 illustrates how the unmounting process happens.

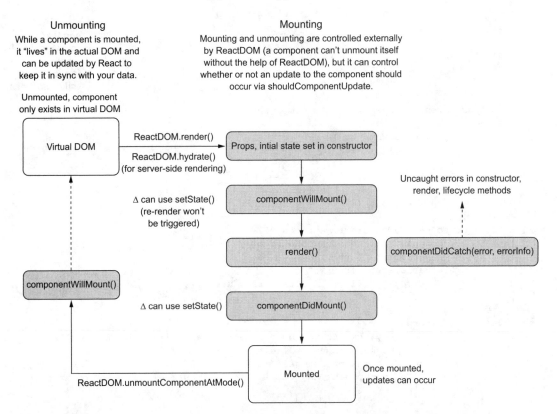

Figure 4.9 React DOM **is responsible for mounting and unmounting components. Mounting is the process of inserting your components into the DOM and unmounting is the opposite: the process of removing your components from the DOM. Once components are unmounted, they no longer exist in the DOM.**

Based on how mounting has worked so far, you might expect a componentDidUnmount method to be available, but there isn't one. That's because once a component is removed, its life is over and thus it shouldn't be able to do anything from beyond the grave. Let's add the componentWillUnmount to our running example so we can get the full picture of a component's lifecycle.

Listing 4.5 Unmounting

```
//...
class ChildComponent extends Component {
    //...
    componentWillUnmount() {
```

```
            console.log('ChildComponent: componentWillUnmount');  ◁──┐
        }                                                            │
        render() {                                                   │
            console.log('ChildComponent: render');                   │
            return [                                                  │
                <div key="name">Name: {this.props.name}</div>        │
            ];                                                        │
        }                                                            │
    }                                                                │
}                                                                    │
                                                                     │
class ParentComponent extends Component {                            │
    //...                                                            │
    componentWillUnmount() {                                         │
        console.log('ParentComponent: componentWillUnmount');  ◁─────┘
    }
    onInputChange(e) {
        const text = e.target.value;
        this.setState(() => ({ text: text }));
    }
    componentDidCatch(err, errorInfo) {
        console.log('componentDidCatch');
        console.error(err);
        console.error(errorInfo);
        this.setState(() => ({ err, errorInfo }));
    }
    render() {
        return [
            <h2 key="h2">Learn about rendering and lifecycle methods!</h2>,
            <input key="input" value={this.state.text}
    onChange={this.onInputChange} />,
            <ChildComponent key="ChildComponent" name={this.state.text} />
        ];
    }
}
//...
```

Add the componentWill-Unmount method to the parent and child components.

4.2.7   Catching errors

Error handling is a first-class part of writing clean programs. So far, we haven't seen any special methods in React for dealing with errors. If you've worked with React for a long time, you may remember that previous versions of React would lock up the entire app if an error occurred in a React component's render or lifecycle methods. This was often a source of frustration, as it meant that an uncaught error could lock up the entire application.

More recent versions of React introduced a new concept called *error boundaries* to help deal with this. If an uncaught exception is thrown within a component's constructor, render, or lifecycle methods, React will unmount the component and its children from the DOM. That may seem confusing at first, but the benefit it offers is the ability to isolate errors in components from breaking the rest of the app.

Exercise 4.2   Differences among components

What are some of the differences between React components created from the abstract base class `React.Component` and components created from plain functions without inheritance?

You can handle these errors by using another method that your components inherit from `React.Component`: `componentDidCatch`. The semantics of the method are similar to the `try...catch` behavior you'd see in JavaScript. `componentDidCatch` gives you access to the error being thrown and an error message. Using these you can ensure your components appropriately respond to errors. In a larger application, you might use this method to set up error state for individual components (maybe a widget, card, or other component) or at an application level. The following listing shows how to add the `componentDidCatch` method to the parent component.

Listing 4.6   Handling errors

```
//...
class ChildComponent extends Component {
    constructor(props) {
        super(props);
        console.log('ChildComponent: state');
        this.oops = this.oops.bind(this);        ◁── Bind the class method.
    }
    //...
    oops() {
        this.setState(() => ({ oops: true }));   ◁── Toggle state so you throw an error.
    }
    render() {
        console.log('ChildComponent: render');
        if (this.state.oops) {
            throw new Error('Something went wrong');   ◁── Throw an error in the render method.
        }
        return [
            <div key="name">Name: {this.props.name}</div>,
            <button key="error" onClick={this.oops}>
                Create error
            </button>
        ];
    }
}

class ParentComponent extends Component {
    //...
    constructor(props) {
        super(props);
        console.log('ParentComponent: state');
        this.state = { text: '' };
        this.onInputChange = this.onInputChange.bind(this);
    }
    //...
```

```
    componentDidCatch(err, errorInfo) {
        console.log('componentDidCatch');
        console.error(err);
        console.error(errorInfo);
        this.setState(() => ({ err, errorInfo }));
    }
    render() {
        console.log('ParentComponent: render');
        if (this.state.err) {
            return (
                <details style={{ whiteSpace: 'pre-wrap' }}>
                    {this.state.error && this.state.error.toString()}
                    <br />
                    {this.state.errorInfo.componentStack}
                </details>
            );
        }
        return [
            <h2 key="h2">Learn about rendering and lifecycle methods!</h2>,
            <input key="input" value={this.state.text}
    onChange={this.onInputChange} />,
            <ChildComponent key="ChildComponent" name={this.state.text} />
        ];
    }
}

render(<ParentComponent />, document.getElementById('root'));
```

Add a componentDidCatch method to the parent and use it to update component state.

If an error is thrown, display the error and error message.

We've looked at the different lifecycle methods provided to you by React and seen how you can use them in a variety of situations. If it seems like there are a lot of methods to keep track of, you'll be relieved to know that these make up the majority of the API for React components (you can also use table 4.1 as a cheat sheet). The core React API doesn't have much more than what we've covered so far. What's more, you don't have to use every one of these methods; use what you need. Table 4.1 shows a summary of the methods covered so far (note that render isn't included).

Table 4.1   Summary of React component lifecycle methods

	Initial	Will	Did
Mounting	defaultProps *Arguments*—None, static property *What*—Static version accessed many times. Sets values to this.props if that prop isn't set by the parent component. *When*—Invoked when a component is created and can't rely on this.props. Returned complex objects	componentWillMount *Arguments*—None *What*—Allows you to operate on component data before the mounting process happens. For example, if you call setState within this method, render() will see the updated state and will be executed only once despite the state change. "Last chance" to change initial render data.	componentDidMount *Arguments*—None *What*—Invoked once the component has been inserted into the DOM. At this point, you can access refs (a way to access the underlying DOM representation discussed in future chapters). Often a good place to perform

Table 4.1 Summary of React component lifecycle methods

	Initial	**Will**	**Did**
Mounting *(continued)*	are shared across instances, not copied.	*When*—Invoked once, both on the client and server (chapter 12 covers server rendering), immediately before the initial rendering occurs.	"impure" actions like integrating with other JavaScript libraries, setting timers (via `set-Timeout` or `set-Interval`), or sending HTTP requests. We'll often use this method to replace placeholder data in our components. *When*—Invoked once, only on the client (not on the server!), immediately after the initial rendering occurs. The `componentDid-Mount()` method of child components is invoked before that of parent components.

Updating	`shouldComponentUpdate`
	
	Arguments—`nextProps`, `nextState`
	
	What—If `shouldComponentUpdate` returns `false`, then `render()` will be completely skipped until the next state change. Also, `componentWillUpdate` and `componentDidUpdate` won't be called. Useful as "escape hatch" for advanced performance tuning.
	
	When—Invoked before rendering when new props or state are being received by your component. Not called for the initial render.
		`componentWillReceiveProps`
		
		Arguments—`nextProps: Object`
		
		What—Use this as an opportunity to react to a prop transition before `render()` is called by updating the state using `this.set-State()`. The old props can be accessed via `this.props`. Calling `this.setState()` within this function won't trigger an additional render.
		
		When—Invoked when a component is receiving new props. This method isn't called for the initial render.
		
		`componentWillUpdate`
		
		Arguments—`nextProps: Object, nextState: Object`
		
		What—Use this as an opportunity to perform preparation before an update occurs. You can't use `setState()`.
		
		When—Invoked immediately before rendering when new props or state are being received. Not called for the initial render.
			`componentDidUpdate`
			
			Arguments—`prev-Props: Object, prevState: Object`
			
			What—Invoked immediately after the component's updates are flushed to the DOM. This method isn't called for the initial render.
			
			When—Use this as an opportunity to operate on the DOM when the component has been updated.

Table 4.1   Summary of React component lifecycle methods

	Initial	Will	Did
Updating *(continued)*		`componentWillUnmount` *Arguments*—None *What*—Perform any necessary cleanup in this method, such as invalidating timers or cleaning up any DOM elements that were created in `componentDidMount`. *When*—Invoked immediately before a component is unmounted.	
Errors	`componentDidCatch` *Arguments*—`error`, `errorInfo` *What*—Handles errors in components. React will unmount components that occur in and below the tree where the error occurred. *When*—Called on an error in `constructor`, lifecycle, or `render` methods		

4.3   *Starting to create Letters Social*

Now that you know a little bit more about React's lifecycle methods and what they do, let's put those skills to use. You're going to start building out the Letters Social application. If you haven't already, make sure you read the first section of this chapter so you know how to use the Letters Social repository. You should be on the start branch when starting out, but if you want to skip to the end of the chapter you can check out the chapter-4 branch (`git checkout chapter-4`).

Up to this point you've been running most of your code in the browser on Code-Sandbox. That's been fine for learning, but you're going to switch context and start creating files on your local computer. You'll want to use the Webpack build process included with the repository, for a few reasons:

- The ability to write JavaScript in many files that are output in one or a small handful of files that have automatically resolved dependencies and import order
- The ability to handle and process different types of files (like SCSS or font files)
- To utilize other build tools like Babel so you can write modern JavaScript that will run on older browsers
- To optimize JavaScript by removing dead code and minifying it

Webpack is an incredibly powerful tool used by many teams and companies. As stated earlier in the chapter, I won't be covering how to use it in this book. One of my hopes for you in this book is to not have to learn React and every related build tool. There's simply too much complexity going on at once instead of making learning easy. But you can learn more about it if you choose. The build process included in the source code can be understood if you spend some time reading about Webpack at https://webpack.js.org.

You'll start building Letters Social by creating an App component and a main index file that will serve as the entry point into the app (where `React DOM`'s `render` method is called). The App component will house some logic for fetching posts from the API and will render a number of Post components—you'll create the component for posts next. The repository also contains a number of components that you won't have to create yourself. You'll use these now and in future chapters. The following listing shows the entrypoint file, src/index.js.

Listing 4.7　Main app file (src/index.js)

```
import React, { Component } from 'react';
import { render } from 'react-dom';

import App from './app';

import './shared/crash';
import './shared/service-worker';
import './shared/vendor';
import './styles/styles.scss';

render(<App />, document.getElementById('app'));
```

Import React and the render method from React DOM—this file will be where the main call to React DOM's render method will be.

Import some files related to error reporting, a service worker register, and styling (handled by repository setup).

Call render with the main app on a target element (the HTML template can be found in src/index.ejs).

Import the default export from the App component—you'll create this in the next listing.

The main app file contains references to some styling that Webpack can import as well as the main call to `React DOM`'s `render` method. This is the main place your React app will "start." When the script is executed by the browser, it will render the main app and React will take over. Without this call, your app won't be executed. You might remember from past chapters that you called this at the bottom of a main app file. It's no different here, really—your app is going to be comprised of many different files that Webpack will know how to bring together (thanks to your `import`/`export` statements) and run in the browser.

Now that you have an entry point for your app, let's create the main App component. You can place this file in the src directory as src/app.js. You'll sketch out a basic skeleton for the App component and then fill it in as you go. In this chapter, your goal is to get the main app running and displaying a number of posts. In the next chapter you'll start to flesh out more functionality and add the ability to create posts as well as add locations to posts. You'll keep adding functionality to the app as you explore different topics in React like testing, routing, and application architecture (using Redux). The following listing shows the basics of the App component.

Listing 4.8   Creating the App component (src/app.js)

```
import React, { Component } from 'react';
import PropTypes from 'prop-types';
import parseLinkHeader from 'parse-link-header';
import orderBy from 'lodash/orderBy';

import ErrorMessage from './components/error/Error';
import Loader from './components/Loader';
import * as API from './shared/http';
import Ad from './components/ad/Ad';
import Navbar from './components/nav/navbar';
import Welcome from './components/welcome/Welcome';

class App extends Component {
    constructor(props) {
        super(props);
        this.state = {
            error: null,
            loading: false,
            posts: [],
            endpoint: `${process.env

.ENDPOINT}/posts?_page=1&_sort=date&_order=DESC&_embed=comments&_expand=
user&_embed=likes`
        };
    }
    static propTypes = {
        children: PropTypes.node
    };
    render() {
        return (
            <div className="app">
                <Navbar />
                {this.state.loading ? (
                    <div className="loading">
                        <Loader />
                    </div>
                ) : (
                    <div className="home">
                        <Welcome />
                        <div>
                            <button className="block">
                                Load more posts
                            </button>
                        </div>
                        <div>
                            <Ad
                                url="https://ifelse.io/book"
                                imageUrl="/static/assets/ads/ria.png"
                            />
                            <Ad
                                url="https://ifelse.io/book"
                                imageUrl="/static/assets/ads/orly.jpg"
                            />
```

Import the libraries you'll need for the App component.

Import the error message and loader components to use.

Import the Letters API module for use in creating and fetching posts.

Import the preexisting Ad, Welcome, and Navbar components.

Set up initial state for the component— you'll keep track of posts and an endpoint to hit for more posts.

If loading, render a loader and not the app body.

This is where you'll add components for displaying posts.

Render the Welcome and Ad components.

```
                        </div>
                    </div>
                )}
            </div>
        );
    }
}
```

```
export default App;
```
| Export the App
| component.

With that, you can run the development command (npm run dev) and your app should at least boot up and be available in the browser. If you haven't already, make sure you run npm run db:seed at least once to generate sample data for your database. Running npm run dev will do a few things for you:

- Start up the Webpack build process and development server
- Start the JSON-server API so you can respond to network requests
- Create a development server (useful for server-side rendering in chapter 12)
- Hot-reload your app when changes occur (so you don't have to refresh the app every time you save a file)
- Notify you of build errors (these should show up in the command line and the browser if and when they occur)

When the app is up and running in development mode, you should be able to view the running app at http://localhost:3000. The API server is running at http://localhost:3500 if you want to make requests to it using things like Postman (www.getpostman.com) or just want to navigate to different resources using your browser.

With those logistical matters out of the way, you should add the ability to fetch post to the App component. To do that, you'll need to send a network request to the Letters Social API using the Fetch API (bundled up in the API module you pulled in). Right now, your component doesn't do much. You haven't defined any lifecycle methods outside of the constructor and render methods, so the component doesn't have any data to work with. You need to fetch data from the API and then update component state with that data. You'll also add an error boundary so that if your component encounters an error you can show an error message instead of the entire app unmounting. The next listing shows how to add the class methods to the App component.

Listing 4.9 Fetching data when the App component mounts

```
//...
    constructor(props) {
        //...
        this.getPosts = this.getPosts.bind(this);
    }

    componentDidMount() {
        this.getPosts();
    }
```
◁ **Bind class method and use it to fetch posts from the API when the component mounts.**

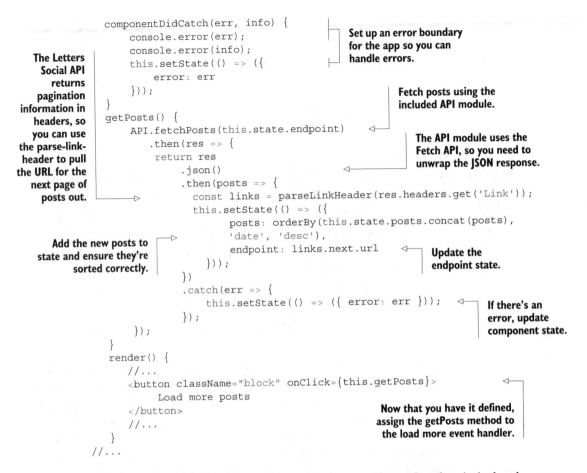

```
        componentDidCatch(err, info) {                    ┐  Set up an error boundary
            console.error(err);                           │  for the app so you can
            console.error(info);                          ┘  handle errors.
            this.setState(() => ({
                error: err
            }));                                              Fetch posts using the
        }                                                     included API module.
        getPosts() {
            API.fetchPosts(this.state.endpoint)     ◁───┘
                .then(res => {                               The API module uses the
                    return res                               Fetch API, so you need to
                        .json()                   ◁───────── unwrap the JSON response.
                        .then(posts => {
                            const links = parseLinkHeader(res.headers.get('Link'));
                            this.setState(() => ({
                                posts: orderBy(this.state.posts.concat(posts),
                                'date', 'desc'),
                                endpoint: links.next.url    ◁───┐  Update the
                        }));                                    │  endpoint state.
                })
                .catch(err => {
                    this.setState(() => ({ error: err }));  ◁───┐  If there's an
                });                                              │  error, update
            });                                                  │  component state.
        }
        render() {
            //...
            <button className="block" onClick={this.getPosts}>  ◁───┐
                Load more posts
            </button>                                 Now that you have it defined,
            //...                                     assign the getPosts method to
        }                                             the load more event handler.
    //...
```

Annotations:
- **The Letters Social API returns pagination information in headers, so you can use the parse-link-header to pull the URL for the next page of posts out.**
- **Add the new posts to state and ensure they're sorted correctly.**

The app should fetch posts when it mounts now and keep that data in its local component state. Next, you need to create a Post component that will house post data. You'll create the Post component from a set of preexisting components that came with the source code. These are mainly stateless functional components, and you'll build on them over the rest of the book. Take a look at the src/components/post directory to familiarize yourself with them.

Your posts will also fetch their own content so you can move the Post component around in future chapters and render it on its own. The App component makes a request to get posts, but all it really cares about is the ID and date of a post, whereas the Post component itself will be responsible for loading the rest of its content. Another way to do this would be to have the App component be responsible for all data fetching and just pass data to the post. One upside to this approach is that fewer network requests are made. You'll make the post responsible for additional data fetching for the purposes of illustration and because we're still focusing on learning lifecycle methods, but I wanted to point out another approach to be clear. The following listing shows the Post component. Create it in src/components/post/Post.js.

Listing 4.10   Creating the Post component (src/components/post/Post.js)

```
import React, { Component } from 'react';          Import the API
import PropTypes from 'prop-types';                module so you
                                                   can fetch a post.

import * as API from '../../shared/http';
import Content from './Content';                   Import the
import Image from './Image';                       constituent
import Link from './Link';                         components
import PostActionSection from './PostActionSection';   for Post.
import Comments from '../comment/Comments';
import Loader from '../Loader';

export class Post extends Component {               You need lifecycle
    static propTypes = {                            methods, so extend
        post: PropTypes.shape({                     React.Component.
            comments: PropTypes.array,
            content: PropTypes.string,
            date: PropTypes.number,                 Declare
            id: PropTypes.string.isRequired,        propTypes.
            image: PropTypes.string,
            likes: PropTypes.array,
            location: PropTypes.object,
            user: PropTypes.object,
            userId: PropTypes.string
        })                              Define a constructor so
    };                                  you can set state and
    constructor(props) {                bind class methods.
        super(props);
        this.state = {                  Set initial state.
            post: null,
            comments: [],
            showComments: false,
            user: this.props.user
        };                                          Bind class
        this.loadPost = this.loadPost.bind(this);   method.
    }
    componentDidMount() {               Load a post
        this.loadPost(this.props.id);   on mount.
    }
    loadPost(id) {
        API.fetchPost(id)
            .then(res => res.json())                Use the API to
            .then(post => {                         fetch a single post
                this.setState(() => ({ post }));    and update state.
            });
    }
    render() {
        if (!this.state.post) {
            return <Loader />;          If the post hasn't
        }                               loaded yet, show a
        return (                        loader component.
            <div className="post">
```

Set up the mock data for your CommentBox component.

```
        <UserHeader date={this.state.post.date}
                    user={this.state.post.user} />
        <Content post={this.state.post} />
        <Image post={this.state.post} />
        <Link link={this.state.post.link} />
        <PostActionSection showComments={this.state.showComments}/>
        <Comments
            comments={this.state.comments}
            show={this.state.showComments}
            post={this.state.post}
            user={this.props.user}
        />
      </div>
    );
  }
}

export default Post;
```

The last thing you need to do is to actually iterate over the posts so they get displayed. Remember that the way to display a dynamic list of components is to construct an array (either through `Array.map` or another method) and use that in a JSX expression. Also, don't forget that React requires you to pass a key prop to each item being iterated so it knows which components to update in a dynamic list. This is true for any array of components that you return in a `render` method. The next listing shows how to update the `render` method of the App component to iterate over posts.

Listing 4.11   Iterating over Post components (src/app.js)

```
//...
import Post from './components/post/Post';        ◁──┐ Import the Post
//...                                                 │ component.
<Welcome />
                   <div>
                     {this.state.posts.length && (
                       <div className="posts">
                         {this.state.posts.map(({ id }) => (
                           <Post id={id} key={id}
                             user={this.props.user} />
                         ))}
                       </div>
                     )}
                     <button className="block" onClick={this.getPosts}>
                       Load more posts
                     </button>
                   </div>
                   <div>
                     <Ad
                       url="https://ifelse.io/book"
                       imageUrl="/static/assets/ads/ria.png"
                     />
                     <Ad
                       url="https://ifelse.io/book"
```

Iterate over the posts you fetched and render a Post component for each one.

Don't forget to add a key prop to each item that you're iterating over.

```
                        imageUrl="/static/assets/ads/orly.jpg"
            />
        </div>
//...
```

With that, you're rendering out posts and have a start on Letters Social, as shown in figure 4.10. There's lots of room for improvements, certainly, but you're on your way. We'll look at adding posts and adding locations to posts in the next chapter. We'll also explore using refs—a way to access underlying DOM elements from your React components.

> ### Exercise 4.3   Uncaught errors
> What happens when an uncaught error occurs in a React component? Are there ways to handle the error?

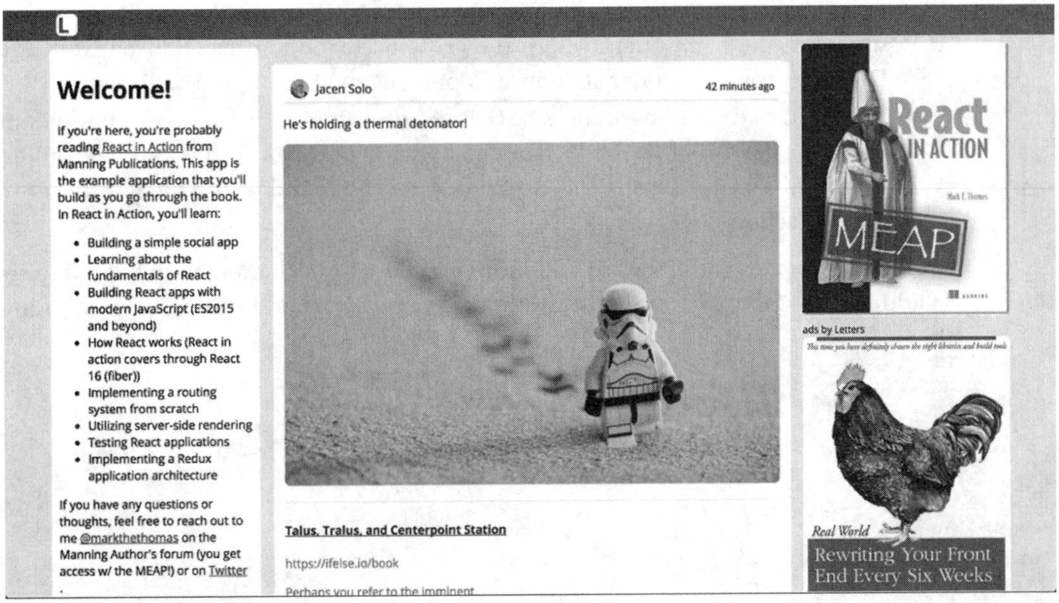

Figure 4.10   Our first pass at Letters Social. Posts are rendering, and you can load more. In the next chapter, you'll add the ability to create posts with locations.

4.4   Summary

Let's go over what you've learned in this chapter:

- React components are created from JavaScript classes that inherit from the `React.Component` class and that have a lifecycle you can hook into. This means they have a beginning, middle, and end of their time being managed by React. Because they inherit from the `React.Component` abstract base class, they also have access to special React APIs that stateless functional components don't.

- React provides lifecycle methods that you can use to hook into different parts of a component's lifetime. This lets your app act appropriately at different parts of React's process of managing the UI. These lifecycle methods don't all have to be used and should only be brought in when you need them. Many times, all you'll need is a stateless functional component.

- React provides a method for handling errors that occur in your component's `constructor`, `render`, or lifecycle methods: `componentDidCatch`. Using this method, you can create *error boundaries* in your application. These behave like `try...catch` statements in JavaScript. When an error is caught by React, it will unmount the component where the error occurred and its children from the DOM to promote render stability and prevent an entire app from breaking.

- You've started building Letters Social, the project we'll use to explore topics in React for the rest of the book. The final version of the project is available online at https://social.react.sh, and the source can be found at https://github.com/react-in-action/letters-social.

In the next chapter, you'll start to add more functionality to Letters Social. We'll focus on adding the ability to create posts dynamically and even add locations to posts using Mapbox.

5

Working with forms in React

This chapter covers

- Using forms in React
- Controlled and uncontrolled form components in React
- Validating and sanitizing data in React

By this point, you've gotten some basics for building simple components with React: lifecycle hooks, PropTypes, and much of the top-level component API. You've had a taste of the fundamentals and can do basic things like update local component state and pass data between components using props. You've also been introduced to component structure, ways to think in terms of components, and lifecycle methods.

In this chapter, you'll put more of that knowledge to work and really start building out the sample app, Letters Social. You'll be creating a component that users can use to create new posts for Letters Social. First, we'll explore the overall problem and review the data requirements. Then we'll talk about forms in React and you'll build out the functionality for the component. By the end of this chapter, you'll have learned how to use forms in your React applications.

How do I get the code for this chapter?

As with every chapter, you can check out the source code for this chapter by going to the GitHub repository at https://github.com/react-in-action/letters-social. If you want to start this chapter with a clean slate and follow along, you can use your existing code from chapter 4 (if you followed along and built out the examples yourself) or check out the chapter-specific branch (chapter-5-6).

Remember, each branch corresponds to the code at the end of the chapter (for example, chapter-5-6 corresponds to the code as it will be at the end of chapters 5 and 6). You can execute one of the following terminal commands in the directory of your choice to get the code for the current chapter. If you don't have the repository at all, type the following:

```
git clone git@github.com:react-in-action/letters-social.git
```

If you already have the repository cloned:

```
git checkout chapter-5-6
```

You may have come here from another chapter, so it's always a good idea to ensure you have all the right dependencies installed:

```
npm install
```

5.1   *Creating posts in Letters Social*

So far, your React application, Letters, doesn't do much except let you read things. A read-only social network is really more like a library, and that's not what your fictional investors want. The first feature you need to create is to the ability to create posts. You'll be creating functionality for users to create posts with forms and display them in the newsfeed. To get started, let's review the data requirements and get an overview of the problem so you understand exactly what you need to accomplish.

5.1.1   *Data requirements*

You'll be starting to use some browser HTTP libraries to send data to your fake API server. You probably already know at least a little bit about how these work and how to communicate with RESTful and other sorts of web APIs from JavaScript, so I won't cover it in depth. If you don't have experience with HTTP in the browser or communication with servers, there are many excellent resources available, for example, *JavaScript Application Design* by Nicolas G. Bevacqua (Manning, 2015).

When working with APIs, you usually need to send data that fulfills a contract of sorts. If a database is expecting user info, you may be required to include things like your name, email, and perhaps a profile picture. Your data will usually need to have a particular shape to it, or the server will reject it. One of the first things you should to is figure out how exactly your data needs to look for the server to be happy.

Listing 5.1 shows the basic schema for posts in Letters Social. We're using a simple JavaScript class here because that's what the server will actually use. When creating a post, the payload you send to the server needs to have most of the things defined in the schema. Note that your post can have a number of useful properties on it, including a location—you'll create a location-adding feature in chapter 6. The server will assign some smart defaults for properties you don't specify but will ignore other properties that aren't defined. One thing you won't need to do in the browser is create a unique ID—the server can do that on its own.

Listing 5.1 Post schema (db/models.js)

```
export class Post {
    constructor(config) {
        this.id = config.id || uuid();
        this.comments = config.comments || [];
        this.content = config.content || null;
        this.date = config.date || new Date().getTime();
        this.image = config.image || null;
        this.likes = config.likes || [];
        this.link = config.link || null;
        this.location = config.location || null;
        this.userId = config.userId;
    }
}
```

5.1.2 Component overview and hierarchy

Now that you know a little about the data you'll be able to work with, you can start to think about how you might be able to express this data in component form. There are plenty of examples of the sort of social networking app you're creating, so it shouldn't be hard to think of examples you've seen. Figure 5.1 shows the final product that you're building toward, so we can look at that for some initial inspiration.

I talked about establishing component hierarchy and relationships earlier in the book and emphasized their importance in creating apps with React. We'll do that again here before you start creating your component. Here's what you have so far in your Letters app:

- Post data available to use from the API; some posts have images, others have links
- User data for each post, with some avatar info
- An App component that serves as the catch-all component for the entire application
- A Post component that you use as you iterate over the data from the API

You need to add the ability to create posts, and these posts can have locations associated with them as well as text content. You'll need to let the user pick this location and then display that location in each of the posts in the newsfeed. Where should the CreatePost component live? Based on the mockups and the user needs, it seems like it

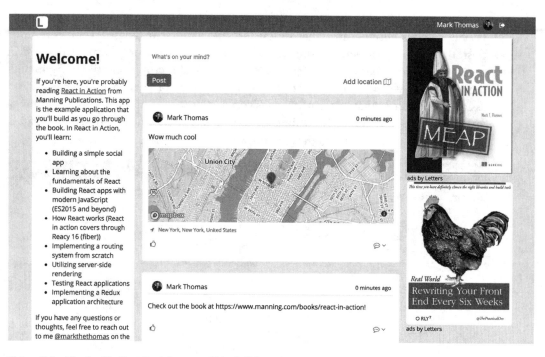

Figure 5.1   The final Letters Social app you'll be building. Can you see any ways you can break things out into components?

makes sense to place it as a sibling to the iterated posts, all within the main App component, as illustrated in figure 5.2.

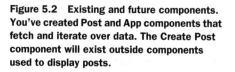

Figure 5.2   Existing and future components. You've created Post and App components that fetch and iterate over data. The Create Post component will exist outside components used to display posts.

Let's see how to create the skeleton for your component. You'll put in just the basics of a component that will render a basic element out, import the right tools, export the

Component class, and set up PropTypes to be defined later. The following listing shows how to create this basic skeleton.

Listing 5.2   Creating a component skeleton (src/components/post/Create.js)

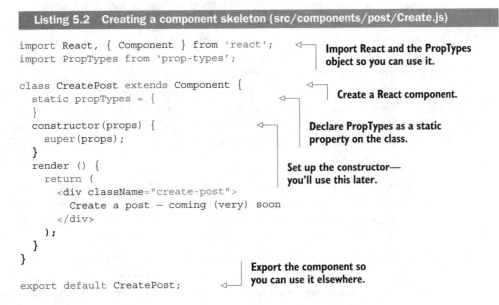

```
import React, { Component } from 'react';          Import React and the PropTypes
import PropTypes from 'prop-types';                 object so you can use it.

class CreatePost extends Component {                Create a React component.
  static propTypes = {
  }                                                 Declare PropTypes as a static
  constructor(props) {                              property on the class.
    super(props);
  }                                                 Set up the constructor—
  render () {                                        you'll use this later.
    return (
      <div className="create-post">
        Create a post — coming (very) soon
      </div>
    );
  }
}
                                                    Export the component so
export default CreatePost;                           you can use it elsewhere.
```

5.2   Forms in React

Both components you're building in this chapter involve the use of forms. Web forms are still similar to paper forms—they're a structured means of receiving and recording input. With paper, you use a pen or pencil to record information. With browser forms, you use a keyboard, mouse, and files on your computer to capture information. There are a number of form elements that you are probably familiar with, like input, select, and textarea, among others.

Most web applications involve forms to one degree or another. I've never worked on an application that was deployed to production that didn't involve forms of some kind. I've also found that forms sometimes have a bad reputation for being difficult to work with. Perhaps it's for this reason that many frameworks have implemented a "magic" approach to forms that seeks to ease the burden on the developer. React doesn't take a magical approach, but it can make forms easier to work with.

5.2.1   Getting started with forms

There's no standard way to do forms across front-end frameworks. In some frameworks and libraries, you can set up a form *model* that's updated as the user changes form values and has special methods built into it for detecting when a form is in different states. Others implement different paradigms and techniques when it comes to forms. What they all have in common is that they do forms slightly differently.

What should we make of the different approaches? Is one better than another? It's hard to say whether one is fundamentally better than another, but sometimes "easier to use" approaches can obscure the underlying mechanisms and logic from you. That's not always a bad thing—sometimes you don't need visibility into the inner workings of the framework. But you do need to have a sufficient understanding to support a mental model that will let you create maintainable code and fix bugs when they arise. That's where React shines, in my opinion. By not giving you too much "magic" when it comes to forms, you get a nice middle ground between having to know too much and knowing too little about the forms.

Fortunately, the mental model for forms in React is more of what you've already learned. There's no special set of APIs to use—forms are just more of what we've seen so far in React: components! You use components, state, and props to create forms. Because we're building on previous learning, let's review some parts of React's mental model before moving on:

- Components have two main ways of working with data: state and props.
- Because they're JavaScript classes, components can have custom class methods in addition to lifecycle hooks that can be used to respond to events and for just about anything else.
- As you might for regular DOM elements, you can listen for events like clicks, input changes, and other events in React components.
- Parent components (such as form elements) can provide callback methods as props to child components, making it possible for components to communicate with each other.

You'll use these familiar React ideas as you build out your component for creating posts.

5.2.2   Form elements and events

To create a post, you'll need to make sure that the post is persisted to your database, that the post UI is updated, and that you update the list of posts for the user. First, you'll scaffold out the form elements that you'll build, just as you might if you were building out a regular HTML form. There's not much to the markup—you're only receiving one input and don't need to display much else. The following listing shows the very beginnings of the component: rendering a `textarea` input.

Listing 5.3   Adding to your CreatePost component (src/components/post/Create.js)

```
//...
class CreatePost extends Component {
  render() {
    return (
      <div className="create-post">
            <textarea
                placeholder="What's on your mind?"
            />
            </div>
            <button>Post</button>
        </div>
```

```
    );
  }
}
//...
```

Now that you've created the bare-bones markup for your basic form, you can start to wire things up. You may remember from earlier chapters that React lets you interact with events like you would in regular browser JavaScript. It lets you listen for regular events like clicks, scrolls, and others and react (no pun intended) to them. You'll take advantage of these events as you work with your forms.

> **NOTE** If you've worked on front-end applications for some time, you'll know that there are many inconsistencies between different browsers, especially when it comes to events. In addition to all the other goodness you get from it, React also does a lot of work to abstract over these differences in browser implementations. That's a benefit that doesn't get much attention, but it can be an incredible help. Not having to worry as much about the differences between browsers tends to let you focus more on other areas of your app and generally results in happier developers.

Many different events can occur in the browser as a result of user interaction—including mouse moves, keyboard typing, clicks, and more. We're concerned with a few of these types of events in particular when it comes to your app. For our purposes, you want to listen with two main event handlers—onChange and onClick:

- onChange—This is fired when an input element changes. You can access the new value of the form element using event.target.value.
- onClick—This is fired when an element is clicked. You'll listen for this so you can know when a user wants to send a post to the server.

Next you'll assign some event handlers for these events. For now, you'll put in some console logging side effects for these functions so we can observe them being fired. You'll replace these with real functionality later. The following listing shows how you can set up the event handlers by binding them in the component class constructor and then assigning them in the components.

Listing 5.4 Adding to your CreatePost component (src/components/post/Create.js)

```
class CreatePost extends Component {
  constructor(props) {
    super(props);
    this.handleSubmit = this.handleSubmit.bind(this);        ◁── Bind class methods for
    this.handlePostChange = this.handlePostChange.bind(this); ◁── handling submission
  }                                                                and post changes.

                                                             Declare method
  handlePostChange(e) {                                      on class to be
        console.log('Handling an update to the post body!'); used when
  }                                                          update occurs to
                                                             body text (the
                                                             onChange event)
```

Declare method for handling submission event, and React will pass event to handler

```
handleSubmit() {
    console.log('Handling submission!');
}

render() {
    return (
        <div className="create-post">
            <button onClick={this.handleSubmit}>Post</button>
            <textarea
                value={this.state.content}
                onChange={this.handlePostChange}
                placeholder="What's on your mind?"
            />
        </div>
    );
}
}
```

Pass event handlers to the button and textarea components.

Value of component will be read from component state

Event handlers receive a synthetic event as an argument, and we have access to a number of available properties on the synthetic event. Table 5.1 shows some of the properties you can access on a synthetic event. By *synthetic* event, I mean that React translates the browser event into something you can work with in your React components.

Table 5.1   Properties and methods available on a synthetic event in React

Property	Return type
bubbles	boolean
cancelable	boolean
currentTarget	DOMEventTarget
defaultPrevented	boolean
eventPhase	number
isTrusted	boolean
nativeEvent	DOMEvent
preventDefault()	
isDefaultPrevented()	boolean
stopPropagation()	
isPropagationStopped()	boolean
target	DOMEventTarget
timeStamp	number
type	string

Before we move on, try something: add `console.log(event)` to the post component's change event handler. If you type something into the `textarea` element and open the developer console for your browser, you should see messages being logged out (see figure 5.3 for an example). If you inspect these objects or try accessing some of the properties in table 5.1, you should get back information about the event. For our purposes, we'll be concerned with the `target` property that you get back. Remember, `event.target` is just a reference to the DOM element that dispatched the event, as it would be in normal JavaScript.

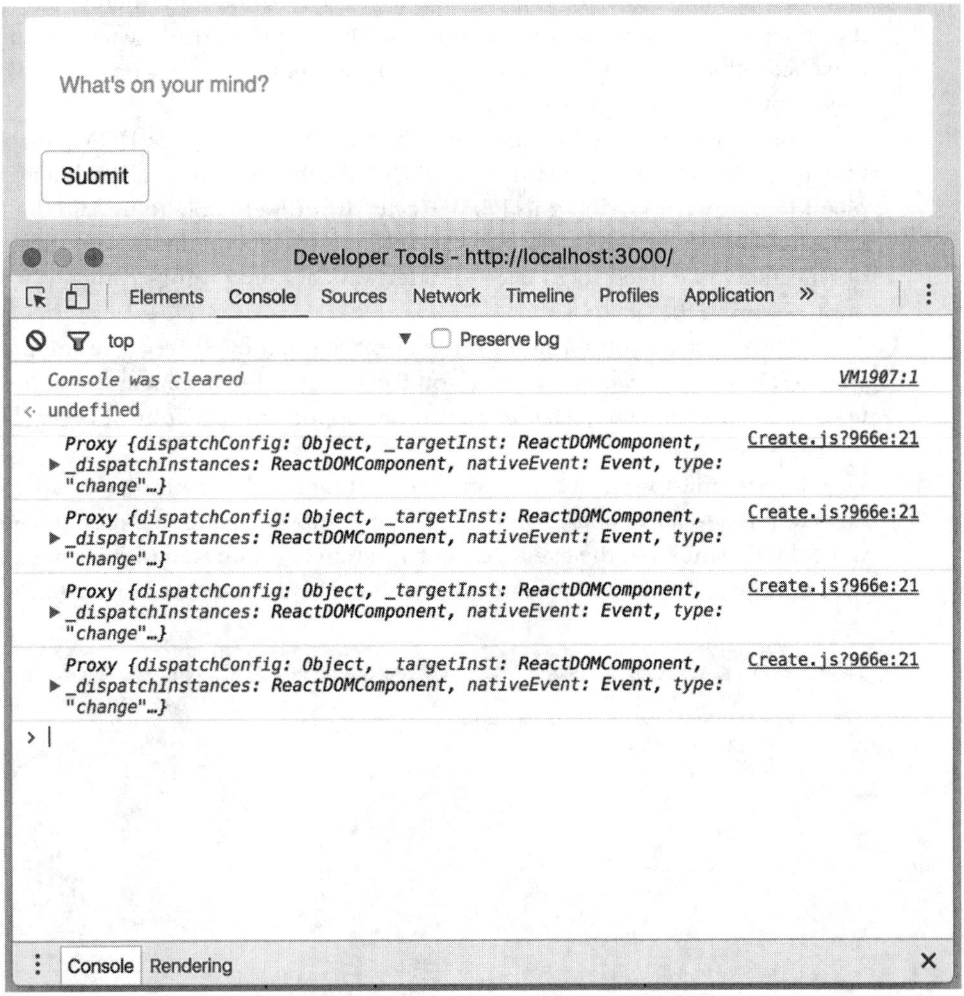

Figure 5.3 React passes a synthetic event to event handlers that you set up. It's a *normalized* event, meaning you can access the same properties and data as you would for a regular browser event.

5.2.3   *Updating state in forms*

You can listen for events now and watch as your component listens to updates and submission events, but you're not doing anything with the data yet. You need to do something with the events to update your application state. This is the key way you work with forms in React: by receiving events from event handlers and then using data from those events to update state or props.

State and props are the two main ways that React lets you work with data. Right now, if you try to type something into the form, nothing happens. That may seem like an error at first, but it's just React doing its job. Think about it: when you're changing the value of the input, you're mutating the DOM, and part of React's main job is to make sure that the DOM stays in sync with the in-memory version of the DOM that gets created from your components.

Because you haven't changed anything in the in-memory DOM (no state was updated), React won't update the actual DOM with any changes. That's a great example of React in action, doing its job perfectly. If you were able to update the form values, you'd be inadvertently putting yourself in a tricky situation where things are out of sync and you'd need to go back to older ways of doing things (which is what React improves on in the first place).

To update state, you'll listen for the event emitted by React when the input value changes. When this event is emitted, you'll extract a value from it and use that value to update component state. That gives you the opportunity to control every step of the update process.

Let's see how to put this into practice. Listing 5.5 shows how to set up event handlers to listen to and update the state of your components when a user changes a data value. Later, you'll use the event.target reference you worked with before and access the value property to update your state with the value from the textarea element.

Listing 5.5   Updating component state using inputs (src/components/post/Create.js)

```
class CreatePost extends Component {
  constructor(props) {
    super(props);

    // Set up state
    this.state = {
      content: '',
    };

    // Set up event handlers
    this.handleSubmit = this.handleSubmit.bind(this);
    this.handlePostChange = this.handlePostChange.bind(this);
  }
```

```
handlePostChange(event) {
  const content = event.target.value;          Grab value of textarea element from
    this.setState(() => {                       value property of DOM element (what
      return {                                  you want to update state with)
        content,
      };                                         Use that value to set
    });                                          state and update it
}                                                with new value

handleSubmit() {
  console.log(this.state);                       To see updated state, hit
}                                                form submission button and
                                                 inspect developer console
render() {
  return (
    <div className="create-post">
        <button onClick={this.handleSubmit}>Post</button>
        <textarea
          value={this.state.content}             New value for
          onChange={this.handlePostChange}       textarea element is
          placeholder="What's on your mind?"     provided to element
        />
    </div>

  );
}
}
```

5.2.4 *Controlled and uncontrolled components*

This approach to updating component state in forms—tightly controlling how updates occur by using events and event handlers to update state—is probably the more common way to handle forms in React. Components that are designed with this process in mind are generally known as *controlled* components. That's because we tightly control the component and how state is changed. But there's another way of designing components that use forms, known as *uncontrolled* components. Figure 5.4 shows an overview of how controlled and uncontrolled components work and illustrates some of their differences.

In an uncontrolled component, rather than use a value property to set data, the component maintains its own internal state. You can still listen for updates to the input using an event handler, but you'll no longer manage the state of the input. Listing 5.6 shows an example of using an uncontrolled component approach. We'll stick to using controlled components in this book, but it's important to at least know what this pattern looks like in practice.

Controlled

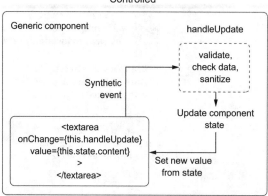

Uncontrolled

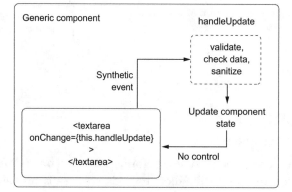

Figure 5.4 Controlled components listen for events emitted by a DOM element, operate on the emitted data, and then update the component state and set the value of the element. This keeps everything in the domain of the component and creates a unified state universe. Uncontrolled components maintain their own internal state and create a situation where a microcosm exists within the component, cutting off access to and control of that state.

Listing 5.6 Using uncontrolled components (src/components/post/Create.js)

```
class CreatePost extends Component {
  constructor(props) {
    super(props);

    this.state = {
      content: '',
    };

    this.handleSubmit = this.handleSubmit.bind(this);
    this.handlePostChange = this.handlePostChange.bind(this);
  }

  handlePostChange(event) {
    const content = event.target.value;
    this.setState(() => {
      return {
        content,
      };
```

Your handlers
are the same as
before, but the
effect that
changing state
has won't be
the same.

```
    });
  }

  handleSubmit() {                      ⊲─┐  Your handlers are the same
    console.log(this.state);              │  as before, but the effect that
  }                                       │  changing state has won't be
                                          │  the same.
  render() {
    return (
<div className="create-post">
              <button onClick={this.handleSubmit}>Post</button>
              <textarea
                onChange={this.handlePostChange}
                placeholder="What's on your mind?"    ⊲─┐  As noted, there's now
              />                                         │  no value element
        </div>                                           │  that will listen to the
      );                                                 │  component state.
  }
}
```

5.2.5 *Form validation and sanitization*

One important part of using forms to record and store user input is letting users know when they're violating any validation rules you've set up and when they're doing anything to provide data that doesn't satisfy your application. Hopefully, the server applications that receive data from your client-side application will have strict data-validation and sanitization procedures in place—you can't rely on a browser app to do all the work in this area. And even if you have good data sanitization and validation in place on your server, you still need to provide and enforce good data practices on the front end in order to help users, to add another level of defense against bad actors, and to promote data integrity. If you don't, you could potentially have confused users, security holes, and meaningless data—all things you don't want.

As we've seen so far, using forms to update component state involves state, props, and component methods, like much else in React. To add validation and sanitization to your component, you need to hook into the update process. To that end, you'll be writing general-purpose validation and sanitization functions that could be used anywhere you can use JavaScript and probably in most other front-end frameworks.

Exercise 5.1   Thinking about React events and forms

Take a minute to think about what you've learned about events and forms in React so far. Are events in React any different from the events you'd deal with in the browser? How are they different, if at all?

Fortunately, the CreatePost component you're creating doesn't require extensive validation. You only need to check for a maximum length and do some additional validation so the component won't submit empty posts to the API server. We're using a simple server setup for the purposes of learning and local development, so it will accept most payloads without doing much validation. Writing applications on the server is another domain outside the scope of this book, so I'll only focus on validation and sanitization on the browser.

You need to ask yourself a few questions when setting up validation for forms and inputs in your applications:

- What are the data requirements for the application?
- Based on these constraints, how can you help your users provide meaningful data?
- Are there ways you can eliminate inconsistencies in data that users provide?

First, you need to find out what the data requirements set by the business or application back end (if one exists) are. You should start there because that knowledge will help you establish basic guidelines for how to treat your data. Because we've already established that your server will willingly accept most things and we've set out the basic data types for a post, we can move on the next question.

Based on the constraints you have, how can you best help your users provide meaningful data and have a good experience in your app? That usually involves checking data for things like size, character type, maybe file type for file uploads, and more. Right now, your CreatePost component is fairly benign, and there's not much to validate beyond length. Next you'll check for a minimum and maximum length and only let the user submit their post if valid. The following listing shows how to set up some basic validation for your component.

Listing 5.7   Adding basic validation (src/components/post/Create.js)

```
//...
class CreatePost extends Component {
  constructor(props) {
    super(props);

    this.state = {              Create a simple valid
      content: '',              property in local
      valid: false,         ◁── component state
    };

    this.handleSubmit = this.handleSubmit.bind(this);
    this.handlePostChange = this.handlePostChange.bind(this);
  }

  handlePostChange(event) {
    const content = event.target.value;
    this.setState(() => {
        return {                              Determine validity of post
            content,                          by setting max length
            valid: content.length <= 280  ◁── here—280 demonstrates
        };                                    usage, but users sometimes
    });                                       want posts to be long
  }
```

```
handleSubmit() {
  if (!this.state.valid) {
    return;
  }
  const newPost = {                          Create a new
    content: this.state.content,             post object.
  };

  console.log(this.state);
}

render() {
  return (
    <div className="create-post">
        <button onClick={this.handleSubmit}>Post</button>
        <textarea
            value={this.state.content}
            onChange={this.handlePostChange}
            placeholder="What's on your mind?"
        />
      </div>
  );
}
}
```

We've worked on answering the first two questions (data constraints and validation). Now we can approach the final aspect: eliminating data inconsistencies with (very) basic data sanitization. Whereas validation is asking the user for *certain* data, sanitization is ensuring that the data you get back is safe and in the right format, and that it exists in a way that it can be persisted. Information security is a huge and very important field, and this book can't begin to really go into proper data handling for security—but we can tackle one smaller area for Letters: offensive content.

You'll use a JavaScript module called bad-words, available from npm (the main JavaScript module registry and service—learn more at www.npmjs.com/about), to help us out. It should already be installed in your project. bad-words takes in a string and replaces any words found on a blacklist (you can create your own and substitute it for the default if you prefer) with asterisks. The example illustrated in the following listing is mostly contrived, but at the very least you can prevent people from posting potentially offensive content on the public app (https://social.react.sh). Remember, this a very contrived example and isn't in any way suggesting or endorsing any kind of censorship.

> **Listing 5.8 Adding basic content sanitization (src/components/post/Create.js)**

```
import PropTypes from 'prop-types';
import React from 'react';
                                           Import default object
import Filter from 'bad-words';            from bad-words module
```

```
const filter = new Filter();
```
◁─┐ **Use a constructor to create
     new instance of filter**

```
class CreatePost extends Component {
  //...
  handlePostChange(event) {
    const content = filter.clean(event.target.value);
      this.setState(() => {
            return {
                content,
                valid: content.length <= 280
            };
        });
  }
//...
  }
export default CreatePost;
```
◁─┐ **Pass form value into
     the .clean() method
     of filter and use
     returned value to
     set state**

5.3   *Creating new posts*

Now that you're performing some basic validation and sanitization of posts, you'll want to create them by sending them to the server. We're going to introduce slightly greater complexity to achieve this, so we'll go over each step briefly and then look at an illustration of what the process will look like all put together.

To send your post up to the API, you'll need to do the following things, in addition to what the CreatePost component is already doing, which includes keeping track of state, doing some basic validation, and performing some basic content sanitization.

Next, you'll need to do the following to send the data up to your API:

1   Capture the user input to be used as the post, updating state and performing the data-checking logic you've implemented so far.
2   Call an event handler function passed from the parent component (the main App component in this case) as a prop and give the post data to it.
3   Reset the CreatePost component's state.
4   In the parent component, use the data passed from the CreatePost child component to perform an HTTP POST to the server.
5   Update the local component state with the new post you receive from the server.
6   To get a better grasp on what you'll be doing, see the illustration in figure 5.5.

You'll start by adding a function that will handle post submission in the parent component (App.js). There are several parts to this function, so you'll add them one at a time and we'll go through each. Listing 5.9 shows how to add the post submission function to the main App component.

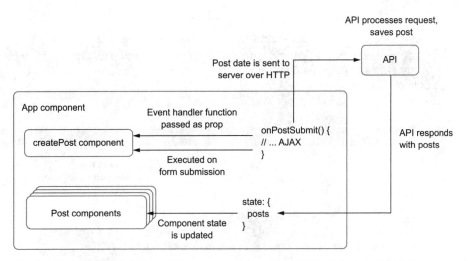

Figure 5.5 The CreatePost component overview. The CreatePost component receives a function as a prop, uses its internal state as an input for that function, and calls it when the user clicks Submit. That function, passed from the parent App component, sends the data to the API, updates the local posts, and initiates a refresh of posts from the API.

Listing 5.9 Handling post submissions (src/app.js)

```
import * as API from './shared/http';          ◁─── Import the Letters
//...                                                API module.
export default class App extends Component {
  //...
  createNewPost(post) {
    this.setState(prevState => {
                  return {
                        posts: orderBy(prevState.posts.concat(newPost),
      'date', 'desc')
                  };                    ◁─── Concat the new post
              });                            and make sure posts
                                             are sorted.
  }
  //...
}
```

You've set up the post-creation handler function in the parent component, but it won't do anything at this point because nothing ever calls it. That's because you need to give it to its child component (the CreatePost component you've been working on). Remember how you can pass data from parent to child as props? You can pass functions, too. That's crucial because it allows components to cooperate and work together. Even though components can interact, they're not so intertwined or coupled that you could never move them around; the CreatePost component could just as easily be moved to another part of the application and emit the same data to another handler. Listing 5.10 shows an example of passing callbacks as props.

> **Exercise 5.2 Controlled and uncontrolled components**
> What are some of the differences between controlled and uncontrolled components in React? What determines whether a component is considered controlled or uncontrolled?

Listing 5.10 Passing callbacks as props (src/app.js)

```
import CreatePost from './post/Create';          ◁─┐  Import the
                                                      component for use.
export default class App extends Component {
  //...
  render() {
   return (
     //...
     <CreatePost onSubmit={this.createNewPost} />   ◁─┐  Pass the
     //...                                                handlePostSubmit
      )                                                   function using
     }                                                    props.
  //...
}
```

At this point, you've set up the basics of the event handler in the parent component and are passing it into the child component. That helps you separate concerns—the CreatePost component is only responsible for bundling up some post data and then sending it to the parent component to do what it wants with it, namely, sending it off to the API. Chapter 6 covers that and more.

5.4 Summary

Here are the main things you learned in this chapter:

- Forms are handled in React much like any other component: you can use events and event handlers to pass data around and submit data.
- React doesn't provide any "magic" ways to work with forms. Forms are just components.
- Form validation and sanitization work within the same React mental model of events, component updates, rerendering, state and props, and so on.
- You can pass functions as props between components, which is a powerful and useful design pattern that prevents coupled components but promotes component communication.
- Data validation and sanitization aren't "magic"—React lets you use regular JavaScript and libraries to work with your data.

In the next chapter, you'll build on what you've created here and start to integrate a third-party library with React to add maps to your app.

Integrating third-party libraries with React

This chapter covers

- Sending form data in JSON format to a remote API
- Building some new kinds of components, including a location-picker, type-ahead, and a display map
- Integrating your React app with Mapbox to search locations and display maps

In chapter 5, we started looking at forms and how they work in React. You added event handlers to update component state in the CreatePost component. In this chapter, you'll build on that previous work and work on adding the ability to create new posts. You'll start interacting more with the JSON API that provided posts to render in the last chapter.

Often, you'll build React applications in a context that involves non-React libraries that also work with the DOM. These might include things like jQuery, jQuery plugins, or even other front-end frameworks. We've seen that React manages the DOM for you and that this can simplify how you think about user interfaces. There are still times, though, where you need to interact with the DOM, and it's often in the context of third-party libraries that use it. We'll explore some ways

129

you can go about doing that with React in this chapter as you add Mapbox maps to posts in Letters Social.

How do I get the code for this chapter?

As with every chapter, you can check out the source code for this chapter by going to the GitHub repository at https://github.com/react-in-action/letters-social. If you want to start this chapter with a clean slate and follow along, you can use your existing code from chapter 4 (if you followed along and built out the examples yourself) or check out the chapter branch (chapter-5-6).

Remember, each branch corresponds to the code at the end of the chapter or chapters indicated—for example, the branch chapter-5-6 corresponds to the code as it will be at the end of this chapter. You can execute one of the following terminal commands in the directory of your choice to get the code for the current chapter.

If you don't have the repository at all, type the following:

```
git clone git@github.com:react-in-action/letters-social.git
```

If you already have the repository cloned:

```
git checkout chapter-5-6
```

You may have come here from another chapter, so it's always a good idea to ensure you have all the right dependencies installed:

```
npm install
```

6.1   *Sending posts to the Letters Social API*

As you'll recall from chapter 2, you created a comment box component that allowed you to add comments. It persisted these locally, only in memory—the moment you refresh the page, any comments you added are gone because they live and die with the state of the page at a given time. You could have chosen to take advantage of local or session storage or used another browser-based storage technology (such as cookies, IndexedDB, WebSQL, and so on). Those would still keep everything local, however.

What you'll do is send the post data formatted as JSON to your API server, as shown in listing 6.1. It will handle storing the post and responding with the new data. When you cloned the repository, there were already-created functions in the shared/ http folder that you can use for the Letters Social project. You're using the isomorphic-fetch library for network requests. It follows the Fetch API of the browser but has the advantage that it can work on the server, too.

Listing 6.1   Sending posts to the server (src/components/ app.js)

```
export default class App extends Component {
//...
createNewPost(post) {
```

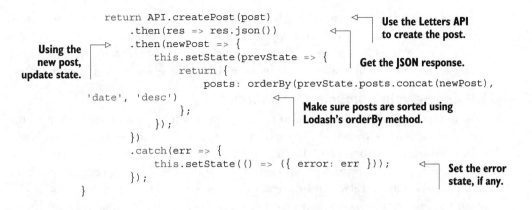

```
            return API.createPost(post)              ◁───   Use the Letters API
                .then(res => res.json())         ◁          to create the post.
                .then(newPost => {
                    this.setState(prevState => {   Get the JSON response.
                        return {
                            posts: orderBy(prevState.posts.concat(newPost),
    'date', 'desc')                        ◁───
                        };                              Make sure posts are sorted using
                    });                                 Lodash's orderBy method.
                })
                .catch(err => {
                    this.setState(() => ({ error: err }));    ◁───   Set the error
                });                                                   state, if any.
    }
```

With that, you only have one last thing to do: invoke the post creation method inside the child component. You've already passed it in, so it's a simple matter of ensuring that the click event triggers an invocation of the parent method and the post data gets passed along. The following listing shows how to call the method passed as a prop inside the child component.

Listing 6.2 Calling functions passed via props

```
class CreatePost extends Component {

// ...

fetchPosts() {/* created in chapter 4 */}
                                            Prevent default event and
                                            create an object to send to
handleSubmit(event) {                       the parent component
    event.preventDefault();            ◁───
    if (!this.state.valid) {
        return;                     Make sure you have
    }                               a callback function
    if (this.props.onSubmit) {   ◁─── to work with.
        const newPost = {
            date: Date.now(),
            // Assign a temporary key to the post; the API will create a real one
    for us
            id: Date.now(),
            content: this.state.content,       Invoke onSubmit callback passed via
        };                                     props from the parent component,
                                               passing in new post
        this.props.onSubmit(newPost);    ◁───
        this.setState({                   Reset state to initial form so
            content: '',                  user has visual cue that post
            valid: null,                  was submitted
        });
    }
  }
// ...
}
```

Now, if you run the application in development mode using npm run dev, you should be able to add posts! They should appear in your feed right away, but if you refresh your page, you should still be able to see your added post. It won't have a profile image or link preview like others, but you'll be adding those features in later chapters.

6.2   *Enhancing your component with maps*

Now that you've added the ability to create posts to your app and send them to the server, you can move on to enhancing it a bit. The fictional investors for Letters Social have been using Facebook and Twitter and have noticed that these let you add locations to your posts. They really want Letters Social to have this capability, so you'll be adding the ability to select and display locations when choosing a post. You'll also reuse the map display component so that the posts in a user's newsfeed can show a location. Figure 6.1 shows what you'll be building.

Figure 6.1   What you'll create for Letters Social. You'll enhance the current ability to post so users can add a location to their posts. Once you're done, you'll be able to search for and choose locations when creating posts.

You might have noticed in figure 6.1 that you're going to use Mapbox to create your maps. Mapbox is a mapping and geoservices platform that provides an incredible variety of map and location-related services. You can customize maps with data, create different styles of maps and overlays, do geographic search, add navigation, and more. I can't cover even close to all of what Mapbox does, but if you'd like to learn more, head to www.mapbox.com.

6.2.1 Creating the DisplayMap component using refs

You'll need a way to display a location to the user both when they're picking a location for a new post and when a post renders in their newsfeed. We're going to see how to create a component that will serve both purposes so you can reuse your code. You may not always be able to do this because each place where a map is needed may have different demands. But for this case, sharing the same component will work and will save you extra effort. Start by creating a new file called src/components/map/Display-Map.js. You'll put both our map-related components in this directory.

Where's the Mapbox library coming from? In most other cases, we've used libraries that we installed from npm. You'll use the Mapbox npm module in the next section, but you'll use a different library to create the maps. If you look in the HTML template included with the source code (src/index.ejs), you'll see a reference to the Mapbox JS library (`mapbox.js`):

```
...
<script src="https://api.mapbox.com/mapbox.js/v3.1.1/mapbox.js"></script>
...
```

This will give your React app the ability to work with the Mapbox JS SDK. Note that the Mapbox JS SDK requires a Mapbox token to work. I've included a public token in the application source code for Letters Social so you don't need a Mapbox account. If you have an account or want to create one for the purposes of customization, you can add your token by changing values in the config directory of the application source.

There are often situations when you're working on a project or feature that requires you to integrate React with a non-React library. You might be working with something like Mapbox (as you are in this chapter), or it could be another third-party library that wasn't written with React in mind. Given how React DOM manages the DOM for you, you may wonder if this is something you can even do. The good news is that React provides some nice escape hatches that make working with these sorts of libraries possible.

This is where refs come into play. I've briefly mentioned refs in past chapters, but they'll be especially useful here. A *ref* is React's way of giving you access to the underlying DOM node. Refs can be useful in React, but you shouldn't overuse them. We still want to use state and props as the primary means for making our apps interactive and for working with data. But there are good cases where refs are useful, including the following:

- To manage focus and imperatively interact with media elements like `<video>`
- To imperatively trigger animations
- To interact with third-party libraries that use the DOM outside of React (this is our use case)

How do you use refs in React? In past versions, you would add a string attribute to React elements (`<div ref="myref"></div>`), but the new approach is to use an inline callback, like so:

```
<div ref={ref => { this.MyNode = ref; } }></div>
```

When you want to refer to the underlying DOM element, you can reference it from your class. You can interact with it in the `ref` callback function, but most of the time you'll want to store the reference on your component class so it's available elsewhere.

I should note a few things. You can't use refs in React on a stateless functional component from the outside because that component doesn't have a backing instance. For example, this won't work:

```
<ACoolFunctionalComponent ref={ref => { this.ref = ref; } } />
```

But if the component is a class, you get a ref to the component because it does have a backing instance. You can also pass refs as props to components that consume them. Most of the time, you'll only want to use refs when you need direct access to a DOM node, so this use case probably won't come up often unless you're building a library that needs refs to work.

You're going to use refs to interact with the Mapbox JavaScript SDK. Mapbox's library handles creating a map for you and setting up lots of things like event handlers, UI controls, and more on the map. Its map API requires using either a DOM element reference or an ID to search the DOM for. You'll use a ref. The following listing shows the skeleton of your DisplayMap component.

Listing 6.3   Adding refs to your map component (src/components/map/DisplayMap.js)

```
import React, { Component } from 'react';
import PropTypes from 'prop-types';

export default class DisplayMap extends Component {
    render() {
        return [                                           Return an array of
            <div key="displayMap" className="displayMap">   elements from render
                <div
                    className="map"
                    ref={node => {                          DOM element that Mapbox
                        this.mapNode = node;                will use to create your map
                    }}
                >
```

```
                        </div>
                    </div>
                ];
            }
        }
```

This is a good start in getting your map to work with React. Next, you'll need to use the Mapbox JS API to create the map. You'll create a method that will use the ref you stored on the class. You'll also need to set up some default properties and state so the map has a default area to pan to and doesn't start by showing the entire world. You'll record a few pieces of state in the component, including whether the map has loaded and some location information (latitude, longitude, and place name). Note how it's a fairly trivial matter to interact with another JavaScript library through React. The hardest part has been using refs, but besides that, the libraries can pretty easily be made to work together. The following listing shows how to set up the DisplayMap component.

Listing 6.4 Creating a map with Mapbox (src/components/map/DisplayMap.js)

```
import React, { Component } from 'react';
import PropTypes from 'prop-types';

export default class DisplayMap extends Component {
    constructor(props) {
        super(props);
        this.state = {                              Set up
            mapLoaded: false,                       initial state
            location: {
                lat: props.location.lat,
                lng: props.location.lng,
                name: props.location.name
            }
        };
        this.ensureMapExists = this.ensureMapExists.bind(this);      ◁─┐
    }                                                                  Bind the
    static propTypes = {                                               ensureMapExists
        location: PropTypes.shape({                                    class method.
            lat: PropTypes.number,
            lng: PropTypes.number,
            name: PropTypes.string
        }),
        displayOnly: PropTypes.bool
    };
    static defaultProps = {
        displayOnly: true,
        location: {
            lat: 34.1535641,
            lng: -118.1428115,
            name: null
        }
    };
    componentDidMount() {
```

Check to see if the map has location information to work with—if it does, set up the map.

Create new map with Mapbox and store reference to it on component (you're disabling map features you don't need)

```
        this.L = window.L;
        if (this.state.location.lng && this.state.location.lat) {
            this.ensureMapExists();
        }
    }
    ensureMapExists() {
        if (this.state.mapLoaded) return;
        this.map = this.L.mapbox.map(this.mapNode, 'mapbox.streets', {
            zoomControl: false,
            scrollWheelZoom: false
        });
        this.map.setView(this.L.latLng(this.state.location.lat,
      this.state.location.lng), 12);

        this.setState(() => ({ mapLoaded: true }));
    }
    render() {
        return [
            <div key="displayMap" className="displayMap">
                <div
                    className="map"
                    ref={node => {
                        this.mapNode = node;
                    }}
                >
                </div>
            </div>
        ];
    }
}
```

Mapbox uses a library called Leaflet (hence the "L").

Update state so you know the map loaded

Set map view to latitude and longitude your component received

Make sure you don't accidentally re-create the map if you've already loaded.

Your component should now display a map that's good enough for display-only purposes. Remember, though, that you want to create a map component that you can indicate specific locations on and update for the user when they're picking a new location. You'll need to do some more work to enable these features: adding methods for adding a marker to the map, updating the map position, and ensuring that the map gets updated correctly. The following listing shows how to add these methods to your component.

Listing 6.5   A dynamic map (src/components/map/DisplayMap.js)

```
import React, { Component } from 'react';
import PropTypes from 'prop-types';

export default class DisplayMap extends Component {
    constructor(props) {
        super(props);
        this.state = {
            mapLoaded: false,
            location: {
                lat: props.location.lat,
                lng: props.location.lng,
                name: props.location.name
```

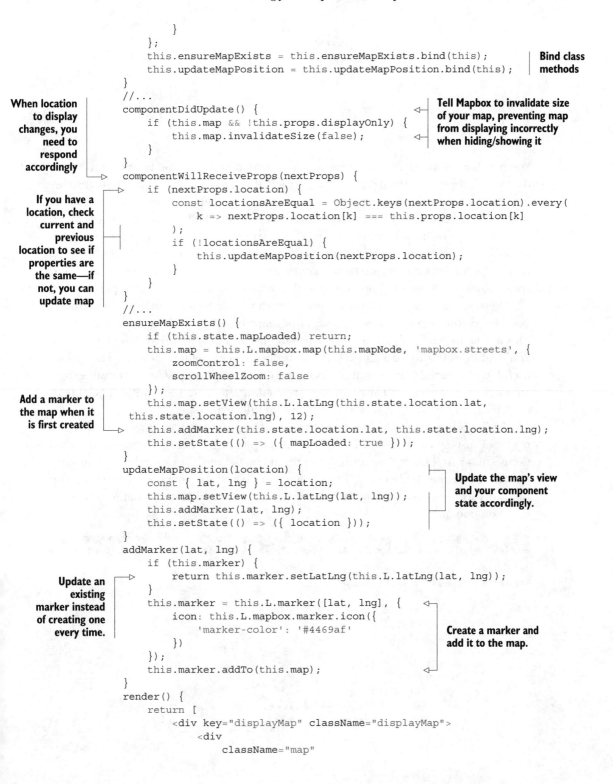

```
                }
            };
            this.ensureMapExists = this.ensureMapExists.bind(this);        Bind class
            this.updateMapPosition = this.updateMapPosition.bind(this);     methods
        }
        //...
        componentDidUpdate() {                                   ◄── Tell Mapbox to invalidate size
            if (this.map && !this.props.displayOnly) {               of your map, preventing map
                this.map.invalidateSize(false);              ◄──    from displaying incorrectly
            }                                                        when hiding/showing it
        }
        componentWillReceiveProps(nextProps) {
            if (nextProps.location) {
                const locationsAreEqual = Object.keys(nextProps.location).every(
                    k => nextProps.location[k] === this.props.location[k]
                );
                if (!locationsAreEqual) {
                    this.updateMapPosition(nextProps.location);
                }
            }
        }
        //...
        ensureMapExists() {
            if (this.state.mapLoaded) return;
            this.map = this.L.mapbox.map(this.mapNode, 'mapbox.streets', {
                zoomControl: false,
                scrollWheelZoom: false
            });
            this.map.setView(this.L.latLng(this.state.location.lat,
        this.state.location.lng), 12);
            this.addMarker(this.state.location.lat, this.state.location.lng);
            this.setState(() => ({ mapLoaded: true }));
        }
        updateMapPosition(location) {
            const { lat, lng } = location;
            this.map.setView(this.L.latLng(lat, lng));
            this.addMarker(lat, lng);
            this.setState(() => ({ location }));
        }
        addMarker(lat, lng) {
            if (this.marker) {
                return this.marker.setLatLng(this.L.latLng(lat, lng));
            }
            this.marker = this.L.marker([lat, lng], {            ◄──
                icon: this.L.mapbox.marker.icon({
                    'marker-color': '#4469af'
                })
            });
            this.marker.addTo(this.map);                         ◄──
        }
        render() {
            return [
                <div key="displayMap" className="displayMap">
                    <div
                        className="map"
```

Annotations (left margin):
- When location to display changes, you need to respond accordingly
- If you have a location, check current and previous location to see if properties are the same—if not, you can update map
- Add a marker to the map when it is first created
- Update an existing marker instead of creating one every time.

Annotations (right):
- Update the map's view and your component state accordingly.
- Create a marker and add it to the map.

```
                        ref={node => {
                            this.mapNode = node;
                        }}
                    >
                    </div>
                </div>
            ];
        }
    }
```

You may have noticed a pattern here as you've added each method to the component: do something with a third-party library, teach React about it, repeat. That's usually how integration with third-party libraries goes in my experience. You tend to want to find an integration point where you can get data out of the library or use its API to tell it to do things—but all within React. There are many exceptions where it can be incredibly difficult, but in my experience, the combination of React's refs and general JavaScript interoperability make working with non-React libraries not as bad as it could otherwise be (and I hope you find the same in your future React apps).

There's still at least one improvement you can make to your component. Mapbox also allows you to generate static images of maps based on geographic information. This can be useful for situations where you might not want to load an interactive map. You'll add this feature as a fallback so that users can see a map right away. This will be useful in chapter 12 when you'll be doing server-side rendering. The server will generate markup that won't call any mounting-related methods, so users will still be able to see a location for posts even before the app has fully loaded.

You'll also need to add one minor bit of UI to your map component so that the map can display the name of its location in display-only mode. We previously mentioned that you'd be adding a sibling to the main elements, and that's why you were returning an array of elements. This is where you'll add this small bit of markup. The following listing shows how to add the image fallback and location name display to your component.

> **Listing 6.6   Adding a fallback map image (src/components/map/DisplayMap.js)**

```
import React, { Component } from 'react';
import PropTypes from 'prop-types';

export default class DisplayMap extends Component {
    constructor(props) {
        super(props);
        this.state = {
            mapLoaded: false,
            location: {
                lat: props.location.lat,
                lng: props.location.lng,
                name: props.location.name
            }
        };
```

```
                    this.ensureMapExists = this.ensureMapExists.bind(this);
Bind                this.updateMapPosition = this.updateMapPosition.bind(this);
the class  ├─▷      this.generateStaticMapImage = this.generateStaticMapImage.bind(this);
method.           }
                  //...
                  generateStaticMapImage(lat, lng) {          ◁─
                      return `https://api.mapbox.com/styles/v1/mapbox/streets-
                  v10/static/${lat},${lng},12,0,0/600x175?access_token=${process  ◁─
                      .env.MAPBOX_API_TOKEN}`;
                  }
                  render() {
                      return [
                          <div key="displayMap" className="displayMap">
                              <div
                                  className="map"
                                  ref={node => {
                                      this.mapNode = node;
                                  }}
                              >
                                  {!this.state.mapLoaded && (       ◁─
                                      <img
                                          className="map"
                                          src={this.generateStaticMapImage(
                                              this.state.location.lat,
                                              this.state.location.lng
                                          )}
                                          alt={this.state.location.name}
                                      />
                                  )}
                              </div>
                          </div>,
If you're in  ├─▷        this.props.displayOnly && (
display-only                 <div key="location-description" className="location-
mode, show                description">
a location                       <i className="location-icon fa fa-location-arrow" />
name and                         <span className="location-
indicator.  └─▷           name">{this.state.location.name}</span>
                             </div>
                         )
                      ];
                  }
              }
```

Comment: **Use latitude and longitude to generate an image URL from Mapbox.**

Comment: **Display the location image.**

6.2.2 Creating the LocationTypeAhead component

You can display maps in your app, but you'll still can't do anything to create them. You need to build another component to support that feature: a *location type-ahead*. In the next section, you'll use this component in the CreatePost component you've been working with to allow users to search for locations. This component will use the browser Geolocation APIs as well as the Mapbox APIs to search for locations.

You can get started by creating another file, src/components/map/LocationType-Ahead.js. Figure 6.2 shows the type-ahead component you'll create in this section.

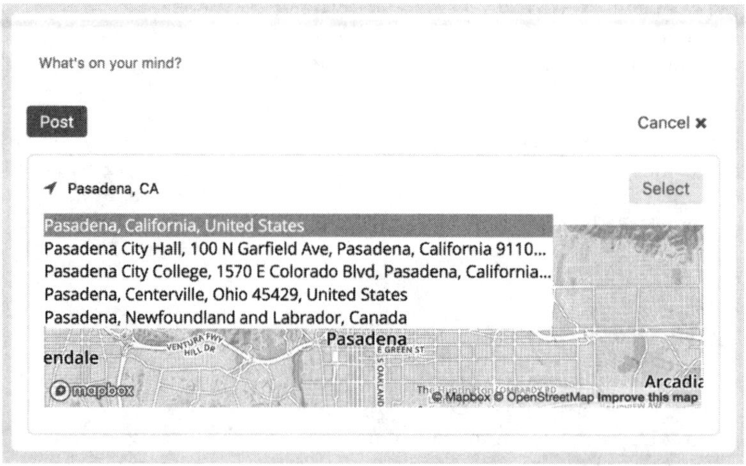

Figure 6.2   A location type-ahead component you can use along with your map component to let the user add locations to their posts

Here's the basic functionality your component will have by the time it's done:

- Display a list of locations for a user to select
- Yield the selected location to a parent component for use
- Use the Mapbox and Geolocation APIs to let users pick their current location or search by address

Next, you'll get started by creating a skeleton of what your component will look like. Listing 6.7 shows the first sketch of it. You'll be using Mapbox again, but this time you're using a different set of APIs. You used the map-display API in the last section, but here you'll use the set of Mapbox APIs that let users do *reverse geocoding*, which is a fancy way of saying "search for a real location by text." The Mapbox module is already installed with the project and will use the same public Mapbox key to work. If you previously added in your API key, the app configuration should use the same key here.

Exercise 6.1   Mapbox alternatives

You've used Mapbox in this chapter, but there are other mapping libraries out there, such as Google maps. How would you go about switching out Mapbox for Google Maps? What would you have to do differently?

Listing 6.7   The beginnings of the LocationTypeAhead component

```
import React, { Component } from 'react';
import PropTypes from 'prop-types';
import MapBox from 'mapbox';                    ⟵┘  Import Mapbox.
```

```
export default class LocationTypeAhead extends Component {
    static propTypes = {
        onLocationUpdate: PropTypes.func.isRequired,
        onLocationSelect: PropTypes.func.isRequired
    };
    constructor(props) {
        super(props);
        this.state = {
            text: '',
            locations: [],
            selectedLocation: null
        };
        this.mapbox = new MapBox(process.env.MAPBOX_API_TOKEN);
    }
    render() {
        return [
            <div key="location-typeahead" className="location-typeahead">
                <i className="fa fa-location-arrow"
    onClick={this.attemptGeoLocation} />
                <input
                    onChange={this.handleSearchChange}
                    type="text"
                    placeholder="Enter a location..."
                    value={this.state.text}
                />
                <button
                    disabled={!this.state.selectedLocation}
                    onClick={this.handleSelectLocation}
                    className="open"
                >
                    Select
                </button>
            </div>
        ];
    }
}
```

Expose two methods, one for location update and one for location selection.

Set up initial state

Create an instance of the Mapbox client.

Return an array of elements that will be the markup for your type-ahead component. You'll need to implement all of the methods referenced in event handlers (onChange, onClick, and so on).

Now you can start filling out the methods you referenced in the render method of the component. Note that you want a way to handle a change in search text, a button that will allow you to choose a location, and an icon that'll let the user pick their current location. I'll cover that functionality next; for now, you need methods that will let a user search for locations using text and choose a location. Listing 6.8 shows how to add these methods. Where are these locations going to come from? You're going to use the Mapbox API to search for locations based on what the user types and use those results to show them addresses. This is just one way you can use Mapbox. You can do the opposite, too—put in coordinates and turn it into an address. You'll use that feature in the next listing to work with the Geolocation API.

Listing 6.8   Searching for locations (src/components/map/LocationTypeAhead.js)

```
//...
constructor(props) {
    super(props);
    this.state = {
        text: '',
        locations: [],
        selectedLocation: null
    };
    this.mapbox = new MapBox(process.env.MAPBOX_API_TOKEN);
    this.handleLocationUpdate = this.handleLocationUpdate.bind(this);
    this.handleSearchChange = this.handleSearchChange.bind(this);
    this.handleSelectLocation = this.handleSelectLocation.bind(this);
    this.resetSearch = this.resetSearch.bind(this);
}
componentWillUnmount() {
    this.resetSearch();
}
handleLocationUpdate(location) {
    this.setState(() => {
        return {
            text: location.name,
            locations: [],
            selectedLocation: location
        };
    });
    this.props.onLocationUpdate(location);
}
handleSearchChange(e) {
    const text = e.target.value;
    this.setState(() => ({ text }));
    if (!text) return;
    this.mapbox.geocodeForward(text, {}).then(loc => {
        if (!loc.entity.features || !loc.entity.features.length) {
            return;
        }
        const locations = loc.entity.features.map(feature => {
            const [lng, lat] = feature.center;
            return {
                name: feature.place_name,
                lat,
                lng
            };
        });
        this.setState(() => ({ locations }));
    });
}
resetSearch() {
    this.setState(() => {
        return {
            text: '',
            locations: [],
            selectedLocation: null
        };
```

Bind class methods.

When the component unmounts, reset the search.

When a location is selected, update local component state

At the same time, pass location up to parent via a props callback

Use Mapbox client to search for locations using user's text

Pull text off the event you receive when a user types into search box

Don't do anything if no results

Transform Mapbox results into a format you can more easily use in your component.

Update state with new locations

Allow resetting component state (see componentWillUnmount)

```
        });
    }
    handleSelectLocation() {
        this.props.onLocationSelect(this.state.selectedLocation);
    }
//....
```

> When location is selected, pass
> currently selected location up

Next, you want to let the user choose their current location for a post. To do that, you'll use the browser Geolocation API. It's okay if you haven't worked with the Geolocation API before. For a long time it was a bleeding-edge feature, and you could only use it on certain browsers. Now it's gained wide adoption and is more broadly useful.

The Geolocation API does pretty much what you think it might: you can ask the user whether you can use their location in your app. Nearly all browsers support the Geolocation API at this point (http://caniuse.com/#feat=geolocation), so you can take advantage of it and let a user choose the current location for a post. Note that the Geolocation API can only be used in secure contexts, so if you try to deploy Letters Social to an unsecured host, it won't work.

You'll need to use the Mapbox API again, since all the Geolocation API gives you back is coordinates. Remember how you used the user's text to search for locations in Mapbox? You can do the inverse: provide coordinates to Mapbox and get back matching addresses. The following listing shows how to use the Geolocation and Mapbox APIs to let the user choose their current location for a post.

Listing 6.9 Adding Geolocation (src/components/map/LocationTypeAhead.js)

```
constructor(props) {
    super(props);
    this.state = {
        text: '',
        locations: [],
        selectedLocation: null
    };
    this.mapbox = new MapBox(process.env.MAPBOX_API_TOKEN);
    this.attemptGeoLocation = this.attemptGeoLocation.bind(this);
    this.handleLocationUpdate = this.handleLocationUpdate.bind(this);
    this.handleSearchChange = this.handleSearchChange.bind(this);
    this.handleSelectLocation = this.handleSelectLocation.bind(this);
    this.resetSearch = this.resetSearch.bind(this);
}
//...
attemptGeoLocation() {
    if ('geolocation' in navigator) {
        navigator.geolocation.getCurrentPosition(
            ({ coords }) => {
                const { latitude, longitude } = coords;
                this.mapbox.geocodeReverse({ latitude, longitude },
    {}).then(loc => {
                    if (!loc.entity.features ||
    !loc.entity.features.length) {
                        return;
```

> Bind class
> method

> Check to see if browser
> supports geolocation

> Get current
> position of
> user's device

> This will yield back
> coordinates that
> you can use.

> Use Mapbox to geocode the
> coordinates and return early
> if nothing is found.

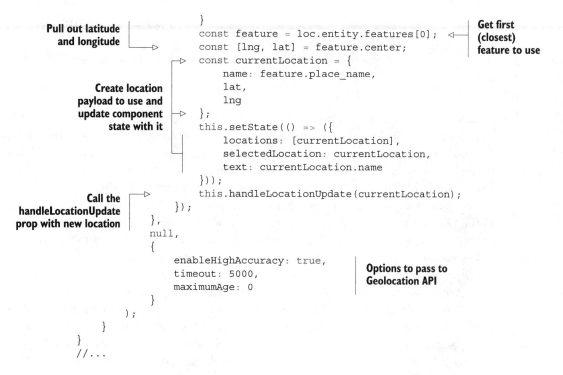

```
                                                }
Pull out latitude                               const feature = loc.entity.features[0];      ◁──    Get first
and longitude                                   const [lng, lat] = feature.center;                  (closest)
                                         ┌─▷     const currentLocation = {                           feature to use
                                         │           name: feature.place_name,
Create location                          │           lat,
payload to use and                       │           lng
update component                         │       };
state with it                            └─▷     this.setState(() => ({
                                                     locations: [currentLocation],
                                                     selectedLocation: currentLocation,
                                                     text: currentLocation.name
                                                 }));
Call the                         ┌─▷             this.handleLocationUpdate(currentLocation);
handleLocationUpdate             │           });
prop with new location           │       },
                                         null,
                                         {
                                             enableHighAccuracy: true,
                                             timeout: 5000,             Options to pass to
                                             maximumAge: 0              Geolocation API
                                         }
                                     );
                                 }
                             }
                             //...
```

Your component can search Mapbox for locations and let the user pick their own location via the Geolocation API. But it's not showing anything to the user yet, so you'll fix
that next. You're going to need to use the location results so the user can click to
select one, as shown in the following listing.

Listing 6.10   Displaying results to the user (src/components/map/LocationTypeAhead.js)

```
//...
render() {
        return [
            <div key="location-typeahead" className="location-typeahead">
                <i className="fa fa-location-arrow"
    onClick={this.attemptGeoLocation} />
                <input
                    onChange={this.handleSearchChange}
                    type="text"
                    placeholder="Enter a location..."
                    value={this.state.text}
                />
                <button
                    disabled={!this.state.selectedLocation}
                    onClick={this.handleSelectLocation}
                    className="open"
                >
                    Select
                </button>
            </div>,
```

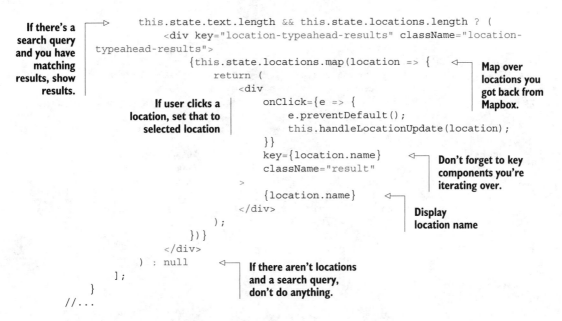

```
            this.state.text.length && this.state.locations.length ? (
                <div key="location-typeahead-results" className="location-
        typeahead-results">
                    {this.state.locations.map(location => {
                        return (
                            <div
                                onClick={e => {
                                    e.preventDefault();
                                    this.handleLocationUpdate(location);
                                }}
                                key={location.name}
                                className="result"
                            >
                                {location.name}
                            </div>
                        );
                    })}
                </div>
            ) : null;
        ];
    }
//...
```

If there's a search query and you have matching results, show results.

Map over locations you got back from Mapbox.

If user clicks a location, set that to selected location

Don't forget to key components you're iterating over.

Display location name

If there aren't locations and a search query, don't do anything.

6.2.3 *Updating CreatePost and adding maps to posts*

Now that you've created the LocationTypeAhead and DisplayMap components, you can integrate these into the CreatePost component you've been working with. This will tie together the functionality you've created and allow the user to create posts that have a location. Remember how the CreatePost component passes its data back up to a parent component to do the actual post creation? You'll do the same thing with the type-ahead and DisplayMap components, but from the CreatePost. They'll work together but not be so tied to each other that you can't move them around or use them elsewhere.

You need to update your CreatePost component to work with the LocationType-Ahead and DisplayMap components you created earlier—which, remember, yield and receive a location, respectively. You'll keep track of a location in the CreatePost component and use the two components you recently created as a source and destination of the location data. The following listing shows how to add the methods you'll need to add locations to posts.

Listing 6.11   Handling locations in CreatePost (src/components/post/Create.js)

```
constructor(props) {
    super(props);
    this.initialState = {
        content: '',
        valid: false,
        showLocationPicker: false,
        location: {
            lat: 34.1535641,
            lng: -118.1428115,
            name: null
        },
        locationSelected: false
```

Add keys to state so you can keep track of location and related data; set up some default location data

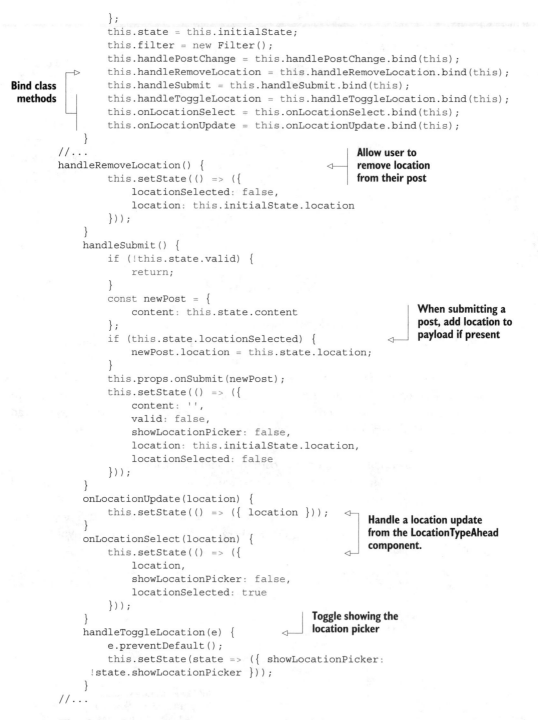

```
        };
        this.state = this.initialState;
        this.filter = new Filter();
        this.handlePostChange = this.handlePostChange.bind(this);
        this.handleRemoveLocation = this.handleRemoveLocation.bind(this);
        this.handleSubmit = this.handleSubmit.bind(this);
        this.handleToggleLocation = this.handleToggleLocation.bind(this);
        this.onLocationSelect = this.onLocationSelect.bind(this);
        this.onLocationUpdate = this.onLocationUpdate.bind(this);
    }
    //...
    handleRemoveLocation() {
        this.setState(() => ({
            locationSelected: false,
            location: this.initialState.location
        }));
    }
    handleSubmit() {
        if (!this.state.valid) {
            return;
        }
        const newPost = {
            content: this.state.content
        };
        if (this.state.locationSelected) {
            newPost.location = this.state.location;
        }
        this.props.onSubmit(newPost);
        this.setState(() => ({
            content: '',
            valid: false,
            showLocationPicker: false,
            location: this.initialState.location,
            locationSelected: false
        }));
    }
    onLocationUpdate(location) {
        this.setState(() => ({ location }));
    }
    onLocationSelect(location) {
        this.setState(() => ({
            location,
            showLocationPicker: false,
            locationSelected: true
        }));
    }
    handleToggleLocation(e) {
        e.preventDefault();
        this.setState(state => ({ showLocationPicker:
    !state.showLocationPicker }));
    }
    //...
```

Bind class methods

Allow user to remove location from their post

When submitting a post, add location to payload if present

Handle a location update from the LocationTypeAhead component.

Toggle showing the location picker

The CreatePost component can now work with locations, so you need to add in the UI to make it happen. Once you add in the associated UI for adding a location, you'll find that the render method has become a little cluttered. This isn't necessarily a bad thing, and the markup isn't so complicated that you have to refactor anything (I've worked with render methods that are hundreds of lines long), but it's a good opportunity to explore a different technique for rendering in React component—which I call *subrendering*.

Exercise 6.2   Using refs elsewhere

We've spent some time exploring how to use refs in React in this chapter. Can you think of other libraries or situations where refs might come in handy? Have you worked on any projects in the past that might require using refs to be integrated with React?

A *subrender* method involves breaking part of your render method into a class method on the component (or a function anywhere, really) and then invoking that within a JSX expression in the main render method. You can use this technique if you need to break up a larger render method, need to isolate the logic for a particular part of the rendered UI, or for other reasons. You'll probably find other cases where it's useful, but the key takeaway is that you can break up your render into multiple parts that don't have to be other components. The following listing illustrates breaking up a render method into smaller parts.

Listing 6.12   Adding a subrender method (src/components/post/Create.js)

```
constructor(props) {
    //...
    this.renderLocationControls = this.renderLocationControls.bind(this);
}
renderLocationControls() {
    return (
        <div className="controls">
            <button onClick={this.handleSubmit}>Post</button>
            {this.state.location && this.state.locationSelected ? (
                <button onClick={this.handleRemoveLocation}
                    className="open location-indicator">
                    <i className="fa-location-arrow fa" />
                    <small>{this.state.location.name}</small>
                </button>
            ) : (
                <button onClick={this.handleToggleLocation}
                    className="open">
                    {this.state.showLocationPicker ? 'Cancel' : 'Add
                    location'}{' '}
                    <i
                        className={classnames(`fa`, {
                            'fa-map-o': !this.state.showLocationPicker,
                            'fa-times': this.state.showLocationPicker
                        })}
                    />
```

- **Bind class method in constructor** → `this.renderLocationControls = this.renderLocationControls.bind(this);` and `renderLocationControls() {`
- **If a location is selected, show button that allows users to remove their location**
- **Bind removeLocation method and display current location**
- **Show button that will toggle location picker components**
- **Show right text and use right bound method based on location state**

```
                            </button>
                        )}
                    </div>
                );
            }
        render() {
            return (
                <div className="create-post">
                    <textarea
                        value={this.state.content}
                        onChange={this.handlePostChange}
                        placeholder="What's on your mind?"
                    />
                    {this.renderLocationControls()}
                    <div
                        className="location-picker"
                        style={{ display: this.state.showLocationPicker ? 'block'
        : 'none' }}
                    >
                        {!this.state.locationSelected && [
                            <LocationTypeAhead
                                key="LocationTypeAhead"
                                onLocationSelect={this.onLocationSelect}
                                onLocationUpdate={this.onLocationUpdate}
                            />,
                            <DisplayMap
                                key="DisplayMap"
                                displayOnly={false}
                                location={this.state.location}
                                onLocationSelect={this.onLocationSelect}
                                onLocationUpdate={this.onLocationUpdate}
                            />
                        ]}
                    </div>
                </div>
            );
        }
```

Invoke subrender method

Show or hide location picker components depending on state

Show location picker components if a location isn't selected

Finally, you need to add the maps to posts that have locations on them. You've already done the work of building out the DisplayMap component and making sure it can work in display-only mode, so all you need to do is include it in the Post component. The following listing shows how to do that.

Listing 6.13 Adding maps to your posts (src/components/post/Post.js)

```
import React, { Component } from 'react';
import PropTypes from 'prop-types';

import * as API from '../../shared/http';
import Content from './Content';
import Image from './Image';
```

```
import Link from './Link';
import PostActionSection from './PostActionSection';
import Comments from '../comment/Comments';
import DisplayMap from '../map/DisplayMap';          ◁─┐  Import the DisplayMap
import UserHeader from '../post/UserHeader';               component for use.
import Loader from '../Loader';

export class Post extends Component {
    static propTypes = {
        post: PropTypes.object
    };
    //...
    render() {
        if (!this.state.post) {
            return <Loader />;
        }
        return (
            <div className="post">
                <UserHeader date={this.state.post.date}
    user={this.state.post.user} />
                <Content post={this.state.post} />
                <Image post={this.state.post} />            If post has location
                <Link link={this.state.post.link} />        associated with it,
                {this.state.post.location && <DisplayMap     show it and turn on
    location={this.state.post.location} />}        displayOnly mode
                <PostActionSection showComments={this.state.showComments} />
                <Comments
                    comments={this.state.comments}
                    show={this.state.showComments}
                    post={this.state.post}
                    handleSubmit={this.createComment}
                    user={this.props.user}
                />
            </div>
        );
    }
}

export default Post;
```

With that, you've added the ability to add and display locations on posts for your users. Your investors will surely be happy and impressed by such a game-changing feature!

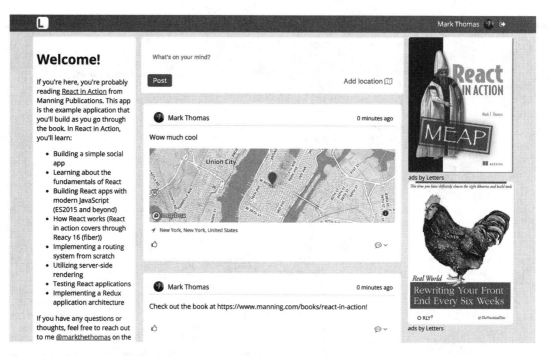

Figure 6.3   The final product of your work in this chapter. You users can create posts and add locations to them.

6.3   *Summary*

Here's what you learned in this chapter:

- In React, a *ref* is a reference to an underlying DOM element. Refs can be useful when you need an escape hatch and need to work with libraries that work with the DOM outside of React.
- Components can be controlled or uncontrolled. *Controlled* components give you full control over the state of the component and involve a complete cycle of listening for and then setting an input's value. *Uncontrolled* components maintain their own state internally and don't provide insight or control.
- Integrating React components with third-party libraries that also use the DOM is often possible through the use of refs. Refs can act as escape hatches when you need to reach out and interact with DOM elements.

In the next chapter, you'll start to add complexity to and create basic routing for your app so you have the possibility of multiple pages.

Routing in React

7

This chapter covers

- More advanced component design and use
- Enabling multi-page React applications with routing
- Building a router from scratch with React

In this chapter, you're going to start making your app more robust and scalable by adding routing. *Routing* means users will be able to navigate to different sections of the app using URLs. The app has been limited to only one page until now, which would hamper growth when you add sections to it. Larger applications would especially suffer from overcrowding without routing or another mechanism to give the app manageable hierarchy. We'll see how to solve this problem for your application using React. You'll build a simple router from scratch in order to better understand how you can do routing with React applications.

151

How do I get the code for this chapter?

As with every chapter, you can check out the source code for this chapter by going to the GitHub repository at https://github.com/react-in-action/letters-social. If you want to start this chapter with a clean slate and follow along, you can use your existing code from chapters 5 and 6 (if you followed along and built out the examples yourself) or check out the chapter-specific branch (chapter-7-8).

Remember, each branch corresponds to the code at the end of the chapter (for example, the branch chapter-7-8 corresponds to the code as it will be at the end of these chapters). You can execute one of the following terminal commands in the directory of your choice to get the code for the current chapter.

If you don't have the repository at all, type the following:

```
git clone git@github.com:react-in-action/letters-social.git
```

If you already have the repository cloned:

```
git checkout chapter-7-8
```

You may have come here from another chapter, so it's always a good idea to ensure you have all the right dependencies installed:

```
npm install
```

7.1   What is routing?

To really get into routing, we first have to have some idea of what it is. Routing is a key part of all websites and web applications in one way or another. It plays a central role in the simplest static HTML pages and the most complex React web applications. Routing comes into play pretty much anytime you want to map a URL to an action. Most applications are chock full of URL links because links are the de facto way of moving around on the web. Think about how effective a system for finding something a URL has become—they're in use almost everywhere. Why are they so useful for finding things on the web? Maybe because we're used to routing systems like addresses, and even though URLs don't require turn-by-turn directions, they help us find what we're looking for—in this case, apps or resources instead of locations.

> **DEFINITION**   *Routing* can have many different meanings and implementations. For our purposes, it's a system for resource navigation. In the abstract, routing is probably a familiar idea to you and is common in web engineering. If you're working in the browser, you're familiar with routing as it relates to URLs and resources in the browser (paths to images, scripts, and so on). On the server, routing can be a focus on matching incoming request paths (like https://ifelse.io/react-ecosystem) to resources from a database. You're learning how to use React, so routing in this book will usually mean matching components (the resources people want) to a URL (the way of telling the system what they want).

Routing is an important part of web applications. Say you want to build a web app where users can create custom fundraising pages to raise money for causes that are important to them. In that case, you'll need routing for quite a few reasons:

- In general, so people can provide external links to your web app. URLs leading to permanent resources should be long-lasting and keep a consistent structure over time.

- Public fundraising pages need to be reliably accessible to everyone, so you need a URL that will route them to the right page.

- Different parts of the admin interface will require it. Users need to be able to move forward and backward in their browsing history.

- Different parts of your site will need their own URLs so you can easily route people to the right section (for example, /settings, /profile, /pricing, and so on).

- Breaking up your code by page helps promote modularity, so you can break up your app as well. Along with dynamic content, that can in turn reduce the size of the app that has to be loaded at a given point.

7.1.1 Routing in modern front-end web applications

In the past, the basic architecture of a web application involved a different approach to routing than the modern way. The older approach involved the server (think something created in Python, Ruby, or, PHP) generating HTML markup and sending it down to the browser. A user might fill out a form with some data, send it back up to the server, and wait for a response. This was revolutionary in making the web more powerful because you could modify data instead of only viewing it.

Since then, web services have undergone many developments in design and construction. Nowadays, JavaScript frameworks and browser technology are advanced enough that web applications can have a more distinct client-server split. The client app (all in-browser) is sent down by the server and then effectively "takes over." The server is then responsible for sending down raw data, usually in the form of JSON. Figure 7.1 illustrates and compares how these two generic architectures work.

So far, you've been using a modern architecture to build the learning app, Letters Social. A node.js server sends down the HTML, JavaScript, and CSS that you need for your app. Once that's loaded, though, React takes over. Further requests for data are sent to the sample API server. But you're missing a key part of that architecture: client-side routing.

> **Exercise 7.1 Ruminating on routing**
> Take a second to reflect on routing before we dive deeper into building your router with React. What are some other examples of routing you've encountered in past projects? What are some other uses for routing?

Old architecture

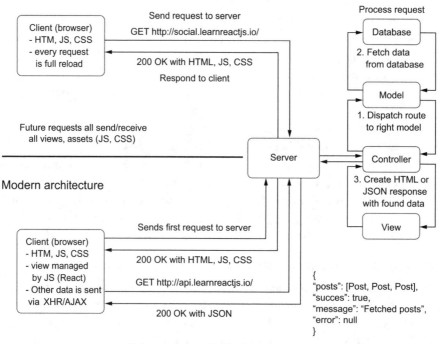

Figure 7.1   Comparing slightly older and modern web application architectures. In the old way, dynamic content would be generated on the server. The server would usually fetch data from a database and use it to populate an HTML view that would be sent down to the client. Now there is more application logic on the client that gets managed by JavaScript (in this case, React). The server initially sends down the HTML, JavaScript, and CSS assets, but after that, the client React app takes over. From there, unless a user manually refreshes the page, the server will only have to send down raw JSON data.

7.2   *Creating a router*

You'll build a simple router from scratch using components in order to better understand how you can do routing with React applications. Here's how you'll proceed at a high level:

- You'll create two components, Router and Route, that will be used together to accomplish client-side routing.
- The Router component will be comprised of Route components.
- Each Route will represent a URL path (/, /posts/123) and map a component to that URL. When your users visit /, they'll see a component for that.
- The Router component will look like a normal React component (it'll have a `render` method and component methods and use JSX) but will let you map components to URLs.

- The Route components can specify parameters like /users/:user, where the :user syntax will denote a value passed to the component.
- You'll also create a Link component that will enable navigation with your client-side router.

If that doesn't all make perfect sense yet, don't worry. We'll work through each step in turn. Let's look at an example of what you'll be working towards as you build the router.

Listing 7.1 shows the Router component you'll build being used in its final form. It's easy to read through and think about: you have a router with routes that are tied to a component. Routing doesn't necessarily have to be hierarchical—you could create chaos and arbitrarily nest resources—but often is. That means it can map relatively easily to React's composition semantics. If you were starting React for the absolute first time, a routing example like the one in the following listing might be one of the easiest components to understand right away.

Listing 7.1   Router end result (src/index.js)

> **Router component handles storing routes and returning the proper component for use in rendering**

> **Each Route component receives a path and a component and matches them together, and you can nest several components within each other.**

```
//...
    <Router location="/">
      <Route path="/" component={App}>
        <Route path="posts/:post" component={SinglePost} />
        <Route path="login" component={Login} />
      </Route>
    </Router>,
//...
```

> **You can pass in parameters to component paths that represent dynamic values, meaning you can get data back from your routes and use it in components.**

This sort of router structure is easy to read and think about. It's also fairly well established in React applications, thanks to React Router. You'll follow suit and build your router with the same basic API in mind. As you do that, we'll draw inspiration and take direction from a small, lightweight router library created by TJ Holowaychuk, called react-enroute. With this library you can explore routing in React without having to re-create an entire open source library like React Router.

We know some more about what you'll be building and how it should look in use, but where do we start? We start with children.

7.2.1   *Component routing*

No, you won't be enlisting youngsters to implement routing in your app. Instead, you'll be using the special component prop children. You may remember the children prop from past chapters, where it was part of the signature for React.createElement(type, props, children) or as the special prop with which you can compose components.

Before, you only cared about children from an input perspective: you would pass in components to another component to compose them together. Now you're going to access children from within a component and use components themselves to set up your routes. This is where you can start to do the work of mapping components to URLs. If routing in web development is the mapping of URLs to behaviors or views, then routing in React is the mapping of URLs to particular components.

7.2.2   Creating the <Route /> component

You're going to create a Router component that will use child components to match URL routes to components and render them out. If you're having a hard time thinking about what this will look like, remember that we'll go through each step deliberately, and you don't have to fully get everything from the start.

Listing 7.2 showed two types of components: Router and Route. Let's start with the Route components, which you can use to associate components with routes. Listing 7.2 shows how to create the Route component. There may not appear to be much to it, but as you'll see shortly, that's fine. The Router component will do most of the heavy lifting, whereas the Route component will serve mainly as a data container for your mappings of URLs and components.

Listing 7.2   Creating a Route component (src/components/router/Route.js)

```
import PropTypes from 'prop-types';
import { Component } from 'react';
import invariant from 'invariant';

class Route extends Component {
    static propTypes = {
        path: PropTypes.string,
        component: PropTypes.oneOfType([PropTypes.element, PropTypes.func]),
    };
    render() {
        return invariant(false, "<Route> elements are for config only and
    shouldn't be rendered");
    }
}

export default Route;
```

Bring in invariant library so you can ensure that the Route component never gets rendered, or if it does, you'll throw an error

Each Route takes a path and a function, so specify these props using PropTypes.

The entire Route component is just a function that returns a call to the invariant library—if ever called, error is thrown and you'll know things aren't behaving correctly

Use a named export to make component available to outside modules

You probably noticed that you're importing a new library here, called `invariant`. This is a simple tool you'll use to ensure that errors get thrown if certain conditions aren't met. To use it, you pass in a value and a message. If that value is *falsey* (`null`, `0`, `undefined`, `NaN`, `''` (empty string), or `false`), it will throw an error. The `invariant` library is often used in React, so if you ever see a warning or error message in the developer tools console that says something like "invariant violation," it's probably involved. You'll use it here to make sure the Route component doesn't render anything.

That's right—the Route component won't render anything. If it does, the `invariant` tool will throw an error. That might sound like a weird thing to do at first. After all, you've been doing lots of rendering in your components so far. But it's just a way of grouping routes and components together in a way that React can understand and that you can take advantage of. You'll use the Route components to store props and pass in the children you want. This will become clearer as you build out your Router component, but take a look at figure 7.2 before moving on to check your understanding.

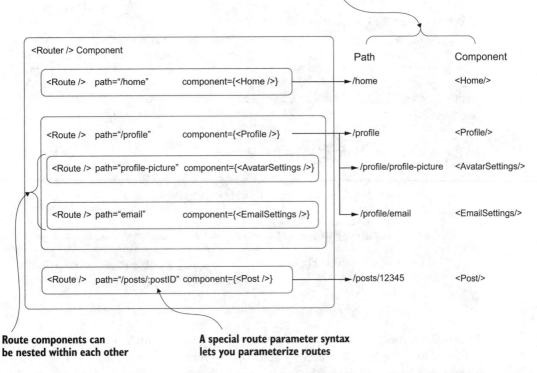

Figure 7.2 Overview of how Route and Router components will work. The Router, which you'll build in the next section, has Route components as its children. Each of these components uses two props: a `path` string and a component. The `<Router/>` will use each `<Route/>` to match a URL and render the right component. Because everything is a React component, you can pass in props to your router when rendering and use those as the initial application state for top-level data like user, authentication state, and more.

7.2.3 *Starting to build the `<Router/>` component*

To get started working on the Router, you'll need to go through the basics of creating a component again. This should be familiar by now, although you'll eventually build a component that does some unique things you haven't seen so far. The good news is that you don't have to do anything "magic" to create your router. You're going to be working with React components, adding some logic to the Router component, and then using it as the main component that your app renders.

This might not seem like a big deal. You may be thinking, "Okay, so it's a component. This is React, after all, so that seems…normal?" I'm pointing it out because it's a good example of something powerful and flexible that you can do with "just" React that isn't something you might immediately think of doing. You don't need any brand-new tools. You just need to find a way to record a mapping of URLs and components and then a way to interact with the right browser APIs. Now you can get to building this thing.

What about React Router?

You might have heard of `React Router` before if you've worked with React at all. It's one of the most popular React projects in open source and is by far the most popular routing solution for React applications. You may wonder why you don't just install `React Router` and learn how to use that API. You could do that, but I think you'd miss out on the chance to see how you can do things with React components that you might not expect (such as mapping URLs to components!). You'll learn far more from building something yourself than you will by simply installing something with npm.

Now, this is different from what you would probably do if you were in a business situation or any kind of production environment. As helpful as building your own router from scratch might be, your primary role as an engineer is (almost always) to deliver value to the company, and you can do that most effectively by either building or using tools that are well tested, performant, and easy to work with.

With that in mind, you and your team would probably choose to use `React Router` instead of building your own. It's often a better engineering and business decision to choose a well-maintained, popular, open source library that fits your needs. When we discuss server-side rendering in chapter 12, you'll swap out your router for `React Router` so we can take advantage of some its features.

Listing 7.3 shows how to scaffold out the Router component. There's little out of the ordinary here aside from the `routes` property that gets set up on the component. Notice that because you don't want to do anything to change the routes on the fly, you're not storing the routes in React's local component state. There may be some cases where you'd want to dynamically change the routes at runtime, such as a user actively customizing the app or something similar. In those cases, you could use the component's `state` interface. You don't have that need here, so you'll stick the routes on the component.

Listing 7.3   Scaffolding out the Router (src/components/router/Router.js)

```
export default class Router extends Component {
  static propTypes = {
    children: PropTypes.object,
```

◁─| The Router component will have a render() method.

```
    location: PropTypes.string.isRequired
};

constructor(props) {              You'll store the routes on
    super(props);                 the router component in
    this.routes = {};    ◁─┘      an object.
}
                          Specify PropTypes—the router
                          will receive children and a
    render() {}  ◁─┘      location to work with.
}
```

Now that you have the bare bones of your Router component, you can start adding some utilities that you'll use later in the core methods of the component.

When working with routes, there are a few things you'll need to do. If you looked carefully at listing 7.2, you probably saw that you could pass in path props that didn't all have a / before them. That may seem like a minor thing, but you need to make sure that users of the router can do this. You also need to make sure that any double // get removed if a user were to include too many forward slashes either by accident or as a result of nesting routes.

Let's see how to create two helper utilities to address these issues. First, you want to create a utility for cleaning a path. This will use a simple regular expression to replace any double forward slashes with a single one. If you're not familiar with regular expressions, you can find many good resources to learn more about them online. They're a powerful way of matching patterns in text and are key to many forms of software development. But they can also seem obscure and difficult to reason about or learn. Fortunately for us, you're only using a simple regular expression to find and replace any double forward slashes (//). The next listing shows how to implement the simple cleanPath method. Note that sanitizing strings with regular expressions can be tricky, so don't expect every case you encounter to be this straightforward.

> **Listing 7.4 Adding the cleanPath utility to the Router (src/components/router/Router.js)**

```
//...
cleanPath(path) {                         cleanPath uses String.replace
    return path.replace(/\/\//g, '/');  ◁─┤ to remove any double slash
}                                         characters from the path (/).
//...
```

We won't go too deep into regular expressions because they deserve serious, in-depth treatment, but we can at least note a few things. First, the basic regex syntax in JavaScript is two forward slashes with an expression inside /<regular expression>/. Second, although the \/\/ series of characters looks arcane and, frankly, kind of like a W, it's only two forward slashes (//) with escape characters (/) added so they don't get interpreted as comments or anything else. Finally, the g character added to the end of the regular expression is a flag meaning *match all occurrences*. To learn more about regular expressions, head to http://regexr.com/3eg8l for detailed insights about what each part of a regular expression means and to practice matching different patterns.

Now that you can clean occurrences of `//`, you need to handle a few other situations for the routes you add. You'll call this utility `normalizeRoute` because it will ensure that parent and child routes get created as the right strings with a forward slash if and where necessary. This function will take a path and an optional parent. With these two inputs, you can handle a few situations. The following listing shows how the `normalizeRoute` method will work.

> **Listing 7.5   Creating the normalizeRoute utility (src/components/router/Router.js)**

```
//...
normalizeRoute(path, parent) {        ◁──┐  Function receives path and
    if (path[0] === '/') {                   parent object—the route
      return path;                           property is a path string.
    }
                                          If the path is just a /, you can
                                          just return it—we don't need
                                          to join it with a parent.

    if (parent == null) {                 If no parent is provided, you
      return path;                        can just return the path since
    }                                     there's nothing to join it with.

    return `${parent.route}/${path}`;     ◁──┐  If there is a parent, you add
  }                                             the path to the parent's path
//...                                           by joining them together.
```

7.2.4 *Matching URL paths and parameterized routing*

You've got some helper tools created, but you aren't doing any routing yet. To start matching URLs to components, you need to add routes to your router. How are you going to do that? Essentially, you need to find a way to render a given component based on what the current URL is—the "matching" part I keep talking about. That may not sound like a lot of work, but more than a few steps are involved.

First, let's look at a key component of a front-end routing system for the browser: *path matching.* You need some way to evaluate path strings and turn them into meaningful data you can use. To accomplish this, you'll use a small package called `enroute`, which is itself a tiny router you'll use to match paths to your components. Internally, enroute converts strings into regular expressions that can be used to match strings (for example, the URLS you'll be checking against). You can also use it to specify path *parameters* so you can create a path like `/users/:user` and get access to the user ID in `/users/1234` as something like `route.params.user` in your code. This approach is common, and you may have seen something similar if you've ever worked with express.js.

The ability to parameterize URLs is useful because that way you can treat the URL like another form of data input you can pass to a router. URLs are powerful, and making them dynamic is part of the reason why. URLs can be meaningful and allow users to visit resources directly without having to first visit one page and then navigate several more times to get where they want to go.

You won't use the full capabilities of parameterizing your routes, but let's look at a few examples to make sure you know what you're working toward. Table 7.1 shows a couple examples of URL paths that might be useful in a common web application.

Table 7.1 Examples of common routes with parameters

Route	Example use
/	Home page for the app.
/profile	Profile page for a user; shows settings.
/profile/settings	Settings route; a child of the profile page; shows user-related settings.
/posts/:postID	postID made available to code; example route would be /posts/2391448. Useful if you wanted to create publicly available links to particular posts.
/users/:userID	:userID is a path parameter; useful to show a particular user based on their ID.
/users/:userID/posts	Show all posts for a user; the :userID part of the URL is dynamic and made available in your code.

You're only taking advantage of one aspect of parameterized routing here with the :name syntax, but there are tools that will let you do much more than that. If you're interested in learning more about parameterized routing, check out the path-to-regexp library, available at www.npmjs.com/package/path-to-regexp. This is a great tool, and there are others we could spend time looking into, but we need to focus on the task at hand: routing with React.

The important takeaway about these routing tools (enroute and path-to-regexp) is that you're going to use them to help match URLs and work with some path parameters in URLs. It doesn't matter so much for now which tool you use or if you want to go build your own; you just need something that lets you focus on the fundamentals. One of the beautiful things about React is that you're free to make your own informed decision about which routing tools you want to use when you're building your own applications.

> ### Exercise 7.2 Pondering parameters
> Parameterizing routes is often a useful way of getting data into your application. Can you think of other ways you might use route parameters besides getting the post ID?

You'll be using your URL-matching library (enroute) to determine which route to render, so next you'll get that set up on your component. Right now, the Router component has a `render` method that doesn't do anything, so that seems like a good place to start. The following listing shows how to integrate `enroute` with your router and the resulting changes to the `render` method.

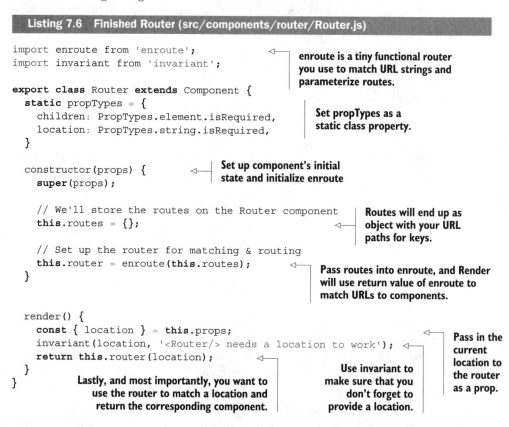

Listing 7.6   **Finished Router (src/components/router/Router.js)**

```
import enroute from 'enroute';                    ◁───┐ enroute is a tiny functional router
import invariant from 'invariant';                     │ you use to match URL strings and
                                                       │ parameterize routes.

export class Router extends Component {
  static propTypes = {
    children: PropTypes.element.isRequired,        ┐ Set propTypes as a
    location: PropTypes.string.isRequired,         │ static class property.
  }

  constructor(props) {            ◁──┐ Set up component's initial
    super(props);                      │ state and initialize enroute

    // We'll store the routes on the Router component    ┐ Routes will end up as
    this.routes = {};                                 ◁──┤ object with your URL
                                                         │ paths for keys.

    // Set up the router for matching & routing
    this.router = enroute(this.routes);     ◁──┐ Pass routes into enroute, and Render
  }                                              │ will use return value of enroute to
                                                 │ match URLs to components.

  render() {
    const { location } = this.props;                                      ◁──┐ Pass in the
    invariant(location, '<Router/> needs a location to work');   ◁──┐        │ current
    return this.router(location);     ◁──┐                            │        │ location to
  }                                                                            │ the router
}                                                                              │ as a prop.
```

Lastly, and most importantly, you want to use the router to match a location and return the corresponding component.

Use invariant to make sure that you don't forget to provide a location.

You didn't add that much code, but some of the most important parts of the router are now in place. Right now, there aren't any routes for `enroute` to work with, but the basic mechanics are there. You want to try to find a component associated with a route and then use the router to render that. In the next section, you'll create those routes so your router can use them.

7.2.5   *Adding routes to the Router component*

To add a route to the router, you need two things: the right URL string to use and the component for that URL. You'll create a method on the Router component that will let you tie these two things together: `addRoute`. If you take a quick look at the `enroute` usage example at https://github.com/lapwinglabs/enroute, you'll see how `enroute` works. It takes an object with URL strings for keys and functions for values, and when one of the paths is matched, it invokes the function and passes in some extra data. Listing 7.7 shows how you'd use the `enroute` library without React. With `enroute` you can match functions that take parameters and any additional data to URL strings.

Listing 7.7 Route configuration example (src/components/router/Router.js)

```
function edit_user (params, props) {
    return Object.assign({}, params, props)
}

const router = enroute({
        '/users/new': create_user,
        '/users/:slug': find_user,
        '/users/:slug/edit': edit_user,
        '*': not_found
    });

enroute('/users/mark/edit', { additional: 'props' })
```

Two parameters are used: route parameters (like /users/:user) and any additional data you pass in.

Pass in an object with paths and functions that you've created to handle those paths.

To use, pass in a location and any additional data and the right function will be executed.

Now that you have some idea of how enroute works apart from React, let's see how to integrate it into your router and give it some life. Instead of returning an object as you did in the preceding listing, you want to return a component. But you currently have no way to get to the paths or components for your routes. Remember how you created a Route component that would store them but didn't render anything? You need to get access to that data from your parent component (Router). That means you're going to need to use the children property.

NOTE You've seen how you can compose components together in React to create new components by creating parent and child relationships between components. So far, you've only used children "externally" by nesting components within each other. Any time you've been nesting and composing components, you've been utilizing React's concept of children. But you haven't dynamically accessed any of those nested children from a parent component yet. You can access the children passed into a parent on the component's props as, you guessed it, children.

The children prop that's available on every React component or element is what we call an *opaque* data structure because it, unlike almost everything else in React, isn't just an array or plain old JavaScript object. This may change in future versions of React, but in the meantime, it means there are a few tools provided by React that let you work with the children prop. A number of methods are available from React.Children you can use to work with the children opaque data structure, including the following:

- React.Children.map—Similar to Array.map in native JavaScript, this invokes a function on every immediate child within children (meaning it won't traverse every possible descendent component, just direct descendants) and returns an array of the elements it traverses. Returns null or undefined rather than an empty array if children is null or undefined:

```
React.Children.map(children, function[(thisArg)])
```

- `React.Children.forEach`—Similar to the way that `React.Chidlren.map` works, but it doesn't return an array:

```
React.Children.forEach(children, function[(thisArg)])
```

- `React.Children.count`—Returns the total number of components found in children. Equal to the number of times either `React.Children.map` or `React.Children.forEach` would invoke their callback on the same elements:

```
React.Children.count(children)
```

- `React.Children.only`—Returns the only child in `children` or throws an error:

```
React.Children.toArray(children)
```

- `React.Children.toArray`—Returns `children` as a flat array with keys assigned to each child:

```
React.Children.toArray(children)
```

Because you want to add route information to `this.routes` on the Router component, you'll use `React.Children.forEach` to iterate over each of the children of Router (remember, those are the Route components) and get access to their props. You'll use these props to set up your routes and tell `enroute` which component should be rendered at which URL.

"Self-eradicating" components in React

When React 16 came out, it enabled components to return arrays from render. This was previously impossible, but it opens up some interesting possibilities. One of them is the idea of a *self-destructing* or *self-eradicating*[1] component. Previously, when you could only return a single node from any given component, you would often find yourself wrapping components in divs or spans just to get valid JavaScript output. A common scenario would look something like this:

```
export const Parent = () => {
    return (
        <Flex>
            <Sidebar/>
            <Main />
            <LinksCollection/>
        </Flex>
    );
}
```

Top-level components, side-by-side, laid out with Flexbox (or CSS grids)

---

[1] Big thanks to Ben Ilegbodu for first introducing this idea to me!

```
export const LinksCollection = () => {
    return (
        <div>
            <User />
            <Group />
            <Org />
        </div>
    );
}
```

Wrapper div added because User, Group, and Org can't be returned together in JavaScript—it doesn't support multiple return values

This was a source of much annoyance for many teams, although it certainly didn't stop people from using React. One major sort of problem it creates, though, isn't merely the fact that the wrapping div seems unnecessary. As you can see here, the app is laid out using Flexbox (or some other CSS layout API that would break in this scenario).

The problem that the wrapping div creates is that it forces you to move components up a level so they aren't grouped within a single node. There are certainly other reasons this caused problems or forced workarounds, but this is one that I've encountered many times.

With the advent of React 16 and following, though, it became possible to return arrays, so now we have a way around this. React 16 introduced many other powerful features, but this one was a welcome change. Developers can now do something like this:

```
export const SelfEradicating = (props) => props.children
```

This component acts as a sort of pass-through, getting out of the way or "self-eradicating" as it renders its children. Using this approach, you can maintain component separation without having to hedge on things like your CSS layout technique. The same scenario might look something like this with a "self-eradicating" component:

```
export const SelfEradicating = (props) => props.children

export const Parent = () => {
    return (
        <Flex>
            <Sidebar/>
            <Main />
            <LinksCollection/>
        </Flex>
    );
}

export const LinksCollection = () => {
    return (
        <SelfEradicating>
            <User />
            <Group />
            <Org />
        </SelfEradicating>
    );
}
```

Remember, enroute expects you to give a function to each route so it can pass in parameter information and other data to it. This function is where you'll tell React to create a component and handle rendering additional child components. Listing 7.8 shows how to add the `addRoute` and `addRoutes` methods to your component. `addRoutes` uses `React.Children.forEach` to iterate over the child Route components, grab their data, and set up the route for enroute to use. This is the core body of the router—once you implement this, the router will be up and running!

Exercise 7.3   props.children

We talked about React's `props.children` in this chapter. Are there any differences between `props.children` and other props? Why might there be any differences?

Listing 7.8   The `addRoute` and `addRoutes` methods (src/components/router/Router.js)

Make sure every Route has a path and component prop or throw an error.

Use destructuring to get component, path, and children props.

render is a function you'll give to enroute that takes route-related params and additional data.

```
addRoute(element, parent) {
    const { component, path, children } = element.props;

    invariant(component, `Route ${path} is missing the "path" property`);
    invariant(typeof path === 'string', `Route ${path} is not a string`);

    const render = (params, renderProps) => {
        const finalProps = Object.assign({ params }, this.props, renderProps);
        const children = React.createElement(component, finalProps);
        return parent ? parent.render(params, { children }) : children;
    };

    const route = this.normalizeRoute(path, parent);

    if (children) {
        this.addRoutes(children, { route, render });
    }

    this.routes[this.cleanPath(route)] = render;
}
//...
```

Merge together props from parent with child component

Create a new component with merged props.

If there are more nested children on current Route component, repeat process and pass in route and parent component

Use cleanPath utility to create path on routes object and assign your finished function to it

Use normalizeRoute helper to make sure the URL path gets set up right

If there's a parent, invoke render method of parent parameter but with children you've created

Whew! There was a lot going on in those few lines of code. Feel free to go back over it a couple of times to make sure you feel comfortable with the concepts. Once you add the `addRoutes` method, we'll recap the steps and review with a visualization. But first you'll add the `addRoutes` method. Comparatively, it's quite short. The following listing shows how to implement it.

> **Listing 7.9 The `addRoutes` method (/components/router/Router.js)**

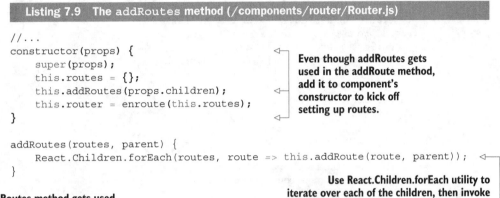

```
//...
constructor(props) {
    super(props);
    this.routes = {};
    this.addRoutes(props.children);
    this.router = enroute(this.routes);
}
```

Even though addRoutes gets used in the addRoute method, add it to component's constructor to kick off setting up routes.

```
addRoutes(routes, parent) {
    React.Children.forEach(routes, route => this.addRoute(route, parent));
}
```

addRoutes method gets used in addRoute any time there are additional children to iterate over

Use React.Children.forEach utility to iterate over each of the children, then invoke addRoute for each child Route component.

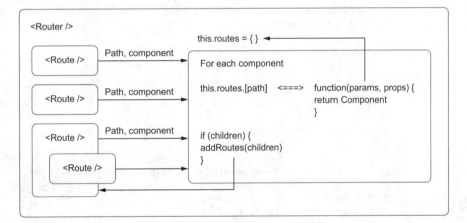

Figure 7.3 The process of adding routes to your router. For each Route component found within your Router component, pull off the path and component props and then use those to create a function you can pair with a URL path for `enroute` to use. If there are child components for a Route, run the same process for those before moving on. When done, the `routes` property will have all the right routes set up.

With that, your router is complete and ready to roll. The next listing shows the Router component in its final state with helper tools (path normalization, invariant uses) left out for brevity. In the next chapter, you'll put the Router component to use.

Listing 7.10   Finished Router (src/components/router/Router.js)

```javascript
import PropTypes from 'prop-types';

import React, { Component } from 'react';
import enroute from 'enroute';
import invariant from 'invariant';

export default class Router extends Component {
    static propTypes = {
        children: PropTypes.array,
        location: PropTypes.string.isRequired
    };

    constructor(props) {
        super(props);

        this.routes = {};

        this.addRoutes(props.children);
        this.router = enroute(this.routes);
    }

    addRoute(element, parent) {
        const { component, path, children } = element.props;

        invariant(component, `Route ${path} is missing the "path" property`);
        invariant(typeof path === 'string', `Route ${path} is not a string`);

        const render = (params, renderProps) => {
            const finalProps = Object.assign({ params }, this.props,
    renderProps);

            const children = React.createElement(component, finalProps);

            return parent ? parent.render(params, { children }) : children;
        };

        const route = this.normalizeRoute(path, parent);

        if (children) {
            this.addRoutes(children, { route, render });
        }

        this.routes[this.cleanPath(route)] = render;
    }

    addRoutes(routes, parent) {
        React.Children.forEach(routes, route => this.addRoute(route,
    parent));
    }

    cleanPath(path) {
        return path.replace(/\/\//g, '/');
    }
```

```
    normalizeRoute(path, parent) {
        if (path[0] === '/') {
            return path;
        }
        if (!parent) {
            return path;
        }
        return `${parent.route}/${path}`;
    }

    render() {
        const { location } = this.props;
        invariant(location, '<Router/> needs a location to work');
        return this.router(location);
    }
}
```

7.3   *Summary*

In this chapter, you started turning your React application from a simple page with some components into a more robust application that handles routing and route configuration. We covered quite a lot of ground and explored an advanced use of components to build an entire router from the ground up:

- Routing in modern client applications doesn't require you to perform a complete page reload. Instead, it can be handled with client-side applications like React. This can decrease browser load time and potentially server load, too.
- React doesn't have a built-in routing library like some frameworks do. Instead, you're free to either pick one from the community or build your own from scratch (like you did!).
- React provides you with several utilities to work with the opaque children data structure. You can iterate over multiple components, check to see how many there are, and more.
- You can use the routing setup you created to dynamically change which children are rendered inside of a component. You're listening for changes in the browser's location and rendering using that data.

In the next chapter, you'll use your Router and add authentication to your app with Firebase.

More routing and integrating Firebase

In the last chapter, you built a simple router from scratch in order to better understand how you can do routing with React applications. In this chapter, you'll start to use the router you built and break up the Letters Social app into better sections. By the end of the chapter, you'll be able to navigate around your app, view individual post pages, and perform user authentication.

> ## How do I get the code for this chapter?
> As with every chapter, you can check out the source code for this chapter by going to the GitHub repository at https://github.com/react-in-action/letters-social. If you want

to start this chapter with a clean slate and follow along, you can use your existing code from chapters 5 and 6 (if you followed along and built out the examples yourself) or check out the chapter-specific branch (chapter-7-8).

Remember, each branch corresponds to the code at the end of the chapter (for example, the branch chapter-7-8 corresponds to the code as it will be at the end of this chapter). You can execute one of the following terminal commands in the directory of your choice to get the code for the current chapter.

If you don't have the repository at all, type the following:

```
git clone git@github.com:react-in-action/letters-social.git
```

If you already have the repository cloned:

```
git checkout chapter-7-8
```

You may have come here from another chapter, so it's always a good idea to ensure you have all the right dependencies installed:

```
npm install
```

8.1 Using the router

In the last chapter, you built a working router with React. In a situation where you're working on a React app in a production setting, you'll probably want to opt for something like React Router. Fortunately, React Router follows a very similar API, but it also comes with more advanced features that let you do even more with routing. Maybe you don't need all those features, though, and something like you've built is enough. That's perfectly fine—pick the tools that best suit the problems you're solving, not the ones with the most GitHub stars or Hacker News upvotes. Your needs will change in chapter 12 as we tackle server-side rendering, so we'll switch to React Router in that chapter.

Let's get started using your shiny new router. First you need to hook up the router to the HTML5 History API (https://developer.mozilla.org/en-US/docs/Web/API/History) so you can take advantage of navigation that doesn't require a full page reload. You'll use *push state* navigation because you don't need to hit the server every time for a full page refresh. But you could also use hash-based routing (see https://github.com/ReactTraining/react-router/blob/v3/docs/guides/Histories.md for more).

We won't spend much time exploring the HTML5 APIs, because they deserve their own treatment. You'll use the well-known history library, available on npm at www.npmjs.com/package/history. This library will let you work with the History API in a reliable and predictable way across browsers. To make sure it's installed, run npm install --save history. Once you've installed it, you'll need to make some changes to your index.js file that currently serves as the root of the entire app. Until now, this file was where React DOM would render your whole app to a DOM element. But you have routing enabled, and your Router component expects a location (see chapter 7). You need to find a way to feed it that location and take advantage of the HTML5 History API using the history library, and index.js is the perfect place to do this.

Exercise 8.1   Comparing client-side and server-side routing

Take a moment to consider the differences between client-side routing and client-server URL-based routing. What is one of the primary differences between client-side routing and server-side routing?

In addition to taking advantage of `history`, you'll need to set up your routes. To do so, you'll need to refactor some of your components, which should give you a sense of the benefits of composability and modularity in React. You'll move things around but won't have to fundamentally change the way your components work. Let's see how to fix the App component first. It needs to serve as a container for the child routes because you want every page to have the same sidebars and navigation bar, changing only what gets passed into the `children` prop. Figure 8.1 shows an example of what this looks like.

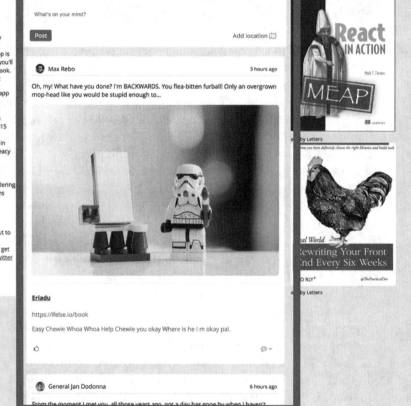

Figure 8.1   The boxed area in the screenshot above will change based on what view you decide to render based on a URL. Over time, you may even do more nesting and expand that area to include the sidebars so you can maintain the same navigation bar across pages and have other routes that have dynamic areas in them.

To achieve this sort of nesting, you need to refactor the App component to dynamically show `children`, as shown in listing 8.1. Fortunately, you won't end up deleting much of the work we've done—you'll just move it around. As you refactor, you're going to do some reorganization of your app files. Create a new directory in `src` called pages. You'll be putting components here that tend to only contain other components and provide them with data. I'll talk about this idea more when we start exploring React application architecture in later chapters.

Listing 8.1 Refactoring the App component (src/app.js)

```
import React, { Component } from 'react';
import PropTypes from 'prop-types';

import ErrorMessage from './components/error/Error';
import Nav from './components/nav/navbar';
import Loader from './components/Loader';

class App extends Component {
    constructor(props) {
        super(props);
        this.state = {
            error: null,
            loading: false
        };
    }
    static propTypes = {
        children: PropTypes.node
    };
    componentDidCatch(err, info) {          Set up top-level error boundary
        console.error(err);                 using componentDidCatch so
        console.error(info);                you can display error if
        this.setState(() => ({              something goes wrong
            error: err
        }));
    }
    render() {                              Render the
        if (this.state.error) {             error, if any.
            return (
                <div className="app">
                    <ErrorMessage error={this.state.error} />
                </div>
            );
        }
        return (                                         Pass user props in—
            <div className="app">                        you'll use this when
                <Nav user={this.props.user} />           you integrate Firebase.
                {this.state.loading ? (
                    <div className="loading">            If app is in a loading
                        <Loader />                        state, render the loader
                    </div>
                ) : (
                    this.props.children                  Use props.children to output
                )}                                       the currently active route.
```

```
          </div>
        );
      }
    }


export default App;
```

You need to create a component for the main page so users can see the posts. Create a file called home.js and place it in the pages directory. This component should look familiar—it was the main component you had before breaking things into pages. Listing 8.2 shows the Home component with the method logic you've implemented before commented out for brevity. Remember, as with all chapters, you can check out different branches for each chapter if you want to see how the app has changed or how it'll be at the end of the chapter at https://github.com/react-in-action/letters-social.

Listing 8.2 The refactored Home component (src/pages/Home.js)

```
import React, { Component } from 'react';
import parseLinkHeader from 'parse-link-header';
import orderBy from 'lodash/orderBy';

import * as API from '../shared/http';
import Ad from '../components/ad/Ad';
import CreatePost from '../components/post/Create';
import Post from '../components/post/Post';
import Welcome from '../components/welcome/Welcome';

export class Home extends Component {
    constructor(props) {
        super(props);
        this.state = {
            posts: [],
            error: null,
            endpoint: `${process.env

    .ENDPOINT}/posts?_page=1&_sort=date&_order=DESC&_embed=comments&_expand=
    user&_embed=likes`
        };
        this.getPosts = this.getPosts.bind(this);
        this.createNewPost = this.createNewPost.bind(this);
    }
    componentDidMount() {
        this.getPosts();
    }
    getPosts() {
        API.fetchPosts(this.state.endpoint)
            .then(res => {
                return res.json().then(posts => {
                    const links = parseLinkHeader(res.headers.get('Link'));
                    this.setState(() => ({
                        posts: orderBy(this.state.posts.concat(posts),
    'date', 'desc'),
```

> **Don't forget to adjust import paths—the component lives in a different directory.**

> **Logic for these is exactly the same—you're only moving components around to accommodate new hierarchy.**

```
                             endpoint: links.next.url,
                     }));
                });
            })
            .catch(err => {
                this.setState(() => ({ error: err }));
            });
    }
    createNewPost(post) {
        post.userId = this.props.user.id;
        return API.createPost(post)
            .then(res => res.json())
            .then(newPost => {
                this.setState(prevState => {
                    return {
                        posts: orderBy(prevState.posts.concat(newPost),
    'date', 'desc')
                    };
                });
            })
            .catch(err => {
                this.setState(() => ({ error: err }));
            });
    }
    render() {                        ◁─────    Logic for these is exactly the same—
        return (                                you're only moving components around
            <div className="home">              to accommodate new hierarchy.
                <Welcome />
                <div>
                    <CreatePost onSubmit={this.createNewPost} />
                    {this.state.posts.length && (
                        <div className="posts">
                            {this.state.posts.map(({ id }) => {
                                return <Post id={id} key={id}
    user={this.props.user} />;
                            })}
                        </div>
                    )}
                    <button className="block" onClick={this.getPosts}>
                        Load more posts
                    </button>
                </div>
                <div>
                    <Ad url="https://ifelse.io/book"
    imageUrl="/static/assets/ads/ria.png" />
                    <Ad url="https://ifelse.io/book"
    imageUrl="/static/assets/ads/orly.jpg" />
                </div>
            </div>
        );
    }
}

export default Home;
```

Now that you have your Home component moved around, you're ready to configure your routes and hook up the `history` tool so your router can respond to browser location changes. It's often helpful to make a single module available to other parts of your application as a utility so you don't duplicate work. You'll do this more later in the book, and you've probably done this on your own, too. You'll do that with the `history` library, as shown in the next listing, because you want to eventually use it to (among other things) create links that work with your Router and don't have to be normal `<a href=""></>` tags.

Listing 8.3 Setting up the history library (src/history/history.js)

```
import createHistory from 'history/createBrowserHistory';
const history = createHistory();
const navigate = to => history.push(to);
export { history, navigate };
```

Make a single instance of history library available to your app.

Export navigate method and history instance (in case you need direct access later).

Now that you have `history` set up, you can set up the rest of index.js and configure your Router. The following listing shows how to do that.

Listing 8.4 Setting up index.js for routing (src/index.js)

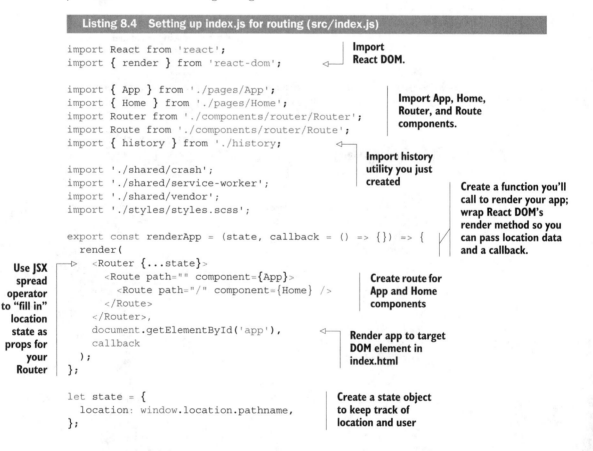

```
import React from 'react';
import { render } from 'react-dom';

import { App } from './pages/App';
import { Home } from './pages/Home';
import Router from './components/router/Router';
import Route from './components/router/Route';
import { history } from './history';

import './shared/crash';
import './shared/service-worker';
import './shared/vendor';
import './styles/styles.scss';

export const renderApp = (state, callback = () => {}) => {
  render(
    <Router {...state}>
      <Route path="" component={App}>
        <Route path="/" component={Home} />
      </Route>
    </Router>,
    document.getElementById('app'),
    callback
  );
};

let state = {
  location: window.location.pathname,
};
```

Import React DOM.

Import App, Home, Router, and Route components.

Import history utility you just created

Create a function you'll call to render your app; wrap React DOM's render method so you can pass location data and a callback.

Use JSX spread operator to "fill in" location state as props for your Router

Create route for App and Home components

Render app to target DOM element in index.html

Create a state object to keep track of location and user

```
history.listen(location => {
    state = Object.assign({}, state, {
        location: location.pathname
    });
    renderApp(state);
});

renderApp(state);
```

Fire when location changes and
update router, causing application
to re-render with new state data

Render
the app.

8.1.1 Creating a page for a post

You're routing! At this point, you've done a lot to get routing enabled and working
in your app. But you haven't done anything to let the user move around different
parts of your application. At this point, your app will probably start to have more
pages and subsections of pages. If you were building out a more complicated version
of a social networking app, you'd probably have sections for a profile page, user set-
tings, messages, and more. But in this case, all you need to do is display individual
posts. How are you going to do this? You'll start with the URL. Remember the
/posts/:postID route used a few times in examples so far? Your post pages are
going to live at this URL.

You'll get started by creating a page component for individual posts. In earlier
chapters, you built a Post component that would fetch its data once it was loaded, so
creating this single-post page shouldn't be too much trouble. You want to create a new
component for this page, ensure the post is included, and make sure you map it to the
route correctly. One thing that will be different is where you get the post ID from.
Rather than an initial fetch from the server, you'll pull it from the URL. You used a
special syntax to set up the URL, and the router will make that parameterized route
data available to your component. The following listing shows how to set up the single-
post page.

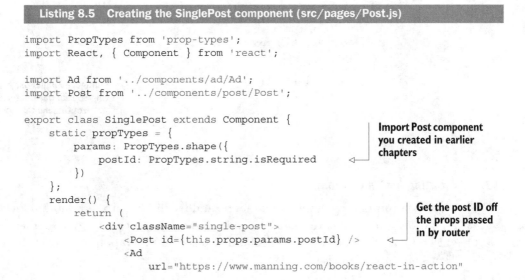

Listing 8.5 Creating the SinglePost component (src/pages/Post.js)

```
import PropTypes from 'prop-types';
import React, { Component } from 'react';

import Ad from '../components/ad/Ad';
import Post from '../components/post/Post';

export class SinglePost extends Component {
    static propTypes = {
        params: PropTypes.shape({
            postId: PropTypes.string.isRequired
        })
    };
    render() {
        return (
            <div className="single-post">
                <Post id={this.props.params.postId} />
                <Ad
                    url="https://www.manning.com/books/react-in-action"
```

Import Post component
you created in earlier
chapters

Get the post ID off
the props passed
in by router

```
                                imageUrl="/static/assets/ads/ria.png"
                        />
                </div>
            );
        }
}

export default SinglePost;
```

Now that you have a component to use, you can integrate it back into your router so users will be able to navigate to individual posts. Listing 8.6 shows how to add the Single-Post component to your router. Notice that you're taking advantage of the *parameterized* routing we've seen in router examples so far. The `:post` part of the path is what gets provided to your component in the `params` prop.

Listing 8.6 Adding individual posts to the router (src/index.js)

```
import React from 'react';
import { render } from 'react-dom';

import * as API from './shared/http';
import { history } from './history';
import Route from './components/router/Route';
import Router from './components/router/Router';       Import SinglePost
import App from './app';                                component for use
import Home from './pages/home';                        in your router
import SinglePost from './pages/post';          ◁─┘

//...

export const renderApp = (state, callback = () => {}) => {
    render(
        <Router {...state}>
            <Route path="" component={App}>
                <Route path="/" component={Home} />
                <Route path="/posts/:postId" component={SinglePost} />    ◁─┐
            </Route>
        </Router>,
        document.getElementById('app'),             Configure SinglePost route
        callback                                    using special parameterized
    );                                              routing syntax (:post)
};

//...
```

8.1.2 Creating a <Link/> component

If you run your app in development mode and try clicking around, you'll notice that even though you still have routes set up for individual posts, you can't get there without knowing the ID of the post in the first place and then putting that in the URL. That's not very useful, is it?

You need to create a custom Link component that will work with your `history` tool and your Router—otherwise, users will probably abandon your app quickly, and your investors will be sad. How can you enable this? A regular anchor tag (`<a href="/">Link!</a>`) won't do because it will try to reload the entire page, which you don't want. You might also want to create links from things that aren't anchor tags at all, such as a post in a list or anything you don't want to wrap in an anchor tag.

> **NOTE** *Accessibility* is the degree to which an interface is usable by someone. You've probably heard people talk about "web accessibility" before, but you may not know much about it. That's okay—it's easy to learn. You want to make sure your app is usable by as many people as possible, whether they're using it with a mouse and keyboard, screen reader, or other devices. I just mentioned making arbitrary elements of an application navigable using a Link component—something that should be done with care when approaching things from an accessibility standpoint. With that in mind, I wanted to briefly mention accessibility with regard to this book. Because building accessible web applications is a huge and important topic, it's beyond the scope of this book. There are companies, apps, and hobby projects that consider it as a first-class dimension of engineering. Although you may be able to reference the source code for Letters Social as a collection of ways to build apps using React components, we haven't handled all the different accessibility concerns that would come up for your app. To learn more about accessibility on the web, check out the WAI-ARIA authoring practices (www.w3.org/WAI/PF/aria-practices) or the MDN documentation on ARIA (https://developer.mozilla.org/en-US/docs/Web/Accessibility/ARIA). Ari Rizzitano has also put together an excellent talk on this topic with a special focus on accessibility in React, called "Building Accessible Components" (https://speakerdeck.com/arizzitano/building-accessible-components).

You'll need to use your `history` utility again here and integrate it into a Link component that you can use to enable push-state linking inside of your application. Remember the `navigate` function you exposed earlier? Using this function, you can now programmatically tell the `history` library to change the location for the user. To turn this functionality into a component, you'll use some React utilities to wrap other components in a clickable Link component. You'll use `React.cloneElement` to create a copy of the target element and then attach a click handler that will perform navigation. The signature for `React.cloneElement` looks like this:

```
ReactElement cloneElement(
  ReactElement element,
  [object props],
  [children ...]
)
```

It takes an element to clone, the `props` to merge into the new element, and any `children` it should have. You'll use this utility to clone the component that you want to turn into a Link. And you'll need to make sure the Link component only has a single child, so you'll bring back the `React.Children.only` tool from earlier in the chapter. All together, these tools will let you turn other components into Link components that help the user get around your app. The following listing shows how to create the Link component.

Listing 8.7   Creating the Link component (src/components/router/Link.js)

Import the libraries
you'll need.

```
import { PropTypes, Children, Component, cloneElement } from 'react';
import { navigate } from '../../history
```

Reuse the history tool
you've been working with.

```
class Link extends Component {
  static propTypes = {
    to: PropTypes.string.isRequired,
    children: PropTypes.node,
  }
```

to and children props will hold
target URL and component
you're Link-ifying, respectively.

Clone
children
of Link
component
to wrap only
one node (it
can have
children)

```
  render() {
    const { to, children } = this.props;
    return cloneElement(Children.only(children), {
      onClick: () => navigate(to),
    });
  }
}
```

In props object, pass onClick
handler that will navigate to
URL using history

Define propTypes

Import the libraries
you'll need.

```
import PropTypes from 'prop-types';
import { Children, cloneElement } from 'react';
import { navigate } from '../../history';

function Link({ to, children }) {
  return cloneElement(Children.only(children), {
    onClick: () => navigate(to)
  });
}

Link.propTypes = {
  to: PropTypes.string,
  children: PropTypes.node
};

export default Link;
```

Reuse the history tool
you've been working with.

Clone children of
Link component to
wrap only one node
(it can have children)

In props object, pass onClick
handler that will navigate to
URL using history

Define
propTypes

to and children props will hold
target URL and component
you're Link-ifying, respectively.

To integrate the Link component, you can wrap individual posts in the reusable Post component and make sure Link gets a `to` prop that will send the user to the right page (see previous Note on accessibility). You can follow this same pattern to wrap other components in a similar manner and turn them into Link-ified components. The following listing shows how to integrate the Link component.

Listing 8.8 Integrating the Link component (src/components/post/Post)

```
import React, { Component } from 'react';
import PropTypes from 'prop-types';

import * as API from '../../shared/http';
import Content from './Content';
import Image from './Image';
import Link from './Link';
import PostActionSection from './PostActionSection';
import Comments from '../comment/Comments';
import DisplayMap from '../map/DisplayMap';
import UserHeader from '../post/UserHeader';

import RouterLink from '../router/Link';          ◁── Import Link component; alias it
                                                      as RouterLink to avoid naming
                                                      conflict with Link component
                                                      used in our posts

export class Post extends Component {

//...

    render() {
        return this.state.post ? (
            <div className="post">
                <RouterLink to={`/posts/${this.state.post.id}`}>
                    <span>
                        <UserHeader date={this.state.post.date}
                            user={this.state.post.user} />
                        <Content post={this.state.post} />
                        <Image post={this.state.post} />
                        <Link link={this.state.post.link} />
                    </span>
                </RouterLink>
                {this.state.post.location && <DisplayMap
                    location={this.state.post.location} />}
                <PostActionSection showComments={this.state.showComments} />
                <Comments
                    comments={this.state.comments}
                    show={this.state.showComments}
                    post={this.state.post}
                    handleSubmit={this.createComment}
                    user={this.props.user}
                />
            </div>
        ) : null;
    }
}

export default Post;
```

Wrap section of Post component you want to be linkable and give it the right ID

With that, you've fully integrated the Router into your application. Users can now view individual posts, which is great for sharing and focusing on one at a time. Your investors will be suitably impressed and excited to invest in your next round of fundraising. You're not done yet, though. In the next section we'll discuss what to do when you can't match a URL to a component.

> ### Exercise 8.2 Adding more links
> Try finding some other areas in the app that might make for good Link candidates and use the Link component to turn them into links. *Hint*: How will users get back to the home page after navigating to an individual post? As you go through, try to think about the user's experience as they move around the application. What would make sense to them? Which ones did you turn into Links? Are there cases where you turned things into Links that weren't already anchor tags? Check out the single post page in the application source code to see an example of adding a simple back button.

8.1.3 Creating a <NotFound/> component

Try navigating to /oops in the Letters app and see what happens. Nothing? Yep, that's what should happen based on your code, but it isn't what you want for users. Right now, your Router component doesn't handle any "not found" or "catch-all" routes. You want to be kind to your users and assume that at some point they (or you) might make a mistake and try to navigate to a route that doesn't exist in your app. To address that, you'll create a simple NotFound component and configure it when creating an instance of your Router. The following listing shows how to create the Not-Found component.

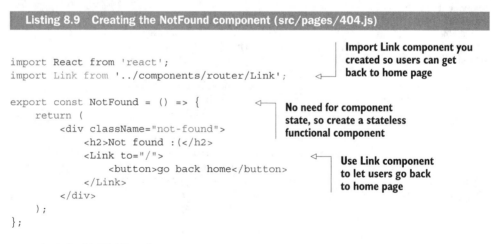

Listing 8.9 Creating the NotFound component (src/pages/404.js)

```
import React from 'react';
import Link from '../components/router/Link';          Import Link component you
                                                         created so users can get
                                                         back to home page

export const NotFound = () => {                          No need for component
    return (                                             state, so create a stateless
        <div className="not-found">                      functional component
            <h2>Not found :(</h2>
            <Link to="/">                                Use Link component
                <button>go back home</button>            to let users go back
            </Link>                                       to home page
        </div>
    );
};

export default NotFound;
```

Now that the NotFound component exists, you need to integrate it into your Router configuration. You may be wondering how you're going to tell the Router that it should send users to the NotFound component. The answer is to use the * character when configuring a router. That character says "match anything," and if you put it at the end of your configuration, any routes that haven't been matched to anything else will go there. Be sure to note that the order here matters: if you put the catch-all route too high up, it'll match anything and not work like you'd want it to. The following listing shows how to configure more routes for your router.

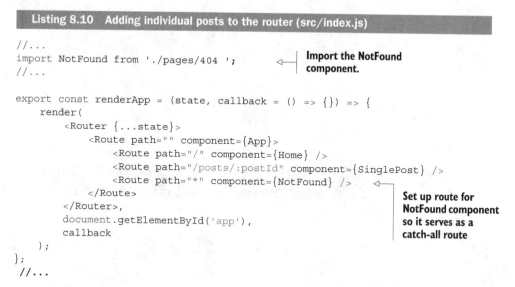

Listing 8.10 Adding individual posts to the router (src/index.js)

```
//...
import NotFound from './pages/404 ';        ←——  Import the NotFound
//...                                               component.

export const renderApp = (state, callback = () => {}) => {
    render(
        <Router {...state}>
            <Route path="" component={App}>
                <Route path="/" component={Home} />
                <Route path="/posts/:postId" component={SinglePost} />
                <Route path="*" component={NotFound} />     ←——
            </Route>                                              Set up route for
        </Router>,                                                NotFound component
        document.getElementById('app'),                           so it serves as a
        callback                                                  catch-all route
    );
};
//...
```

8.2 Integrating Firebase

With your router fully built and functioning, there's one more area we want to tackle in this chapter that we couldn't have before: enabling user login and authentication. You'll do this using the popular and easy-to-use "back-end as a service" platform Firebase (https://firebase.google.com). Firebase offers services that abstract away or take the place of a back-end API that handles user data, authentication, and other concerns. For our purposes, you can think of it as a drop-in replacement for a back-end API.

You won't be using it to completely replace the back end of your application (you're still using your API server), but you will be using Firebase to handle user login and user management. To get started with Firebase, head to https://firebase.google.com and create an account if you don't have one already. Once you're signed up, go to the Firebase console at https://console.firebase.google.com and create a new project to use in Letters Social. Once you've done that, click the Add Firebase to Your Web App button to open up a modal overlay. You'll see some configuration information for your app that you'll use in just a bit. See figure 8.2.

Once you've created a project and have access to your project configuration values, you're ready to get started. The Firebase SDK is already installed with the sample application code, so you can move ahead and create a new file called core.js in a new back-end directory inside of src (src/backend/core.js). Listing 8.11 shows how you'll set up core.js with the values from the app configuration. I've included the public Firebase API

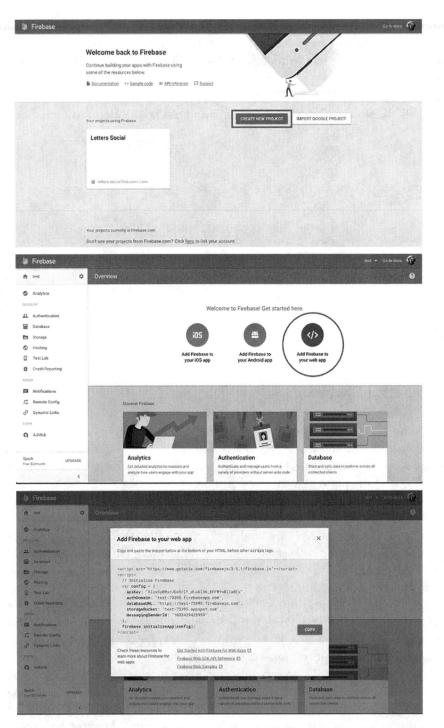

Figure 8.2   The Firebase console. Create a new project to be used with your instance of the Letters Social app.

key in the source code so you can run the app without an account, but if you want to replace it with your own, you can easily change the values in the config directory.

Listing 8.11 Configuring the Firebase back end (src/backend/core.js)

```
import firebase from 'firebase';

const config = {
    apiKey: process.env.GOOGLE_API_KEY,
    authDomain: process.env.FIREBASE_AUTH_DOMAIN
};

try {
    firebase.initializeApp(config);
} catch (e) {
    console.error('Error initializing firebase — check your source code');
    console.error(e);
}

export { firebase };
```

Values are injected by Webpack—change values in config directory if you want to include your own

Initialize Firebase with your credentials.

Export configured firebase instance for use elsewhere

Because you'll be using Firebase for authentication, you'll need to set up some code that will let you take advantage of that functionality. To get started, pick a platform to use for your authentication, as shown in figure 8.3. Choosing GitHub, Facebook, Google, or Twitter will let users that already have one of those accounts sign in without

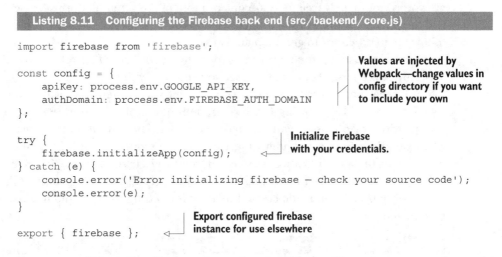

Figure 8.3 Setting up an authentication method with Firebase. Navigate to the Authentication section and pick any of the social providers. Then follow the instructions for the social authenticator you picked and make sure Firebase has access to the right credentials to authenticate with your chosen platform.

having to manage another username/login combination. I suggest picking GitHub because you and most people who will see your app will likely have GitHub accounts, but you're completely free to set up one or more of the other platforms to use. I'll use GitHub in our examples for simplicity. Once you've decided, click the provider and follow the instructions to get the platform set up.

Once you've set up the platform of your choice for use with Firebase, you'll need to set up some more code that will let you interact with `firebase` to perform user login. Firebase comes with built-in tools that let you authenticate with a variety of social platforms. I'll be using GitHub, as mentioned, but you're free to use whichever provider or providers you set up on your own. They all follow the same pattern (for example, create a provider object, set up the scope, and so on). You can find more about the authentication services offered by Firebase at https://firebase.google.com/docs/auth/. The next listing shows setting up the authentication utilities in `src/backend/auth.js`. You'll create functions for getting the user and token and logging in and out.

Listing 8.12   Setting up authentication tools (src/backend/auth.js)

```
import { firebase } from './core';          ←  Import Firebase library
                                               you've recently configured

const github = new firebase.auth.GithubAuthProvider();   ⎫ Use Firebase to set up
github.addScope('user:email');                           ⎬ GitHub authentication
                                                         ⎭ provider

export function logUserOut() {
    return firebase.auth().signOut();        ←  Create function that wraps
}                                               Firebase logout method

export function loginWithGithub() {                          ⎫ Create simple loginWith-
    return firebase.auth().signInWithPopup(github);  ←       ⎬ Github utility that returns
}                                                            ⎬ a Firebase authentication
                                                             ⎭ action Promise

export function getFirebaseUser() {
    return new Promise(resolve => firebase.auth().onAuthStateChanged(user =>
      resolve(user)));
}

export function getFirebaseToken() {                    ←  You'll need the token
    const currentUser = firebase.auth().currentUser;       later, so create a method
    if (!currentUser) {                                    that helps you get it.
        return Promise.resolve(null);
    }
    return currentUser.getIdToken(true);
}
```
Create wrapper method to get Firebase user (annotation for getFirebaseUser)

Now that we have everything set up and ready, we can create a new component that will handle login. Create a new file called src/pages/Login.js. Here, we'll create a straightforward component that tells your user how they can log in to Letter Social. The following listing shows the Login page component.

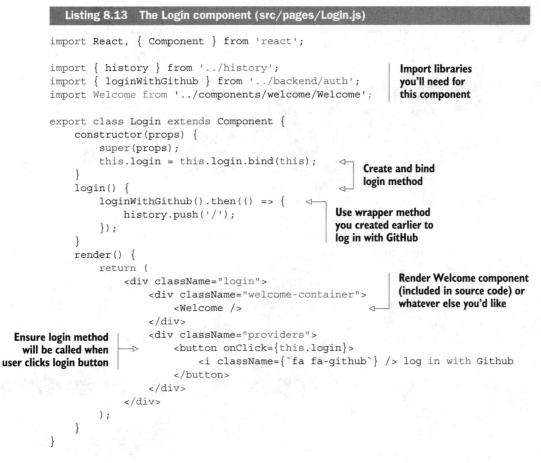

Listing 8.13   The Login component (src/pages/Login.js)

```
import React, { Component } from 'react';

import { history } from '../history';
import { loginWithGithub } from '../backend/auth';        ← Import libraries
import Welcome from '../components/welcome/Welcome';          you'll need for
                                                             this component

export class Login extends Component {
    constructor(props) {
        super(props);
        this.login = this.login.bind(this);         ←┐ Create and bind
    }                                                 ┘ login method
    login() {
        loginWithGithub().then(() => {               ← Use wrapper method
            history.push('/');                          you created earlier to
        });                                             log in with GitHub
    }
    render() {
        return (
            <div className="login">                     Render Welcome component
                <div className="welcome-container">     (included in source code) or
                    <Welcome />                    ←    whatever else you'd like
                </div>
                <div className="providers">
                    <button onClick={this.login}>
                        <i className={`fa fa-github`} /> log in with Github
                    </button>
                </div>
            </div>
        );
    }
}

export default Login;
```

Ensure login method will be called when user clicks login button →

8.2.1   Ensuring a user is logged in

Your last task is to make sure an unauthenticated user is redirected to the login page. For the current state of your app, it would make little difference whether a user is logged in or out because they can only see dummy data that isn't related to anything in real life (they'll just be happy to see all the random Star Wars quotes and avatars). But in a production situation, it's likely that a user absolutely needs to only be able to see data if they have an account and are logged in. This is a basic requirement of almost all web applications, and though we won't focus on security here, we do need to make sure a user can only see the social network if they're logged in.

There are different approaches to making this functionality possible. In more robust and developed tools like React Router, there are *hooks* you can execute when a particular route is navigated to—you can check to see if the user is logged in and can proceed. This is only one approach, and you don't have hooks functionality set up in your Router component, but you can add some logic to your main file (index.js) to check for a user's presence and determine where they should be routed. You'll transition to using React Router and these hooks in later chapters. You also need to add the Login component to your Router.

> **Exercise 8.3   Firebase alternatives**
>
> We're using Firebase in this book as a "back-end as a service." That dramatically simplifies things for learning purposes, but it's not necessarily how you might approach things on a team. Without having to go into depth, what do you think would take the place of Firebase for your application?

When a user signs in, you want to make sure that they also get recorded with your API. We're using Firebase for authentication, but you still want to store the user's information so they can create posts and comments and can like posts (you'll add comment and like functionality in later chapters). You'll need to account for whether a user exists and, if they don't, create them as a user in your system. The authentication logic you'll build out will take all this into account. We'll also slightly modify the browser history listener function so it can redirect people based on whether or not they're logged in.

The following listing shows how to add this logic and modify the history listener in the main index file for your app (src/index.js).

Listing 8.14   Adding the Login container to the Router (src/index.js)

```
export const renderApp = (state, callback = () => {}) => {
    render(
        <Router {...state}>
            <Route path="" component={App}>
                <Route path="/" component={Home} />
                <Route path="/posts/:postId" component={SinglePost} />
                <Route path="/login" component={Login} />          ◁──┐ Add Login page
                <Route path="*" component={NotFound} />               │ to your routes
            </Route>
        </Router>,
        document.getElementById('app'),
        callback
    );
};

let state = {
    location: window.location.pathname,
    user: {                                          ◁──┐ Keep track of user and
        authenticated: false,                           │ update state object you
        profilePicture: null,                           │ created accordingly
        id: null,
        name: null,
        token: null
    }
};
```

```
renderApp(state);

history.listen(location => {
    const user = firebase.auth().currentUser;
    state = Object.assign({}, state, {
        location: user ? location.pathname : '/login'
    });
    renderApp(state);
});

firebase.auth().onAuthStateChanged(async user => {
    if (!user) {
        state = {
            location: state.location,
            user: {
                authenticated: false
            }
        };
        return renderApp(state, () => {
            history.push('/login');
        });
    }
    const token = await getFirebaseToken();
    const res = await API.loadUser(user.uid);
    let renderUser;
    if (res.status === 404) {
        const userPayload = {
            name: user.displayName,
            profilePicture: user.photoURL,
            id: user.uid
        };
        renderUser = await API.createUser(userPayload).then(res => res.json());
    } else {
        renderUser = await res.json();
    }
    history.push('/');
    state = Object.assign({}, state, {
        user: {
            name: renderUser.name,
            id: renderUser.id,
            profilePicture: renderUser.profilePicture,
            authenticated: true
        },
        token
    });
    renderApp(state);
});
```

In your history listener, check to see first if there's a Firebase user

Use async function to respond to Firebase user state changing

If no user, update state and render app appropriately

Try to load user from our API

If there is a user, get their token using await and Firebase utility we created

Declare a user variable to assign to

If no user, you need to sign them up

Create user payload your API will understand

Send request to API and use the response

If user already exists, use them for rendering app

Update app state

Push user to the main page

Render app with new state

Now your users can sign in and have an account created for them on the fly. You should update the navbar so they know how to do that and so they can see the logout option, too. You may remember that you were passing in a user prop to the Navbar component earlier in the chapter even though it didn't exist yet. Now that it does, the Navbar component can conditionally show different views based on their authentication state. The following listing shows how to make these changes to the Navbar component.

Listing 8.15   Updating the Navbar component with (src/components/nav/navbar.js)

```
import React from 'react';
import PropTypes from 'prop-types';

import Link from '../router/Link';
import Logo from './logo';
import { logUserOut } from '../../backend/auth';

    export const Navigation = ({ user }) => (
     <nav className="navbar">
         <Logo />
         {user.authenticated ? (
             <span className="user-nav-widget">
                 <span>{user.name}</span>
                 <img width={40} className="img-circle"
     src={user.profilePicture} alt={user.name} />
                 <span onClick={() => logUserOut()}>
                     <i className="fa fa-sign-out" />
                 </span>
             </span>
         ) : (
             <Link to="/login">
                 <button type="button">Log in or sign up</button>
             </Link>
         )}
     </nav>
    );

    Navigation.propTypes = {
        user: PropTypes.shape({
            name: PropTypes.string,
            authenticated: PropTypes.bool,
            profilePicture: PropTypes.string
        }).isRequired
    };

export default Navigation;
```

If user is authenticated, show info about their profile (name, profile picture)

Give user option to log out (using Firebase utility we created earlier)

If they're not logged in, show a helpful link.

Declare proptypes

Export component for use

8.3   *Summary*

In this chapter, you started using the Router component you built, added a few more routing-related components to your application, did some refactoring, and added user authentication with Firebase. Here are some things to take away:

- Firebase is a "back-end-as-a-service" tool that lets you authenticate users, store data, and more. It can get you pretty far without having to do any back-end development and is a great place to start for many hobby projects.

- You can integrate browser history APIs with your router. This also enables you to create Link components that don't require a full page reload in lieu of regular anchor tags.
- Firebase can handle authentication and user session data for you. We'll explore more advanced methods of handling changing state like this in later chapters when we look at Flux, Redux, and even using Firebase on the server for server-side rendering.

Testing is an incredibly important part of developing good software. In the next chapter, we'll look at testing your React component using Jest and Enzyme.

Testing React components

In the last chapter, you added some significant functionality to your application. It now has routing and user state, and you've broken it up into smaller pieces. You even added some basic authentication so users could log in using their GitHub profile. Your application is starting to look more robust, even if it's probably not going to worry anyone at Facebook or Twitter. You can do lots more with React than you could when we first started. But as we've focused on learning the basics, we've omitted an important part of the development process: *testing*.

I didn't cover testing from the start to spare you the mental overload of learning React and testing fundamentals at the same time. But that doesn't mean it's an unimportant part of either learning or web development. In this chapter, we'll focus on testing because it's a fundamental part of developing high-quality software solutions. Instead of demonstrating tests for every single one of your components, though, we'll go through a representative sample so you'll understand the important principles at work and be able to write your own tests.

By the end of this chapter, you'll understand some of the basic principles of testing web applications. You'll also have set up tests and a test runner, worked with Jest, Enzyme, and the React test renderer, and learned to use and understand test coverage tools. You'll be equipped to start testing your applications, which will add another level of confidence to your React development skills.

How do I get the code for this chapter?

As with every chapter, you can check out the source code for this chapter by going to the GitHub repository at https://github.com/react-in-action/letters-social. If you want to start this chapter with a clean slate and follow along, you can use your existing code from chapters 7 and 8 (if you followed along and built out the examples yourself) or check out the chapter-specific branch (chapter-9).

Remember, each branch corresponds to the code at the end of the chapter (for example, the branch chapter-7 corresponds to the code as it will be at the end of this chapter). You can execute one of the following terminal commands in the directory of your choice to get the code for the current chapter.

If you don't have the repository at all, type the following:

```
git clone git@github.com:react-in-action/letters-social.git
```

If you already have the repository cloned:

```
git checkout chapter-9
```

You may have come here from another chapter, so it's always a good idea to ensure you have all the right dependencies installed:

```
npm install
```

Testing in software development is the process of validating assumptions. For example, say you're building an application (like Medium, Ghost, or WordPress) that lets users write and create blog posts. Users pay a monthly fee and get the hosting and the tools to run their own blog. When creating the front-end of the application, there are several key things it *must* do (among others), including correctly displaying those posts and letting users edit them.

How can you be sure your app is doing what it needs to do? You can try it out yourself and see if it works. Click around, edit things, and use the application in as many ways as you can think of. This manual process works reasonably well and is a first line of defense against bugs and regressions. You should always take care to inspect what you're working on, but you can't test things quickly and or in a perfectly consistent manner.

Also, as your application grows, the number of situations and features you'll need to manually test increases at an incredible rate. I've worked on applications with thousands of tests, but there are many applications where that number would be easily dwarfed. The React library itself has 4,855 tests at the time of writing. There's no chance someone wanting to test React would be able to validate by hand the assumptions involved in all those tests.

Fortunately, instead of testing everything by hand, you can use software to test software. Computers excel where we fail in at least two important areas: speed and consistency. We can use software to test our code in ways that we never could by hand, even with an army of people trying things out in every possible way. You may be thinking, "My project is small and really straightforward—there's not much that could go wrong." But even as great as your coding skills may be, bugs are inevitable. Your apps will break and work in unpredictable ways when you change things (and sometimes even when you don't).

But instead of despairing about the inevitability of bugs, we can accept that they'll happen and take steps to minimize their impact and frequency. That's where testing comes in. You may have some general idea about what testing is, but to get started we'll need to explore some different types of testing. Bear in mind that the world of testing is huge, and I can't cover even close to everything here. I won't be doing any in-depth coverage of testing as a domain. I also won't be deeply covering several types of testing, including integration testing, regression testing, testing automation, and others. But by the end of the chapter, you should be familiar enough to get started testing React components in a few different ways.

9.1   *Types of testing*

As I said, testing software is the process of using software to validate your assumptions. Because you're using software to test software, you'll ultimately be using the same primitives you use when building software: Booleans, numbers, strings, functions, objects, and the like. It's important to remember that there's no magic here—just more code.

There are different types of testing, and you'll use a few to test your React application. They encompass different aspects of an application, and when used together and in the right proportions, they should give you a significant degree of confidence in your application. Different types of tests address different parts and scopes of an application. A well-tested app will test the individual units of functionality that make up the basic parts of the app. It will also test the collections of these units of functionality and, at the highest level, the points at which everything comes together (such as the user interface).

Here are a few types of testing:

- *Unit*—Unit tests focus on individual units of functionality. For example, say you have a utility method for fetching new posts from the server. A unit test will focus only on that one function. It doesn't care about anything else. Like components, these tests allow for refactoring and promote modularity.
- *Service*—Service tests focus on bundles of functionality. This part of the "testing spectrum" can include a variety of granularities and focuses. The point, though,

is that you're testing things that aren't at the highest level (see integration tests, next) or the lowest levels of functionality. An example of a service test might be something like a tool that uses several units of functionality but is not itself at the level of an integration test.

- *Integration*—Integration tests focus on an even higher level of testing: the integration of various parts of an application. They test the way that services and lower-level functionality come together. Typically, these tests test an application through its user interface, not through the individual code behind the user interface. These tests may simulate clicks, user input, and other interactions that drive the application.

You may be wondering what these tests will look like in code; we'll get into that shortly, but first we need to talk about how these tests work together in the overall testing approach. If you've done testing before, you may have heard of the *testing pyramid*. This pyramid, illustrated in figure 9.1, generally refers to the proportion of different types of tests you should write. In this chapter, you'll only be writing unit tests for your components.

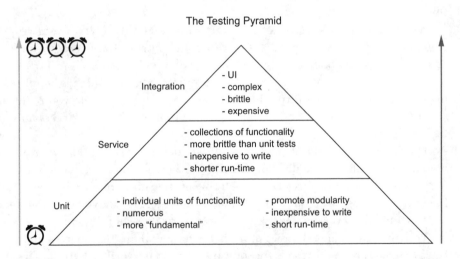

Figure 9.1 The testing pyramid is a way of guiding how many and which types of tests you write as you test your applications. Notice that certain types of tests take longer and are thus more "expensive" in terms of time (and therefore also financial cost).

9.1.1 Why test?

There are some software development paradigms where testing is a "first-class citizen" of the entire development process. That means testing is important, is considered at the beginning and throughout the development process, and usually plays a role in determining when something is considered complete. Granted, the consensus is that testing is a good thing for software development, but there are certain paradigms where it takes on a central role. For example, you may have heard of *test-driven develop-ment* (TDD). When practicing TDD, as its name suggests, the very process of writing software is driven by testing. When working, a developer will usually write a *failing* test (a test that makes assertions that haven't yet been met), write just enough code to get it to pass, refactor any duplication, and then move on to the next feature, repeating the process.

Although you don't have to be a strict practitioner of TDD to write great software, consider some of the benefits before moving on. If you're already wise to the upsides of testing, feel free to move on to the next section where we get started with testing in React. But I want to ask an important question: why do we test at all?

First and foremost, we want to write software that works. There are so many inter-connected parts of modern software that it would be foolish to assume that every part of the software stack will reliably work all the time. Things will break, and it's better to assume things will fail than to assume they'll work all the time. We can do our part to minimize the ways that our own software can break by testing our assump-tions. Testing forces you to visit (or revisit) your assumptions about your software. You walk it through the different cases it can handle and ensure that it handles them all appropriately.

Secondly, the process of testing your software tends to help you write better code. Going through the process of writing out your tests encourages you to think through what your code does, especially if you do it beforehand (as in TDD). Though it's far less preferable, you can write tests after the fact, too, which is better than hav-ing no tests at all. Going through the process of testing will help you better under-stand the code you write and will validate assumptions you and others make about how things work.

Third, integrating testing into your software development workflow means you can release code more frequently. You may have heard people in the tech industry men-tion "shipping often" before. That usually means releasing software incrementally and frequently. In the past, companies tended to only release software after an extensive process and only several times a year (or at least relatively infrequently).

Thinking has changed today, and people have realized that incremental iteration leads to generally better results for software: you can get feedback from users and oth-ers on it sooner, experiment more easily, and more. The confidence you can have in a well-tested app is a key part of this process. Using *continuous integration* (CI) or *continu-ous deployment* tools like Circle CI (https://circleci.com), Travis CI (https://travis-ci.org), or others, you can make testing part of the deployment process for your software. The idea is this: *if the tests pass, it gets deployed.* These tools usually run your tests in a pris-tine environment and, if they pass, send the code off to whatever system runs your application. Figure 9.2 shows the process that the Letters Social app uses to get tested and deployed.

Finally, tests also help you when going back and refactoring your code or moving it around. Say, for example, your requirements change, and you need to move some

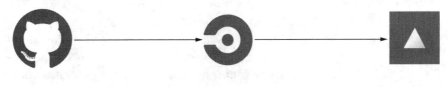

Code is stored
Receives code from `git push`
Lets interested services know

Runs code in test environment
Runs all tests for every single commit
If tests pass, deploy to Heroku
If they fail, let me know and no deploy

Hosts and runs
application code

Figure 9.2   The Letters Social deploy pipeline. A CI build process is triggered when I (or anyone who contributes to the repository) *push* **code. The CI provider (Circle, in this case) uses Docker containers to run your tests quickly and reliably. If the tests pass, the code will be deployed to whatever service you use to run your code. In our case, that's Now.**

components around. If you've kept your components modular and they have good tests, moving them should be easy. Untested code can be moved around, of course, but you have much less of a firm idea of whether it broke other parts of your system than you do when your code is tested.

There's more to be said about the benefits and theory of testing in software, but it's beyond the scope of this book. If you want to learn more, I recommend checking out *The Art of Unit Testing, Second Edition* (Manning Publications, 2013) by Roy Osherove and *Growing Object-Oriented Software: Guided by Tests* by Nat Pryce and Steve Freeman (Addison-Wesley, 2009).

9.2 *Testing React components with Jest, Enzyme, and React-test-renderer*

Testing software is just more software, made from the same primitives and basic elements that your normal programs are, though people have developed special tools to aid in the testing process. You could try to create the necessary tools to run all your tests, but the open source community has already put an incredible amount of work into a huge number of powerful tools—so you'll use those instead.

You'll need a few types of libraries to test your React applications:

- *Test runner*—You'll need something to run your tests. Most tests could be executed as regular JavaScript files, but you'll want to take advantage of some of the added features of test runners, such as running more than one test at a time and reporting back error or success information in a nicer way.

  For this book, you'll use Jest for most aspects of your testing. Jest is a testing library developed by engineers at Facebook. Some popular alternatives with fewer features built in that you might consider include Mocha (https://mochajs.org) and Jasmine (https://jasmine.github.io). Jest is often used for testing React apps, but adapters are being created for other frameworks, too. The source code includes a setup file (test/setup.js) that invokes the adapter for React.

- *Test doubles*—When writing tests, you want to avoid tying your tests to other fragile or unpredictable parts of your infrastructure as much as possible; other tools you rely on should be *mocked out*—replaced with a "fake" function that behaves in an expected way. Testing this way promotes a focus on the code under test and modularity because your tests aren't tied to the exact structure of your code at a given time. You'll use Jest for mocking and test doubles, but there are other libraries that also do this, such as Sinon (http://sinonjs.org).

- *Assertion libraries*—You can use JavaScript to make assertions about your code (for example, does *X* equal *Y*?), but there are plenty of edge cases that you'll need to account for. Developers have created solutions to make writing assertions about your code easier. Jest comes with assertion methods built in, so you'll rely on those.

- *Environment helpers*—Running tests on code that needs to run in a browser environment places slightly different demands on you. The browser environment is unique and includes things like the DOM, user events, and other normal parts of web applications. These testing tools will help ensure that you can successfully emulate a browser environment. You'll be using Enzyme and the React test renderer to aid in testing your React components. Enzyme makes testing React components easier. It provides a robust API that lets you query for different types of components and HTML elements, set and get props of components, inspect and set component state, and more. The React test renderer does similar things and can also generate snapshots of your components. We won't go into every aspect of Enzyme or the React test renderer APIs, but feel free to explore more at http://airbnb.io/enzyme and www.npmjs.com/package/react-test-renderer.

- *Framework-specific libraries*—There are libraries specifically made for React (or other frameworks) that make writing tests for a particular framework easier. These abstractions are usually developed to aid in the testing of a library or framework and handle setting up anything needed by the framework. In React, almost everything is "just JavaScript," so there's still little "magic" to be seen even in these tools.

- *Coverage tools*—Thanks to the deterministic nature of code, people have figured out ways to determine which parts of your code are "covered" by tests. That's great because you can get a metric that serves as a guideline in determining how well tested your code is. It's no substitute for logic and basic analysis (100% code coverage doesn't mean you can't have bugs), but it can guide how you test your code. You'll use Jest's built-in coverage tool, which utilizes a popular tool called Istanbul (https://github.com/gotwarlost/istanbul).

Next, you'll get started by installing the tools you'll be using for your tests. If you cloned the book repository from GitHub, these tools should already be installed. Make sure to run `npm install` again when changing chapters to make sure you have all the libraries for that chapter.

9.3 Writing your first tests

Once you've installed the tools you'll need, you're ready to start writing some tests. In this section, you're going to set up commands to run your tests and start testing some basic React components. You'll make assertions about your components and look at ways to test rendered output of components.

But before diving in, I should note a few things about Jest and where the code for your tests will run. Jest can be configured to run in different environments depending on the sort of tests you're writing. If you're writing tests for React applications that run in the browser, you'll want to tell Jest that so it can provide the virtual browser environment you need to properly emulate a real browser. Jest uses another library, `jsdom`, to accomplish that. If you're writing tests for node.js applications, you don't want the extra memory and baggage of the `jsdom` environment—you just want to test your server-side code. Jest is configured to run browser-oriented tests by default, so you don't need to override anything.

> ### Exercise 9.1 Reviewing types of testing
> There are a few different types of testing. To review, try matching the type with the description of the type of testing.
>
> 1 Unit
> 2 Service
> 3 Integration
>
> __ Complex, often brittle tests that take a long time to write and run. They test the way different systems work together at a high level. There are often fewer of these types of tests than others.
>
> __ Less complex tests that test the way a particular system works, but without interacting with other systems.
>
> __ Low-level, focused tests that focus on testing small bits of functionality. These should be the most numerous tests in a suite.

9.3.1 Getting started with Jest

To run your tests, as mentioned, you'll use Jest. You can run Jest from the command line, and it will execute your tests, so you're going to add a script to your package.json file so you can run it. The next listing shows how to add the custom script to your package.json. If you cloned the repository from GitHub, this script should already be available.

Listing 9.1 Setting up a custom npm script (package.json)

```
{
  //...
  "scripts": {
```

```
//...
  "test": "jest --coverage",
  "test:w": "jest -watch --coverage",
"jest": {
  "testEnvironment": "jsdom",
  "setupFiles": ["raf/polyfill", "./test/setup.js"]
},
"repository": {
  "type": "git",
  "url": "git+ssh://git@github.com/react-in-action/letters-social.git"
},
"author": "Mark Thomas <hello@ifelse.io>",
// ...
```

Run your tests and output test coverage.

Run the tests in watch mode.

Configure Jest; some testing helpers and stubs are included with the sample code.

Now that you have a command in place to run your tests (`npm test`), try it out. You shouldn't get any helpful info back yet because there are no tests to run (Jest should warn you accordingly in your terminal). You can also run `npm run test:w` to run Jest in watch mode. That's helpful when you don't want to manually run your tests every time. Jest's immersive watch mode makes it especially useful to work with—it will do some work to run only tests that relate to changed files. That's helpful if you have a large test suite and don't want to run every test every time. You can also provide regex patterns or search by text string to run only particular tests.

Tooling matters

Testing libraries and even testing as a whole sometimes get last consideration when it comes to evaluating libraries. That's unfortunate for at least two reasons. First, unusable testing libraries can make it more difficult for teams to buy into testing their code, potentially causing them to forgo it altogether. That, in turn, generally results in code that's harder to maintain, less stable, and more difficult to work with overall.

Another downside is that if you or your team spends a lot of time writing tests, your tools can have a substantial impact on your time. That can quickly translate to money lost by the business because its engineers are taking longer to do the work they need to do. I've seen both results firsthand. If testing wasn't considered a top priority from the beginning, it became more and more difficult over time and was treated as a "one day" kind of thing. The result was code that could be more difficult to change with confidence because assumptions about functionality were no longer backed by tests.

Another reason it pays to treat your testing tools as important is that if you do test your code, a significant time investment will be involved. If you have flaky tests or a testing setup that takes a long time to run, you can end up losing large chunks of time on a daily basis. There's no magic solution to this problem, but treating your testing tools and setup as first-class issues will often help you greatly in the long run.

9.3.2 Testing a stateless functional component

Time to get started writing some tests. First, we'll focus on a relatively straightforward example of testing a component. You're going to test the Content component. It doesn't do much; it just handles rendering a paragraph with content inside of it. The next listing shows the structure of the component.

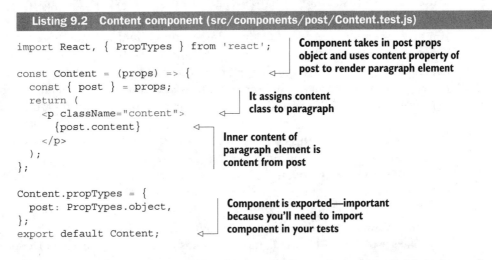

> **Listing 9.2 Content component (src/components/post/Content.test.js)**

```
import React, { PropTypes } from 'react';          ┐ Component takes in post props
                                                    │ object and uses content property of
const Content = (props) => {                      ◄─┘ post to render paragraph element
  const { post } = props;
  return (                                          ┐ It assigns content
    <p className="content">                       ◄─┘ class to paragraph
      {post.content}                              ◄─┐
    </p>                                            │ Inner content of
  );                                                │ paragraph element is
};                                                  ┘ content from post

Content.propTypes = {                               ┐ Component is exported—important
  post: PropTypes.object,                           │ because you'll need to import
};                                                ◄─┘ component in your tests
export default Content;
```

One of the first things you can do when starting to write tests is to think about what assumptions you want to validate. That is, once all the tests pass, they should confirm certain things to you and act as a sort of guarantee. In fact, one of my favorite things about tests is that I rely on them to fail when I'm making changes to a particular feature or part of a system. They back up my assumption that the changes I made represent a change to the application or system. This makes me much more comfortable when writing my code because on the one hand I have a record of how things were supposed to work beforehand, and on the other because I can get a sense of how my changes affect the application as a whole.

Let's look at your component and think about how you might test it. There are a few assumptions you want to validate about this component. For one, it needs to render some content that got passed in as a prop. It also needs to assign a class name to a paragraph element. Aside from that, there's not much to the component that you need to focus on. These things should be enough to get you started writing a test.

You may notice that "React works properly" isn't one of the things you're trying to test here. We also excluded things like "A function can be executed," "The JSX transpiler will work," and some other fundamental assumptions about the technologies you're using. These things are important to test, but the tests you're writing could never adequately or accurately validate these assumption. These other projects are responsible for writing their own tests and ensuring that they work. This underscores the importance of choosing software that's reliable, well-tested, and kept up-to-date. If you have serious doubts about React's reliability, those doubts may be unfounded.

Although not perfect, React is used on some of the most popular web apps in the world, including Facebook.com and Netflix.com, to name two. There are certainly bugs, but it's highly unlikely that you'd encounter them in our straightforward situation.

You know a few things about the component you want to validate, but you could have also gone about this the other way if you were starting from scratch and had written the test first. You may have thought to yourself, "We need a component that displays content, has a certain type, and has a certain class name so our CSS works." You may have then proceeded to write the test that would validate these conditions. You're going about it the other way due to how you've been learning about React, but you can see how starting with a test can make things easy: you start out by having to think through and plan your component. As mentioned, test-driven development (TDD) is a school of thought that makes writing tests first a central part of software development.

Let's see how to test this component. To do that, you'll need to write a test *suite*, which is a group of tests. Individual tests make *assertions* (statements about code that can be true or false) to validate assumptions. For example, a test for your component would *assert* that the right class name is set up. If any of your assertions fail, the test fails. That's how you know something has inadvertently changed or no longer works in your app. Listing 9.3 shows how to set up the skeleton of the test.

Notice that the file for the component ends with *.test.js*. That's a convention that you can choose to follow if you like. Jest will look for files that end in .spec.js or .test.js and run those tests by default. If you choose to follow a different convention, you'll need to explicitly tell Jest about which files you want to run by adding them to the command line invocation (`jest --watch ./my.cool.test.file.js`, for example). You'll follow the .test.js convention for all your tests.

It's also good to note where the test files are placed. Some people choose to place all their tests in a "mirror" directory called test, usually located in the root directory of their project. For every file that gets tested, they'll create a corresponding file in the test directory. That's a fine way to structure things, but you can also locate your test files right next to their source files. You'll go with this method, but either way is perfectly fine.

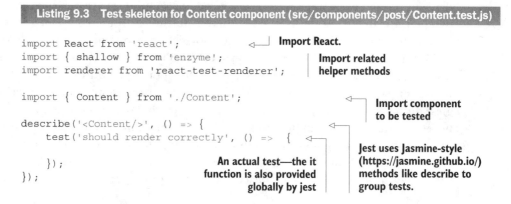

Listing 9.3   Test skeleton for Content component (src/components/post/Content.test.js)

```
import React from 'react';                        ⎯⎤ Import React.
import { shallow } from 'enzyme';                 ⎮ Import related
import renderer from 'react-test-renderer';       ⎮ helper methods

import { Content } from './Content';              ⎯⎤ Import component
                                                     to be tested
describe('<Content/>', () => {
    test('should render correctly', () => {

    });
});
```

An actual test—the it function is also provided globally by jest

Jest uses Jasmine-style (https://jasmine.github.io/) methods like describe to group tests.

You may have noticed that there's nothing special about the describe functions so far. They're primarily for organization and for ensuring that you can split your tests into the appropriate chunks to test different parts of your code. It may not seem like a huge need for such a small file, but I've worked with test files that are 2,000–3,000 lines long (or more), and I can speak from experience: readable tests help make good tests.

> ### Write clean tests!
> Have you ever read test code that hasn't gotten the same treatment as the code that it's testing? I've had this happen to me more than once. It can be confusing or even frustrating to read through test code that isn't clean. Tests are just more code, so they still need to be clean and readable, right? I've already mentioned in this chapter that testing can sometimes take second priority to writing application code. Test code can be treated as a task that has to be done or even a barrier between you and the application code, and so standards are lowered. This tendency can be easy to slip into, but the reality is that poorly written tests can be as bad as poorly written application code. Tests should serve as another form of documentation for your code, and one that still has to be read by developers. Remember that test code should still be clean code.

Jest will look for files to test and then execute these different describe and it functions, calling the callback functions you've provided to them. But what do you need to put inside them? You need to set up *assertions*. To do that, you need something to assert on. This is where Enzyme comes in; it lets you create a testable version of your component that you can inspect and make assertions about. You'll use Enzyme's *shallow rendering*, which will create a lightweight version of your component that doesn't perform full mounting or insertion into the DOM. You also need to provide some *mock* (fake) data for the component to use. The next listing shows how to add the test version of the component to your test suite. Before you start writing your tests, make sure to run the npm run test:w command in your terminal to start the test runner.

Listing 9.4 Shallow rendering (src/components/post/Content.test.js)

```
import React from 'react';
import { shallow } from 'enzyme';
import renderer from 'react-test-renderer';

import { Content } from './Content';

describe('<Content/>', () => {
  describe('render methods', () => {
    it('should render correctly', () => {
      const mockPost = {
        content: 'I am learning to test React components',    Create dummy
      };                                                        post object that
                                                                component can use
```

```
      const wrapper = shallow(<Content post={mockPost} />);     ◁─┐
    });                                                            │
  });                                                              │
});                            Perform shallow rendering of        │
                               component and save returned         │
                                     wrapper for later use         │
```

You now have a test component set up that you can make assertions about. To do this, you'll use the built-in expect() function from Jest. If you were using a different assertion library, you might use something else. Remember from earlier that these assertion libraries are for making assertions easier. For example, checking whether an object is *deeply equal* (meaning equal in every one of its properties) can be an involved task. When writing your tests, you shouldn't be focusing on implementing tons of new functionality just to write them—you should be focusing on the code under test. Assertion helpers and open source libraries make that easier.

To test the component at hand, you want to make a few assertions we mused about earlier: class name, inner content, and element type. You'll also create a snapshot test using the React test renderer. *Snapshot testing* is a feature of Jest that allows you to test the render output of your components in a unique way. Snapshot testing is closely related to *visual regression testing*, a process where the visual output of an application can be compared and checked for differences.

If a difference in images is found, you know that your test failed and needs adjusting or at least that the output snapshot needs to be updated. Rather than images, Jest will create JSON outputs for tests and store them in specially named directories. These should be added to version control along with all your other code. The following listing shows how to use Jest, Enzyme, and the React test renderer to make those assertions.

> ### Listing 9.5   Making assertions (src/components/post/Content.test.js)

```
import React from 'react';
import { shallow } from 'enzyme';          Import enzyme and       Import
import renderer from 'react-test-renderer';   react-test-renderer.  component
                                                                     you want
import Content from '../../../src/components/post/Content';     ◁─   to test

describe('<Content/>', () => {                Use Jasmine-style describe function
    test('should render correctly', () => {    to group tests together
Create     const mockPost = {
mock          content: 'I am learning to test React components'
post        };                                                Use Enzyme's
        const wrapper = shallow(<Content post={mockPost} />);  ◁─  shallow method
        expect(wrapper.find('p').length).toBe(1);                 to render
        expect(wrapper.find('p.content').length).toBe(1);         component
        expect(wrapper.find('.content').text()).toBe(mockPost.content);
        expect(wrapper.find('p').text()).toBe(mockPost.content);
    });
```

```
          ┌▷ test('snapshot', () => {
Create    │      const mockPost = {
snapshot  │          content: 'I am learning to test React components'
test using │     };
Jest and  ├▷     const component = renderer.create(<Content post={mockPost} />);
react-test-│     const tree = component.toJSON();
renderer  └▷     expect(tree).toMatchSnapshot();
              });
          });
```

If your test runner is running, you should see a passing result from Jest. The Jest command-line tools have greatly improved since the test runner came out, and you should be able to see important information about your tests in the terminal.

9.3.3 Testing the CreatePost component without Enzyme

Now that you have your first test working, you can move on to testing more complex components. For the most part, testing React components should be straightforward. If you find yourself creating a component that has tons of functionality built into it and subsequently huge tests associated with it, you may want to consider breaking it into several components (although that's not always possible).

The next component you want to test, the CreatePost component, has more functionality than the Content component did, and your tests will need to address this added functionality. Listing 9.6 shows the CreatePost component so you can review it before writing out tests for it. The CreatePost component is used by the Home component to trigger the submission of new posts. It renders out a `textarea` that gets updated when the user types in it and a button that submits the form with data when a user clicks it. When the user clicks, it invokes a callback function passed by a parent component. You can test all these assumptions and make sure that things work as you expect.

Listing 9.6 CreatePost component (src/components/post/Create.js)

```
import PropTypes from 'prop-types';
import React from 'react';
import Filter from 'bad-words';
import classnames from 'classnames';
import DisplayMap from '../map/DisplayMap';
import LocationTypeAhead from '../map/LocationTypeAhead';
class CreatePost extends React.Component {
    static propTypes = {
        onSubmit: PropTypes.func.isRequired
    };
    constructor(props) {
        super(props);
        this.initialState = {
            content: '',
            valid: false,
            showLocationPicker: false,
```

```
                location: {
                    lat: 34.1535641,
                    lng: -118.1428115,
                    name: null
                },
                locationSelected: false
        };
        this.state = this.initialState;
        this.filter = new Filter();
        this.handlePostChange = this.handlePostChange.bind(this);
        this.handleRemoveLocation = this.handleRemoveLocation.bind(this);
        this.handleSubmit = this.handleSubmit.bind(this);
        this.handleToggleLocation = this.handleToggleLocation.bind(this);
        this.onLocationSelect = this.onLocationSelect.bind(this);
        this.onLocationUpdate = this.onLocationUpdate.bind(this);
        this.renderLocationControls = this.renderLocationControls.bind(this);
    }
    handlePostChange(event) {
        const content = this.filter.clean(event.target.value);
        this.setState(() => {
            return {
                content,
                valid: content.length <= 300
            };
        });
    }
    handleRemoveLocation() {
        this.setState(() => ({
            locationSelected: false,
            location: this.initialState.location
        }));
    }
    handleSubmit(event) {
        event.preventDefault();
        if (!this.state.valid) {
            return;
        }
        const newPost = {
            content: this.state.content
        };
        if (this.state.locationSelected) {
            newPost.location = this.state.location;
        }
        this.props.onSubmit(newPost);
        this.setState(() => ({
            content: '',
            valid: false,
            showLocationPicker: false,
            location: this.defaultLocation,
            locationSelected: false
        }));
    }
    onLocationUpdate(location) {
        this.setState(() => ({ location }));
    }
```

```
onLocationSelect(location) {
    this.setState(() => ({
        location,
        showLocationPicker: false,
        locationSelected: true
    }));
}
handleToggleLocation(event) {
    event.preventDefault();
    this.setState(state => ({ showLocationPicker:
 !state.showLocationPicker }));
}
renderLocationControls() {
    return (
        <div className="controls">
            <button onClick={this.handleSubmit}>Post</button>
            {this.state.location && this.state.locationSelected ? (
                <button onClick={this.handleRemoveLocation}
 className="open location-indicator">
                    <i className="fa-location-arrow fa" />
                    <small>{this.state.location.name}</small>
                </button>
            ) : (
                <button onClick={this.handleToggleLocation}
 className="open">
                    {this.state.showLocationPicker ? 'Cancel' : 'Add
 location'}{' '}
                    <i
                        className={classnames(`fa`, {
                            'fa-map-o': !this.state.showLocationPicker,
                            'fa-times': this.state.showLocationPicker
                        })}
                    />
                </button>
            )}
        </div>
    );
}
render() {
    return (
        <div className="create-post">
            <textarea
                value={this.state.content}
                onChange={this.handlePostChange}
                placeholder="What's on your mind?"
            />
            {this.renderLocationControls()}
            <div
                className="location-picker"
                style={{ display: this.state.showLocationPicker ? 'block'
 : 'none' }}
            >
                {!this.state.locationSelected && (
                    <LocationTypeAhead
                        onLocationSelect={this.onLocationSelect}
```

```
                                onLocationUpdate={this.onLocationUpdate}
                        />
                    )}
                    <DisplayMap
                        displayOnly={false}
                        location={this.state.location}
                        onLocationSelect={this.onLocationSelect}
                        onLocationUpdate={this.onLocationUpdate}
                    />
                </div>
            </div>
        );
    }
}

export default CreatePost;
```

This was a slightly more complicated component than you created in previous chapters. With it you can create posts and add a location to those posts. In my experience, testing larger and more complex components further highlights the importance of clean, readable tests. If you can't read or reason through your test file, how is a future-you or another developer going to?

Listing 9.7 shows a suggested skeleton of tests for the CreatePost component. You don't have enough methods to make it difficult to read through the tests, but if a component had more to it, you might even add nested `describe` blocks to make it easier to reason about. The functions in listing 9.7 will be executed by the test runner (Jest in this case), and within those tests you can make your assertions. Most tests follow this same sort of pattern. You import the code under test, mock out any dependencies to isolate your tests to one unit of functionality (hence *unit tests*), and then a test runner and assertion library will work together to run your tests.

> **Listing 9.7   Testing the CreatePost component (src/components/post/Create.test.js)**

```
jest.mock('mapbox');
import React from 'react';
import renderer from 'react-test-renderer';

import CreatePost from '../../../src/components/post/Create';

describe('CreatePost', () => {          ◁──┐  Using one describe call here, but
    test('snapshot', () => {                   in larger test files you can have
                                               many and even nest them
    });
    test('handlePostChange', () => {     ◁──┐
                                              Create a test for
    });                                       each method in your
    test('handleRemoveLocation', () => {  ◁── component, including
                                              a snapshot to ensure
    });                                       it renders correctly
    test('handleSubmit', () => {          ◁──┘
```

```
    });
    test('onLocationUpdate', () => {

    });
    test('handleToggleLocation', () => {

    });
    test('onLocationSelect', () => {

    });
    test('renderLocationControls', () => {

    });
});
```

If you follow a consistent pattern of considering each part of your component that needs to be tested, you'll be more thorough in developing and testing your components. Feel free to follow whatever structure makes the most sense to you—this is just one that has been helpful for me and for teams I've been on. I've also found it helpful to start writing tests by writing out the different `describe` and `test` blocks for a component or module before writing any other tests. I find that I can more easily think through the cases I want to cover (with an error, without an error, with a condition, and so on) if I'm doing that all at once.

What about other types of testing?

You may be wondering about testing such things as user flows, cross-browser testing, and other types of testing I'm not covering here. These other sorts of testing will generally be focused on by an engineer or engineering team dedicated to specialized forms of testing. QA teams and SETs (*software engineers in test*) will generally have a host of specialized tools that allow them to take your application and simulate all the complicated flows that might exist.

These types of testing (*integration testing*) may involve the interaction of one or more disparate systems. If you remember the testing pyramid from figure 9.1, these tests can take a lot of time to write, are hard to maintain, and tend to cost a lot of money. When you think of "testing front-end applications," you may think these sorts of tests are what would be involved. We've seen that this isn't the case (most tests that non-QA engineers write are unit or low-level integration tests). If you're interested in learning more about these sorts of tools, here are a few you could use as a springboard to learn more about higher-level testing:

- *Selenium*—www.seleniumhq.org
- *Puppeteer*—https://github.com/GoogleChrome/puppeteer
- *Protractor*—www.protractortest.org/#/

With this skeleton setup in place, you can begin testing the CreatePost component, starting with the constructor. Remember, the constructor is where initial state gets set up, class methods get bound, and other setup can occur. To test this part of the CreatePost component, we need to introduce another tool I mentioned earlier: Sinon. You need some test functions that you can give to your component for use that aren't dependent on other modules. With Jest you can create mock functions for your test that help keep your tests focused on the component itself and prevent you from tying all your code together. Remember how I said tests should break when you change your code? That's true, but changing one test also shouldn't break other tests. As with regular code, your tests should be decoupled and only care about the slice of code they're testing.

Jest's mock functions not only help us isolate our code, they help us make more assertions. You can make assertions about how your component used the mock function, whether it was called, what arguments it was called with, and more. The following listing shows setting up the snapshot test for your component and mocking some basic props your component needs using Jest.

Listing 9.8   Writing your first test (src/components/post/Create.test.js)

```
jest.mock('mapbox');
import React from 'react';
import renderer from 'react-test-renderer';
```
Use jest.mock function to tell Jest to use a mock instead of the module when running tests

```
import CreatePost from '../../../src/components/post/Create';

describe('CreatePost', () => {
  test('snapshot', () => {
    const props = { onSubmit: jest.fn() };
    const component = renderer.create(<CreatePost {...props} />);
    const tree = component.toJSON();
    expect(tree).toMatchSnapshot();
  });
  //...
});
```
Create test block within outer describe block you created earlier

Use React test renderer to create your component and pass in props

Call toJSON method to generate a snapshot

Assert that snapshot matches

Create mock props object and use Jest's to create mock function

Now that you have one test under your belt, you can test some other aspects of the component. The component is primarily responsible for allowing users to create posts and attach locations to them, so you need to test those areas of functionality. You'll start by testing post creation. The next listing shows how to test post creator methods in your component.

Listing 9.9   Testing post creation (src/components/post/Create.test.js)

```
jest.mock('mapbox');
import React from 'react';
import renderer from 'react-test-renderer';

import CreatePost from '../../../src/components/post/Create';
```

```
describe('CreatePost', () => {
    test('snapshot', () => {
        const props = { onSubmit: jest.fn() };
        const component = renderer.create(<CreatePost {...props} />);
        const tree = component.toJSON();
        expect(tree).toMatchSnapshot();
    });
    test('handlePostChange', () => {
        const props = { onSubmit: jest.fn() };
        const mockEvent = { target: { value: 'value' } };
        CreatePost.prototype.setState = jest.fn(function(updater) {
            this.state = Object.assign(this.state, updater(this.state));
        });

        const component = new CreatePost(props);
        component.handlePostChange(mockEvent);
        expect(component.setState).toHaveBeenCalled();
        expect(component.setState.mock.calls.length).toEqual(1);
        expect(component.state).toEqual({
            valid: true,
            content: mockEvent.target.value,
            location: {
                lat: 34.1535641,
                lng: -118.1428115,
                name: null
            },
            locationSelected: false,
            showLocationPicker: false
        });

    });
    test('handleSubmit', () => {
        const props = { onSubmit: jest.fn() };
        const mockEvent = {
            target: { value: 'value' },
            preventDefault: jest.fn()
        };
        CreatePost.prototype.setState = jest.fn(function(updater) {
            this.state = Object.assign(this.state, updater(this.state));
        });

        const component = new CreatePost(props);
        component.setState(() => ({
            valid: true,
            content: 'cool stuff!'
        }));
        component.state = {
            valid: true,
            content: 'content',
            location: 'place',
            locationSelected: true
        };
        component.handleSubmit(mockEvent);
        expect(component.setState).toHaveBeenCalled();
        expect(props.onSubmit).toHaveBeenCalledWith({
```

Create mock set of props to use

Mock setState so you can make sure your component calls it and that updating post updates state in the right way.

Directly instantiate component and call its methods

Assert that your component invokes the right methods and that method updated state correctly

Create another mock event to simulate what your component will receive from an event

Mock setState again.

Instantiate another component and set state of component to simulate user entering post content

Directly modify component's state (for testing purposes)

Handle post submission with mock event you created and assert that mocks were called

```
                content: 'content',
                location: 'place'
            });
        });
    });
```

Finally, you want to test the remainder of the component's functionality. Aside from letting users create posts, the CreatePost component also handles the user picking a location. Other components handle updating the location via callbacks passed as props, but you still need to test the component methods on CreatePost related to this feature.

Remember you implemented a subrender method on CreatePost, which you used to make reading the render method's output of CreatePost easier and to reduce clutter. You can test this in a similar way that you've been testing components with Enzyme or the React test renderer. The following listing shows the rest of the tests for the CreatePost component.

Listing 9.10   Testing post creation (src/components/post/Create.test.js)

```
jest.mock('mapbox');
import React from 'react';
import renderer from 'react-test-renderer';

import CreatePost from '../../../src/components/post/Create';

describe('CreatePost', () => {
    test('handleRemoveLocation', () => {
        const props = { onSubmit: jest.fn() };
        CreatePost.prototype.setState = jest.fn(function(updater) {
            this.state = Object.assign(this.state, updater(this.state));
        });
        const component = new CreatePost(props);
        component.handleRemoveLocation();
        expect(component.state.locationSelected).toEqual(false);
    });
    test('onLocationUpdate', () => {
        const props = { onSubmit: jest.fn() };
        CreatePost.prototype.setState = jest.fn(function(updater) {
            this.state = Object.assign(this.state, updater(this.state));
        });
        const component = new CreatePost(props);
        component.onLocationUpdate({
            lat: 1,
            lng: 2,
            name: 'name'
        });
        expect(component.setState).toHaveBeenCalled();
        expect(component.state.location).toEqual({
            lat: 1,
            lng: 2,
            name: 'name'
        });
    });
});
```

Annotations:
- **Mock setState** → points to `CreatePost.prototype.setState = jest.fn(function(updater) {`
- **Invoke handleRemoveLocation function** → points to `component.handleRemoveLocation();`
- **Assert that you updated state in correct manner** → points to `expect(component.state.locationSelected).toEqual(false);`
- **Repeat same process for rest of your component methods** → points to `test('onLocationUpdate', () => {`

**Repeat
same
process for
rest of your
component
methods**

```
test('handleToggleLocation', () => {
    const props = { onSubmit: jest.fn() };
    const mockEvent = {
        preventDefault: jest.fn()
    };
    CreatePost.prototype.setState = jest.fn(function(updater) {
        this.state = Object.assign(this.state, updater(this.state));
    });
    const component = new CreatePost(props);
    component.handleToggleLocation(mockEvent);
    expect(mockEvent.preventDefault).toHaveBeenCalled();
    expect(component.state.showLocationPicker).toEqual(true);
});
test('onLocationSelect', () => {
    const props = { onSubmit: jest.fn() };
    CreatePost.prototype.setState = jest.fn(function(updater) {
        this.state = Object.assign(this.state, updater(this.state));
    });
    const component = new CreatePost(props);
    component.onLocationSelect({
        lat: 1,
        lng: 2,
        name: 'name'
    });
});
test('onLocationSelect', () => {
    const props = { onSubmit: jest.fn() };
    CreatePost.prototype.setState = jest.fn(function(updater) {
        this.state = Object.assign(this.state, updater(this.state));
    });
    const component = new CreatePost(props);
    component.onLocationSelect({
        lat: 1,
        lng: 2,
        name: 'name'
    });
    expect(component.setState).toHaveBeenCalled();
    expect(component.state.location).toEqual({
        lat: 1,
        lng: 2,
        name: 'name'
    });
});
test('renderLocationControls', () => {
    const props = { onSubmit: jest.fn() };
    const component = renderer.create(<CreatePost {...props} />);
    let tree = component.toJSON();
    expect(tree).toMatchSnapshot();
});
});
```

**Create another snapshot
test for subrender
method you created**

9.3.4 *Test coverage*

Now that you've gotten your hands dirty testing some components, let's look at test coverage and see what progress you've made. In your terminal, stop the test runner and execute the command shown in the next listing. This command will turn on the coverage option included in Jest.

> **Listing 9.11 Enabling test coverage (project root)**

```
> npm run test:w
```

Once your test runner finishes executing tests, it should output a colored table that should look something like figure 9.3 (with less coverage). The figure shows the Jest

% of statements covered by tests	% of logical branches covered by tests	% of functions covered by tests	Total % lines of the file covered	Lines of source files that tests don't run through at all

File		% Stmts	% Branch	% Funcs	% Lines	Uncovered Lines
All files		78.76	67.19	66.27	80.18	
db		85.71	100	87.5	85.71	
constants.js		100	100	100	100	
models.js		85.29	100	87.5	85.29	69,70,71,72,73
src/backend		68.42	100	0	68.42	
auth.js		64.71	100	0	64.71	... 18,19,20,25
core.js		100	100	100	100	
index.js		100	100	100	100	
src/components/ad		100	100	100	100	
Ad.js		100	100	100	100	
src/components/comment		69.23	58.33	63.64	69.23	
Comment.js		100	100	100	100	
Comments.js		81.82	58.33	66.67	81.82	38,47
Create.js		45.45	100	50	45.45	... 14,15,16,19
src/components/nav		83.33	50	71.43	90	
logo.js		100	50	100	100	
navbar.js		75	50	66.67	83.33	20
src/components/post		89.36	62.5	81.25	89.36	
Avatar.js		50	100	0	50	4
Content.js		100	100	100	100	
Controls.js		100	62.5	100	100	
Create.js		93.75	50	100	93.75	32
Image.js		80	75	100	80	5
Link.js		100	100	100	100	
Post.js		100	50	100	100	
Posts.js		33.33	100	0	33.33	5,7
User.js		100	50	100	100	
index.js		100	100	100	100	
src/components/router		97.44	91.67	90.91	97.3	
Link.js		66.67	100	50	66.67	13
Route.js		100	100	100	100	
Router.js		100	91.67	100	100	
index.js		100	100	100	100	
src/components/welcome		100	100	100	100	
Welcome.js		100	100	100	100	
index.js		100	100	100	100	

Source files

Figure 9.3 Test coverage output from Jest shows coverage stats for the different files in your project. Each column reflects a different aspect of coverage. For each type of coverage, Jest shows a percentage covered. Statements and functions are simply JavaScript statements and functions, whereas branches are logical branches. If your test doesn't address one part of an if statement, that should be reflected in the code coverage both in the uncovered lines column and in the percent-covered stat for branches.

coverage output with annotations about each of the columns. There are different forms of readable code coverage reports (HTML, for example), but the terminal output is most useful during development because it provides immediate feedback.

Istanbul is the tool generating the stats in figure 9.3. If you want to see more detailed coverage information, open the coverage directory that should have been generated by the `jest` command that included the coverage option. In this directory, Istanbul should have created a few files. If you open ./coverage/lcov-report/index.html in a browser, you should see something like figure 9.4.

All files

78.76% Statements 178/226 **68.75%** Branches 44/64 **66.27%** Functions 55/83 **80.18%** Lines 174/217

File ▲		Statements		Branches		Functions		Lines	
db		85.71%	30/35	100%	4/4	87.5%	7/8	85.71%	30/35
src/backend		68.42%	13/19	100%	0/0	0%	0/5	68.42%	13/19
src/components/ad		100%	3/3	100%	0/0	100%	1/1	100%	3/3
src/components/comment		69.23%	18/26	58.33%	7/12	63.64%	7/11	69.23%	18/26
src/components/nav		83.33%	10/12	50%	2/4	71.43%	5/7	90%	9/10
src/components/post		89.36%	42/47	66.67%	16/24	81.25%	13/16	89.36%	42/47
src/components/router		97.44%	38/39	91.67%	11/12	90.91%	10/11	97.3%	36/37
src/components/welcome		100%	2/2	100%	0/0	100%	1/1	100%	2/2
src/containers		50%	20/40	50%	4/8	50%	11/22	52.78%	19/36
src/history		66.67%	2/3	100%	0/0	0%	0/1	100%	2/2

Figure 9.4   Istanbul generates coverage metadata in computer-readable and human-readable formats. The coverage report shown here is useful for more detailed exploration of code coverage. You can even sort by different columns and prioritize files with low coverage. Note that there are columns for statements, branches (if/else statements), functions (which functions were called), and lines (lines of code).

The Istanbul output is useful, but you can also drill down into different files and get more in-depth information about individual files. Each file should display information about how many times different lines were covered and which ones weren't. Most of the time the top-level summary is good enough, but sometimes you may want to inspect individual reports, like the one in figure 9.5. When I'm writing tests, I like to take at least one look at these files once I've covered all my cases to make sure I didn't miss any edge cases or logical branches.

Test coverage is an important and useful tool for software development, but don't treat it as a magical guarantee that your code works. You can get to 100% coverage and still have code that breaks. You can technically also have code that works with 0% code coverage. *Coverage* is about making sure your tests are executing all the different parts of your code—not guaranteeing a lack of errors or things like performance—but it's useful for that and should be treated as an important data point when considering how "complete" your code is. I've been on teams where our definition of success for a particular user story or task included, among other things, code coverage above

```
All files / src/components/post Content.js

100% Statements 4/4    100% Branches 0/0    100% Functions 1/1    100% Lines 4/4


  1      import React, { PropTypes } from 'react';
  2
  3  3x  const Content = (props) => {
  4  2x    const { post } = props;
  5  2x    return (
  6          <p className="content">
  7            {post.content}
  8          </p>
  9        );
 10      };
 11
 12  3x  Content.propTypes = {
 13        post: PropTypes.object,
 14      };
 15      export { Content };
 16
```

Figure 9.5   Individual file coverage report generated by Istanbul. You can see how many times different lines were or weren't covered and get a sense for exactly which parts of your code were covered.

80% and no decreased coverage overall. Use coverage as a guideline for which parts of your code you have or haven't tested and to check your testing progress.

> **Exercise 9.2   Considering coverage**
>
> We talked about test coverage in this chapter. Does 100% test coverage mean that your code is perfect? What role should code coverage play in your testing?

9.4   Summary

In this chapter, you learned about some of the principles behind testing and how to test React applications:

- *Testing* is the process of validating assumptions made about software. It helps you better plan your components, prevents breakage in the future, and helps increase confidence in your code. It also plays an important role in a rapid development process.
- Manual testing doesn't scale well because no number of people could ever quickly or adequately test complex software well.
- We use a variety of tools in the software testing process, ranging from tools that run our tests to tools that determine how much of our code is covered by tests.
- Different types of tests should occur in different proportions. *Unit* tests should be the most common and are easy, cheap, and quick to write. *Integration* tests test the interaction of many different parts of the system and can be brittle and take longer to write. They should be less common.
- You can test React components using a variety of tools. Because they're just functions, you could test them strictly as such. But tools like Enzyme make testing React components easier.

- Clean tests, like any clean code, are easy to read and well organized and use appropriate proportions of unit, service, and integration tests. They should provide meaningful assurance that things function in a particular manner and should guarantee that changes to your component can be evaluated.

In the next chapter, we'll look at a more robust implementation of the Letters Social app and explore the Redux architectural pattern. Before moving on, see if you can keep honing your testing skills and get test coverage for the app up above 90%!

Part 3

React application architecture

By the end of part 2, you will have transformed the Letters Social sample application from a bare-bones static page to a dynamic user interface with routing, authentication, and dynamic data. In part 3, you'll add to what you've created by exploring some advanced topics in React.

In chapters 10 and 11, you'll explore the Flux application architecture and implement Redux. Redux is a variation of the Flux pattern that has become the de facto state management solution for sizeable React applications. You'll explore the concepts of Redux and transition your React application to use Redux as the state management solution. As you do this, you'll continue to add features to Letters Social, including comments and the ability to like posts.

In chapter 12, we'll take things a step further and explore how you can use React on the server. Thanks to the availability of the node.js server runtime, you can execute React code on the server. You'll explore server-side rendering with React and even integrate your Redux state management into the process. You'll also integrate React Router, a popular routing library for React.

Finally, you'll make a minor departure from React for the web in chapter 13 and explore React Native. React Native is another React project that gives you the ability to write React applications that can run on iOS and Android mobile devices.

By the end of part 3, you'll have created an entire application that takes full advantage of React, Redux, and server side rendering. You'll have completed your initial foray into React, but you'll be able to further your abilities with React and explore other advanced topics like React Native.

Redux application architecture

10

By this point, you can create React applications that are tested, handle dynamic data, accept user input, and can communicate with remote APIs. That's a lot and covers most of what a typical web app will do; you may feel like the only thing left to do is practice. Putting your skills to use will help you master React, but there's still an important area you'll need to cover to build larger, more complex applications: application architecture. *Application architecture* is "the process of defining a structured solution that meets all of the technical and operational requirements, while optimizing common quality attributes such as performance, security, and manageability" (from *Microsoft Application Architecture Guide*, 2nd Edition). Architecture asks, "Okay, we can do this, but now how do we do it better and consistently?" It's about how and how well the application is organized, how data moves around, and how responsibility is delegated to different parts of a system.

Every application has an implicit architecture of sorts simply because it has a structure and does things in a particular way. What I'm talking about here are strategies and paradigms for building complex applications. React errs on the side of being a more minimal or unopinionated framework focused on UI, so it doesn't come with a built-in strategy for you to follow as you build more complex applications.

Just because there isn't a built-in strategy for you to use doesn't mean there aren't options out there, though. There are many approaches to building complex applications with React, and many of them are based on the Flux model popularized by engineers at Facebook. Flux differs from the popular MVC architecture by promoting unidirectional data flow, introducing new concepts (dispatchers, actions, stores), and in other ways. Flux and MVC are concerned with things "above" what an application looks like or even some of the specific libraries or technologies it is built with. They are more concerned with how the application is organized, how data moves around, and how responsibility is delegated to different parts of a system.

This chapter explores one of the most widely used and well-regarded variants of the Flux pattern: Redux. It's extremely common to see Redux used with React applications, but in fact it can be used with most JavaScript frameworks (in-house or otherwise). This chapter and the next cover the core concepts of Redux (actions, middleware, reducers, the store, and others) and then the integration of Redux with your React app. *Actions* in Redux represent work being done (fetching user data, logging the user in, and so on), *reducers* determine how state should change, the *store* holds a centralized copy of state, and *middleware* allows you to inject custom behavior into the process.

How do I get the code for this chapter?

As with every chapter, you can check out the source code for this chapter by going to the GitHub repository at https://github.com/react-in-action/letters-social. If you want to start this chapter with a clean slate and follow along, you can use your existing code from chapter 9 (if you followed along and built out the examples yourself) or check out the chapter-specific branch (chapter-10-11).

Remember, each branch corresponds to the code at the end of the chapter (for example, the branch chapter-10-11 corresponds to the code as it will be at the end of these chapters). You can execute one of the following terminal commands in the directory of your choice to get the code for the current chapter.

If you don't have the repository at all, type the following:

```
git clone git@github.com:react-in-action/letters-social.git
```

If you already have the repository cloned:

```
git checkout chapter-10-11
```

You may have come here from another chapter, so it's always a good idea to ensure you have all the right dependencies installed:

```
npm install
```

10.1 *The Flux application architecture*

Modern applications must do more than ever before and are correspondingly more complex—internally and externally. Developers have long been aware of the mess that can be made of a complex application that grows without coherent design patterns in place. Spaghetti-code codebases aren't only not fun to work with, they slow down developers and thus business units. Remember the last time you had to work in a large codebase full of one-off solutions and jQuery plugins? Probably not fun. To combat disorganization, developers have developed paradigms like MVC (Model-View-Controller) to organize the functionality of an application and guide development. Flux (and by extension Redux) is an effort in the same vein that helps you deal with increased complexity in an application.

Don't worry if you're not especially familiar with the MVC paradigm; we won't spend much time getting into it. But before we talk about Flux and Redux, it might be helpful to briefly discuss MVC for the sake of comparison. If you're interested in learning more, Jeff Atwood has some helpful thoughts at https://blog.codinghorror .com/understanding-model-view-controller/, and there are many other resources available online. Here are the basics:

- *Model*—The data for your application. Usually a noun like User, Account, or Post, for example. Your model should at least have the basic methods to manipulate associated data. In the most abstract sense, the model represents raw data or knowledge. It's where the data intersects with your application code. For example, the database might store several properties like `access-Scopes`, `authenticated`, and so on. But the model will be able to use this data for a method like `isAllowedAccessForResource()` on it that will act on the underlying data to model. The model is where raw data converges with your application code.
- *View*—A representation of your model. The view is often the user interface itself. The view shouldn't have any logic in it that isn't related to presentation of the data. For front-end frameworks, this would generally mean that a particular view was directly associated with a resource and would have CRUD (create, read, update, delete) actions associated with it. This isn't how front-end applications are always built anymore.
- *Controller*—Controllers are the "glue" that binds the model and view together. Controllers should usually be only glue and not much more (for example, they shouldn't have complex view or database logic in them). You should generally expect controllers to have far less ability to mutate data than the models they interact with.

The paradigms we're going to focus on in this chapter (Flux and Redux) depart from these concepts but still have the goal of helping you create a scalable, sensible, and effective application architecture.

Redux owes its origin and design to a pattern popularized at Facebook, called *Flux*. If you're familiar with the popular MVC pattern that Ruby on Rails and other application frameworks use, Flux might be a departure from what you're used to. Rather than break parts of your application into models, views, and controllers, Flux defines several different parts to it:

- *Store*—Stores contain the application state and logic; they're somewhat like a model in a traditional MVC. However, instead of representing a single database record, they manage the state of many objects. Unlike a model, you represent the data however it makes sense, unconstrained by resources.
- *Actions*—Rather than update state directly, Flux apps modify their state by creating actions that modify state.
- *View*—The user interface, usually React, but Flux doesn't require React.
- *Dispatcher*—A central coordinator of actions and updates to stores.

Figure 10.1 shows an overview of Flux.

Figure 10.1   A simple Flux overview

In the Flux pattern, as shown in figure 10.1, actions are created from views—this might be a user clicking something. From there, the dispatcher handles incoming actions. Actions are then sent to the appropriate store to update state. State, having changed, notifies a view that new data should be used (if applicable). Notice how this would differ from a typical MVC-style framework, where the view and a model (like the store here) would both be able to update the other. This bidirectional data flow differs from the more unidirectional flow typical in Flux architectures. Also, note that middleware is missing here: although possible to create in Flux, it is less of a first-class citizen than in Redux, so we omit it here.

If some of these parts sound familiar, the way data flows in Flux might not be if you've worked with MVC-style applications before. As mentioned, data flows more unidirectionally in the Flux paradigm, which differs from the bidirectional manner MVC-type implementations tend to enforce. This usually means that there's no single place in an app where data flows from; many different parts of the system have authority to modify state, and state is often decentralized throughout the application. This approach works well in many cases, but in larger apps, it can be confusing to debug and work with.

Think what this might look like in a medium-to-large application. Say you had a collection of models (user, account, and authentication) that were associated with their own controllers and views. At any given place in the application, it could be difficult to pin down the exact location of state because it's distributed across parts of the application (information about a user could be found on any of the three models I mentioned).

This might not necessarily be a problem for smaller apps and can even be made to work well for larger applications, but it can become more difficult in nontrivial client-side applications. For example, what happens when things you need in order to modify a model's use in 50 different locations and 60 different controllers need to know about changes to state? Making matters more complicated is the fact that views sometimes act like models in some front-end frameworks (so state is even more decentralized). Where's the source of truth for your data? If it's spread across views and many different models, and all in a moderately complex setup, mentally keeping track of everything is going to be difficult. This can also result in inconsistent application state that causes application bugs, so it's not just a "developer-only" problem—end-users are directly affected as well.

Part of the reason why this is difficult is that people generally aren't good at reasoning about change that occurs over time. To drive this home, imagine a checkers board in your head. It's not so hard to hold maybe one or even a few snapshots of the board in your head. But would you be able to keep track of every snapshot of the board after 20 turns? Thirty? The entire game? We should be building systems that are easier for us to think about and use because keeping mental track of asynchronous changes to data over time is hard. For example, think of calling a remote API and using the data to update your application state. Simple for a handful of cases, but what if you have to call 50 different endpoints and need to keep track of the incoming responses while a user is still using the app and making changes that could result in more API interaction? It can be hard to mentally line them all up in a row and predict what the result of changes would be.

You may already notice some similarities between React and Flux. They're both relatively new approaches to building user interfaces and they both aim to improve the mental model a developer works with. In each, changes should be easy to reason about, and you should be able to build your UI in a way that empowers you instead of hinders you.

What does Flux look like in code? It's primarily a paradigm, so there are plenty of libraries available that implement the core ideas of Flux. They're all slightly different from one another in how they implement Flux. Redux does this, too, even though its particular flavor of Flux has gained the most use and mindshare. Other Flux libraries include Flummox, Fluxxor, Reflux, Fluxible, Lux, McFly, and MartyJS (though in practice you'll see little use of these compared to Redux).

10.1.1 *Meet Redux: A variation on Flux*

Perhaps the most widely used and well-known library that implements the ideas behind Flux is Redux. Redux is a library that implements the ideas of Flux in a slightly modified way. Redux is described by its own documentation as "a predictable state container for JavaScript apps." In concrete terms, this means it's a library that puts into practice the concepts and ideas of Flux in its own way.

Nailing down exact definitions of what is and isn't considered Flux is not important here, but I should cover some of the important differences between the Flux and Redux paradigms:

- *Redux uses a single store*—Rather than locate state information in multiple stores across the app, Redux apps keep everything in one place. In Flux, you can have many different stores. Redux breaks from this and enforces a single global store.
- *Redux introduces reducers*—Reducers are a more immutable approach to mutation. In Redux, state is changed in a predictable and deterministic way, one part of state at a time, and only in one place (the global store).
- *Redux introduces middleware*—Because actions and data flow in a unidirectional way, you can add middleware to your Redux app and inject custom behavior as data is updated.
- *Redux actions are decoupled from the store*—Action-creators don't dispatch anything to the store; instead, they return action objects that a central dispatcher uses.

These may be subtle differences to you, and that's okay—your goal is learning about Redux, not doing a "spot the differences" exercise. Figure 10.2 shows an overview of the Redux architecture. You'll dive into each of the different sections, explore how they work, and develop a Redux architecture for your app.

As you can see in figure 10.2, actions, a store, and reducers make up the bulk of the Redux architecture. Redux uses a single centralized state object that's updated in specific, deterministic ways. An action is created when you want to update state (usually due to an event like a click). The action will have a type that a certain reducer will handle. The reducer that handles the given action type will make a copy of the current state, modify it with data from the action, and then return the new state. When the store is updated, view layers (React in our case) can listen to updates and respond accordingly. Also note that in the figure the views are just reading in updates from the store—they don't care about the data being communicated to them. The `React-redux` library handles passing new props to components when the store changes, but views still just receive and display data.

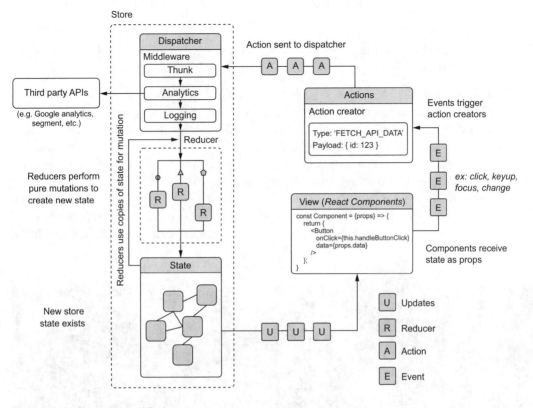

Figure 10.2   **An overview of Redux**

10.1.2 *Getting set up for Redux*

Redux is a paradigm for your application architecture, but it's also a library you can install. This is one area where Redux shines over a "raw" Flux implementation. There are so many implementations of the Flux paradigm—Flummox, Fluxxor, Reflux, Flux-ible, Lux, McFly, and MartyJS, to name a few—and they all have varying degrees of community support and different APIs. Redux enjoys strong community support, but the Redux library itself has a small, powerful API that has helped it become one of the most popular and relied-upon libraries for React application architecture. In fact, it's so common to see Redux used with React that the core teams for each library often interact with each other and ensure compatibility and feature-awareness. Some people are even on both teams, so there's generally great visibility and communication between the projects.

To get set up to use Redux, you're going to need to do a few things:

- Make sure you've run `npm install` with the source code from the current chapter so all the right dependencies are installed locally. In this chapter, you'll start to take advantage of some new libraries, including `js-cookie`, `redux-mock-store`, and `redux`.

- Install the Redux developer tools. You can use them to inspect the Redux store and actions in the browser.

Redux is predictable by design and that makes it easy to create some amazing debugging tools. Engineers like Dan Abramov and others who work on the Redux and React libraries have helped create some powerful tools for working with Redux applications. Because the state in Redux changes in predictable ways, debugging in new ways is possible: you can track individual changes to your app state, inspect differences between changes, and even rewind and replay your app state over time. The Redux Dev Tools extension lets you do all this and more and comes bundled as a browser extension. To install it for your browser, follow the instructions at https://github.com/zalmoxisus/redux-devtools-extension. Figure 10.3 shows a sneak peek of what's available with the Redux Dev Tools.

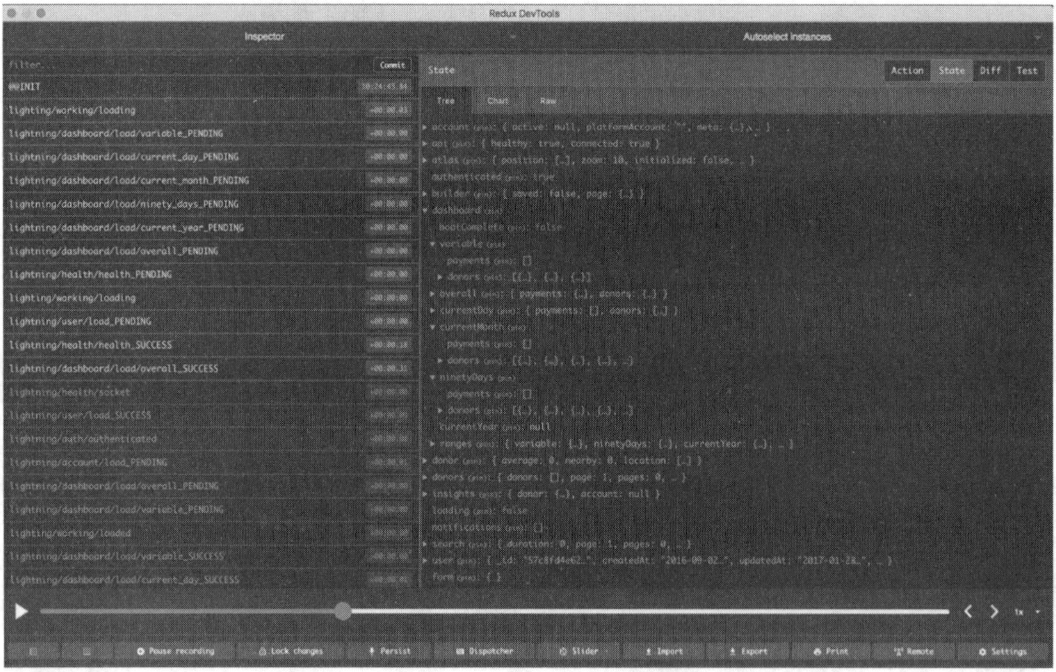

Figure 10.3   The Redux Dev Tools extension bundles the popular Redux Dev Tools library from Dan Abramov in a convenient browser extension. With it, you can rewind and replay your Redux app, inspect changes one by one, examine diffs between changes in state, review your entire app state in one area, generate testing boilerplate, and more.

After installing the extension, you should see the new Dev Tools icon in your browser toolbar. As of the time of writing, it only appears colorized when it detects a Redux app instance in development mode, so if you visit the app or other sites that don't have Redux set up, the extension won't work yet. But once you configure the app, you'll see the icon appear with color, and clicking it will open the tools.

10.2 Creating actions in Redux

In Redux, actions are payloads of information that send data from your application to your store. Apart from an action, the store doesn't have any other way to get data. Actions are used throughout a Redux application to initiate changes in data, although they themselves are not responsible for updating the state (store) of the app. Reducers are more involved with that part of the architecture, and we'll look at those after actions. If you're used to being able to update the state of your app however you like, you may not like actions at first. They can take some getting used to, but they lead to apps that are usually more predictable and easier to debug. If the way data changes in your app is tightly controlled, you can easily predict what should and shouldn't have changed in your app. Figure 10.4 shows where actions fit into the broader picture. We're starting with actions and will work our way through the Redux flow, through the store, reducers, and eventually back to React to complete the data flow.

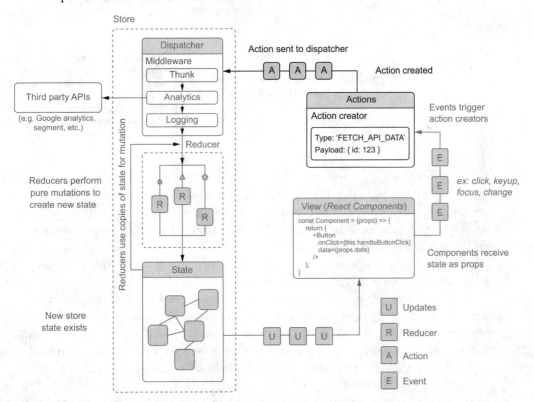

Figure 10.4   Actions are how your Redux application knows to change; they have a type and any additional information that your app needs.

What does a Redux action look like? It's a plain old JavaScript object (POJO) with a required *type* key and anything else you want on it. The type key will be used by reducers and other Redux tools to associate a set of changes together. Every unique type of action should have a unique type key. Types should typically be defined as string constants, and you're free to use whatever unique names you like for these, although coming up with a naming pattern to follow is a good idea. Listing 10.1 shows a few examples of the action type names you might come up with.

In general, you should keep your actions so they only have the information on them that they absolutely need. That way, you'll avoid passing extra data around and have less information to think about. The next listing shows two simple actions, one with additional data on it and one without. Note that you can name the additional keys on actions whatever you want, but this can be confusing if you aren't consistent and is especially problematic for teams.

Listing 10.1   Some simple Redux actions

```
{
    type: 'UPDATE_USER_PROFILE',
    payload: {
        email: 'hello@ifelse.io'
    }
}

{
    'type: 'LOADING'
}

{
    type: appName/dashboard/insights/load'
}
```

An action can contain info that will tell your application about how it should change, like a new user email address, error diagnostics, or other info.

Every action must have a type—without a type, your app doesn't know what sort of changes you need to make to the store.

Types are usually uppercase string constants so you can tell them apart from regular values in your app, but here I use a name-spacing scheme to ensure actions are unique but readable.

10.2.1   *Defining action types*

Although you may add more later in the chapter, you can start transitioning your Letters Social app to a Redux architecture by laying out some action types. These will usually map to user actions such as logging in, logging out, changing a form value, and so on, but they don't necessarily have to be user actions. You may want to create action types for an opened, resolved, or errored network request or any other number of things that don't directly pertain to a user.

It's also worth noting that in a smaller app, you might not necessarily have to define your action types in a constants file; you could just as well remember to pass them in when you create actions or hardcode them yourself. The downside is that as your app grows, keeping track of action types will be a pain point and could lead to difficult debugging or refactoring situations. In most real-world cases, you'll define your actions, so that's what you'll do here, too.

You'll sketch out a few action types that you can expect to use, but you can feel free to add or remove them over time as needed. You'll use the name-spacing approach to action types here, but remember when creating your own actions that you can follow whatever pattern you feel is best as long as they are unique. You'll also "bundle" similar action types together in objects, but they could just as easily be spread out and exported as individual constants. The advantage to bundling is that you can group them together and use shorter names (GET, CREATE, and so on) without having to build those into the variable names themselves (UPDATE_USER_PROFILE, CREATE_NEW _POST, and so on). Listing 10.2 shows how to create your initial action types. You'll put these in src/constants/types.js. You're creating all the actions you'll need for this chapter right now so you can reference them and don't have to constantly go back to the file.

Listing 10.2 Defining action types (src/contstants/types.js)

```
export const app = {
    ERROR: 'letters-social/app/error',
    LOADED: 'letters-social/app/loaded',
    LOADING: 'letters-social/app/loading'
};

export const auth = {
    LOGIN_SUCCESS: 'letters-social/auth/login/success',
    LOGOUT_SUCCESS: 'letters-social/auth/logout/success'
};

export const posts = {
    CREATE: 'letters-social/post/create',
    GET: 'letters-social/post/get',
    LIKE: 'letters-social/post/like',
    NEXT: 'letters-social/post/paginate/next',
    UNLIKE: 'letters-social/post/unlike',
    UPDATE_LINKS: 'letters-social/post/paginate/update'
};

export const comments = {
    CREATE: 'letters-social/comments/create',
    GET: 'letters-social/comments/get',
    SHOW: 'letters-social/comments/show',
    TOGGLE: 'letters-social/comments/toggle'
};
```

When using the Redux developer tools, these action types will show up in a timeline of your app's state changes, so grouping names in a URL-like fashion like in listing 10.2 can make them easier to read when you have many actions and action types. You could also use : characters to separate them (namespace:action_name:status) or use whatever convention makes the most sense to you.

10.2.2 *Creating actions in Redux*

Now that you have some types defined, you can start doing something with actions. You'll reuse logic from preexisting parts of the app, so a lot of the code may look familiar to you. This is actually a good point to reflect on briefly: most of a Redux app shouldn't be a complete redo of any existing application logic. Hopefully, you're able to clean it up, but the main work of converting it to use Redux can potentially just be mapping the different aspects of your application state to the patterns Redux enforces. At any rate, we need to get started with actions.

Actions are how you initiate state changes in Redux applications; you can't just modify a property directly like you might in other frameworks. Actions are created with *action creators*—functions that return an action object—and dispatched by the store using a `dispatch` function.

We don't want to get too far ahead of ourselves here. I'll just cover the action creators themselves first. You'll start simple and create some actions that should indicate to your app when loading has started and completed. You won't need to pass any additional information in this time, but I'll cover parameterized action creators next. The next listing shows how to create two action creators for loading and loaded actions. To keep things organized, you'll put any action creators under the actions directory. The same will go for other Redux-related files; reducers and the store will get their own directories, too.

> **Listing 10.3** `loading` and `loaded` action creators (src/actions/loading.js)

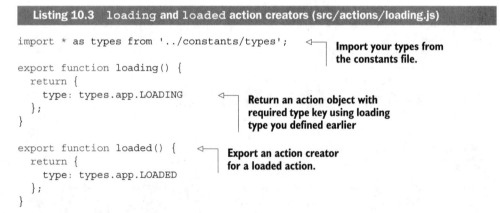

```
import * as types from '../constants/types';        ◁──┐  Import your types from
                                                          the constants file.
export function loading() {
  return {
    type: types.app.LOADING      ◁──┐  Return an action object with
  };                                   required type key using loading
}                                      type you defined earlier

export function loaded() {        ◁──┐  Export an action creator
  return {                              for a loaded action.
    type: types.app.LOADED
  };
}
```

10.2.3 *Creating the Redux store and dispatching actions*

Action creators won't do anything by themselves to change your app state (they just return objects). You need to use the dispatcher provided by Redux in order for the action creators to have any effect. The `dispatch` function is provided by the Redux store itself and will be the way you send actions into Redux to be handled. You'll set up the Redux store next so you can use its `dispatch` function with your actions.

Before you set up your store, you'll need to create a root reducer file that will allow you to create a valid store; the reducer won't do anything until later when you look at reducers and build them out. You'll create a folder called reducers in src and inside it a file, root.js. In this file, you'll use the `combineReducers` function provided by Redux to set up where your future reducers will go. This function does exactly what it sounds like it does: combines multiple reducers into one.

Without the ability to combine reducers, you'd run into issues with conflicts between multiple reducers and would have to find ways to merge reducers or route actions. This is one area where the benefits of Redux can be tangibly observed. There's a bit more work in setting everything up, but once the work is done, Redux makes it easier to scale application state management. The next listing shows how to create the root reducer file.

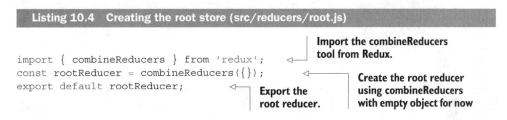

Listing 10.4 Creating the root store (src/reducers/root.js)

```
import { combineReducers } from 'redux';        ⊲── Import the combineReducers
const rootReducer = combineReducers({});        ◁   tool from Redux.
export default rootReducer;          ◁              Create the root reducer
                      Export the                    using combineReducers
                      root reducer.                 with empty object for now
```

Now that you have a reducer set up for Redux to use, you'll configure and set up the store. Create a folder called store and create several files inside it: store.js, stores/store .prod.js, and stores/store.dev.js. These files are responsible for exporting a function that creates your store for you and, if you're in development mode, integrates the developer tools. Listing 10.5 shows creating the store-related files side by side in the same listing. You're using different files for each environment here because you might want to include different middleware and other libraries for development and production environments. This just a convention—there's nothing about Redux that requires you to put functions in many files or one.

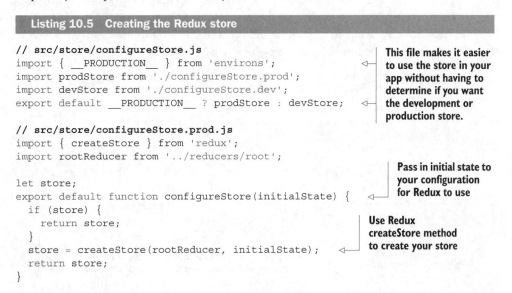

Listing 10.5 Creating the Redux store

```
// src/store/configureStore.js
import { __PRODUCTION__ } from 'environs';           ◁── This file makes it easier
import prodStore from './configureStore.prod';            to use the store in your
import devStore from './configureStore.dev';              app without having to
export default __PRODUCTION__ ? prodStore : devStore;  ◁  determine if you want
                                                          the development or
                                                          production store.

// src/store/configureStore.prod.js
import { createStore } from 'redux';
import rootReducer from '../reducers/root';
                                                   Pass in initial state to
let store;                                         your configuration
export default function configureStore(initialState) {  ◁─ for Redux to use
  if (store) {
    return store;                                  Use Redux
  }                                                createStore method
  store = createStore(rootReducer, initialState);  ◁─ to create your store
  return store;
}
```

```
// src/store/configureStore.dev.js
import thunk from 'redux-thunk';
import { createStore, compose} from 'redux';      ⟵  Import compose utility
import rootReducer from '../reducers/root';            from Redux, which will let
                                                       you combine middleware

let store;
export default initialState => {
    if (store) {                              ⟵  Make sure you're accessing the same
        return store;                            store consistently—this ensures you
    }                                            return the same store if another file
    const createdStore = createStore(            accesses an already-created store.
        rootReducer,
        initialState,
        compose(window.devToolsExtension())   ⟵  If dev tools extension
    );                                            is installed, this will
    store = createdStore;                         hook into it
    return store;
};
```

Now that you have a store configured and ready to use, you can try dispatching some
actions and see how they work. Before long, you'll hook Redux up to React, but
remember that you don't have to use Redux with React or with any library or framework. There are other open-source projects using Redux to integrate with frameworks
like Angular, Vue, and more.

The Redux store exposes a couple of important functions that you'll use throughout working with Redux: getState and dispatch. getState will be used to grab a
snapshot of your Redux store state at a given point in time, and dispatch is how you'll
send actions to the Redux store. When calling the dispatch method, you pass in an
action that's the result of calling an action creator. Using the store.dispatch()
method is the only way to trigger a state change in Redux, so you'll be using it all over
the place. Next you'll try using the store to dispatch a few actions using the loading
action creators that you set up before. The following listing shows how to dispatch a
few actions using a temporary file (src/store/exampleUse.js). This file is just for
demonstration purposes and won't be needed to make the main app work.

> **Listing 10.6 Dispatching actions (src/store/exampleUse.js)**

```
import configureStore from './configureStore';         ⟵  Import configureStore
import { loading, loaded } from '../actions/loading';      method and use it to
const store = configureStore();                            create a store

console.log('========== Example store ==========');
store.dispatch(loading());
store.dispatch(loaded());          ⟵  Dispatch
store.dispatch(loading());            another action.
store.dispatch(loaded());
console.log('========== end example store ==========');
```

          Call store's dispatch method and pass in invoked action
          creator; will return object for dispatch method to use

To dispatch these actions, all you need to do is import the exampleUse file into your main app file, and it will run when you open the app. Listing 10.7 shows the minor modification you need to make to src/index.js. Once you connect Redux to React, you'll interact with Redux through React components and won't need to manually dispatch actions like you are here for demonstration purposes.

Listing 10.7   Importing the exampleUse file (src/index.js)

```
import React from 'react';
import { render } from 'react-dom';

import { App } from './containers/App';
import { Home, SinglePost, Login, NotFound, Profile } from './containers';
import { Router, Route } from './components/router';
import { history } from './history';
import { firebase } from './backend';
import configureStore from './store/configureStore';
import initialReduxState from './constants/initialState';

import './store/exampleUse';        ⊲——┤  Import the store file so it will
//...                                      run when you open the app.
```

If you load the app in development mode (using npm run dev), you should see that the Redux dev tools icon is enabled. When the app runs now, the imported file that you've created will run and invoke the store dispatcher several times, sending actions off to the store. Right now, there isn't any handling set up for the actions (via reducers), and you haven't hooked anything up to React, so there won't be any meaningful changes. But if you open the developer tools and look at the action history, you should see an action dispatched and recorded for each of the loading actions you dispatched. Figure 10.5 shows the actions being dispatched in the context of your diagram and the results you should see in the Redux developer tools.

10.2.4   Asynchronous actions and middleware

You can dispatch actions, but right now they're only synchronous. There are many cases where you'll want to make a change to your app based on an *asynchronous* action. These might be a network request, reading a value back from the browser (via local storage, cookie stores, and so forth), working with WebSockets, or any other async action. Redux doesn't have support for asynchronous actions out of the box because it expects actions to just be objects (not Promises or anything else). But you can enable it by integrating a library you've already installed: redux-thunk.

redux-thunk is a Redux *middleware* library, which means it works as a sort of "on the way" or pass-through mechanism for Redux. You've probably used other APIs that make use of this concept, like Express or Koa (server-side frameworks for Node.js). Middleware works by letting you hook into a cycle or process of some kind in a composable way, meaning that you can create and use multiple middleware functionalities independent of each other in a single project.

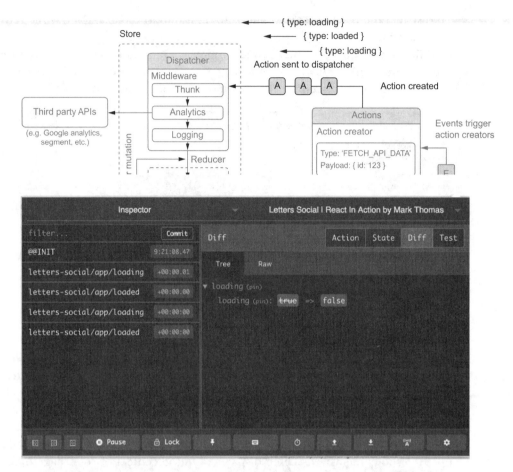

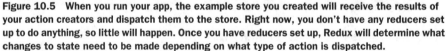

Figure 10.5   When you run your app, the example store you created will receive the results of your action creators and dispatch them to the store. Right now, you don't have any reducers set up to do anything, so little will happen. Once you have reducers set up, Redux will determine what changes to state need to be made depending on what type of action is dispatched.

Redux middleware is, in the words of the Redux docs, a "third-party extension point between dispatching an action and the moment it reaches the reducer." This means you have one or more opportunities to act on or because of an action before it gets handled by a reducer. You'll use Redux middleware to create an error-handling solution next, but right now you can use the `redux-thunk` middleware to enable asynchronous action creation in your application. Listing 10.8 shows how to integrate the `redux-thunk` middleware into your app. Note that you should add the middleware to both your production and development stores (configureStore.prod.js and configureStore.dev.js). Remember, you can choose whatever production/development store setup makes the most sense for your situation—I only broke them into two here to make clear which one gets used for each environment.

Listing 10.8   Enabling asynchronous action creators via redux-thunk

```
import thunk from 'redux-thunk';
import { createStore, compose, applyMiddleware } from 'redux';
import rootReducer from '../reducers/root';

let store;
export default (initialState) => {
  if (store) {
    return store;
  }
  const createdStore = createStore(rootReducer, initialState, compose(
    applyMiddleware(
      thunk,
    ),
    window.devToolsExtension()
    )
  );
  store = createdStore;
  return store;
};
```

To integrate middleware into your Redux store, pull in applyMiddleware utility

Insert and order middleware in Redux within the applyMiddleware function—here you're inserting the redux-thunk middleware into your store.

You can create async action creators now that you have the `redux-thunk` middleware installed. Why do I say *async action creators* and not *asynchronous actions*? Because even when you're doing asynchronous things like making network requests, the actions you create aren't the asynchronous tasks themselves. Instead, `redux-thunk` teaches your Redux store to evaluate a Promise when it comes through. The course of that Promise is how you dispatch actions for your store. Nothing has really changed about Redux. The actions are still synchronous, but Redux now knows to wait for Promises to resolve when you pass them into the dispatch function.

In earlier chapters, you created some logic to fetch posts from your API using the `isomorphic-fetch` library and display them using React. Actions like these that perform asynchronous work will often require multiple actions to be dispatched (usually loading, success, and failure actions). For example, say you want to let a user upload files to a server that sends back progress data over the duration of the upload. One way of mapping actions to the different parts of this process would be to create an action to indicate that the upload has started, an action to tell the rest of the app that something is loading, an action for progress updates from the server, an action for the completion of the upload, and an action to handle errors.

`redux-thunk` works by wrapping the dispatch method of a store so that it will handle dispatching something other than plain objects (like Promises, an API dealing with asynchronous flows). The middleware will dispatch created actions asynchronously (at the beginning and end of a request, for example) as the Promise is executed and let you handle those changes appropriately. As already noted, the key distinction here is that actions themselves are still synchronous, but when they get dispatched and sent to reducers they are asynchronous. Figure 10.6 shows how this works.

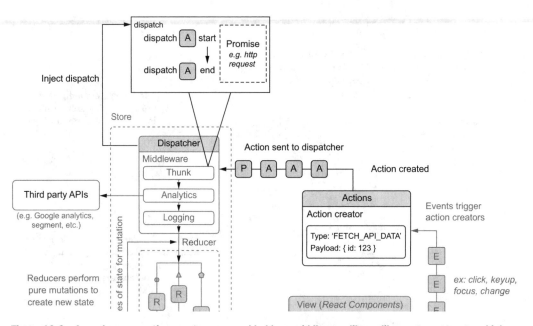

Figure 10.6 Asynchronous action creators are enabled by a middleware library like `redux-thunk`, which allows you to dispatch something besides an action like a Promise (a way to do asynchronous work that's part of the JavaScript specification). It will resolve the Promise and let you dispatch actions at different points over the lifetime of the Promise (before execution, on completion, on error, and so on).

Next you'll use what you know about async action creators to write some action creators that will handle fetching and creating posts. Because `redux-thunk` wraps the store's dispatch method, you can return a function from your action creator that receives the dispatch method as a function, allowing you to dispatch multiple actions over the course of a Promise execution. Listing 10.9 shows what this sort of action creator looks like. You'll create several async action creators and a synchronous one. You'll start by creating a handful of actions you'll need to handle user interactions with posts and comments. First up is an error action that you'll use to show the user error information if something goes wrong. In a larger application, you'll probably need to create more than one way to handle errors, but for our purposes this should suffice. You can use this error action here and also in any component error boundaries. `componentDidCatch` will provide error information you can dispatch to the store.

Listing 10.9 Creating the error action (src/actions/error.js)

```
import * as types from '../constants/types';
export function createError(error, info) {        ◁⟶ This action creator is
    return {                                           parameterized—you want to send
        type: types.app.ERROR,       ◁⟶                error information to your store.
        error,
        info              ⟍  Pass along actual        This action has generic app error
    };                        error and info          type—in larger apps you'll have
}                                                      many types of errors
```

Now that you have a way to handle errors, you can start to write some async action creators. You'll start with comments and move on to posts. The posts and comments actions should look similar overall with some minor differences in how each set of actions works. You want the ability to do a few things related to comments: show and hide them, load them, and create a new comment for a given post. Listing 10.10 shows the comment actions you'll create.

As you create these and other actions, you'll continue to use the isomorphic-fetch library to do network requests, but the Fetch API that it follows is becoming more standard in browsers and is now the de facto way to do network requests. When possible, you'll keep using the Web platform APIs or libraries that follow the same specifications.

Listing 10.10 Creating comment actions (src/actions/comments.js)

```
import * as types from '../constants/types';
import * as API from '../shared/http';              Import your
import { createError } from './error';              API helpers.

export function showComments(postId) {              Create parameterized action
    return {                                        creator so you can show a
        type: types.comments.SHOW,                  particular comments section.
        postId
    };
}
export function toggleComments(postId) {            You want the ability to
    return {                                        toggle a comment section.
        type: types.comments.TOGGLE,
        postId
    };
}
                                                    Create ability to get
                                                    comments—your async
export function updateAvailableComments(comments) { action creators in this file
    return {                                        will use this function
        type: types.comments.GET,
        comments
    };
}                                                   Create comment from a given
                                                    payload; return a function
export function createComment(payload) {            instead of a plain object
    return dispatch => {
        return API.createComment(payload)           The Fetch API implements Promise-
            .then(res => res.json())                based methods like json() and blob().
            .then(comment => {
                dispatch({                          Dispatch create comment
                    type: types.comments.CREATE,    action with comment JSON
                    comment                          you get back from server
                });
            })
                                                    If you receive an error,
            .catch(err => dispatch(createError(err)));   send it to store using
    };                                              createError action
}
export function getCommentsForPost(postId) {        Fetch comments for a particular
    return dispatch => {                            post and use updateAvailable-
        return API.fetchCommentsForPost(postId)     Comments action
```

```
                  ┌──▷  .then(res => res.json())
Handle the        │     .then(comments => dispatch(updateAvailableComments(comments)))
error, if any.    └──▷  .catch(err => dispatch(createError(err)));
            };
    }
```

Now that you've created actions for comments, you can move on to creating actions for posts. The actions for posts will be similar to the ones you've just created but will also use some comment actions. The ability to mix and match different actions across your application is another reason Redux works well as your application architecture. It provides a structured, repeatable way to create functionality with actions and then utilize that functionality across your app.

Next you'll keep creating actions and add some functionality to your posts. In earlier chapters, you created functionality for fetching and creating posts. Now you'll also create ways to like and unlike posts. The next listing shows the action creators related to posts in your application. You'll start with four action creators for now and then explore a few more in the next listing.

Listing 10.11   Creator async and synchronous actions (src/actions/posts.js)

```
import parseLinkHeader from 'parse-link-header';        ◁──┐  JSON API uses Link
                                                           │  headers to indicate
import * as types from '../constants/types';              │  paging options
import * as API from '../shared/http';
import { createError } from './error';
import { getCommentsForPost } from './comments';


export function updateAvailablePosts(posts) {     ◁──┐  As you did with
    return {                                          │  comments, this action
        type: types.posts.GET,                        │  creator will pass along
        posts                                         │  new comments to store.
    };
}
export function updatePaginationLinks(links) {    ◁──┘  Update pagination links
    return {                                             in store accordingly
        type: types.posts.UPDATE_LINKS,
        links
    };
}                                         ┌──  Like a particular
export function like(postId) {        ◁──┘    post using its ID.
    return (dispatch, getState) => {
        const { user } = getState();                 ┐  Return function will have the
        return API.likePost(postId, user.id)         │  dispatch and getState methods
            .then(res => res.json())                 │  injected into it by Redux
            .then(post => {
                dispatch({                 ◁──┐  Dispatch LIKE action
                    type: types.posts.LIKE,     │  with post attached
                    post                        │  as metadata
                });
            })
```

```
                .catch(err => dispatch(createError(err)));
        };
    }
    export function unlike(postId) {                    ⟵⎤  Unliking a post involves
        return (dispatch, getState) => {                    │  same flow, but dispatches
            const { user } = getState();                    │  a different action type
            return API.unlikePost(postId, user.id)
                .then(res => res.json())
                .then(post => {
                    dispatch({
                        type: types.posts.UNLIKE,
                        post
                    });
                })
                .catch(err => dispatch(createError(err)));
        };
    }
```

You still need to create a few more action types for posts. You can like and unlike posts, but you still haven't ported over the post creation you previously created. You also need a way to fetch a number of posts and single posts individually. Listing 10.12 shows the corresponding action creators you'll need to create.

Hopefully by now you're starting to get the hang of asynchronous action creators. In many apps, these sorts of action creators are pretty common. But the possibilities don't end here. I've found using redux-thunk by itself to be sufficient for most applications that need asynchronous action creation, but people have created plenty of other libraries to address this need. For example, check out Redux Saga at https://github.com/redux-saga/redux-saga.

Listing 10.12 Creating more post action creators (src/actions/posts.js)

```
//...

export function createNewPost(post) {
    return (dispatch, getState) => {              ⟵⎤  As before, use getState function
        const { user } = getState();                  │  to access snapshot of state
        post.userId = user.id;                    ⟵⎤
        return API.createPost(post)                   │  Embed user ID
            .then(res => res.json())                  │  on new post
            .then(newPost => {
                dispatch({                        ⟵⎤  Dispatch a create
                    type: types.posts.CREATE,         │  post action.
                    post: newPost
                });
            })
            .catch(err => dispatch(createError(err)));
    };
}
    export function getPostsForPage(page = 'first') {
        return (dispatch, getState) => {          ⟵⎤  Grab pagination
            const { pagination } = getState();        │  state object
            const endpoint = pagination[page];
```

```
            return API.fetchPosts(endpoint)
                .then(res => {
                    const links = parseLinkHeader(res.headers.get('Link'));
                    return res.json().then(posts => {
                        dispatch(updatePaginationLinks(links));
                        dispatch(updateAvailablePosts(posts));
                    });
                })
                .catch(err => dispatch(createError(err)));
        };
    }
    export function loadPost(postId) {
        return dispatch => {
            return API.fetchPost(postId)
                .then(res => res.json())
                .then(post => {
                    dispatch(updateAvailablePosts([post]));
                    dispatch(getCommentsForPost(postId));
                })
                .catch(err => dispatch(createError(err)));
        };
    }
```

Use link header parser and pass in Link header

Dispatch link action

Dispatch update posts action

Load post from API and fetch its associated comments

10.2.5 *To Redux or not to Redux?*

With those action creators done, you've created the initial functionality for creating posts and comments. You're still missing one area, though: authentication for the user. In previous chapters, you were using Firebase helpers to check for the user's authentication state and update the local component state with that. Do you need to do the same thing with authentication? That brings up another good question: what belongs in Redux and what doesn't? Let's look at this somewhat contentious question before moving on.

Opinions in the React/Redux community vary from "put whatever you want in the store" to "absolutely everything must go in the store." There's also a tendency for engineers who have only worked with React in a Redux context to see that as the only way to go and think of React and Redux as one and the same. People are often limited by their experience, but my hope is that we can take time to consider the facts and tradeoffs before forming an immovable opinion.

For one, it's important to remember that although React and Redux fit well together, the technologies themselves aren't intrinsically linked. You don't need Redux to build React applications. I hope you've seen that in this book. Redux is just another tool available to engineers—it's not the only way to build your React applications and is certainly not something that invalidates "normal" React concepts (local component state, for example). There are some cases where you might simply be adding overhead by bringing a component's state into Redux.

What should you do? So far, Redux has proven to be a great way to give your application a robust architecture that has already helped you better organize code and functionality (and we haven't even gotten to reducers yet!). Based on your experience so far, you may be tempted to quickly agree with the "absolutely everything should be in the Redux store" point of view. But I want to caution against this impulse and look at the tradeoffs instead.

In my experience, there are a couple questions we can ask to guide decisions about what does and doesn't belong in the Redux store. The first one is this: do many other parts of the application need to know about this piece of state or functionality? If so, it should probably go in the Redux store. If the state is completely localized to a component, you should consider leaving it out of the Redux store. One example is something like a dropdown menu that doesn't need to be controlled except by the user. If your app needs to control whether the dropdown is open or closed and respond to it opening or closing, those state changes should probably go through the store. But if not, keeping the state local to the component is fine.

Another question is whether the state you're dealing with would be simplified or better expressed in Redux. If you're taking the state and actions for a component and translating them into Redux for the sake of doing so, you're probably introducing additional complexity for yourself and not getting much for it. But if your state is complicated or particular enough that Redux would make it easier to work with, you might want to include it in the store.

With those things in mind, let's revisit the question of whether you should integrate the user and authentication logic into Redux. Do other parts of the application need to know about the user? They certainly do. Would you be able to better express the user logic in Redux? Without centralizing it in the store, you might need to replicate the logic across different pages in your application, and that might not be ideal. For the time being it looks like it makes sense to integrate the user and authentication logic into Redux.

Let's see how to create some actions! Listing 10.13 shows the user-related actions you'll create. You'll use a modern feature of the JavaScript language in these examples, async/await. If you're unfamiliar with how this part of the language works, it might help to read through the Mozilla Developer Network documentation (https://developer.mozilla.org/en-US/docs/Web/JavaScript/Reference/Statements/async_function) and the chapter on async/await in *Exploring ES2016 and ES2017* by Dr. Axel Rauschmayer (Leanpub, 2017; http://exploringjs.com/es2016-es2017/ch_async-functions.html).

Listing 10.13 Creating user-related actions (src/actions/auth.js)

```
import * as types from '../constants/types';
import { history } from '../history';
import { createError } from './error';
import { loading, loaded } from './loading';
import { getFirebaseUser, loginWithGithub, logUserOut, getFirebaseToken }
    from '../backend/auth';
```

> Import modules you'll need for
> your auth-related actions.

```
export function loginSuccess(user, token) {
    return {
        type: types.auth.LOGIN_SUCCESS,
        user,
        token
    };
}
export function logoutSuccess() {
    return {
        type: types.auth.LOGOUT_SUCCESS
    };
}
export function logout() {
    return dispatch => {
        return logUserOut()
            .then(() => {
                history.push('/login');
                dispatch(logoutSuccess());
                window.Raven.setUserContext();
            })
            .catch(err => dispatch(createError(err)));
    };
}
export function login() {
    return dispatch => {
        return loginWithGithub().then(async () => {
            try {
                dispatch(loading());
                const user = await getFirebaseUser();
                const token = await getFirebaseToken();
                const res = await API.loadUser(user.uid);
                if (res.status === 404) {
                    const userPayload = {
                        name: user.displayName,
                        profilePicture: user.photoURL,
                        id: user.uid
                    };
                    const newUser = await API.createUser(userPayload).then(res
                        => res.json());
                    dispatch(loginSuccess(newUser, token));
                    dispatch(loaded());
                    history.push('/');
                    return newUser;
                }
                const existingUser = await res.json();
                dispatch(loginSuccess(existingUser, token));
                dispatch(loaded());
                history.push('/');
                return existingUser;
            } catch (err) {
                createError(err);
            }
        });
    };
}
```

Create login and logout action creators—login action will be parameterized to accept user and token

Log user out using Firebase

Push user to login page, dispatch logout action, and clear user context (for error-tracking library)

Log user in with Firebase

Async/await uses try...catch error-handling semantics

Try finding user you got back from Firebase with API—if they don't exist (404), must sign them up using info from Firebase

Get user and token from Firebase using await

Create new user

Dispatch login actions with new user and return from function

If user already existed, dispatch appropriate login actions and return

Catch error in login process and dispatch it to store

After all that, you've created actions for user-related actions, comments, posts, loading, and errors. If that seemed like a lot, you'll be glad to know that what you've done is create the bulk of the raw functionality of the app. You still need to teach Redux how to respond to state changes with reducers in the next section and then wire everything up to React, but the actions you've re-created represent all the basic ways you (or a user) can interact with your application. This is another strength of Redux: you end up doing work to turn functionality into actions, but in the end you have a pretty comprehensive collection of what actions someone could take in your app. This can be much clearer than spaghetti-code–filled codebases where there's no way to get an accurate way of the application, much less the different actions you can take.

10.2.6 *Testing actions*

Next you'll write some quick tests for these actions before we move on to reducers. For the sake of expediency, I won't cover writing the tests for every single reducer or action that you set up, but I want to make sure you have some representative examples to get an idea of how to test different parts of a Redux app. If you'd like to see more examples, check out the application source code and look in the test directory.

Redux makes testing action creators, reducers, and other parts of your Redux architecture straightforward. Even better, they can be tested and maintained mostly independently of your front-end framework. This can be especially important in larger applications where testing is a nontrivial endeavor (say, a business application instead of a weekend side project). For actions, the general idea is to assert that expected action type or types, and any necessary payload information is created based on a given action.

Most action creators can be easily tested because they usually return an object with a type and payload information. Sometimes, though, you need to do some additional setup to accommodate things like async action creators. To test async action creators, you'll use the mock store you installed at the beginning of the chapter (`redux-mock-store`—see more at https://github.com/arnaudbenard/redux-mock-store) and configure it with `redux-thunk`. That way, you can assert that an async action creator dispatches certain actions and verify that it's working as expected. The next listing shows how you can go about testing actions in Redux.

Listing 10.14   Testing actions in Redux (src/actions/comments.test.js)

```
jest.mock('../../src/shared/http');
import configureStore from 'redux-mock-store';
import thunk from 'redux-thunk';
import initialState from '../../src/constants/initialState';
import * as types from '../../src/constants/types';
import {
    showComments,
    toggleComments,
    updateAvailableComments,
    createComment,
```

◁─┐ Use Jest to mock HTTP file so you don't make network requests

Import mock store and redux middleware so you can create mock store to mirror yours

Import actions you'll need to test

import API so you can mock out specific functions on it

Create mock store and reinitialize it before each test

Assert that an action creator will output an action with the right type and data

Create mock comment to pass to action creator

Dispatch action and use await to wait for promise to resolve

Mock out createComment method from API module using Jest

Assert that actions were created as expected

```javascript
        getCommentsForPost
    } from '../../src/actions/comments';
    import * as API from '../../src/shared/http';

    const mockStore = configureStore([thunk]);
    describe('login actions', () => {
        let store;
        beforeEach(() => {
            store = mockStore(initialState);
        });
        test('showComments', () => {
            const postId = 'id';
            const actual = showComments(postId);
            const expected = { type: types.comments.SHOW, postId };
            expect(actual).toEqual(expected);
        });
        test('toggleComments', () => {
            const postId = 'id';
            const actual = toggleComments(postId);
            const expected = { type: types.comments.TOGGLE, postId };
            expect(actual).toEqual(expected);
        });
        test('updateAvailableComments', () => {
            const comments = ['comments'];
            const actual = updateAvailableComments(comments);
            const expected = { type: types.comments.GET, comments };
            expect(actual).toEqual(expected);
        });
        test('createComment', async () => {
            const mockComment = { content: 'great post!' };
            API.createComment = jest.fn(() => {
                return Promise.resolve({
                    json: () => Promise.resolve([mockComment])
                });
            });
            await store.dispatch(createComment(mockComment));
            const actions = store.getActions();
            const expectedActions = [{ type: types.comments.CREATE, comment:
        [mockComment] }];
            expect(actions).toEqual(expectedActions);
        });
        test('getCommentsForPost', async () => {
            const postId = 'id';
            const comments = [{ content: 'great stuff' }];
            API.fetchCommentsForPost = jest.fn(() => {
                return Promise.resolve({
                    json: () => Promise.resolve(comments)
                });
            });
            await store.dispatch(getCommentsForPost(postId));
            const actions = store.getActions();
            const expectedActions = [{ type: types.comments.GET, comments }];
            expect(actions).toEqual(expectedActions);
        });
    });
```

10.2.7 *Creating custom Redux middleware for crash reporting*

You have some actions created, but before you move on to reducers you can add some of your own middleware. *Middleware* is Redux's way of letting you hook into the data flow process (actions dispatched to store, handled by reducer, state updated, listeners notified). Redux's approach to middleware is similar to other tools like Express or Koa (web server frameworks for Node.js), although it solves a different problem. Figure 10.7 shows an example of a middleware-focused flow as it might appear in something like Express or Koa.

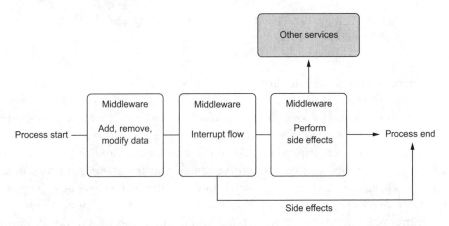

Figure 10.7   Middleware sits between a process's start and end points and lets you do various things in between.

Sometimes you may want to interrupt the flow, send data off to another API, or solve any other application-wide problems. Figure 10.7 shows a few different use cases for middleware: data modification, flow interruption, and performing side effects. One key point here is that the middleware should be composable—you should be able to reorder any of these and not worry about them affecting each other.

Redux middleware lets you act between the point that an action is dispatched and when it reaches a reducer (see the "Middleware" section of figure 10.7). It's a great place to focus on issues that are common to all parts of your Redux app and would otherwise require duplicate code in many places.

Exercise 10.1   Definitions

Match the term to its definition:

A. Store

B. Reducer

C. Action

D. Action creator

___ The central state object in Redux; source of truth.

___ Objects that contain change-related information. They must have a type and can contain any additional information needed to communicate that something happened.

___ Functions used by Redux to compute changes to state based on something happening.

___ Functions that are used to create type and payload information about something that happened in the application.

For example, using middleware can be a great way to centralize error handling, send analytics data off to a third-party API, do logging, and more. You'll implement a simple crash-reporting middleware that will make sure that any unhandled exceptions get reported to your error-tracking and management system. I'm using Sentry (https://sentry.io), an app that tracks and records exceptions for later analysis, but you could use whatever option is best for you or your team (Bugsnag is another great option—check it out at https://bugsnag.com). Listing 10.15 shows how to create some basic error-reporting middleware that will log out errors and send them to Sentry when they're encountered by Redux. Usually, engineers will get notifications of some kind (immediately or in a dashboard) when exceptions occur in an app; Sentry records those errors and lets you know when they happened.

Listing 10.15   Creating simple crash-reporting Redux middleware

```
// ... src/middleware/crash.js
import { createError } from '../actions/error';
export default store => next => action => {        ◁──  Redux middleware is
    try {                                                comprised of composed
        if (action.error) {                              functions that Redux
            console.error(action.error);                 will inject into.
            console.error(action.info);        │ If no errors, move
        }                                      │ to the next action
        return next(action);               ◁──┘ Report error, if any
    } catch (err) {                      ◁──┘
        const { user } = store.getState();              ◁─
        console.error(err);                                  Get user and send along
        window.Raven.setUserContext(user);          ◁──      with error; dispatch
        window.Raven.captureException(err);                  error to store
        return store.dispatch(createError(err));    ◁──
    }
};
```

```
//... src/store/configureStore.prod.js
```

```
import thunk from 'redux-thunk';
import { createStore, compose, applyMiddleware } from 'redux';

import rootReducer from '../reducers/root';
import crashReporting from '../middleware/crash';

let store;
export default function configureStore(initialState) {
  if (store) {
    return store;
  }
  store = createStore(rootReducer, initialState, compose(
    applyMiddleware(thunk, crashReporting)
  ));
  return store;
}
```

> **Pull in middleware to be used in production.**

> **Add middleware for production environment**

This is only a taste of what you can do with Redux middleware. The extensive documentation contains a wealth of Redux information and insight into design and API usage as well as offering excellent examples. See http://redux.js.org/docs/advanced/Middleware.html#seven-examples for more great examples of Redux middleware.

10.3 Summary

Here are the main points covered in this chapter:

- Redux is a library and application architecture that doesn't have to be used with any particular library or framework. It works especially well with React and enjoys immense popularity as the tool of choice for state management and application architecture in many React apps.
- Redux focuses on predictability and enforces strict ways of working with data.
- A *store* is an object that serves as the source of truth for an application; it is the global state of the app.
- Flux allows you to have multiple stores, but Redux only allows one.
- Reducers are functions used by Redux to compute changes to state based on a given action.
- Redux is similar to Flux in many ways, but introduces the idea of reducers, has a single store, and its action creators don't directly dispatch actions.
- Actions contain information about something that happened. They must have a type but can contain any other information that your store and reducers will need to determine how state should be updated. In Redux, there's a single state tree for the entire application; state all lives in one area and can only be updated through specific APIs.
- Action creators are functions that return actions that can be dispatched by the store. With certain middleware (see next item) in place, you can create asynchronous action creators that are useful for doing things like calling remote APIs.

- Redux allows you to write middleware, a place for injecting custom behavior into the Redux state management process. Middleware is executed before reducers are fired off and allow you to perform side effects or implement global solutions for your app.

In the next chapter, you'll continue to work with Redux as you learn about reducers and integrate them into your React app.

11

More Redux and integrating Redux with React

This chapter covers

- Reducers, Redux's way of determining how state should change
- Using Redux with React
- Converting Letters Social to use the Redux application architecture
- Adding like and comment functionality to your app

In this chapter, you'll continue the work you did in the last chapter to build out the basic elements of your Redux architecture. You'll work to integrate React with your Redux actions and store, and explore how reducers work. Redux is a variant of the Flux pattern that was designed with React in mind, and it works well with React's unidirectional data flow and APIs. Although it's not the universal choice, many large React applications will consider Redux as one of the top choices when implementing a state management solution. You'll follow suit and do so for Letters Social.

How do I get the code for this chapter?

As with every chapter, you can check out the source code for this chapter by going to the GitHub repository at https://github.com/react-in-action/letters-social. If you want to start this chapter with a clean slate and follow along, you can use your existing code from chapters 7 and 8 (if you followed along and built out the examples yourself) or check out the chapter-specific branch (chapter-10-11).

Remember, each branch corresponds to the code at the *end* of the chapter (for example, the branch chapter-10-11 corresponds to the code as it will be at the end of this chapter). You can execute one of the following terminal commands in the directory of your choice to get the code for the current chapter.

If you don't have the repository at all, type the following:

```
git clone git@github.com:react-in-action/letters-social.git
```

If you already have the repository cloned:

```
git checkout chapter-10-11
```

You may have come here from another chapter, so it's always a good idea to ensure you have all the right dependencies installed:

```
npm install
```

11.1 *Reducers determine how state should change*

You can create and dispatch actions and handle errors, but these don't do anything to change your state yet. To handle the incoming actions, you need to set up reducers. Remember, actions are just ways to describe that something happened and specify some info about what happened, but nothing more. The job of reducers is to specify how the store state should change in response to these actions. Figure 11.1 shows how reducers fit into the broader picture of Redux we've been looking at.

But what are reducers? If you've enjoyed the straightforward simplicity of Redux so far, you won't be disappointed by reducers: they're just more simple functions that have a single purpose. *Reducers* are pure functions that receive the previous state and an action as arguments and return the next state. According to the Redux documentation, they're called reducers because their method signature looks like what you would pass to `Array.prototype.reduce` (for example, `[1,2,3].reduce((a, b) => a + b, 0)`).

Reducers must be *pure* functions, meaning that given an input they will produce the same associated output every time. This contrasts with actions or middleware, where side effects are produced and API calls are often made. Doing anything asynchronous or impure (like calling `Date.now` or `Math.random()`) in reducers is an anti-pattern and could degrade performance or reliability in your app. The Redux docs drive this point home: "Given the same arguments, it should calculate the next state and return it. No

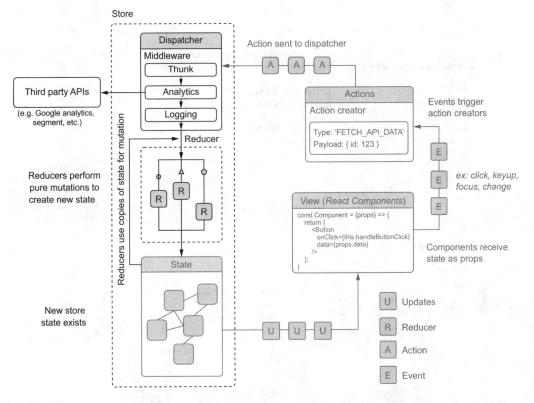

Figure 11.1   Reducers are just functions that help determine what changes should be made to the state. You can think of them as sort of a gateway to your app state that tightly controls incoming changes.

surprises. No side effects. No API calls. No mutations. Just a calculation." For more on this, see https://redux.js.org/basics/reducers.

11.1.1   *State shape and initial state*

Reducers will start to work on modifying the single Redux store, so it's a good time to talk about what shape that store will take. Designing the state shape of any app will both affect and be affected by how the UI of your app works, but it's generally a good idea to keep the "raw" data separated from the UI data as much as possible. One way to do this is to store things like IDs separate from their counterparts and use the IDs to look up data.

You'll create an initial state file that will help you determine your state shape and structure. In the constants folder, create a file named initialState.js. This will be the state of your Redux app before any actions have been dispatched or any changes have been made. You'll include information for error and loading states, as well as some information about posts, comments, and the user. You'll store the IDs for comments and posts in arrays and the main information for these in objects that you can easily reference. The following listing shows an example of setting up the initial state.

Listing 11.1   Initial state and state shape (src/constants/initialState.js)

```
export default {            ◁──┐  Object that Redux will
    error: null,               │  use for its initial state
    loading: false,
    postIds: [],               Store comment
    posts: {},                 and post IDs
    commentIds: [],            separate from
    comments: {},              the actual data.
    pagination: {                                            Store pagination
        first: `${process.env                      ◁──       links (received via
              .ENDPOINT}/posts?_page=1&_sort=date&_order=DESC&   HTTP headers)—
    _embed=comments&_expand=user&_embed=likes`,    ◁──       this is just one
        next: null,                                          approach to
        prev: null,                                          pagination.
        last: null
    },
    user: {                    ◁──  Store information
        authenticated: false,       about user's
        profilePicture: null,       authentication state
        id: null,
        name: null,
        token: null
    }
};
```

11.1.2 *Setting up reducers to respond to incoming action*

With your initial state set up, you should create some reducers to handle incoming actions so your store can be updated. Reducers usually use a `switch` statement to match incoming action types to make updates to state. They return a new copy of the state (not the same version with changes) that will then be used to update the store. Reducers also perform catch-all behavior to ensure that unknown actions just return the existing state. We've noted it before, but it's important to say again that reducers are performing calculations and should return the same output every time based on a given input; no side effects or impure processes should be initiated.

Reducers are responsible for calculating how the store should change. In most apps, you'll have many reducers that will each be responsible for a slice of your store. This helps keep files uncluttered and focused. You'll ultimately use the `combine-Reducers` method available from Redux to, well, combine your reducers into one. Most reducers use a `switch` statement with cases for different action types and a default catch-all at the bottom to ensure that unknown action types (probably created by accident, if anything) don't have any unintentional effects on state.

Reducers also make copies of state and don't directly mutate the existing store state. If you look back at figure 11.1, you'll see that the reducers use state as they perform their jobs. This approach is similar to the way that immutable data structures generally work; modified copies are made instead of direct mutations. Listing 11.2 shows how to set up the loading reducer. Note that in this case you're only dealing with a "flat" slice of state—the Boolean `loading` property—so you just return either `true` or `false` for the new state. You'll frequently be working with a state object that has many keys or nested properties, and your reducer will need to do more than just return `true` or `false`.

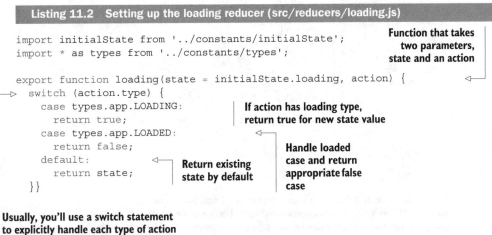

Listing 11.2 Setting up the loading reducer (src/reducers/loading.js)

```
import initialState from '../constants/initialState';
import * as types from '../constants/types';
```
Function that takes two parameters, state and an action

```
export function loading(state = initialState.loading, action) {
  switch (action.type) {
    case types.app.LOADING:
      return true;
    case types.app.LOADED:
      return false;
    default:
      return state;
  }}
```
If action has loading type, return true for new state value

Handle loaded case and return appropriate false case

Return existing state by default

Usually, you'll use a switch statement to explicitly handle each type of action and return state by default.

Now when a loading-related action gets dispatched, the Redux store will be able to do something about it. When an action comes in and has made it through any existing middleware, Redux will invoke reducers to determine what new state should be created based on the action. There wasn't a way for your store to know about change information contained in an action before you had set up any reducers. To visualize this, figure 11.2 cuts out the reducers from the flow; see how there's no way for actions to reach the store?

Next, you'll create another reducer to put your Redux skills to work. After all, many reducers won't be just returning a `true` or `false` value, or at the very least if they do, there will probably be more that goes into calculating that `true` or `false` value. Another key part of the Letters Social app is showing and creating posts, and you need to migrate it to Redux. Like you might if you were migrating a real-life React app to use Redux, you should be able to preserve much of the existing logic that your app uses and translate it into a Redux-friendly form. You'll create two reducers to handle the posts themselves and one for keeping track of the post IDs. In a larger app, you might combine these together under another key, but keeping them separate is fine for now. This also serves as an example of how multiple reducers can be set up to handle a single action. Listing 11.3 shows how to create the reducer for comments. You'll be creating quite a few reducers here, but once that's done, your app will not only have a comprehensive description of actions that can occur but also of ways that the state can change.

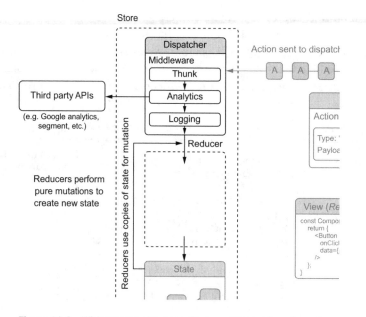

Figure 11.2   **With reducers in place, Redux will know how to make changes to the store when actions are dispatched. In a moderately complex app, you'll usually have many different reducers that are each responsible for their own "slice" of the store state.**

Listing 11.3   **Creating the comments reducer (src/reducers/comments)**

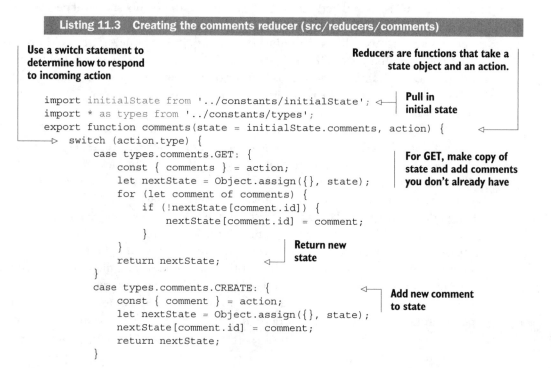

Use a switch statement to determine how to respond to incoming action

Reducers are functions that take a state object and an action.

```
import initialState from '../constants/initialState';
import * as types from '../constants/types';
export function comments(state = initialState.comments, action) {
    switch (action.type) {
        case types.comments.GET: {
            const { comments } = action;
            let nextState = Object.assign({}, state);
            for (let comment of comments) {
                if (!nextState[comment.id]) {
                    nextState[comment.id] = comment;
                }
            }
            return nextState;
        }
        case types.comments.CREATE: {
            const { comment } = action;
            let nextState = Object.assign({}, state);
            nextState[comment.id] = comment;
            return nextState;
        }
```

Pull in initial state

For GET, make copy of state and add comments you don't already have

Return new state

Add new comment to state

```
        default:
            return state;                    ◁─┐  By default return
    }                                           │  same state
}

export function commentIds(state = initialState.commentIds, action) {
    switch (action.type) {
        case types.comments.GET: {
            const nextCommentIds = action.comments.map(comment =>
        comment.id);                                ◁─┐ You only want IDs here
            let nextState = Array.from(state);         │ because you'll store
            for (let commentId of nextCommentIds) {    │ them separately from
                if (!state.includes(commentId)) {      │ main objects.
                    nextState.push(commentId);
                }
            }
            return nextState;
        }
        case types.comments.CREATE: {              ◁─┐ Push new
            const { comment } = action;               │ ID in
            let nextState = Array.from(state);
            nextState.push(comment.id);
            return nextState;
        }
        default:
            return state;
    }
}
```

Create copy of previous state →

Now when you dispatch actions related to comments, your store state will update appropriately. Did you notice how you were able to respond to actions that weren't strictly of the same type? Reducers can respond to actions that are within their purview, even if they aren't of an identical type. This has to be possible because even though the "posts" slice of state manages posts, there are other actions in the realm of the act that might affect it. The takeaway here is that a reducer is responsible for deciding how a particular aspect of state should change, regardless of which action or which type of action is coming through. Some reducers might need to know about many different types of actions that aren't specifically related to the resource (posts) they're modeling.

Now that you've created the comments reducer, you can create the one that will handle posts. It will be very similar to the comments one because you're employing the same strategy for storing them as IDs and objects separately. It will also need to know how to handle liking and unliking posts (you created the actions for this functionality in chapter 10). The following listing shows how to create these reducers.

Listing 11.4   Creating the posts reducers (src/reducers/posts.js)

```
import initialState from '../constants/initialState';
import * as types from '../constants/types';
export function posts(state = initialState.posts, action) {
```

```
switch (action.type) {
    case types.posts.GET: {
        const { posts } = action;
        let nextState = Object.assign({}, state);
        for (let post of posts) {
            if (!nextState[post.id]) {
                nextState[post.id] = post;
            }
        }
        return nextState;
    }
    case types.posts.CREATE: {
        const { post } = action;
        let nextState = Object.assign({}, state);
        if (!nextState[post.id]) {
            nextState[post.id] = post;
        }
        return nextState;
    }
    case types.comments.SHOW: {
        let nextState = Object.assign({}, state);
        nextState[action.postId].showComments = true;
        return nextState;
    }
    case types.comments.TOGGLE: {
        let nextState = Object.assign({}, state);
        nextState[action.postId].showComments =
            !nextState[action.postId].showComments;
        return nextState;
    }
    case types.posts.LIKE: {
        let nextState = Object.assign({}, state);
        const oldPost = nextState[action.post.id];
        nextState[action.post.id] = Object.assign({}, oldPost, action.post);
        return nextState;
    }
    case types.posts.UNLIKE: {
        let nextState = Object.assign({}, state);
        const oldPost = nextState[action.post.id];
        nextState[action.post.id] = Object.assign({}, oldPost, action.post);
        return nextState;
    }
    case types.comments.CREATE: {
        const { comment } = action;
        let nextState = Object.assign({}, state);
        nextState[comment.postId].comments.push(comment);
        return state;
    }
    default:
        return state;
    }
}

export function postIds(state = initialState.postIds, action) {
    switch (action.type) {
```

Handle getting new posts

Show or toggle comments for a post

Liking/unliking a post involves updating specific post in state with new data from API

Handle new IDs same way you did for comments

```
case types.posts.GET: {
    const nextPostIds = action.posts.map(post => post.id);
    let nextState = Array.from(state);
    for (let post of nextPostIds) {
        if (!state.includes(post)) {
            nextState.push(post);
        }
    }
    return nextState;
}
case types.posts.CREATE: {
    const { post } = action;
    let nextState = Array.from(state);
    if (!state.includes(post.id)) {
        nextState.push(post.id);
    }
    return nextState;
}
default:
    return state;
}
}
```

I included two reducers in these files because they were so closely related and both act on the same fundamental data (posts and comments), but you'll probably find that most of the time you want to have one reducer per file to keep things simple. Most of the time your reducer setup will mirror or at least follow the structure of your store. You may have noticed the subtlety that how you design your store state shape (see the initial state you set up earlier in the chapter) will greatly influence how your reducers and, to a lesser degree, your actions are defined. One takeaway from this is that it's generally better to spend too much time on designing state shape than to gloss over it. Too little time spent on design will probably result in lots of rework to improve the state shape, whereas solid design plus the patterns Redux gives you can make adding new functionality easier than not adding it.

Migrating to Redux: worth it?

I've mentioned a few times in this chapter that Redux can be a lot of work to initially set up (perhaps you're feeling that right now!) but in the end it's often worthwhile. Obviously, that can't be true in every possible case, but I've found it to be true in the projects I've worked on and for other engineers I know who've done the same. One project I worked on involved a complete migration of the app from a Flux to Redux architecture. It took the entire team working for maybe a month or so, but we were able to launch the rewrite of the app with minimal instability and bug creation.

The greater overall outcome, however, was the ability to more rapidly iterate on the product due to the patterns that Redux helped us put in place. Months after the Redux migration, we ended up doing a series of complete redesigns of the application. Even though we ended up rebuilding large portions of the React portion of the application, the Redux architecture meant that we had to make relatively few changes to any of the state management and business-logic portions of the application. What's more, the patterns Redux provided for us made it trivial to add to the state of the application where necessary. Integrating Redux was worth the initial work to set it up and transition the app over to it and it continues to pay dividends long after.

With some of the more complicated reducers taken care of, you can finish the reducers portion of our Redux work by creating reducers for errors, pagination, and the user. Start with the error reducer in the following listing.

Listing 11.5   Creating the error reducer (src/reducers/error.js)

```
import initialState from '../constants/initialState';
import * as types from '../constants/types';
export function error(state = initialState.error, action) {
    switch (action.type) {
        case types.app.ERROR:
            return action.error;              ◁⎺⎤ This slice of state isn't
        default:                                 │ complicated; sends
            return state;                        │ through error on action
    }
}
```

Next, you need to ensure that your pagination state can get updated. Right now, the pagination is only related to posts, but in a larger application you might have to set up pagination for many different parts of your application (for example, when you have a post with too many comments to sensibly show at once). You only need to handle simple pagination for your sample application, so create the pagination reducer in the following listing.

Listing 11.6   Creating the pagination reducer (src/reducers/pagination.js)

```
import initialState from '../constants/initialState';
import * as types from '../constants/types';
export function pagination(state = initialState.pagination, action) {
    switch (action.type) {
        case types.posts.UPDATE_LINKS:                    Create new copy of
            const nextState = Object.assign({}, state);   previous state and
            for (let k in action.links) {                 merge in URLs from
                if (action.links.hasOwnProperty(k)) {     action's payload
                    if (process.env.NODE_ENV === 'production') {   ◁⎺
                        nextState[k] =
            action.links[k].url.replace(/http:\/\//, 'https://');  ◁⎺
                    } else {
                        nextState[k] = action.links[k].url;
                    }
                }
            }
        }
    }
```

Update those link URLs with new pagination info

Update URL for each link type

Quirk due to how Letters Social terminates SSL when deployed to Zeit (https://zeit.co/now)—ignore if you don't deploy app yourself

```
            return nextState;
        default:
            return state;
    }
}
```

Now you need to create a reducer that will let you respond to user-related events like logins and logouts. In this reducer you'll also handle storing some cookies on the browser so you can use them later when you do server-side rendering in chapter 12. *Cookies* are small pieces of data that the server can send to a user's web browser. You're probably familiar with cookies from using computers every day (you get notified about them on some sites for legal reasons), but maybe you've never worked with them in a programmatic way before. That's okay. You'll use the `js-cookie` library to interact with cookies, and all you'll do with them is set and unset one particular cookie when the user's authentication state changes. The following listing shows creating the user reducer to do this.

Listing 11.7 Creating the user reducer (src/reducers/user.js)

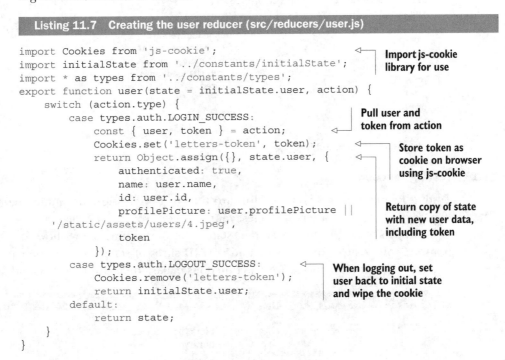

```
import Cookies from 'js-cookie';                              Import js-cookie
import initialState from '../constants/initialState';        library for use
import * as types from '../constants/types';
export function user(state = initialState.user, action) {
    switch (action.type) {
        case types.auth.LOGIN_SUCCESS:                       Pull user and
            const { user, token } = action;                 token from action
            Cookies.set('letters-token', token);            Store token as
            return Object.assign({}, state.user, {          cookie on browser
                authenticated: true,                        using js-cookie
                name: user.name,
                id: user.id,
                profilePicture: user.profilePicture ||       Return copy of state
    '/static/assets/users/4.jpeg',                           with new user data,
                token                                        including token
            });
        case types.auth.LOGOUT_SUCCESS:                      When logging out, set
            Cookies.remove('letters-token');                user back to initial state
            return initialState.user;                       and wipe the cookie
        default:
            return state;
    }
}
```

11.1.3 Combining reducers together in our store

Lastly, you need to make sure that your reducers are integrated with your Redux store. Even though you've created them, they're not connected in any way right now. Let's revisit the root reducer you created in chapter 10 and see how to add new reducers to it. Listing 11.8 shows how to add the reducers you created to the root reducer. It's important to note here that the way that `combineReducers` will create keys on your store is based on the reducers you pass in. For the case in listing 11.8, your store's state will have `loading` and `posts` keys, each managed by their respective reducer. I'm using the ES2015 property shorthand here, but could have named the final keys differently if I wanted to. This is important to note so you don't feel as though your function names must be directly tied to keys on your store.

> **Listing 11.8   Adding new reducers to existing root reducer (src/reducers/root.js)**

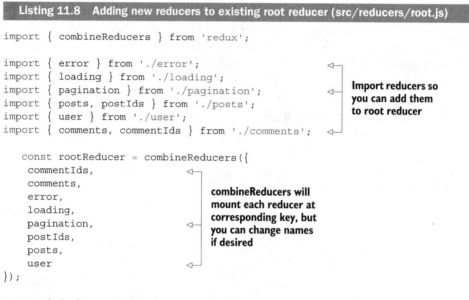

```
import { combineReducers } from 'redux';

import { error } from './error';
import { loading } from './loading';
import { pagination } from './pagination';          Import reducers so
import { posts, postIds } from './posts';           you can add them
import { user } from './user';                      to root reducer
import { comments, commentIds } from './comments';

  const rootReducer = combineReducers({
    commentIds,
    comments,
    error,                      combineReducers will
    loading,                    mount each reducer at
    pagination,                 corresponding key, but
    postIds,                    you can change names
    posts,                      if desired
    user,
});

export default rootReducer;
```

11.1.4   Testing reducers

Testing Redux reducers is straightforward thanks to their pure, decoupled nature—they're just functions, after all. To test your reducers, you'll assert that given a certain input, they should produce a certain state. The next listing shows how to test the reducers you created for the posts and post ID slices of state. As with other parts of Redux, the fact that reducers are also functions makes them easy to isolate and test.

> **Listing 11.9   Testing reducers (src/reducers/posts.test.js)**

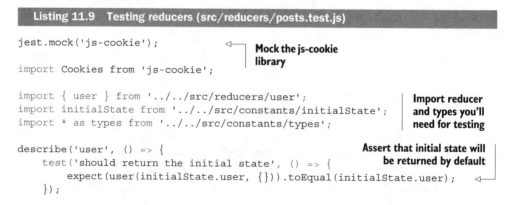

```
jest.mock('js-cookie');                          Mock the js-cookie
                                                 library
import Cookies from 'js-cookie';

import { user } from '../../src/reducers/user';              Import reducer
import initialState from '../../src/constants/initialState';  and types you'll
import * as types from '../../src/constants/types';           need for testing

describe('user', () => {                          Assert that initial state will
    test('should return the initial state', () => {  be returned by default
        expect(user(initialState.user, {})).toEqual(initialState.user);
    });
```

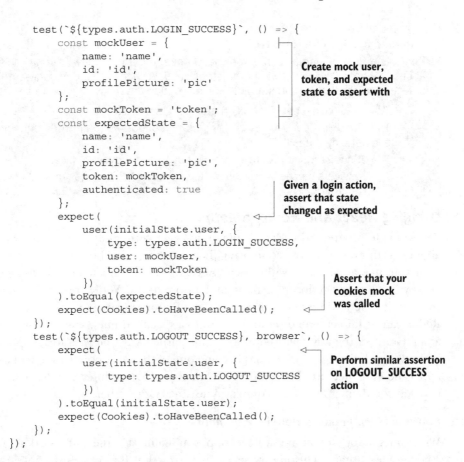

```
test(`${types.auth.LOGIN_SUCCESS}`, () => {
    const mockUser = {
        name: 'name',
        id: 'id',
        profilePicture: 'pic'
    };
    const mockToken = 'token';
    const expectedState = {
        name: 'name',
        id: 'id',
        profilePicture: 'pic',
        token: mockToken,
        authenticated: true
    };
    expect(
        user(initialState.user, {
            type: types.auth.LOGIN_SUCCESS,
            user: mockUser,
            token: mockToken
        })
    ).toEqual(expectedState);
    expect(Cookies).toHaveBeenCalled();
});
test(`${types.auth.LOGOUT_SUCCESS}, browser`, () => {
    expect(
        user(initialState.user, {
            type: types.auth.LOGOUT_SUCCESS
        })
    ).toEqual(initialState.user);
    expect(Cookies).toHaveBeenCalled();
});
});
```

Create mock user, token, and expected state to assert with

Given a login action, assert that state changed as expected

Assert that your cookies mock was called

Perform similar assertion on LOGOUT_SUCCESS action

With that, we've covered most of the basics of a Redux application: the store, reducers, actions, and middleware! The Redux ecosystem is robust, and there are many more areas you can explore yourself. We've omitted some parts of the API and/or Redux ecosystem like advanced middleware usage, selectors (optimized ways of interacting with store state), and more. We also specifically omitted extensively covering the store API (like, for example, working with store.subscribe() to interact with update events). That's because the nuts and bolts of working with this part of Redux will be abstracted over with the react-redux library. (If you're interested in going into more depth in these areas and learning more about Redux, see https://redux.js.org.) I've also put together a guide to the React ecosystem on my blog at https://ifelse.io/react-ecosystem that covers Redux as well.

> **Exercise 11.1   True or false**
>
> Redux is a relatively small library for what it does, but it has a few "strong" opinions about how data flow works within the store, reducer, actions, and middleware. Take a second to check your understanding by evaluating the following statements:
>
> - T | F Reducers should modify the existing state directly.
> - T | F Redux includes a way of doing asynchronous work (network requests, for example) by default.
> - T | F It's a good idea to include an initial state for every reducer by default.
> - T | F Reducers can be combined, making it easier to separate out slices of state.

11.2   *Bringing React and Redux together*

You've made progress with Redux, but your React components don't know anything about it at this point. You need to bring them together somehow. You can start to integrate your new architecture with React now that you've completed the Redux setup process by building out reducers, actions, and a store to use. You've probably noticed that you didn't have to do much with React to get Redux up and running. That's because Redux can be implemented without regard to a specific framework—or any framework at all. Granted, the way that Redux works fits particularly well with React applications, and this is at least in part why it has become one of the most popular choices for React application architecture. But remember even as you start to integrate React and Redux that you could integrate it with Angular, Vue, Preact, or Ember.

11.2.1   *Containers vs. presentational components*

When integrating Redux into a React app, you'll almost certainly be working with the `react-redux` library. This library serves as abstraction that covers the integration of the Redux store and actions into your React components. I'll cover some of the ways you can use `react-redux`, including how to bring actions into your components, and discuss some new types of components: presentational and container components. You no longer need to distribute state among your many components because Redux is responsible for managing the application state via actions, reducers, and the store. Note again that there's nothing inherently wrong with creating a React app that doesn't use Redux; you still get all the other good things that come from using React. Redux's predictability and added structure make designing and maintaining a large, complex React app easier, and that's why many teams will choose to go with it over "vanilla" React.

These two new categories of components (presentational and container) are really just two more-focused expressions of what your components are already doing. The difference between "any old" component and a presentation or container component is in what it does. Rather than allowing any component to handle styling, UI data, *and* application data, presentational components handle UI and UI-related data, and container components handle application data (à la Redux).

It's important to understand the difference between containers and presentational components, but your application is still doing the same things it was doing with better separation of concerns. You haven't introduced anything fundamentally new into the application with Redux; your React components will still receive props, maintain state, respond to events, and render with the same lifecycle as before. The key difference that `react-redux` provides is in integrating your store, reducers, and actions with your components. And the new divide between presentational and container components is just a pattern that can make your life easier.

Let's look at these two general sorts of components used in a React app with a Redux architecture. As noted, presentational components are "UI-only" components. This means they should generally not have much to do with determining how application data is changed, updated, or emitted.

Here are some basics on presentational components:

- They deal with how things look instead of how data flows or is determined.
- They only have their own state (they're React classes with a backing instance) if necessary; most of the time they should be stateless, functional components that receive props from Redux via `react-redux` bindings.
- When they *do* have their own state, it should be UI-related data, not application data. For example: an open/closed dropdown menu item and its state.
- They don't determine how data gets loaded or changed—that should happen primarily in containers.
- They're usually created "by hand" instead of by the `react-redux` library.
- They may contain style information, things like CSS classes, other style-related components, and any other UI-related data.

If you're exploring the React/Redux ecosystems, you may sometimes see references to *smart* (containers) and *dumb* (presentational) components. This way of referring to them has fallen out of favor, as it was found to be unhelpful and had a pejorative bent, but if do you see that terminology used you'll be able to map it to the presentational/container dichotomy. With that in mind, container components do all of the following:

- Serve as a data source and can be stateful; the state will usually come from your Redux store.
- Provide data and behavior information (like actions) to presentational components.
- Can contain other presentational *or* container components; it's common for a container to be a parent with many presentational child components.
- Are usually created using `react-redux`'s *connect* method (more on that shortly) and are usually higher-order components (components that create new components from other components).
- Usually don't have style information that doesn't have to do with application data. For example, the user profile state slice on the Redux store might have "red" recorded for the user's "favorite color", but the container wouldn't use that data for any styling—it would only ever pass it down to a presentational component.

In this chapter, we'll take a sort of middle approach to breaking down your components into presentational and connected or container components. For each component you want to connect to the Redux store, you'll do the following:

- Modify it by exporting a connected component in addition to the regular component.
- Move any props and state into special functions that `react-redux` can use (more on that shortly).
- Bring in any actions you need and bind those to an `actions` prop the component will have.
- Replace local state where appropriate with props mapped to Redux store state.

Figure 11.3 should help you get a better sense of how a connected component typically works; the same Redux aspects exist, but are essentially "rearranged" around a React component so updates from the store are communicated to components.

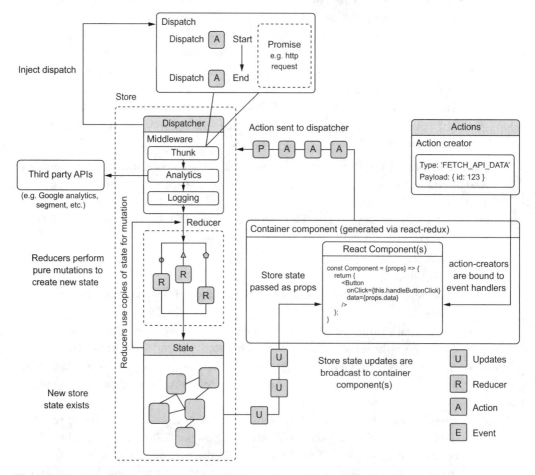

Figure 11.3   **Redux integrated with React.** `react-redux` **provides utilities that will help you generate components (higher-order components; components that generate other components).**

This chapter doesn't have the space to cover converting every component we've touched in this book, but the difference between containers and presentational components as well as the way you integrate Redux with React should give you some good starting practice to point you in the right direction.

11.2.2 Using <Provider /> to connect components to the Redux store

The first step in integrating your Redux setup into your React app is to wrap the entire app with the Provider component provided by `react-redux`. This component accepts a Redux store as a prop and will make that store available to your "connected" components—another way to describe components that are hooked up to Redux. In almost every case, this is the central point of integration between your React components and Redux. A store will have to be available to your containers or your app won't function properly (or probably at all). The following listing shows how to use the Provider component and update the authentication listener to handle your Redux actions.

> **Listing 11.10   Wrapping your app with `react-redux`'s `<Provider />`**

```
import React from 'react';
import { render } from 'react-dom';
import { Provider } from 'react-redux';
import Firebase from 'firebase';

import * as API from './shared/http';
import { history } from './history';

import configureStore from './store/configureStore';
import initialReduxState from './constants/initialState';

import Route from './components/router/Route';
import Router from './components/router/Router';
import App from './app';
import Home from './pages/home';
import SinglePost from './pages/post';
import Login from './pages/login';
import NotFound from './pages/404';

import { createError } from './actions/error';
import { loginSuccess } from './actions/auth';
import { loaded, loading } from './actions/loading';
import { getFirebaseUser, getFirebaseToken } from './backend/auth';

import './shared/crash';
import './shared/service-worker';
import './shared/vendor';
import './styles/styles.scss';

const store = configureStore(initialReduxState);

const renderApp = (state, callback = () => {}) => {
    render(
        <Provider store={store}>
```

Import redux-related modules you'll need here

Create Redux store using initial state

Wrap your router with Provider from react-redux and pass it the store

```
                <Router {...state}>
                    <Route path="" component={App}>
                        <Route path="/" component={Home} />
                        <Route path="/posts/:postId" component={SinglePost} />
                        <Route path="/login" component={Login} />
                        <Route path="*" component={NotFound} />
                    </Route>
                </Router>
            </Provider>,
            document.getElementById('app'),
            callback
        );
};

const initialState = {
    location: window.location.pathname
};

// Render the app initially
renderApp(initialState);

history.listen(location => {                                    History listener
    const user = Firebase.auth().currentUser;                   stays the same
    const newState = Object.assign(initialState, { location: user ?
     location.pathname : '/login' });
    renderApp(newState);
});

getFirebaseUser()
    .then(async user => {                                       Get user from
        if (!user) {                                            Firebase and dispatch
            return history.push('/login');                      loading action
        }
        store.dispatch(loading());
        const token = await getFirebaseToken();
        const res = await API.loadUser(user.uid);
        if (res.status === 404) {
            const userPayload = {
                name: user.displayName,
                profilePicture: user.photoURL,
                id: user.uid
            };
            const newUser = await API.createUser(userPayload).then(res =>
     res.json());
            store.dispatch(loginSuccess(newUser, token));
            store.dispatch(loaded());
            history.push('/');
            return newUser;
        }
        const existingUser = await res.json();
        store.dispatch(loginSuccess(existingUser, token));
        store.dispatch(loaded());
        history.push('/');
        return existingUser;
    })
```

Create new
user if you
don't have
one already
and dispatch
user/token

Load existing
user and
dispatch

```
    .catch(err => createError(err));
//...
```

Now that a store will be available to your components, you can connect them to your store. You'll remember from figure 11.3 that `react-redux` will inject store state into your components as props and change those props when the store gets updated. If you weren't using `react-redux`, you'd need to manually subscribe to updates from the store on a component-by-component basis.

To make this happen, you need to use the `connect` utility from `react-redux`. It will generate a container component that's connected (hence the name) to the Redux store and apply updates when the store changes. The `connect` method only has a few arguments, but there's more to it than might first appear; you can read up on it more thoroughly at https://github.com/reactjs/react-redux. For your purposes, you'll use both the ability to subscribe to the store and to inject the store's `dispatch` function so you can create actions for your components.

To inject state, you'll pass a function (`mapStateToProps`) that will receive `state` as a parameter and will return an object that will be merged into the props for the component; `react-redux` will re-invoke this function whenever the component receives new props. Once you're using `connect` to wrap your component, you'll need to adjust the way props are used in the component (I cover actions next); `state` shouldn't be used unless it relates to UI-specific data. Remember that although this is considered a best practice, it doesn't mean that there are no valid cases for blurring the lines between presentational and container components. They exist, even if they're rare; make the best engineering decisions for your team and specific situation.

Listing 11.11 shows how to use `connect` and how to adjust the way you're accessing props in our Home component and convert it to a stateless function comp. You'll use the first of the two parameters that you'll end up passing to connect: `mapStateTo-Props`. This function will receive `state` (the store state) and can have an additional argument, `ownProps`, that will pass in any additional props passed to the container component. You won't use that parameter right now, but the API provides it in case you need it.

> **Listing 11.11** `mapStateToProps` **(src/pages/Home.js)**

```
import PropTypes from 'prop-types';
import React, { Component } from 'react';
import { connect } from 'react-redux';
import orderBy from 'lodash/orderBy';        ◁── Use Lodash's orderBy function for sorting posts

import Ad from '../components/ad/Ad';
import CreatePost from '../components/post/Create';        Import
import Post from '../components/post/Post';                components
import Welcome from '../components/welcome/Welcome';       Home page displays

export class Home extends Component {
    render() {
```

```
        return (
            <div className="home">
                <Welcome />
                <div>
                    <CreatePost />                                    ← Map over
                    {this.props.posts && (                              posts
                        <div className="posts">
                            {this.props.posts.map(post => (
                                <Post
                                    key={post.id}                    Pass in post and post
                                    post={post}                      ID (mapStateToProps
                                />                                   will further handle)
                            ))}
                        </div>
                    )}
                    <button className="block">
                        Load more posts
                    </button>
                </div>
                <div>
                    <Ad url="https://ifelse.io/book" imageUrl="/static/
        assets/ads/ria.png" />
                    <Ad url="https://ifelse.io/book" imageUrl="/static/
        assets/ads/orly.jpg" />
                </div>
            </div>
        );
    }
}
//...
export const mapStateToProps = state => {
    const posts = orderBy(state.postIds.map(postId => state.posts[postId]),
        'date', 'desc');
    return { posts };                                    ← mapStateToProps
};                                                         function returns props
export default connect(mapStateToProps)(Home);  ←         for connected component
```

Map in posts and sort   Export connected
them using orderBy   component

When you run the app now (using npm run dev), you shouldn't encounter any runtime errors, but you shouldn't see any posts, either, because there are no actions
doing anything. But if you open the React developer tools, you should be able to see
react-redux at work creating your connected component. Notice how connect created another component that wraps the one you passed in and gave it a new set of
props. Behind the scenes, it's also going to subscribe to updates from the Redux store
and pass them in as new props to your container. Figure 11.4 shows what you should
see when you open the dev tools and your app side by side.

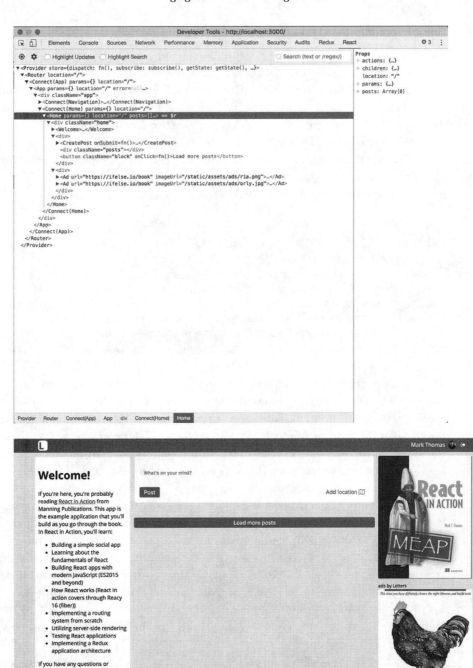

Figure 11.4 If you open the React developer tools, you'll be able to pick out the newly connected component and the props that it had passed into it by `connect`. Notice how the `connect` function created a new component that wrapped the component you passed to it.

11.2.3 *Binding actions to component event handlers*

You need to get your app to respond to user actions again. You'll use a second function to do that: mapDispatchToProps. This function does just what it sounds like—it has a dispatch argument that will be the store's dispatch method, injected into your component. You might have noticed in figure 10.3 from chapter 10 or in your React developer tools that the container has a dispatch method injected into its props already; you can use that function as is because it gets automatically injected if you don't provide a mapDispatchToProps function. But using mapDispatchToProps has the advantage that you can use it to separate out the component-specific action logic from the component itself, and it makes testing easier.

> ### Exercise 11.2   Source code assignment
> The react-redux library provides some nice abstractions that have been battle-tested by many companies and individuals using Redux with React. But you don't have to use this library to get React and Redux to work together. As an exercise, take some time to read through the source code for React-Redux at https://github.com/reactjs/react-redux/tree/master/src. It's not recommended that you create your own way to connect React and Redux, but you should be able to see that it's not "magic."

The mapDispatchToProps function will be invoked by react-redux and the resulting object will be merged into your components' props. You'll use it to set up your action creators and make them available to your component. You'll also take advantage of the bindActionCreators helper utility from Redux. The bindActionCreators utility transforms an object whose values are action creators into an object with identical keys—with the difference being that every action creator is wrapped in a dispatch call, so they may be invoked directly.

You probably noticed in listing 11.11 that you used a React class instead of a stateless functional component. It's common to create stateless functional components, but in this case you need a way to initially load posts, so you require lifecycle methods that can dispatch actions when the component has mounted. One way around this is to offload initiation events to the routing layer and coordinate loading data when certain routes are entered or exited. Your current router isn't built with lifecycle hooks in mind, but other routers like React-router do have this as a feature. We'll explore switching to React Router in the next chapter and you'll take advantage of this feature.

All that's left, then, is to use mapDispatchToProps to pull in your actions and bind them in your components. You can also create an object with functions assigned to whatever key you like. This pattern can make it easier to directly reference your actions if the functions on the mapDispatchToProps object don't have any additional logic between them and the dispatch invocation. The next listing shows how to use mapDispatchToProps to set up your actions.

Listing 11.12 Using `mapDispatchToProps` (src/containers/Home.js)

```
// ...
import { createError } from '../actions/error';                          Import actions
import { createNewPost, getPostsForPage } from '../actions/posts';       you'll need for
import { showComments } from '../actions/comments';                      this component
import Ad from '../components/ad/Ad';
import CreatePost from '../components/post/Create';
import Post from '../components/post/Post';
import Welcome from '../components/welcome/Welcome';
export class Home extends Component {
    componentDidMount() {                          Load posts when
        this.props.actions.getPostsForPage();      component mounts
    }
    componentDidCatch(err, info) {                 If error occurs in your
        this.props.actions.createError(err, info); component, use
    }                                              componentDidCatch to
    render() {                                     handle it, dispatch error
        return (                                   to store
            <div className="home">
                <Welcome />
                <div>
                    <CreatePost onSubmit={this.props.actions.createNewPost} />
                    {this.props.posts && (
                        <div className="posts">
                            {this.props.posts.map(post => (
                                <Post
                                    key={post.id}
                                    post={post}
                                    openCommentsDrawer=          Pass showComments
    {this.props.actions.showComments}                           action via props
                                />
                            ))}
                        </div>
                    )}
                    <button className="block"                   Pass load more
    onClick={this.props.actions.getNextPageOfPosts}>            posts action
                        Load more posts
                    </button>
                </div>
                <div>
                    <Ad url="https://ifelse.io/book" imageUrl="/static/
    assets/ads/ria.png" />
                    <Ad url="https://ifelse.io/book" imageUrl="/static/
    assets/ads/orly.jpg" />
                </div>
            </div>
        );
    }
}
//...
export const mapDispatchToProps = dispatch => {
    return {
```

Use bindAction-Creators to bind wrap your actions in a dispatch call

```
actions: bindActionCreators(
    {
        createNewPost,
        getPostsForPage,
        showComments,
        createError,
        getNextPageOfPosts: getPostsForPage.bind(this, 'next')
    },
    dispatch
    )
};
};
```

Use .bind() to ensure getPostsForPage action is called with 'next' argument every time

```
export default connect(mapStateToProps, mapDispatchToProps)(Home);
```

With that, you've connected your component to Redux! As I mentioned earlier, there isn't sufficient space to cover converting every single one of the components in your application to use Redux. The good news is they all follow the same pattern (create `mapStateToProps` and `mapDispatchToProps`, export using `connect`), and you should be able to convert them to interact with Redux in the same way you did here for the home page. Here are the other components you've connected to the Redux store in the application source:

- *App*—src/app.js
- *Comments*—src/components/comment/Comments.js
- *Error*—src/components/error/Error.js
- *Navigation*—src/components/nav/navbar.js
- *PostActionSection*—src/components/post/PostActionSection.js
- *Posts*—src/components/post/Posts.js
- *Login*—src/pages/login.js
- *SinglePost*—src/pages/post.js

With all these components integrated, your application will be transitioned to using Redux! Now that you know how to add a Redux "loop" (action creator, reducer to handle action, and connecting any components), how would you go about adding a new feature like a user profile? What other features could you add to Letters Social? Fortunately, the Letters Social application has many areas for extension and ways in which you can try new things with Redux.

11.2.4 *Updating your tests*

When you converted your Home component to React, you ended up breaking the tests that you had previously written for it. You're going to fix that now. Fortunately, the bulk of the testing logic should now live elsewhere, so if anything, these tests should have gotten simpler than they were before. The following listing shows the updated test file for the Home component.

Listing 11.13 Updating the Home component tests (src/containers/Home.test.js)

```
jest.mock('mapbox');                                    ←┐  Mock Mapbox because
import React from 'react';                                │  CreateComment component will
import renderer from 'react-test-renderer';         ←┐   │  try to use it, bring in test renderer
import { Provider } from 'react-redux';               │   │  from react-test-renderer

import { Home, mapStateToProps, mapDispatchToProps } from
    '../../src/pages/home';                                      ←┐
import configureStore from '../../src/store/configureStore';
import initialState from '../../src/constants/initialState';     Create initial
                                                                  state with
const now = new Date().getTime();                    ←┐          some posts
describe('Single post page', () => {
    const state = Object.assign({}, initialState, {     ←
        posts: {
            2: { content: 'stuff', likes: [], date: now },
            1: { content: 'stuff', likes: [], date: now }
        },
        postIds: [1, 2]                               ┌─ Use initial state to
    });                                                │  create a store
    const store = configureStore(state);       ←─────┘
    test('mapStateToProps', () => {                       ←┐  To test mapState-
        expect(mapStateToProps(state)).toEqual({          │  ToProps, assert a
            posts: [                                       │  particular state
                { content: 'stuff', likes: [], date: now },│ will result in the
                { content: 'stuff', likes: [], date: now } │ right props
            ]
        });
    });                                        ┌─ Assert mapDispatchToProps function
});                                            │  has all the right properties
    test('mapDispatchToProps', () => {    ←───┘
        const dispatchStub = jest.fn();
        const mappedDispatch = mapDispatchToProps(dispatchStub);
        expect(mappedDispatch.actions.createNewPost).toBeDefined();
        expect(mappedDispatch.actions.getPostsForPage).toBeDefined();
        expect(mappedDispatch.actions.showComments).toBeDefined();
        expect(mappedDispatch.actions.createError).toBeDefined();
        expect(mappedDispatch.actions.getNextPageOfPosts).toBeDefined();
    });                                              ┌─ Perform snapshot test to
    test('should render posts', function() {   ←─────┤  assert that component's
        const props = {                               │  output hasn't changed
            posts: [
                { id: 1, content: 'stuff', likes: [], date: now },
                { id: 2, content: 'stuff', likes: [], date: now }
            ],
            actions: {
                getPostsForPage: jest.fn(),
                createNewPost: jest.fn(),
                createError: jest.fn(),
                showComments: jest.fn()
            }
        };
        const component = renderer.create(
            <Provider store={store}>
```

```
                <Home {...props} />
              </Provider>
      );
      let tree = component.toJSON();
      expect(tree).toMatchSnapshot();     ◁──┐  Perform snapshot test to
  });                                          assert that component's
});                                            output hasn't changed
```

11.3 Summary

Here are the main things you learned in this chapter:

- Reducers are functions used by Redux to compute changes to state based on a given action.
- Redux is similar to Flux in many ways but introduces the idea of reducers, has a single store, and its action creators don't directly dispatch actions.
- Actions contain information about something that happened. They must have a type but can contain any other information that your store and reducers will need to determine how it should be updated. In Redux, there's a single state tree for the entire application; state all lives in one area and can only be updated through specific APIs.
- Action creators are functions that return actions that can be dispatched by the store. With certain middleware (see next bullet point) in place, you can create asynchronous action creators that are useful for doing things like calling remote APIs.
- Redux allows you to write middleware, a place for injecting custom behavior into the Redux state management process. Middleware is executed before reducers are fired off and allow you to perform side effects or implement global solutions for your app.
- react-redux provides bindings for React components that enable you to connect your components to store, handle the passing of new props, and check for updates from Redux (when the store changes).
- Container components are components that only deal with data and nothing UI-related (think "application data only").
- Presentational components are only concerned with what you can see or UI-specific data, such as whether a dropdown menu is open (think "what you see").
- Redux enforces a unidirectional data flow pattern where data changes are computed by reducers responding to actions and applied to the store.

In the next chapter, you'll explore the possibilities of server-side rendering in modern web applications and you'll start using React on the server.

12

React on the server and integrating React Router

This chapter covers

- Server-side rendering with React
- When to and when *not* to add server-side rendering to your application
- Transitioning your routing setup to React Router
- Handling authenticated routes with React Router
- Fetching data during server-side rendering
- Using Redux in the server-side rendering process

Did you know you can use React outside the browser? That's because some parts of the react-dom library don't require a browser environment to work and can run on the node.js runtime (or almost any JavaScript runtime with sufficient language support). To be fair, most JavaScript that isn't platform-specific can run on the browser or server; that would exclude IO-related features like reading files or cryptography for the node.js platform and user-related events or DOM-related aspects for browser platforms. But with the robustness and prevalence of the node.js platform, more and more frameworks are starting to be written with server and browser support in mind.

This is true for React, too; it supports server-side rendering (SSR) via React DOM's server APIs. What does that mean? SSR is generally the generation of static HTML markup that can be sent to the browser via HTTP or another protocol; it's still "rendering," but in a server context. Integrating SSR in your application can be useful in certain circumstances and unnecessary in others. In this chapter, we'll explore some of the historical context of server-side rendering, look at when it might make sense to implement, integrate it into your Letters Social app, and replace the router you created in chapters 7 and 8 to better support SSR and allow for future improvements. You'll implement a simple version of server-side rendering using React to get familiar with the basic concepts.

How do I get the code for this chapter?

As with every chapter, you can check out the source code for this chapter by going to the GitHub repository at https://github.com/react-in-action/letters-social. If you want to start this chapter with a clean slate and follow along, you can use your existing code from chapters 10 and 11 (if you followed along and built out the examples yourself) or check out the chapter-specific branch (chapter-12).

Remember, each branch corresponds to the code at the end of the chapter (for example, the branch chapter-12 corresponds to the code as it will be at the end of this chapter). You can execute one of the following terminal commands in the directory of your choice to get the code for the current chapter.

If you don't have the repository at all, type the following:

```
git clone git@github.com:react-in-action/letters-social.git
```

If you already have the repository cloned:

```
git checkout chapter-12
```

You may have come here from another chapter, so it's always a good idea to ensure you have all the right dependencies installed:

```
npm install
```

12.1   What is server-side rendering?

Let's take a brief look at the historical context of rendering in web applications before we explore using React on the server. If you're already familiar with how SSR works (maybe you've worked with frameworks like Ruby on Rails or Laravel before or already understand the mechanics), feel free to move ahead to section 12.1.4, where you start to implement SSR for your application.

In the past (and still today for many applications), applications with only server-rendered views were the widespread norm. Generally, these apps would create HTML strings interspersed with user-related or other data and send that down to the browser over HTTP. Things would eventually improve, but at first even the server-side aspect was primitive. Simple server-side scripts were created that would manually concatenate parts of HTML strings together and then send that down as a response. This worked but made things more difficult than they had to be since manually creating concatenated views was time-consuming and could be hard to change. Over time, frameworks and even languages developed or were created to better enable developers to build user interfaces that were primarily rendered on the server.

Figure 12.1 shows a rough overview of this process. The basic idea is that servers respond to requests from the browser with dynamically generated HTML that, for example, contains information specific to the requesting user in some way. The example ERB template shows an example of what an engineer might work with as they create HTML markup. You might be familiar with the Pug (née Jade) templating language if you've worked in the node.js community before.

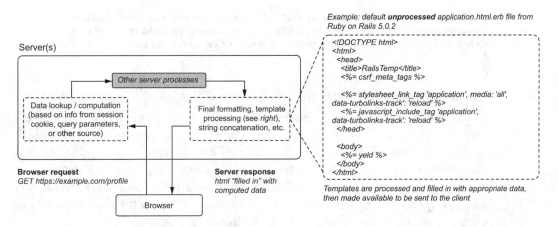

Figure 12.1   A simplified overview of server-side rendering

Frameworks like Ruby on Rails, WordPress (a PHP-based content-management framework), and others developed and grew to fill the need of building applications in this manner. This server-centric approach has worked well and still does. But as client-side JavaScript became more robust and browsers became more powerful, developers eventually started using JavaScript for more than just adding basic interactivity to their apps. They started using it to generate and update interfaces with dynamic data. This meant the server was utilized less for templating and more as a source of data. Today you'll find that many apps (like yours) use a robust client-side application to manage the UI and a remote (usually REST) API to provide dynamic data. This paradigm is the one you've been using in the book so far. But this chapter starts to change that slightly as you blend server-rendered and client-rendered patterns. The next section will show a more concrete example of some of what goes into server-side rendering. Figure 12.2 shows an example of this setup as compared to the one in figure 12.1.

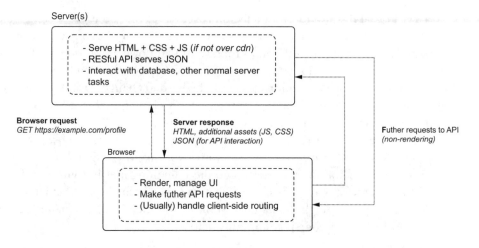

Figure 12.2   As browsers and JavaScript evolved (sometimes slowly), client-side JavaScript took on more responsibilities. In both figure 12.1 and this one, the same basic tasks are being accomplished (fetch or compute data; show it to the user), but client and server take on differing responsibilities.

12.1.1   Digging into server-side rendering

Before you start implementing SSR, we'll look at a few more aspects of it in non-React contexts so that when you do start building it into your app, your task will make more sense. Let's look at an example of SSR that uses ERB (Embedded Ruby). We saw ERB referenced in figure 12.1. ERB is a feature of the Ruby programming language that can be used to create templates for HTML (or other types of text like XML for RSS feed generation). If you're curious, you can learn more about ERB and Ruby on Rails at http://guides.rubyonrails.org/layouts_and_rendering.html.

Many Ruby on Rails apps will incorporate views generated using ERB templates. The framework will read the .erb template files created by developers and populate them using data from a server or elsewhere. Filled with data, the resulting text will be sent to the user's browser. The ability to template HTML views is similar to JSX, albeit with a different syntax and semantics. React creates and manages the UI, whereas templating approaches like ERB only cover the "creation" half. Listing 12.1 shows a simple example of an ERB file to demonstrate the sort of templating that's often used in server-rendered applications. Aside from the syntax differences, it shouldn't be too dissimilar from what you're used to in other templating languages like Handlebars, Jade, EJS, or even in React. Many of these templating languages allow you to use many of the basic constructs available in programming languages like looping, variable access, and more; React's JSX is no different.

Listing 12.1   ERB templating

```
<h1>Listing Books</h1>
<table>
```

```
  <tr>
    <th>Title</th>
    <th>Summary</th>
    <th></th>
    <th></th>
    <th></th>
  </tr>
<% @books.each do |book| %>                                              #A
  <tr>
    <td><%= book.title %></td>
    <td><%= book.content %></td>
    <td><%= link_to "Show", book %></td>
    <td><%= link_to "Edit", edit_book_path(book) %></td>
    <td><%= link_to "Remove", book, method: :delete, data: { confirm: "Are
     you sure?" } %></td>
  </tr>
<% end %>
</table>
<br>
<%= link_to "New book", new_book_path %>
```

It might be helpful to take a quick look at what gets sent to the browser in the server-rendering process to get a feel for the mechanics of what you want to build. After the server processes a template like in listing 12.1, it sends a text response to the browser. The result will look something like listing 12.2, which shows a text representation of an HTTP (version 1/1.1) response. This is similar to what you'll be sending down to your browser when you're rendering the Letters Social app on the server.

I used a common command-line tool, cURL, to fetch the web page at http://example.com so we could see a raw HTTP request. You probably already have cURL installed on your machine, but if you don't, head over to https://github.com/curl/curl and follow the instructions there to install it. Listing 12.2 shows the "raw" HTTP response sample output from running `curl -v https://example.com`. I omitted some content for brevity and left in the > and < symbols from cURL to indicate outgoing (>) and incoming (<) messages. If you don't want to use cURL, you can always navigate to http://example.com in your browser and open the developer tools. Chrome, Firefox, and Edge all have network sections that let you inspect HTTP requests, too.

Listing 12.2 Sample HTTP request

```
> GET / HTTP/1.1
> Host: example.com                          Request you sent to
> User-Agent: curl/7.51.0                     server using cURL
> Accept: */*

< HTTP/1.1 200 OK
< Cache-Control: max-age=604800               Response headers provide
< Content-Type: text/html                     information like status of
< Date: Mon, 01 May 2017 16:34:13 GMT         response and other helpful
< Etag: "359670651+gzip+ident"                info (Cache-Control, Expires,
< Expires: Mon, 08 May 2017 16:34:13 GMT      and so on)
```

```
< Last-Modified: Fri, 09 Aug 2013 23:54:35 GMT
< Server: ECS (rhv/81A7)
< Vary: Accept-Encoding
< X-Cache: HIT
< Content-Length: 1270
<
<!doctype html>
<html>
<head>
    <title>Example Domain</title>

    <meta charset="utf-8" />
    <meta http-equiv="Content-type" content="text/html; charset=utf-8" />
    <meta name="viewport" content="width=device-width, initial-scale=1" />
</head>

<body>
<div>
    <h1>Example Domain</h1>
    <p>This domain is established to be used for illustrative examples in
      documents. You may use this
    domain in examples without prior coordination or asking for
      permission.</p>
    <p><a href="http://www.iana.org/domains/example">More
      information...</a></p>
</div>
</body>
</html>
```

Response headers provide information like status of response and other helpful info (Cache-Control, Expires, and so on)

Response body— what you'll use React to generate

By the end of this chapter, you want the server portion of your application to be able to create the same sort of result as in listing 12.2 (but specific to your app, of course). Hopefully by now the general idea of server rendering is making sense. In the next two sections, we'll explore when it does and doesn't make sense to build this functionality into your application.

12.2   *Why render on the server?*

Why would you want to do SSR? There might be some very compelling reasons, depending on your use case. For example, there's some anecdotal evidence that a server-rendered app fares better when it comes to being indexed and crawled by search engines. Although it seems that large search engines like Google can execute or at least emulate JavaScript and the DOM on the server, it also seems as if sites that render dynamic content without requiring the DOM tend to fair better. It's difficult to ascertain the exact impact of SSR versus non-SSR apps on search engine optimization (SEO) because Google and other companies' site-ranking algorithms are closely held, but there's at least anecdotal evidence from people and teams in the industry that it can have a positive effect. If you have a highly public app that heavily depends on showing up in search engine results, you might consider SSR to increase crawler-friendliness in addition to all your other SEO optimizations.

In this book, you've been building an app that requires interactivity and allows users to dynamically create content, but not every app has those requirements. If you only want the static aspects of React, you could easily use React-DOM's static rendering abilities to create a static page generator or templating library.

Another reason you might want to render on the server is to optimize your users' experience. If your app needs to show content to users as quickly as possible, rendering on the server might allow you to present that content to them more quickly than waiting on a client-side render might. This could be the case if your app is something that depends heavily on showing ads or other static paid content to people and if the size of the payload isn't substantially large. In cases where you want to show content quickly without interaction, you tend to be more concerned about the *first paint*, which is when a user is first able to see something in their browser.

The first paint is one of many metrics you can use to determine how well an app is being rendered by the browser. Another one is the *perceptual speed index* (usually just *speed index* or *SpeedIndex*). This is calculated by recording how much of the page has finished rendering over time. Browsers will record a video of the page as it is loading and determine what percent of the page has loaded at a given interval. This metric can be useful for understanding at an aggregate level how quickly a given page appears to load for a user. SSR can potentially contribute to a faster speed index by allowing more of your site to be renderable by the browser earlier in the loading process. Learn more about speed index at https://sites.google.com/a/webpagetest.org/docs/using-webpagetest/metrics/speed-index.

Most apps will benefit from a faster speed index and quick first paint. But in other cases, you may not care as much about showing something to a user as quickly as possible because you care more about how quickly they can use your app. The time it takes until a user can interact with your application or page, called *time to interactive* (TTI), might be more important if your app is a highly interactive, feature-rich application like Basecamp or Asana. For these applications, SSR might not make sense because they aren't public-facing and rely more heavily on interactivity than on showing their users something quickly.

Let's look at a couple of applications and see how TTI could hypothetically factor in:

- *Basecamp (project management app)*—Users want to be able to search for issues, update to-dos, and check project statuses. In this case, you would want to optimize your app to load JavaScript as quickly as possible instead of trying to show the user content as quickly as possible.

- *Medium (blog/writing app)*—Users want to be able to read and browse articles as quickly as possible. Their ability to do so doesn't depend on the interactivity of the app, so in this case you might want to optimize for the first paint.

When considering SSR you'll also want to weigh the resource-usage tradeoffs between rendering on the server and on the client. If you're rendering a huge amount of data (maybe thousands of rows in an online spreadsheet), doing that on the server will probably require you to send down a much larger initial payload to the browser. This, in turn, will probably mean a longer TTI that could be detrimental to your users and will probably use more server resources. Getting the same amount of data in JSON format after the app has loaded, for example, would probably result in a smaller payload size and potentially better user experience.

Server rendering with enterprise and consumer applications

You may feel like our discussion of server rendering in this chapter is something theoretical that you'll never have to deal with. But I believe you'll find that server rendering is more common than you think and is an option many teams will actively consider. I've seen this to be true in my own experience and in the experiences of other engineers I've met. I've worked on public-facing consumer products and walled-off enterprise applications and had the chance to see server rendering considered in diverse business scenarios. In both sorts of cases, we wanted to do the best thing for our users and we considered server-side rendering as an option.

In the enterprise application, we were dealing with users who wanted the application to be interactive quickly, not just quickly rendered. We also had to serve pages that were potentially filled with hundreds or even thousands of rows of financial data (which could potentially obviate gains achieved by server rendering). The application was comprised of several smaller applications, and we served different JavaScript bundles depending on which of the apps were in use at a given time. To make matters even more complicated, data integrity and security were of the topmost concern for us, so server rendering would potentially introduce a new area to secure and evaluate from a security perspective.

These factors made server rendering a "nice to have" that would be saved for some future time when it could be reevaluated. We found that we could do other things to help our users, like improving our server performance, optimizing how we serve application assets, and defer data fetching on the client until necessary. Interestingly, people also tend to have different expectations about different sorts of applications. Consumer applications like Facebook, Twitter, and Amazon all compete for users that have a wide variety of choices they can make and so directly compete with others on many fronts. In my experience, enterprise users tend to have a slightly different set of expectations for an application they use for work. Speed is, of course, incredibly important, but so are stability, reliability, clarity, and other important aspects of a business application. It might make sense for an engineering team to optimize on these dimensions instead of spending the equivalent time optimizing on a less impactful metric. That's not always the case, but it has been for some projects I've worked on.

Other projects I've worked on had very different demands. Another application was in the e-commerce space. Server rendering of pages made sense because time to first paint and SEO considerations were extremely important. We worked to minimize the size of bundled assets and show content to the user as quickly as possible. Any appearance of sluggishness would potentially dissuade a user from continuing in their shopping experience. The applications were also tightly integrated with marketing efforts, so working to guarantee stable SEO performance was a priority.

There are still other sorts of cases where server rendering can be applied, but I hope that these two simpler examples help shed a little light on some of the practicalities of what we're discussing in this chapter.

You don't necessarily have to go all-or-nothing in your SSR implementation. If you must render thousands of rows in a spreadsheet, it might make sense to let the client handle that aspect of rendering but render the signup and login pages on the server since those are smaller and rely more on first paint than on time to interactivity. You could also choose to render certain portions of pages on the web but allow the client to handle all further data fetching and rendering. If you're interested in learning more about thinking through different aspects of web performance, a great place to start is Google's Web Fundamentals guide: https://developers.google.com/web/fundamentals/performance/.

12.3 *You might not need SSR*

Even though there are some potential benefits to SSR, you should only build it into your app when the need really exists. That's because it can, depending on how deeply integrated it is, introduce significant complexity. In this chapter, we'll implement a basic, even simplistic, version of SSR (server-side rendering) to get familiar with the concepts, but building a robust, purpose-built implementation that handles all the different nuances of doing SSR can represent a significant technical involvement.

There are at least a few reasons why integrating server-side rendering can add complexity. Here are a few of them:

- You'll need to synchronize the server and client in a way that your client can understand when it takes over. This can involve setting up markup, event handlers, and more that a client might need. Your authentication implementation will also need to account for requests coming from either the server or the client, which may require changes.
- The client and server operate within different paradigms that don't always easily map to one another (for example, no DOM, no filesystem, and so on). You must coordinate handoff and rendering and make sure you either don't use, or else properly handle, components that depend on a browser environment.
- Although there are a few exceptions, React (and any JavaScript) is most reliably run on Node.js runtime. This can tend to couple your client and the server that renders it because they now both need to support JavaScript. That can be a good thing, but it does mean you're tying yourself to the JavaScript language/platform more than you would otherwise.
- Fine-tuning SSR can require special tuning of your client and server. Performance gains are usually realized in small, incremental wins that focus on specific

functionality and almost always involve tradeoffs. This can sometimes mean less flexibility in making rapid changes and a more complex maintenance process. Server-side rendering adds one more aspect to this process.

Overall, the main reason for caution here is the "use only what you need" idea. I don't want you to come away with the idea that your React app isn't complete or is somehow "not React-y enough" unless it's using SSR. The best engineering decision-making processes involve a thorough consideration of the tradeoffs involved (not just what other people are using or what's popular!), and that applies here, too. An example might be the case where you're writing a simple blogging app as a personal side project. The reality is that you don't need the infrastructure and orchestration technology of, say, Netflix, if you're not Netflix. Even so, not all large companies are doing SSR. At the present time of writing, for instance, even Instagram doesn't seem to be using React to do SSR, and that company is heavily invested in React. Use what you need.

12.4   *Rendering components on the server*

Now that we've briefly looked at some of the tradeoffs of server-side rendering, we can start to dig in and see how it works with React. Let's start with the React API that you'll use. ReactDOMServer (accessed via `require('react-dom/server')` or import React-DOM from `'react-dom/server'`) exposes four important methods that you can use to generate the initial HTML for your components:

- renderToString
- renderToStaticMarkup
- renderToNodeStream
- renderToStaticNodeStream

Let's look at each method in turn.

First, we have ReactDOMServer.renderToString. renderToString does what it sounds like: it takes a React element and generates the corresponding HTML markup from the component based on initial state and props (either default or passed) that exist when the method is called. React elements, as you'll remember from earlier chapters, are the smallest building blocks of React apps. They're created with React.createElement (or, more commonly, from JSX) and they're created from either a string type or a React component class. The method looks like this:

```
ReactDOMServer.renderToString(element) string
```

When you're rendering on the server, you're using components and passing props as usual. The key difference between what you're used to so far and using React on the server is the lack of a DOM and browser environment. This means React won't run lifecycle methods like componentWillMount or persist state or utilize other DOM-specific features.

> ### Exercise 12.1
>
> Server rendering can involve a significant amount of complexity and shouldn't be treated as a standard or "must-have" feature for all applications. Take some time to think through how you might approach implementing (or choosing not to implement) server-side rendering for the following types of apps:
>
> - Enterprise application with no public-facing portions
> - Social media site that depends heavily on advertising
> - E-commerce application
> - Video-hosting platform

`ReactDOM.renderToStaticMarkup` will do the same thing as `renderToString`, but without attaching any extra DOM attributes for React to use when "taking over" on the client side. This is useful for cases when you want to do basic templating or static site generation and don't need any of the extra attributes. `renderToStaticMarkup` is almost identical to `renderToString`:

```
ReactDOMServer.renderToStaticMarkup(element) string
```

You won't be using `renderToStaticMarkup` beyond this point, but once you're done learning about how to implement SSR with React it should be simple to use it in future projects where appropriate.

You may have noticed that the first two methods have apparent complements in `renderToNodeStream` and `renderToStaticNodeStream`. If so, you've guessed correctly. These methods are identical to the others except they use node's Streams API and were introduced in React 16 along with the fiber reconciler and many other changes. Streams are commonly used in node.js, and if you've done any work with node, you've probably heard of them. If you haven't, that's fine too, and you can learn more at https://nodejs.org/api/stream.html. The takeaway for our purposes is that these stream-based methods are asynchronous. This gives them a significant advantage over their synchronous counterparts. For some time, one of the minor disadvantages of server rendering with React was that these methods were synchronous. That presented a challenge for applications that must render complex pages with many components. We'll explore these methods later in the chapter when we look at data fetching on the server as part of server rendering.

We can focus on `renderToString` now that you know a little bit more about the API methods available to us. `renderToString` will generate code that React can work with and use on the client. React-DOM has another method, `hydrate`, that works almost exactly like the regular `render` method you're so used to. The main difference is that `hydrate` specifically handles markup generated by server-side rendering.

If you call `ReactDOM.hydrate()` on a node that already has the markup created by React-DOM on the server, React will preserve the existing HTML and do less work than it would otherwise. This should generally mean even less work for React to do on initial startup in addition to being a quicker initial load (depending on how much data you're sending down and other factors like server load, network, weather, and so forth). I won't note it again, but remember that SSR isn't magic, and you can easily obviate any performance gains if you do things like load huge JavaScript files, don't split your code, or go against other best practices.

Till now, you haven't touched any server files. Aside from the limited scope of this chapter, server programming is generally outside the scope of this book, so we won't cover much about the node.js runtime or web server programming paradigms. If you're curious to learn more about node and server-side programming, check out *Node.js in Action*, 2nd Edition by Alex Young, et al. (Manning Publications, 2017): www.manning.com/books/node-js-in-action.

You're going to start building SSR by focusing on the server changes you need to make. Listing 12.3 shows the state of the main app server code as it is before you do anything to get it to work with React. I've included all of it so you can get a sense of what it's doing. Most of the code is boilerplate middleware that a simple Express application might use, but most of it isn't directly related to SSR. Figure 12.3 puts the code in listing 12.3 into context of the rendering approaches we've discussed so far in this chapter.

Server(s)

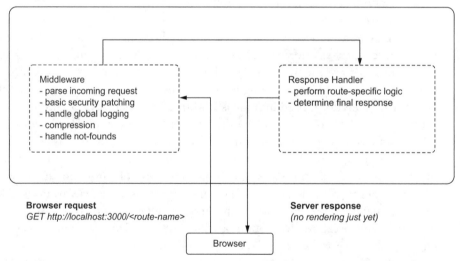

Figure 12.3   As of listing 12.3, this is the basics of what the server code is doing. It sets up your server, adds some boilerplate middleware, and then serves a stripped-down HTML file that in turn downloads your app.

Listing 12.3 shows the (basic) server setup for your app. When you put it into the context of the SSR approaches we've been looking at in this chapter, it matches with the client-focused paradigm. In this sort of approach, the server will usually only send down an HTML file that has no pre-rendered content in it. Your build tools are currently taking care of generating and serving the HTML file. That file contains references to scripts that will download and execute to do the work of rendering and managing the application, but no rendering is done on the server (yet!).

Listing 12.3   Starting out on the server (server/server.js)

```
import { __PRODUCTION__ } from 'environs';
import { resolve } from 'path';
import bodyParser from 'body-parser';
import compression from 'compression';
import cors from 'cors';
import express from 'express';
import helmet from 'helmet';
import favicon from 'serve-favicon';
import hpp from 'hpp';
import logger from 'morgan';
import cookieParser from 'cookie-parser';
import responseTime from 'response-time';
import * as firebase from 'firebase-admin';
import config from 'config';

import DB from '../db/DB';

const app = express();
const backend = DB();

app.use(logger(__PRODUCTION__ ? 'combined' : 'dev'));
app.use(helmet.xssFilter({ setOnOldIE: true }));
app.use(responseTime());
app.use(helmet.frameguard());
app.use(helmet.ieNoOpen());
app.use(helmet.noSniff());
app.use(helmet.hidePoweredBy({ setTo: 'react' }));
app.use(compression());
app.use(cookieParser());
app.use(bodyParser.json());
app.use(hpp());
app.use(cors({ origin: config.get('ORIGINS') }));

app.use('/api', backend);
app.use(favicon(resolve(__dirname, '..', 'static', 'assets', 'meta',
    'favicon.ico')));

app.use((req, res, next) => {
    const err = new Error('Not Found');
    err.status = 404;
    next(err);
});

app.use((err, req, res) => {
    console.error(err);
```

Using ES modules syntax, available in node 8.5 and higher via ESM

Setting up middleware that will apply to all incoming requests; handles logging, some basic security protections, parsing of incoming requests.

Respond to requests, where you'll integrate with React DOM

Error-handling code that will catch forwarded errors from other routes and send to the client

```
        return res.status(err.status || 500).json({
            message: err.message
        });
    });
});

module.exports = app;
```

The first step you want to take is to bring in React-DOM and try rendering a simple component. You'll render a simple `div` first with some text inside it before you move on to integrating your app. You'll use `React.createElement` for this small example so you don't have to deal with transpiling your server file, but you'll be able to use JSX in other files later when you pull your components in to be used. That's because you'll use `babel-register`, a Babel library for development that transpiles your code on-the-fly. You can see us pulling in `babel-register` in index.js. In a production environment you wouldn't do that. Instead, you'd be using something like Webpack and Babel to compile your code into a bundle. I can't cover tooling in-depth here, but you can learn more at https://webpack.js.org and https://babeljs.io.

For this first pass, all you'll do is insert a simple message as the child content of a `div` and send it to the client. Once you have that in place, you'll run the server and check to see what you get back. Figure 12.4 shows what the code in listing 12.4 does.

Listing 12.4   Trying out server-side rendering

```
//...
app.use('/api', backend);                                         Within request handler, create
app.use(favicon(resolve(__dirname, '..', 'static', 'assets', 'meta',     HTML string and send it down
    'favicon.ico')));
app.use('*', (req, res, next) => {
    const componentResponse = ReactDOMServer.renderToString(      Use renderToString
        React.createElement(                                      and pass in bare-
            'div',                                                bones React
            null,                                                 element
            `Rendered on the server at ${new Date()}`
        )
    );                                                            Pass in simple string
    res.send(componentResponse).end();          Send              with timestamp as
});                                              response          child content
//...                                            to client
```

Create element with type of div and no props

If you make the change in listing 12.4, run only the server with `node server/run.js` in a terminal, and use another session to send a request with cURL, then you should see a response coming back from the server. Before, you were sending down the same HTML string every time, and that document would load your application scripts after the fact. React would then run and render your application into the DOM (creating DOM nodes, assigning event listeners, and so on). With this new approach, you can delegate that first render to the server and let React take over. Listing 12.5 shows how to run the server and use cURL to inspect responses coming back from the server.

Server(s)

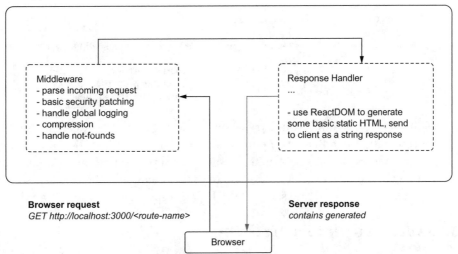

Figure 12.4   You're now using React-DOM to render a simple HTML string and send it to the client. In some sense, this is all SSR is (create static markup, send it to the client). The complexity I've mentioned tends to come from, among other things, getting all the data you need to create the text, coordinating the process with the client, and then optimization.

```
$ npm run server:dev

// ... in a different terminal session

$  curl -v http://localhost:3000
> GET / HTTP/1.1
> Host: localhost:3000
> User-Agent: curl/7.51.0
> Accept: */*
>
< HTTP/1.1 200 OK
< X-Powered-By: react
< X-XSS-Protection: 1; mode=block
< X-Frame-Options: SAMEORIGIN
< X-Download-Options: noopen
< X-Content-Type-Options: nosniff
< Access-Control-Allow-Origin: *
< Content-Type: text/html; charset=utf-8
< Content-Length: 144
< ETag: W/"90-gXhNJUy73fc2MSrpr7eaKDZ7OV8"
< Vary: Accept-Encoding
< X-Response-Time: 0.795ms
< Date: Mon, 08 May 2017 10:26:55 GMT
< Connection: keep-alive
```

Hit running server with request, inspect what you get back

You should get headers back in your request, but you care most about response body.

```
<
* Curl_http_done: called premature == 0
* Connection #0 to host localhost left intact

<div data-reactroot="">Rendered on the server at Mon May 08 2017 03:26:55
    GMT-0700 (PDT)</div>
```

Special react-root and react-checksum properties on outermost HTML element

With that, you've done your first server rendering. You used React to create a string representation of a React component and send it to the client. Right now, React isn't being loaded so it can't pick up from where the server left off, but once it's included it will be able to take over. Try running the same commands but opt to use `renderTo-StaticMarkup` instead and see how the HTTP response from your server differs.

12.5   *Switching to React Router*

The router you built in earlier chapters was optimized for handling routing in the browser, but it wasn't designed with server-side rendering in mind. The chance to dig in and see what's possible with React was a large part of building it yourself and not just installing a third-party library, and I hope that it gave you the chance to see how components can be used in different ways.

It may be useful enough for the relatively simple needs of the sample application, but your router is lacking in a few areas. It has a pretty bare-bones API, and it would be nice if it supported things like routing hooks (transitions between routes), middleware (logic that can be applied to multiple routes), and more. And as you dig into server-side rendering with React, you're going to need more functionality, like the ability to generate a component tree to render based on a request URL. That's why you'll switch to using React Router V3.

React Router (https://github.com/ReactTraining/react-router) seems to be the single most-used and most-developed routing solution for React. It enjoys a robust following and community of contributors on GitHub and has gone through several major revisions.

As of the time of writing, the most recent major version for React Router is 4. It's currently in flux and may have been replaced by a new major version by the time you read this. You'll use version 3 because its API is similar to the router that you created, and you should be able to use it with few changes. You'll also use it because it's a robust technology that has been developed by the React open source community. It can do more than your simpler router can and even exceeds the needs you have here.

It's worth noting that React Router is a substantial technology, and we'll only be dipping into its potential here. The project has come to include a wide variety of routing features for many situations. The latest major version (4 at time of writing) even has solutions for routing with the React Native platform. The number of developers

> ## Choosing third-party libraries vs. building in-house
>
> Another reason you're switching over to React Router instead of sticking with your homegrown solution is that it's a more likely candidate for any business situations you or your team will be in. You may often opt for an open source solution like React Router over writing your own. That's because, depending on your needs, the time required to build and maintain a robust solution to a problem may or may not be worthwhile. Navigating the build-or-buy decision can be tricky when it comes to external dependencies, too. My two cents here are to keep two things in mind: 1) you don't have to use something because everyone else does, and 2) there's often much more work in building your own solution than just the initial work—maintenance is usually the biggest time sink. A large community of open source contributors will often catch many bugs before you encounter them yourself.

using and working on React Router has helped make the project incredibly useful, but it also has the drawback of sometimes changing substantially between major versions. It's for this reason, and the similarity to the router you built from scratch, that you won't use the latest version of React Router. If you find yourself wanting to use the latest version of React Router, I have a post on my blog that covers using React Router v4 with React 16: https://ifelse.io/2017/09/07/server-rendering-with-react-router-and-react-16-fiber. I'll also note that even though APIs have changed between versions of React Router, most of the same concepts apply—you'll just need to do the work of remapping functionality to new APIs when transitioning.

12.5.1 Setting up React router

We've decided on React Router as a production-ready replacement for your own router, so let's see how to get it set up. The first step is to make sure you have React Router installed and swapped out with your current router. Even though the technologies are different, the APIs that you'll use should be similar.

React Router should already be installed with the project dependencies. Now you need to start transitioning your project over to React Router and a setup that will allow you to do SSR. Start with your current src/index.js file. This is an entry-point file where you've been setting up the main parts of your app, including listening to browser history, rendering your router component, and activating your authentication events listener.

This won't work for your SSR setup because so much of the code there depends on a browser environment and because you won't need all the functionality of React Router to get the app working. All you really need to keep is your authentication listener. Before you add anything in, create a helper tool for later. Listing 12.6 shows how to create a simple utility to check whether you're in a browser environment. Some tooling technologies like Webpack can help you bundle code that's environment aware, but for our purposes, stick to this simpler approach.

Listing 12.6   Checking for browser environment (src/utils/environment.js)

```
export function isServer() {
    return typeof window === 'undefined';
}
```

Now you can use this helper to determine what environment you're in and execute code conditionally depending on your needs. It doesn't do exhaustive checks to ensure you're in a browser environment, but it should suffice for your needs. Having to account for the environment your code is running in is a pretty common aspect of building apps with SSR capabilities or apps that share code between client and server (sometimes referred to as *universal* or *isomorphic*). In my experience, this can also be a common source of bugs that can be hard to track down, especially if you install third-party dependencies that aren't built with environment awareness in mind.

By now, lots of the existing technology in the React community will usually either have support for SSR or indicate where it might cause problems. That wasn't always the case. When using earlier versions of React several years ago, I ran into bugs in React itself that made some aspects of certain libraries fail unpredictably. Things are much better now, though, and SSR is a consideration not only of the React community but also the core team.

Before moving on, you need to make a minor adjustment to one of your reducers to take the server environment into account. The user reducer will set a cookie on the browser using `js-cookie`. The server doesn't normally allow you to store cookies (although there are libraries that can emulate this behavior, like `tough-cookie` (https://github.com/salesforce/tough-cookie)), so you need to use your environment helper to adjust this code. The following listing shows the modifications you'll need to make.

Listing 12.7   Modifying the user reducer

```
export function user(state = initialState.user, action) {
    switch (action.type) {
        case types.auth.LOGIN_SUCCESS:
            const { user, token } = action;
            if (!isServer()) {                                  Only attempt to use
                Cookies.set('letters-token', token);            browser cookies if you're
            }                                                   in a browser environment.
            return Object.assign({}, state.user, {
                authenticated: true,
                name: user.name,
                id: user.id,
                profilePicture: user.profilePicture ||
    '/static/assets/users/4.jpeg',
                token
            });
        case types.auth.LOGOUT_SUCCESS:
            Cookies.remove('letters-token');
            return initialState.user;
```

```
        default:
            return state;
    }
}
```

Back to the task at hand. You need to get React Router set up. Much like your router, React Router (version 3) allows you to use a nested hierarchy of <Route/> components to indicate which components should be mapped to which URLs. As I've noted, React Router is an incredibly widely used and battle-tested solution with many features that you didn't add to your own router; you'll stick to directly swapping it in for your own router instead of exploring all it can do.

Create a new file, src/routes.js, for your routes. You're breaking your routes into their own file because they'll need to be accessed by your server and your client. This is convenient for apps where client code sits alongside server code, but you might need to find another way to bring in your routes to your server if they're hosted elsewhere (via npm, a Git submodule, and so on). Your routes file should look like the router you created, with a few minor differences. You added the ability to specify an index component in the same <Route/> component, while React Router exposes a separate component for that purpose. Figure 12.5 shows the high-level role of your routes configuration; it works in the same general manner as your router did and serves to map URLs to components or component trees (when nesting). Listing 12.8 shows how to integrate React Router into your routing setup.

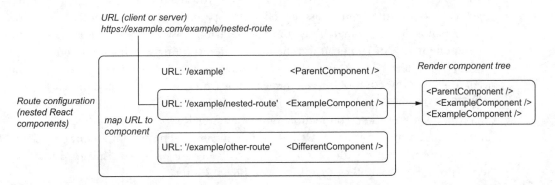

Figure 12.5 In the same way as the router you built, the routes configuration for React Router maps URLs to components. You can nest components in order to share certain parts of the UI across pages or subsections (like a navbar or other shared component).

Listing 12.8 Creating routes for React Router (src/routes.js)

```
import React from 'react';

import App from './pages/app';
import Home from './pages/index';
import SinglePost from './pages/post';
```

```
import Login from './pages/login';
import NotFound from './pages/404';

import { Route, IndexRoute } from 'react-router';

export const routes = (
    <Route path="/" component={App}>
        <IndexRoute component={Home} />
        <Route path="posts/:post" component={SinglePost} />
        <Route path="login" component={Login} />
        <Route path="*" component={NotFound} />
    </Route>
);
```

Use App to wrap the entire app.

Use React Router's IndexRoute component to make sure you can show components at index (/) paths.

Match components with paths as you did with your own router.

Now that you have some routes set up, you can import them into your main app file for use with React Router. The same routes will get used on the client and server, which is where part of the *universal* or *isomorphic* aspect of SSR you may have heard about comes into play. Reusing code on the client and the server can be a big deal, but you probably won't start to see the more significant benefits of it here in such a limited case. The advantage you do gain here is in easily exposing your client components to your server in the "normal" React way.

Now import your routes into your server. Listing 12.9 shows how to bring your routes into the server and use them in the rendering process. How is your server going to grab the right component(s) to render? Because routing is just mapping URLs to actions (HTTP responses, in this case), you need to be able to look up the right component that you've associated with a path. In your own router, you were using a basic URL-regex-matching library to determine whether a URL was mapped to a component in your router. It did the work of determining which component, if any, should be rendered based on a URL (refer to figure 12.5). React Router will allow you to do the same thing but on the server. That way, you can use the incoming URL from the HTTP request to the server to match the component(s) to render into static markup. That's the key connection point between React Router and your goal of doing SSR. React Router uses a URL to render a component or component tree like it normally would, but on the server. The next listing shows how to set up the initial server portion of your SSR capabilities with React Router.

Listing 12.9   Using React Router on the server (server/server.js)

```
//...
import { renderToString } from 'react-dom/server';
import React from 'react';
import { match, RouterContext } from 'react-router';
import { Provider } from 'react-redux';

import configureStore from '../src/store/configureStore';
import initialReduxState from '../src/constants/initialState';
import { routes } from '../src/routes';
```

Import some utils from React Router, renderToString from React DOM, Redux Provider component, your store, and your routes

```
//...
app.use('*', (req, res) => {
    match({ routes: routes, location: req.originalUrl },
    (err, redirectLocation, props) => {
        if (redirectLocation && req.originalUrl !== '/login') {
            return res.redirect(302, redirectLocation.pathname +
    redirectLocation.search);
        }
```

Pass URL to match function as well as routes

Match gives error, redirect (if any), and props; would be used to render custom error page or redirect

```
        const store = configureStore(initialReduxState);
        const appHtml = renderToString(
            <Provider store={store}>
                <RouterContext {...props} />
            </Provider>
        );
```

Pass in RouterContext component you imported from React Router and wrap it in usual Redux Provider component

Using string template literal to create HTML document with your app HTML inserted inside it

```
        const html = `
            <!doctype html>
            <html>
                <head>
                    <link rel="stylesheet"
    href="http://localhost:3100/static/styles.css" />
                    <meta charset=utf-8/>
                    <meta http-equiv="X-UA-Compatible" content="IE=edge">
                    <title>Letters Social | React In Action by Mark
    Thomas</title>
                    <meta name="viewport" content="width=device-
    width,initial-scale=1">
                </head>
                <body>
                    <div id="app">
                        ${appHtml}
                    </div>
                    <script src="http://localhost:3000/bundle.js"
    type='text/javascript'></script>
                </body>
            </html>
        `.trim();
        res.setHeader('Content-type', 'text/html');
        res.send(html).end();
    });
});

//... Error handling

export default app;
```

Set headers on response and send back to browser

12.6 Handling authenticated routes with React router

Now that you have your server set up, you can clean up the client-side of your app a bit. You need to make sure you're using your new routing setup. You also need to move around some of the logic you built related to authentication so you can better utilize React Router. To do that, you'll use a set of features available from React

Router: hooks. Similar to the way lifecycle methods work for mounting, updating, and unmounting components, React Router exposes certain hooks for transitions between routes. There are quite a few ways you can use these hooks, including the following:

- You can trigger data fetching for a page or check if a user is logged in before allowing them to finish the URL transition.
- You can handle any cleanup or maybe end an analytics session when a user leaves a page—you're not restricted to entry-related events.
- With React Router's hooks you can even do synchronous *or* asynchronous work, so you're not restricted to either one.
- Send pageview events to an analytics platform such as Google Analytics.

Figure 12.6 shows the basic flow of the hooks you can use in React Router v3. React Router interacts with the History API (https://developer.mozilla.org/en-US/docs/Web/API/History_API) under the hood, but exposes these hooks to make routing easier in your applications. If you'd like to learn about more about the React Router V3 API and explore other helpful guides written by the community, check the docs out on GitHub at https://github.com/ReactTraining/react-router/blob/v3/docs/API.md.

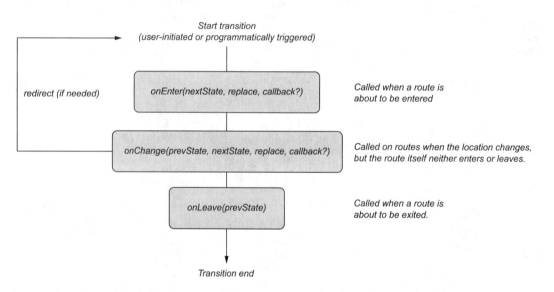

Figure 12.6 React Router exposes a few event handlers on Route components. You can use these to hook into the route transitions that occur when a user or your code causes a transition. Note that the "redirect" is not an HTTP redirect with a 3XX status code.

You'll use the onEnter hook to check for a logged-in user for certain routes and redirect them to the login page if there is no authenticated user. In practice, you'd want to think through your application from a security perspective and put some serious time into how you prevent a user from transitioning to pages they shouldn't be able to transition to. You'd also need to ensure your security strategy extends to your server as well. But for now, Firebase and route hooks should be sufficient to protect some of your routes. The next listing shows how you can set up the onEnter hook for protected pages. You might recognize the authentication logic from the last chapter, where used it in the login action. Figure 12.6 shows how this process works.

Listing 12.10 Setting up an `onEnter` hook (src/routes.js)

```
import React from 'react';

import { Route, IndexRoute } from 'react-router';

import App from './pages/app';
import Home from './pages/index';
import SinglePost from './pages/post';
import Login from './pages/login';
import Profile from './pages/profile';
import NotFound from './pages/error';
import { firebase } from './backend';
import { isServer } from './utils/environment';
import { getFirebaseUser, getFirebaseToken } from './backend/auth';

async function requireUser(nextState, replace, callback) {
    if (isServer()) {
        return callback();
    }
    try {
        const isOnLoginPage = nextState.location.pathname === '/login';
        const firebaseUser = await getFirebaseUser();
        const fireBaseToken = await getFirebaseToken();
        const noUser = !firebaseUser || !fireBaseToken;

        if (noUser && !isOnLoginPage && !isServer()) {
            replace({
                pathname: '/login'
            });
            return callback();
        }
        if (noUser && isOnLoginPage) {
            return callback();
        }
        return callback();
    } catch (err) {
        return callback(err);
    }
}

export const routes = (
    <Route path="/" component={App}>
        <IndexRoute component={Home} onEnter={requireUser} />
        <Route path="/posts/:postId" component={SinglePost}
      onEnter={requireUser} />
```

Annotations:
- React Router hooks take three arguments: nextState, a replace function, and a callback.
- Import Firebase and isServer utilities.
- If you're on server, proceed
- You need to know if you're on login page so you don't infinitely redirect
- If no token or user and you're not on login page, redirect user
- Use Firebase utility functions included in sample repository to get Firebase user and token
- If no user but they're on login page, allow them to proceed
- If error, callback with it
- Add hook to appropriate components using prop

```
        <Route path="/login" component={Login} />
        <Route path="*" component={NotFound} />
    </Route>
);
```

The final bit of setup you need to do before moving on is to clean up the main app file and replace your link components. The following listing shows the stripped-down version of the main client-side file.

Listing 12.11   Cleaning up your app index (src/index.js)

```
import React from 'react';
import { hydrate } from 'react-dom';
import { Provider } from 'react-redux';

import { Router, browserHistory } from 'react-router';      ◁──┐  Import router and
import configureStore from './store/configureStore';              browserHistory
import initialReduxState from './constants/initialState';
import { routes } from './routes';                           ◁──   Import your
                                                                   routes.
import './shared/crash';
import './shared/service-worker';
import './shared/vendor';
// NOTE: this isn't ES*-compliant/possible, but works because we use
//     Webpack as a build tool
import './styles/styles.scss';

// Create the Redux store
const store = configureStore(initialReduxState);             ┐ Wrapping your
                                                             │ app in Redux
hydrate(                                                     │ Provider
    <Provider store={store}>                             ◁──┘
        <Router history={browserHistory} routes={routes} />  ◁──┐ Pass in your routes
    </Provider>,                                                │ and browser-
    document.getElementById('app')                             │ History to Router
);                                                              │ component
```

Import and use hydrate method from React-DOM so it can work with server-rendered markup

You've set up React Router using `browserHistory`, but you could have also set it up using either a hash-based or in-memory history. These are slightly different from your browser history in that they don't use the same browser History API. The hash-based history works by changing a hashed fragment in the URL but not changing the user's browser history. The in-memory history API doesn't manipulate the URL at all and is more suited for things like local development or React Native (covered in the next chapter). For more information on the different history implementations available, see https://github.com/ReactTraining/react-router/blob/v3/docs/guides/Histories.md.

If you run the app locally, you should be able to see everything getting rendered on the server and sent down to the client. React should take over, and things should be interactive as you'd expect. You may notice one thing, though: routing with links seems to be broken. That's because you built your own link components that integrate with your old router. Fortunately, all you'll need to do to remedy this problem is swap out the history module you've been using for the one React Router uses. The change-over here should be easy, but it's also worth pointing out that when you choose or build a router it can affect large portions of your application. Links, changing between pages, how props are accessed—they can all be affected by routing and you should take that into consideration.

The main change you need to make is swapping out the history your links use. React Router still uses the browser History API, but you can sync things up with your router by using the one React Router provides instead of what you were using before. Since you centralized your navigation wrapper, any actions that need to route users around should work fine within your new setup. The next listing shows the lines you'll need to change. Aside from that, you shouldn't have to change anything else.

Listing 12.12 Swapping histories out (src/history/history.js)

```
import { browserHistory } from 'react-router';
const history = typeof window !== 'undefined'
    ? browserHistory
    : { push: () => {} };
const navigate = to => history.push(to);
export { history, navigate };
```

Only lines you'll need to change; let React Router know about your transitions

With those changes in place, you should be rendering on the server using React Router! Let's recap as we wrap up:

- When a request comes in, you pass the URL of the request to React Router's match utility to get the component(s) you want to render.
- Using the results from match, you use React DOM's renderToString method to build an HTML response and send it back down to the client.
- If you use cURL or the developer tools to inspect your dev server (running with npm run server:dev), you should see the HTML for your components in the response (see figure 12.7).

12.7 Server rendering with data-fetching

You've integrated server rendering into your application. This can potentially have benefits with regard to app engagement and performance. There's still room to improve, however. You're not currently doing anything to render the app in its full state before sending it down. The payload that you're sending down is the same whether a user is logged in or not. It's currently up to the browser to then do things like start the authentication flow and loading posts. Your server rendering is also synchronous because you're not yet using renderToNodeStream. In this section, you'll improve your server rendering to take advantage of this API and integrate Firebase on your server so you can do rendering that's aware of authentication state. Figure 12.8 shows an overview of server-rendering with data-fetching integrated.

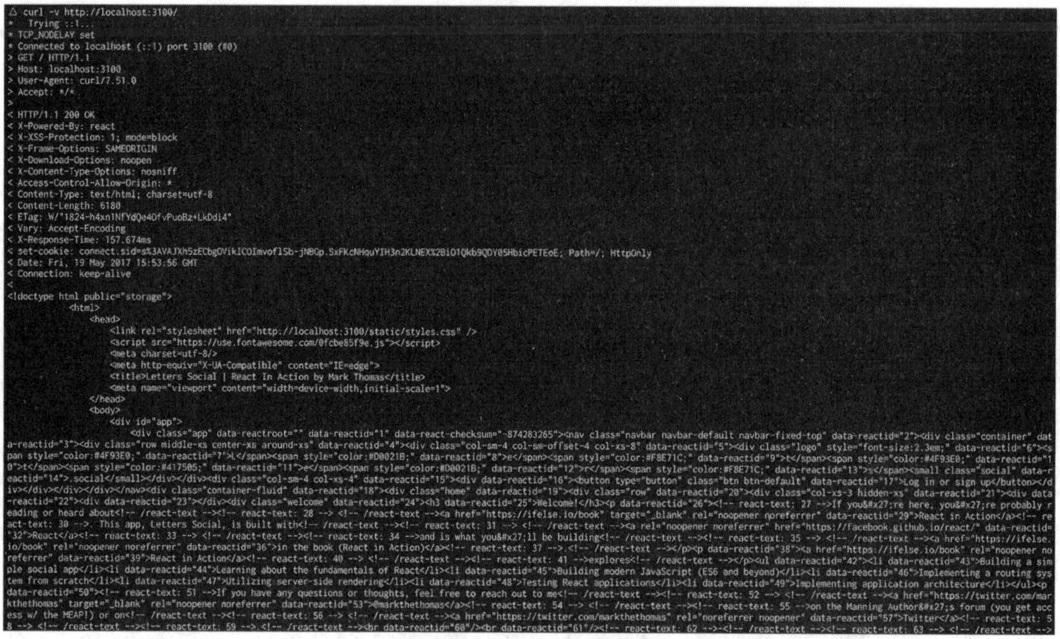

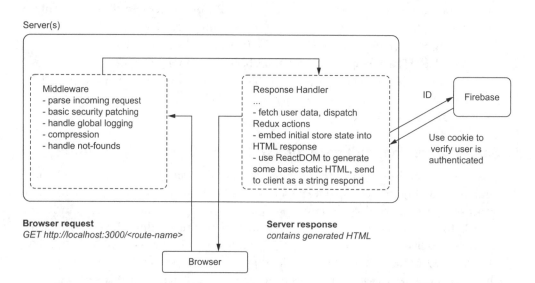

Figure 12.7   Inspecting your server-rendered app. With React-DOM you can create the HTML of your app that you can then send down to the client. Notice that because you haven't done any server-side data fetching, you won't expect to see any dynamic data populating your app (like posts).

Server(s)

Middleware
- parse incoming request
- basic security patching
- handle global logging
- compression
- handle not-founds

Response Handler
...
- fetch user data, dispatch Redux actions
- embed initial store state into HTML response
- use ReactDOM to generate some basic static HTML, send to client as a string respond

ID

Firebase

Use cookie to verify user is authenticated

Browser request
GET http://localhost:3000/<route-name>

Server response
contains generated HTML

Browser

Figure 12.8   Server rendering with data fetching. This is similar overall to how you've been doing rendering, with the main difference being that you'll need to do some data fetching as part of the rendering process. The rendering output will change based on whether or not a user is logged in, what that user's data looks like, and when they log in.

Firebase provides a way to interact with their APIs from the server in a similar way to how you have from the browser. This will enable you to continue to treat Firebase as your database even on the server. In other situations, you might do something like make an HTTP call to a microservice or database that would allow you to determine if a user exists and if they're in a currently authenticated state. You'll stick with Firebase because you're focusing on React, but note that this is one place where you might swap in one of these systems under different circumstances.

If you haven't already created a Firebase account, this is a great time to do so. I've distributed the application source with the public token for the account, but to use the Firebase user admin APIs you need to have a real account (you can use it to access user information, something I don't want people doing). To get set up with a Firebase account, head to https://firebase.google.com and sign up for an account (you should be able to use an existing Google account). From there, create a project named whatever you like.

After that, you'll need to walk through the Firebase admin SDK setup. This process might change over time, so I won't specify it exactly here. The setup and installation instructions can be found at https://firebase.google.com/docs/admin/setup and should be relatively straightforward to follow. We're most interested in the User Management API. You shouldn't need to install anything else in the project because the node.js Firebase SDK is already included in your project dependencies.

As a final bit of setup, you'll need to replace the included Firebase keys in the application, since they're related to the Letters Social project and will likely conflict with your own. You can find them in the source code by looking in the config directory. Two files, development.json and production.json, contain the configuration variables for the development and production environments, respectively. Feel free to edit those or other variables as you see fit (maybe you want to customize the application yourself and deploy it on a site!). Figure 12.9 shows the Firebase console and the service account page. Generate a new private key and move the downloaded file into the main app repository—you'll use it shortly.

You can get back to coding now that you have those logistical bits out of the way. You want to authenticate your server application with the Firebase platform so you can verify and fetch Firebase users for the purposes of rendering the complete application state. You may have already seen the example snippet showing how to do this on the Firebase page, but listing 12.13 shows how to configure the Firebase Admin SDK in your server.

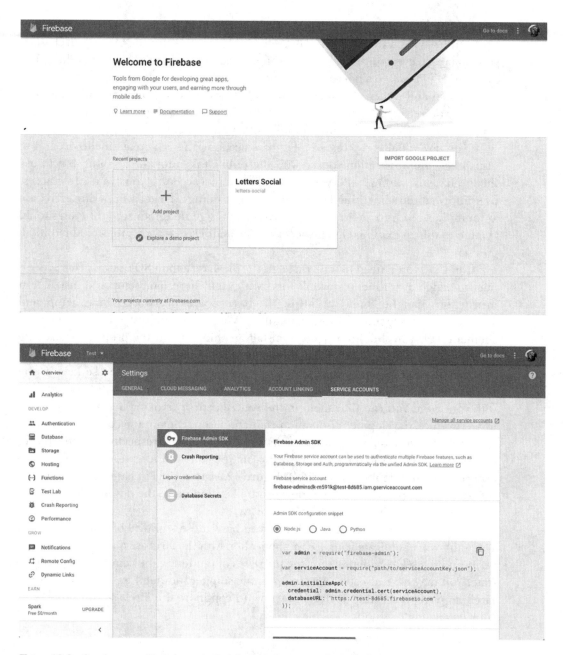

Figure 12.9   Create a new Firebase project and generate a new private key. This will allow you to authenticate to the Firebase platform and use the SDK to manage users on the server.

Listing 12.13   Integrating Firebase on the server (server/server.js

```
// ...
import * as firebase from 'firebase-admin';
import config from 'config';

// Initialize Firebase
firebase.initializeApp({
    credential: firebase.credential.cert(JSON.parse(process.env.LETTERS_
    FIREBASE_ADMIN_KEY) ),
    databaseURL: 'https://letters-social.firebaseio.com'
});

// const serviceAccount = require("path/to/serviceAccountKey.json");
// admin.initializeApp({
//   credential: firebase.credential.cert(serviceAccount),
//   databaseURL: "https://test-8d685.firebaseio.com"
// });


// Our dummy database backend
import DB from '../db/DB';

//...
```

Import Firebase admin SDK

Set stringified version of JSON file as environment variable; parse it so Firebase can work

Another way to authenticate with Firebase

Now when the server runs it will automatically connect to Firebase and enable you to use the Admin SDK to interact with users. That way you can do data fetching on the server in a way that knows about the user making the request. Why does that matter? You might remember from earlier in the chapter that I said server-side routing can be complicated because it can involve synchronizing your client and server. You're not going to do anything terribly complicated, but this is what I was referring to. Server-side rendering can quickly become extremely complicated.

Fortunately, you won't be doing anything so daunting. What you're going to do is use Redux in a way you may not have used it before. Because there's nothing about Redux that constrains it to running in the browser, you can use it for state management on the server too. Here's a brief outline of what you'll do to accomplish rendering that allows for data fetching:

- Get the user's token from a cookie you stored in earlier chapters.
- Verify the token with Firebase and fetch the user if they exist.
- If they don't have a valid token (maybe it expired), clear the cookie and send them to the login page.
- If they're a valid user, fetch their information from your server and dispatch actions to the store.
- Render the appropriate route component based on the state of the store.
- JSON.stringify the current store state and embed it in the HTML that you need to send down to the browser.

If that sounds complicated, don't fret. You're adding a minor step to the same flow of server rendering you were doing before. Instead of rendering the same content every time, you're fetching data from Firebase and using that information to do rendering. Remember, the benefit here is that you can "fully" render the application so the user can immediately see content.

Your use of Redux on the server is a great example of "universal" JavaScript in action. If Redux depended heavily on browser APIs, it might be difficult or impossible to integrate it on the server, and you'd have to take a different approach altogether. As it is, though, you can re-create a store on demand, update it based on responses from your APIs and Firebase, and then use the store to render your application just as you would in the browser. Figure 12.10 shows this process in the context of server rendering that we've been looking at for this chapter.

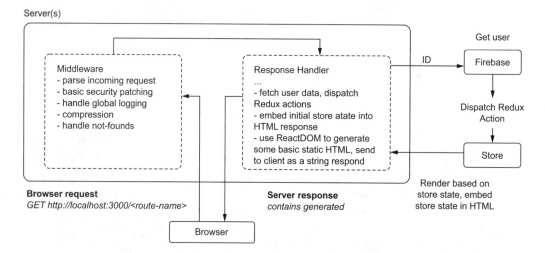

Figure 12.10   Server rendering with data fetching as part of the render process

In this flow, you use a cookie coming from the browser to verify that the user's token is valid. Then you get the user from Firebase and dispatch actions to a Redux store created server-side. You still render to static HTML, but this time you render using updated state so the app can be rendered with new data. You also embed the state in the HTML response so the browser can pick up where the server left off. One thing to watch out for when doing this is your Redux store not being recreated or persisting in memory on the server. I've worked on projects where this was briefly happening during local development, and it was hard to track down. Aside from being annoying, it meant that the server would render the same user data for everyone making requests because the store's state hadn't been wiped. That would've been an unacceptable security breach in a production environment. I mention this to help drive home the reality that coordinating browser and client can be complex and must be done carefully to avoid tricky bugs or security holes.

Let's take a look at the code you'll need to do this data fetching and rendering process. Listing 12.14 shows the initial steps of fetching data and handling some basic errors that might arise from an expired or invalid token. In the next step, you'll integrate asynchronous server rendering with React-DOM's `renderToNodeStream` and even further improve your server rendering.

Listing 12.14 Fetching data for server rendering (server/server.js)

```
// ...
    const store = configureStore(initialReduxState);     ◁── Create instance of
    try {                                                     your Redux store
        const token = req.cookies['letters-token'];      ◁── Get user token off
        if (token) {                                          requests' cookies
            const firebaseUser = await firebase.auth()
                                      .verifyIdToken(token);
            const userResponse = await fetch(
                `${config.get('ENDPOINT')}/users/${firebaseUser.uid}`
            );
            if (userResponse.status !== 404) {
                const user = await userResponse.json();
                await store.dispatch(loginSuccess(user));
                await store.dispatch(getPostsForPage());.
            }
        }
    } catch (err) {
        if (err.errorInfo.code === 'auth/argument-error') {
            res.clearCookie('letters-token');
        }
        // dispatch the error
        store.dispatch(createError(err));
    }
    //...
```

Verify token with Firebase and use response to fetch user from your JSON API

If user exists, unwrap JSON response from API (you're using isomorphic-fetch library and async/await syntax here)

Thanks to Redux-thunk, you can dispatch your asynchronous action creators that you use in login and wait for them to finish before moving on.

If there's an error like token being expired, dispatch error to store

That's most of the work you'll need to do fully render the application with user context! One downside to this approach is that if you had many pages with different data-fetching requirements, it would be difficult to fit those in. You don't have a way of saying, "Ah, we're requesting page X, page X needs Y data." There are ways to do that, though, and I cover them briefly on my blog at https://ifelse.io/2017/09/07/server-rendering-with-react-router-and-react-16-fiber (if you're interested in learning more about this and some of the newer React Router versions).

To finish your rendering improvements, you'll need to do a few more things. First, you'll need to find a way to inject the HTML string that React-DOM will give back to us. Because it works with streams, your string template approach from before will need to change. Instead of directly injecting the resulting HTML, you'll use two functions to write down HTML for your app. One will contain the header information that your app will need (metadata about the app, Open Graph data, CSS links, and so on). The other will embed the Redux store state in the HTML response. You want to embed the state so that when the browser takes over it doesn't redo any of the work the server already did. You want to do less rendering, not more! The next listing shows the HTML wrapper component that you'll pass your component and Redux store state into.

Listing 12.15   Embedding Redux state

Basic metadata about the app—some boilerplate code is omitted as not relevant to current discussion

```
const ogProps = {
    updated_time: new Date(),
    type: 'website',
    url: 'https://social.react.sh',
    title: 'Letters Social | React in Action by Mark Thomas from Manning
      Publications',
    description:
        'Letters Social is a sample application for the React.js book React in
        Action by Mark Thomas from Manning Publications. Get it today at
        https://ifelse.io/book'
};

export const start = () => {
    return `<!DOCTYPE html><html lang="en-us">
        <head>
            <link rel="stylesheet" href="/static/styles.css" type="text/css" />
            <link rel="stylesheet" href="https://api.mapbox.com/map-
box.js/v3.1.1/mapbox.css" />
            <meta http-equiv="X-UA-Compatible" content="IE=edge" />
            <title>
                Letters Social | React in Action by Mark Thomas from Manning
Publications
            </title>
            <link rel="manifest" href="/static/manifest.json" />
            <meta name="viewport" content="width=device-width,initial-scale=1" />
            <meta name="ROBOTS" content="INDEX, FOLLOW" />
            <meta property="og:title" content="${ogProps.title}" />
            <meta property="og:description" content="${ogProps.description}" />
            <meta property="og:type" content="${ogProps.type}" />
            <meta property="og:url" content="${ogProps.url}" />
            <meta property="og:updated_time" content="${ogProps.updated_time}" />
            <meta itemProp="description" content="${ogProps.description}" />
            <meta name="twitter:card" content="summary" />
            <meta name="twitter:title" content="${ogProps.title}" />
            <meta name="twitter:description" content="${ogProps.description}" />
            <meta property="book:author" content="Mark Tielens Thomas" />
            <meta property="book:tag" content="react" />
            <meta property="book:tag" content="reactjs" />
            <meta property="book:tag" content="React in Action" />
            <meta property="book:tag" content="javascript" />
            <meta property="book:tag" content="single page application" />
            <meta property="book:tag" content="Manning publications" />
            <meta property="book:tag" content="Mark Thomas" />
            <meta name="HandheldFriendly" content="True" />
```

Inject your app into main div so when React-DOM takes over on browser, it won't have to redo work server did

```
                <meta name="MobileOptimized" content="320" />
                <meta name="theme-color" content="#4469af" />
                <link
                    href="https://fonts.googleapis.com/css?fam-
    ily=Open+Sans:400,700,800"
                    rel="stylesheet"
                />
            </head>
            <body>
                <div id="app">
        `;
};
```

Redux store in browser should be able to take over where server left off, so embed store in JSON-stringified format;

```
export const end = reduxState => {
    return `</div>
        <script id="initialState">
            window.__INITIAL_STATE__ = ${JSON.stringify(reduxState)};
        </script>
        <script src="https://cdn.ravenjs.com/3.17.0/raven.min.js"
    type="text/javascript"></script>
        <script src="https://api.mapbox.com/mapbox.js/v3.1.1/mapbox.js"
    type="text/javascript"></script>
        <script src="/static/bundle.js" type="text/javascript"></script>
        </body>
    </html>`;
};
```

With that, you need to modify the Redux store so it can take over. In this listing, you'll do two main things: make sure the Redux store is created from scratch every time on the server (to prevent the potential bugs mentioned earlier) and teach it to read the initial state from the DOM. The following listing shows these minor modifications that you'll make to your production store (the development version isn't being rendered by the server, so there's no initial state to pick up).

> **Listing 12.16 Modifying the Redux store for SSR (src/store/configureStore.prod.js)**

```
//...
let store;
export default function configureStore(initialState) {
    if (store && !isServer()) {
        return store;
    }
    const hydratedState =
        !isServer() && process.env.NODE_ENV === 'production'
            ? window.__INITIAL_STATE__
            : initialState;
    store = createStore(
        rootReducer,
        hydratedState,
        compose(applyMiddleware(thunk, crashReporting))
    );
    return store;
}
```

If you're on server, you want to return new store every time

If you're not on server and app is in production mode, check DOM for state and use if possible

Now your store will be able to read initial state from data embedded by your server and won't have to do double work. What's left? You may remember from the beginning of the chapter that you had asynchronous options available to use when rendering on the server. You're currently using the `renderToString` method from React-DOM, but it's synchronous, and that could be a bottleneck for your server if many users visit the app at once. In React 16, an asynchronous option for server rendering was introduced, and you'll use it here. The usage is identical except node.js streams can be used instead of the synchronous method.

Exercise 12.2   Open source libraries

You've done some work to integrate server-side rendering into the Letters Social application. You got it working with Redux, but scaling to a very large application or introducing new data-fetching requirements (data for other pages, for example) might require some refactoring and reconsidering how you approach server rendering. There are open source libraries for doing server rendering with React that help address issues of uniformly allowing components to be rendered on the server. As an exercise in improving your understanding of what's possible with server rendering with React, take some time to look at them and their source code. You'll probably be pleasantly surprised at what you can accomplish with server rendering (optimized rendering, in the case of react-server https://github.com/redfin/react-server) and how much easier an abstraction can make implementing server rendering (in the case of Next.js: https://github.com/zeit/next.js/).

You may be familiar with streams if you've worked with node.js before. If not, that's fine. Streams in node.js are an abstract interface for working with streaming data. That can include things like reading or writing a file, transforming and compressing images, or working with HTTP requests and responses. You can learn more about streams in node.js at https://nodejs.org/api/stream.html. The next listing illustrates taking advantage of the new `renderToNodeStream` API in React-DOM.

Listing 12.17   Async server rendering (server/server.js)

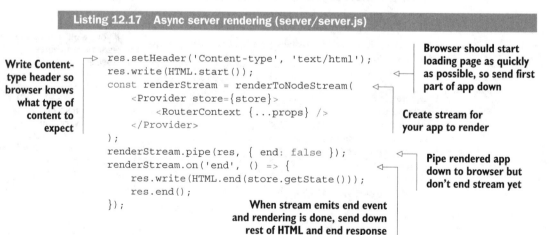

```
res.setHeader('Content-type', 'text/html');
res.write(HTML.start());
const renderStream = renderToNodeStream(
    <Provider store={store}>
        <RouterContext {...props} />
    </Provider>
);
renderStream.pipe(res, { end: false });
renderStream.on('end', () => {
    res.write(HTML.end(store.getState()));
    res.end();
});
```

Write Content-type header so browser knows what type of content to expect

Browser should start loading page as quickly as possible, so send first part of app down

Create stream for your app to render

Pipe rendered app down to browser but don't end stream yet

When stream emits end event and rendering is done, send down rest of HTML and end response

With that, Letters Social is now being fully rendered to users. You can directly observe this if you use the developer tools to inspect the document loading process and look at what the server sends down (figure 12.11 shows something similar to what you should see). You may be able to see the difference in speed if you run the application in production mode, but looking at the development tools in Chrome or Firefox will allow you to inspect the app loading on a frame-by-frame basis. You'll be able to see that a full web page is being sent down by the server and not just rendered after the application has loaded.

Without server rendering, the user would see a gray screen and no content yet

Initial render includes markup before script bundle has loaded

Images haven't loaded yet but can start loading more quickly because their corresponding tags are already available to the brouser

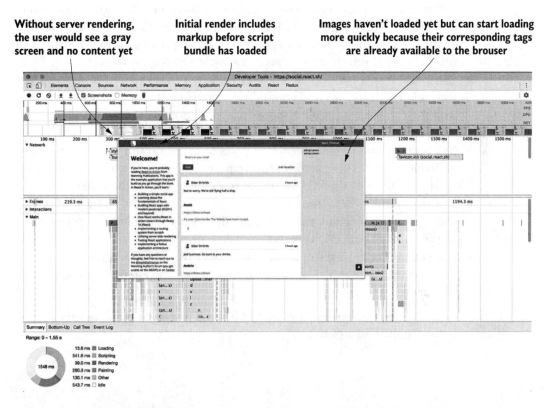

Figure 12.11 If we inspect the performance tab for social.react.sh using the Chrome developer tools, you'll see that the server is sending down fully rendered HTML and not waiting till the application bundle has loaded to render the application.

12.8 Summary

In this chapter, we looked at how you might approach building server-side rendering functionality into your app. As we saw, it can involve quite a few aspects of your application, including routing, data fetching, and state management (Redux):

- Server-side rendering (SSR) is generating the static markup for a UI on a server that is sent to a client. SSR with React involves using React-DOM to either render an HTML string that React can reuse when running on the client-side or static markup (`ReactDOM.renderToString()`) that's meant to remain static on the browser (`ReactDOM.renderToStaticMarkUp()`).

- Not all JS frameworks or libraries are built to handle SSR; React is and can "take over" markup that was generated on the server without having to initially re-render existing elements on the browser.

- Using a routing solution like React Router can allow you to share routes between the client and server, allowing you to share some code across platforms.

- SSR can be complex to implement and only makes sense in certain cases. Some situations where it might make sense include when you're especially concerned about SEO, when you have an app whose critical path needs to involve a quick first paint, or if you're using React as a static markup generator.

- The performance gains SSR can offer are often only realized if the page payload sent down by a server is not overly large (so as to not take even longer to load than before). A longer response time and more data may obviate the quick first paint you would otherwise get.

- SSR requires you to consider which parts of your app will work on the server and which won't. Those features that require a browser environment need to be patched to work or should be handled so as not to run on the server.

- You can accomplish a "complete" render on the server by doing work to synchronize authentication state between client and server and doing any necessary fetching of data on the server.

- Although other JS platform implementations exist, SSR practically requires you to run a node.js server or at least call out to one to generate your HTML for sending to the client.

In the next chapter, we'll take a brief look at React Native and complete your journey toward learning the basics of React.

13
An introduction
to React Native

This chapter covers

- An overview of React Native
- Differences between React and React Native
- Ways to learn more about React Native

At this point, you've been over the basics of using React, implemented a router, explored Redux, looked at server-side rendering, and even transitioned to using React Router. What's left? There's still plenty to learn and explore in the React ecosystem and community. This chapter takes a high-level look at React Native, another project in the React ecosystem developed by Facebook. With React Native, you can write React applications that run on mobile platforms like iOS and Android. This means you can write applications that run on smartphones and any other platforms that React Native targets now or in the future. React Native provides an excellent developer experience when building these mobile applications in a React-like way, and this is a large part of why it's becoming increasingly important and popular in the React community.

Because React Native and getting started with mobile development encompass a substantially large domain, I'll keep our discussion of React Native concise and focused mainly on higher-level concepts. By the end of the chapter, you should have an idea of what React Native is and why you might want to use it, and you'll know how to get started on learning more about it.

13.1 Introducing React Native

Before React Native came on the scene, you had a few options when it came to creating mobile applications. You could either use the iOS and Android platforms and languages available to you or you could opt for one of the hybrid approaches available. These vary in how they're implemented, but they would often utilize a web view (think "mobile browser") and expose some interfaces to the native SDKs. One downside to this approach is that although you can write native applications that allow you to use many familiar web APIs and idioms, the app wasn't "really native," and there would sometimes be a noticeable difference in performance and overall feel. The benefit was that teams or developers without expertise in mobile development could transfer their web-related skills and be able to create a mobile app.

The subject of mobile development and how platforms, languages, and hardware in this world all play their different roles is beyond the scope of this book. But the choice between hybrid and all-native approaches is relevant to our discussion of React Native because React Native offers a new alternative. With React Native, you can build apps that are "really native" but you can use a combination of JavaScript and platform-specific code (like Swift or Java).

React Native aims to bring the idioms and concepts of building user interfaces with React to mobile application development and blend the best aspects of mobile and browser development. It encourages code-sharing across platforms (there are components that target both iOS and Android devices), allows you to write native code where appropriate, and compiles to a native application—all while using many of the same idioms familiar to React.

Let's glance at a few top-level features of React Native:

- With React Native, you can write JavaScript applications that can also use native code (Swift or Java) and compile to native applications that run on iOS or Android.
- React Native can handle creating the same UI elements on Android and iOS, potentially simplifying the development of mobile applications.
- You can add your own native code when you need to, so you aren't constrained to using only JavaScript.
- React Native apps share idioms with React and provide the same component-driven, declarative concepts, and even APIs in some cases, to work with when designing your UI.
- The developer tooling for building React Native applications allows you to reload your application with changes without having to wait for a long compile cycle. This often saves developers time and can make for a more pleasant experience.
- The ability to share code and target multiple platforms can sometimes reduce the number of engineers dedicated to building a particular app or project. It

can lead to fewer codebases to maintain, and engineers can more easily move between web and native platforms.

- You can share logic and other aspects of React web apps with React Native apps, such as business logic and even styles in some cases.

How does React Native work? It may seem like a mysterious, black-box process for something to take your JavaScript and output a compiled, native application. You don't need to know how every part of React Native works in order to work with it, just like you don't need to know the ins and outs of React-DOM to write great React applications. But it's often helpful to have at least a working understanding of the technology you're using.

With React Native, you can create applications that are a blend of JavaScript and native code. React Native makes this possible by creating a bridge of sorts between your application and the underlying mobile platform. Most mobile devices can execute JavaScript, and React Native takes advantage of that to run your JavaScript. When your JavaScript is executed alongside any native code, React Native's bridging system uses the React core library, among others, to translate the component hierarchy (with event handlers, state, props, and styles) into a view on the mobile device.

When updates occur (for example, a user presses a button), React Native translates the native event (a press, a shake, a geolocation event, or whatever it is) into an event your JavaScript or native code can handle. It also renders the proper UI based on changes to state or props. React Native will also bundle all your code and do any necessary compilation so you can release your app to the Apple App Store or Google Play Store.

There's much more to these processes and to how React Native works, but the basic process of translating between the JavaScript running on the device and the native platform APIs and events is where the "magic" of React Native happens. The result is a platform that you can work with but that also doesn't compromise when it comes to performance. It's a happy medium between the problems of previous hybrid approaches to mobile apps, and it also avoids some of the pain points of traditional mobile development. Figure 13.1 illustrates an overall view of how it works.

If that sounds like a departure from the React you've been learning in this book, well, it is in many ways. But more important than the differences are the similarities. I'll cover those more in the next section, but you can look at the code in listing 13.1 to see how similar a React Native component is to the components you've worked with so far.

You can still see what the code in listing 13.1 does even though I'm not covering how to set up a React Native project in this chapter. Visit https://repl.it/KOAE/3 if you want to see what the code is doing and play around with React Native. Repl.it is an online platform for running and sharing code in an interactive way, and it has support for React Native. You'll be able to scan a QR code with your phone to view your React Native playground app. It's a great way to experiment with React Native without having to do any setup or configuration.

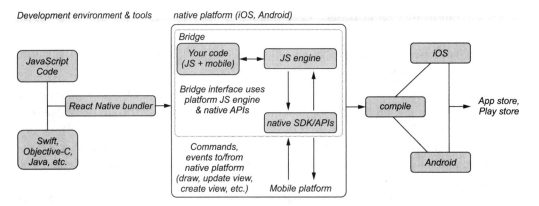

Figure 13.1   React Native works by creating a bridge between your JavaScript and the underlying native platform. Most native platforms implement a JavaScript virtual machine or other way of running JavaScript natively. The bridge enables execution of your application's JavaScript. The React Native bridging system will relay messages between the underlying platform and your JavaScript so that native events can be translated into ones your React components can understand and respond to.

One important thing you might notice is that the elements of the component (View, Text) are analogous to the div and span elements in your components from earlier chapters. This is an example of the broad React concepts persisting across platforms. It doesn't matter so much what the individual elements of a component are as much as that you can reuse and compose them, as shown in this listing.

Listing 13.1   React Native example component

You can still use regular React.Component, even in native app

React Native comes with basic ingredients to build mobile applications.

You can compose components with React Native; view component here is like a div in browser (common layout component)

Text is more like span in browser

```
import React, { Component } from 'react';
import { Text, View } from 'react-native';

export default class WhyReactNativeIsSoGreat extends Component {
    render() {
        return (
            <View>
                <Text>
                    If you like React on the web, you'll like React Native.
                </Text>
                <Text>
                    You just use native components like 'View' and 'Text',
                    instead of web components like 'div' and 'span'.
                </Text>
            </View>
        );
    }
}
```

There are other projects like React VR where the focus is even more divergent from the web UIs you've been working with but that use the same patterns and concepts.

This is one of the most powerful aspects of the React platform and is especially apparent when you see it across platforms. Learn more about React VR at https://facebook .github.io/react-vr.

13.2 *React and React Native*

How similar are React and React Native? Beyond sharing a name, they both use the `React` core library but target different platforms (browsers and mobile devices). This section will briefly look at some of their differences and similarities. Let's compare some of the important aspects of React and React Native:

- *Runtime*—React and React Native target different platforms. React targets browsers and thus heavily uses the browser-specific APIs. You can see some of the results of this in each API. For example, properties like class, ID, and others are commonly seen in web-based React components. Native platforms use different layout and styling semantics, so you won't see many of these properties on React Native components. Browser-based and mobile applications also run on different types of devices, so things like threading, CPU utilization, and other differences in the underlying technology shouldn't be ignored when thinking about React and React Native.

- *Core APIs*—Many of the React-specific APIs (like those used in component lifecycles, state, props, and so on) are similar across React and React Native. But each platform implements different APIs for networking, layout, geolocation, resource management, persistence, events, and other important areas. React Native aims to import some familiar APIs from the browser-oriented world, like the Fetch API for networking (https://developer.mozilla.org/en-US/docs/Web/ API/Fetch_API) and the Flexbox API for layout (https://developer.mozilla.org/ en-US/docs/Web/CSS/flex). React Native also exposes events, but they're more specific to mobile platforms (`onPress`, for instance). These differences can be a minor hurdle, but fortunately there are libraries that help to eliminate differences between web and native APIs, like `react-primitives` (https://github .com/lelandrichardson/react-primitives).

- *Components*—The web-based React project doesn't have "built-in" components (for example, for images, text layout, or other UI elements). You create these yourself. React Native, on the other hand, does include components for things like text, views, images, and more. These are primitives you need to create UIs for mobile applications and are similar to what DOM elements are for browser environments.

- *Use of `React` core library*—Both React and React Native use the `React` core library for component definition. Each project utilizes a different rendering system to wire everything together and interact with the device (browser or mobile). React for web uses the `react-dom` library, whereas React Native implements its own system. This approach enables you to write components in similar ways across platforms.

- *Lifecycle methods*—React Native components also have lifecycle methods since they inherit from the same `React` base class, and those methods are also handled by the platform-specific system (React-DOM or React Native).

- *Event types*—Whereas React-DOM implements a synthetic event system that allows your components to work with browser events in a standard way, mobile applications expose other events. One example is gestures. You can pan, zoom, drag, and more on touch devices. Components written in React Native components allow you to respond to these events.

- *Styling*—Because React Native doesn't target browsers, you'll need to style your components in slightly different ways. There is no CSS API in regular mobile development, but you can use most CSS properties with React Native. React Native provides a specific API where 1:1 correspondence between properties isn't possible. Take CSS animations, for example. The CSS specification and the ways browsers implement it are different than how iOS and Android enable and implement animations, so you'll need to animate differently and use the right API for each platform. Learning new APIs for styling can take time and can prevent directly sharing CSS styling across web and native projects. Thankfully, though, there are libraries that work with React and React Native, like `styled-components` (www.styled-components.com). With the increasing popularity of React Native, you should expect to see more of these cross-platform libraries being developed.

- *Third-party dependencies*—As with React, you can still use third-party component libraries for React Native. Many popular libraries, like `React Router` and `styled-components`, even include variants that target React Native (as noted earlier). One of the most appealing aspects of React Native is that it can still take advantage of the JavaScript module ecosystem.

- *Distribution*—Although you can deploy React applications to almost any modern browser, React Native applications require platform-specific distribution tooling for both development and final release (Xcode, for example). You'll usually need to use the React Native build process to compile your application for final upload. The "walled garden" nature of the iOS and Android tooling is a well-known tradeoff to developing mobile applications.

- *Development tooling*—React for web runs in browsers, so you have the benefit of any browser-specific tools to help with debugging and development. For React Native, you aren't required to have the platform-specific tooling available, but it can still be useful. One key difference between the projects is that React Native has a focus on hot reloading that isn't part of React by default. *Hot reloading* can speed up mobile development because you don't have to wait for your app to compile. Figure 13.2 shows an example of some of the developer tools you get access to when working with React Native.

Figure 13.2 React Native comes with a number of additional developer tools that help with performance, debugging, and other functionality. These tools also mean you have less of a strict reliance on tools like Xcode for development, although you can certainly still use your platform-specific tools for development. Although there are many reasons, the excellent developer experience provided by React Native seems to be one reason why it's been received especially well as a technology.

13.3 When to use React Native

Not every developer and not every team has a need for React Native. Let's imagine a few scenarios you could find yourself in and see how React Native might or might not be something you should consider:

- *Solo developer*—If you're learning React for the first time or just using it for side projects, you'll probably learn React Native for fun or if you work on any mobile projects. React Native is also something to consider if you aren't deeply experienced with native development but want to ease into it or have a more straightforward app. If you already know React, it can make sense to dive into using React Native for mobile development with some familiar concepts at your disposal.

- *Small cross-functional team*—Small startups are often in a position where engineers will work on a broad slice of the stack, ranging from server to client applications (web, mobile, or otherwise). In situations like this, React Native can sometimes present a way for engineers who wear many hats for the organization to work on a mobile app without deep mobile experience and have their React momentum carry over. This could also apply to large organizations that want to easily move engineers between apps or projects.

- *Team with little to moderate native expertise*—If you or your team have little to moderate expertise with mobile development but are familiar with React and Java-

Script, React Native may make it easier for you to get your product together quickly. There's no substitute for experience, but not having to go all-in on Swift (iOS) or Java (Android) could potentially save you time.

- *Deep native expertise*—Some teams will choose React Native not because it lowers the barrier to mobile development in some ways, but because it helps standardize idioms and patterns across the various implementations of an app for a business (mobile and desktop). But if that's not a problem and you already have significant expertise and time invested in mobile development, React Native may need closer evaluation to see whether your team would benefit from the available abstractions and patterns.

Aside from the team and expertise considerations you might make when thinking about React Native, you should also be aware of some of the limitations that are inherent to the technology as it exists today:

- *Use of JavaScript*—If your team or organization doesn't have any JavaScript-focused developers or is already highly experienced with mobile development, it may not make sense to transition engineers to a JavaScript and JavaScript-focused ecosystem, and that's okay. Like React for web, React Native is not a silver bullet and should be evaluated based on tradeoffs, not the hype around it.

- *Specific performance needs*—React Native is performant, but as an abstraction it can present another barrier to achieving specific performance goals that you or your team might have. For example, if rendering 3D scenes is the primary goal of an application, React Native will probably not be the best fit. Other frameworks (like Unity) are probably better suited. This is in keeping with the "React is not a silver bullet" idea I just mentioned and that I've tried to maintain in earlier chapters.

- *Highly specialized app*—Some application types aren't a good fit for the React model. Augmented reality (AR), graphics-intensive, or other highly specialized applications often require special libraries and skills that most web engineers aren't equipped with. This isn't to say that it can't be done, but as of now React Native doesn't focus on addressing these needs.

- *Internal application*—Sometimes larger companies develop apps for internal use that help employees do their job better in a variety of ways. React Native can be well suited for these sorts of apps because such apps usually involve a relatively simple UI and can be iterated on quickly by engineers who don't specialize in mobile development.

Of course, it's ultimately up to you and your team to evaluate whether a technology makes sense for your use case, but hopefully you now have a better sense of when it might or might not make sense to use React Native.

13.4   *The simplest "Hello World"*

Even though I won't cover how to integrate React Native with Letters Social, this section spends a little time walking through a basic "Hello World" example so you can see it in action. You'll work outside the Letters Social repository, so feel free to place the app code wherever you like to keep track of code on your computer. Run the commands in the following listing to get started.

Listing 13.2   Installing `create-react-native-app`

```
cd ./path-to-your-react-native-sample-folder

npm install -g create-react-native-app

create-react-native-app .
```

After you've run these commands, you should be able to see a number of files created in your desired directory and some instructions. These commands are similar to those available in Create React App, a similar project focused just on React.js for the web platform. You can learn more about Create React App at https://github.com/facebookincubator/create-react-app. Figure 13.3 shows what you should see when getting started with the Create React Native App library.

The Create React Native App tool installed dependencies, created some boilerplate files, set up a build process, and integrated the Expo React Native toolkit into the project. The Expo SDK extends React Native's functionality and makes working with the hardware technologies easier, among other things. The Expo XDE development environment makes it easy to manage multiple React Native projects as well as build and deploy them.

You won't build anything substantial, but you can tinker around and get a sense for how easy it might be to start building applications with React Native. Once you have the React Native packager running with `yarn start`, open one of the emulators (Android or iOS) so you can see the running app. Swap out some of the boilerplate code and see the hot reloading happening. Listing 13.3 shows a simple component that fetches some data from the Star Wars API when it's mounted. Notice that React Native is already using modern web APIs like Flexbox and Fetch (which you used a polyfill for in earlier chapters).

```
~/Code/oss/letters-native 6s
△ yarn start
yarn start v1.0.2
$ react-native-scripts start
00:16:28: Starting packager...
Packager started!
```

To view your app with live reloading, point the Expo app to this QR code.
You'll find the QR scanner on the Projects tab of the app.

Or enter this address in the Expo app's search bar:

exp://10.0.1.5:19000

Your phone will need to be on the same local network as this computer.
For links to install the Expo app, please visit https://expo.io.

Logs from serving your app will appear here. Press Ctrl+C at any time to stop.

› Press a to open Android device or emulator, or i to open iOS emulator.
› Press q to display QR code.
› Press r to restart packager, or R to restart packager and clear cache.
› Press d to toggle development mode. (current mode: **development**)

Figure 13.3 When you start the application in development mode, you should see the React Native packager start and see a message like the one shown here. Follow the instructions to make sure you have the Expo XDE set up on your local machine. Depending on what environment you'd like to target, open either the Android or iOS simulator.

Listing 13.3 Simple React Native example (App.js)

```
import React from 'react';
import { StyleSheet, Text, View } from 'react-native';

export default class App extends React.Component {
    constructor(props) {
        super(props);
        this.state = {
            people: []
        };
    }
    async componentDidMount() {
        const res = await fetch('https://swapi.co/api/people');
        const { results } = await res.json();
        this.setState(() => {
            return {
                people: results
            };
        });
    }
    render() {
        return (
            <View style={styles.container}>
                <Text style={{ color: '#fcd433', fontSize: 40, padding: 10 }}>
                    A long time ago, in a Galaxy far, far away...
                </Text>
                <Text>Here are some cool people:</Text>
                {this.state.people.map(p => {
                    return (
                        <Text style={{ color: '#fcd433' }} key={p.name}>
                            {p.name}
                        </Text>
                    );
                })}
            </View>
        );
    }
}

const styles = StyleSheet.create({
    container: {
        flex: 1,
        backgroundColor: '#000',
        alignItems: 'center',
        justifyContent: 'center'
    }
});
```

Unlike React, React Native comes with primitive components for your UI.

Constructor, state initialization, and lifecycle methods are the same in React and React Native

You can use modern JavaScript features like async/await in React Native apps too.

Even though styles appear similar in React Native, you're not using CSS.

JSX expressions are the same in React Native and React

Creating a stylesheet in React Native requires use of its Stylesheet API to style your components.

If you make changes to the app, you should see the packager respond and update your running app in real time, as shown in figure 13.4. I hope this gives you a sense of how easy it can be to build applications in React Native. You may be used to hot reloading on the web, but for mobile development the compile-inspect-recompile cycle can take up a significant amount of time.

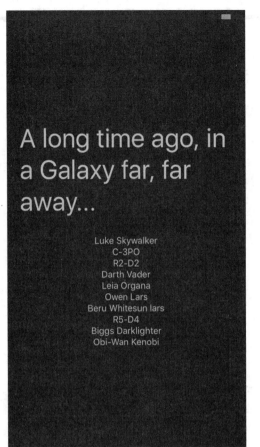

Figure 13.4   **You should be able to see changes being instantly reflected in the simulator running your application code.**

With that, you've created your first React Native component and code, which should give you a brief glimpse into how the technology works and how easy it can be to work with.

13.5   *Where to go next*

One of the phrases you'll see in the React docs, library ecosystem, and community is *learn once, write anywhere*. This is an homage of sorts to the *write once, run anywhere* phrase that's popular within the Java community and that is one of the hallmarks of the React paradigm. As we've seen in this chapter, you can learn React concepts and apply them to a variety of platforms, ranging from web to mobile to VR. There will be platform-specific differences and nuances whenever you learn how to use React on a new platform, but much of your React knowledge will easily transfer. That's one of the reasons why working with React can be such a pleasure.

There are many resources you can look into if you'd like to keep learning about React Native. One is *React Native in Action* by Nader Dabit (Manning Publications,

2018), shown in figure 13.5, which pairs nicely with this book because it allows you to pick up right where you leave off in learning React and is an excellent introduction to React Native. You'll apply your knowledge from your work in this book so far and use the momentum to dive into building mobile applications with React Native. It's also a good resource to look into next if your team is considering React Native for an upcoming project.

Figure 13.5 *React Native in Action* by Nader Dabit gives iOS, Android, and web developers the skills they need to build robust, complex React Native applications. If you're still curious about React, it's the perfect book to transition to next. Learn more at www.manning .com/books/react-native-in-action.

Another great resource to get you started with React Native is the Create React Native App project. Create React Native App provides an excellent starting place for a new React Native project or an excellent sample application for those just starting out with it. It includes a few preset libraries and tools for building React Native apps, but allows you to "eject" and reset to the default. If you're curious about Create React App or Create React Native App, check them out online:

- *Create React Native App*—https://github.com/react-community/create-react-native-app
- *Create React App*—https://github.com/facebook/create-react-app
- *React Native documentation*—https://facebook.github.io/react-native

13.6 *Summary*

Here's a recap of what you learned in this chapter:

- React Native is a technology in the React ecosystem that developers can use to write React applications that run on mobile iOS and Android devices.
- React Native uses the React core library for component creation but uses a different set of libraries to handle rendering your application on the native platform and to handle interactions with the underlying platform (touch events, geolocation, cameras access, and so on).
- React Native handles bridging between your JavaScript and the underlying mobile platform.
- React Native uses many APIs that are identical or similar to web APIs. It uses Flexbox for layout, Fetch for network requests, and other familiar APIs.
- You can mix JavaScript and native code when building React Native applications.
- React Native provides a robust set of tools for developing and compiling your applications.
- React Native's hot-reload developer tools save you time by not making you wait for your application to recompile every time.
- Using React Native can help lower the barrier to mobile development for you or your team.
- You won't want to use React Native for absolutely every type of mobile application, but it should be sufficient for most typical mobile applications.
- *React Native in Action* by Nader Dabit (Manning, 2018) is a great next resource to consider in your React journey—check it out at www.manning.com/books/react-native-in-action.

index

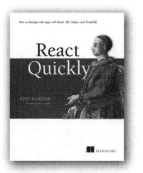

React Quickly
Painless web apps with React, JSX, Redux, and
GraphQL
by Azat Mardan

ISBN: 9781617293344
528 pages, $49.99
August 2017

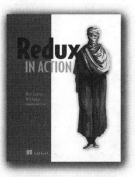

Redux in Action
by Marc Garreau and Will Faurot

ISBN: 9781617294976
312 pages, $44.99
May 2018

Redux in Motion
A test-driven approach
by Thomas Tuts

Course duration: 3h 11m
47 exercises
Live video: $49.99

Functional Programming in JavaScript
How to improve your JavaScript programs
using functional techniques
by Luis Atencio

ISBN: 9781617292828
272 pages, $44.99
August 2009

For ordering information go to www.manning.com

YOU MAY ALSO BE INTERESTED IN

Vue.js in Action
by Erik Hanchett with Benjamin Listwon

> ISBN: 9781617294624
> 375 pages, $44.99
> July 2018

Secrets of the JavaScript Ninja,
Second Edition
by John Resig, Bear Bibeault, and Josip Maras

> ISBN: 9781617292859
> 464 pages, $44.99
> August 2016

Angular Development with Typescript,
Second Edition
by Yakov Fain and Anton Moiseev

> ISBN: 9781617295348
> 568 pages, $49.95
> July 2018

Angular in Action
by Jeremy Wilken

> ISBN: 9781617293313
> 320 pages, $44.99
> March 2018

For ordering information go to www.manning.com